R. B. Cunninghame Graham and Scotland

Gente Scotus, Anima Orbis Terrarum Civis.

R. B. CUNNINGHAME GRAHAM AND SCOTLAND

Party, Prose, and Political Aesthetic

LACHLAN MUNRO

EDINBURGH
University Press

Edinburgh University Press is one of the leading university presses in the UK. We publish academic books and journals in our selected subject areas across the humanities and social sciences, combining cutting-edge scholarship with high editorial and production values to produce academic works of lasting importance. For more information visit our website: edinburghuniversitypress.com

Edinburgh University Press Ltd
The Tun – Holyrood Road
12 (2f) Jackson's Entry
Edinburgh EH8 8PJ

First published in paperback by Edinburgh University Press 2022

Typeset in 10.5/13pt Sabon by
IDSUK (DataConnection) Ltd, and
printed and bound by CPI Group (UK) Ltd,
Croydon, CR0 4YY

A CIP record for this book is available from the British Library

ISBN 978 1 4744 9826 5 (hardback)
ISBN 978 1 4744 9827 2 (paperback)
ISBN 978 1 4744 9828 9 (webready PDF)
ISBN 978 1 4744 9829 6 (epub)

Contents

Acknowledgements

I wish to express my deep appreciation for the wisdom, knowledge, and encouragement of Dr Catriona M. M. MacDonald and Professor Gerard Carruthers of the University of Glasgow, Professor Cedric Watts of the University of Sussex, and Laurence Davies of King's College London.

I would also like to acknowledge the friendship and support of Professor Duncan Ross and Professor Niall MacKenzie (University of Glasgow), Dr Kathryn Castle and Dr Kelvin Knight (London Metropolitan University), Professor Barry Menikoff (University of Hawaii), Dr Elspeth King, Cally Wight, Gerry Cairns, David McCann, Gerry McGarvey, Frank McNab, and Cunninghame Graham's great-great nephews, Robin Cunninghame Graham, and Jamie Jauncey.

Finally, to my wife Lesley, whose intelligence and wit are a constant source of inspiration and strength.

Dedicated to the memory of Craig Munro, 1961–2020

'When will we see your like again?'

The crying need of the nation is not for better morals, cheaper bread,
temperance, liberty, culture, redemption of fallen sisters and erring
brothers, not the grace, love, and fellowship of the Trinity,
but simply for enough money.
And the evil to be attacked is not sin, suffering, greed, priestcraft,
kingcraft, demagogy, monopoly, ignorance, drink, war, pestilence,
nor any other of the scapegoats which reformers sacrifice,
but simply poverty.

George Bernard Shaw, Preface to *Major Barbara*

~

The silent spirit of collective masses is the source of all great things.
But the mass has no voice. It can only feel and stammer.
It must have an interpreter, a prophet who can speak for it.
What manner of man should this prophet be? Who shall tell of those
sufferings, denied by those whose interest it is not to behold them,
those secret longings that derange the beatific optimism of the satisfied?
The great man, when he is at the same time a man of genius,
is a man of feeling. That is why the great man is of all men the least free.
He does not do, he does not say, what he wills.
God speaks in him; ten centuries of sorrow and hope possess and
command him. At times it happens to him, as to the seer in the
old biblical narrative, that being called to curse, he blesses;
the tongue obeys not himself,
but the Spirit that breathes upon it.

Ernest Renan, *Farewell to Tourgenief*

~

Do the duty that lies nearest thee which thou knowest to be a duty.
The second duty will already become clearer.
And in the doing of that duty comes the only reward
of recompense that endures.

Thomas Carlyle, *Sartor Resartus*

~

To hold a pen is to be at war.

Voltaire

Abbreviations

ASLS	Association of Scottish Literary Studies
BSP	British Socialist Party
EUL	Edinburgh University Library
ILP	Independent Labour Party
NAVSR	National Association for the Vindication of Scottish Rights
NLS	National Library of Scotland
NPS	National Party of Scotland
PP	Parliamentary Papers
SDF	Social Democratic Federation
SHRA	Scottish Home Rule Association
SNP	Scottish National Party
SPLP	Scottish Parliamentary Labour Party

Note on Correspondence

The Cunninghame Graham family archives are deposited in the National Library of Scotland (NLS), but a large collection of Graham's letters, photographs, newspaper cuttings, and other memorabilia were accumulated by his first biographer, Herbert Faulkner West, and are preserved in the Rauner Library, Dartmouth College, Hanover, New Hampshire.[1] According to Anne Taylor, Graham was complicit in ensuring that this archive reflected him as he wished to be perceived,[2] and Aimé Félix Tschiffely reported that much of the notable correspondence to him was destroyed by Graham himself.[3] Other universities hold small collections, including the University of Michigan and the University of Texas.

Two limited editions of correspondence have been published – *W. H. Hudson's Letters to R. B. Cunninghame Graham* (1941), edited by Richard Curle,[4] and *A Selection of Letters to Edward Garnett* (1981), edited by Edward Thomas.[5] In addition, Professor Cedric Watts edited *Joseph Conrad's Letters to R. B. Cunninghame Graham* (1969),[6] containing over eighty of Conrad's letters, mostly dealing with literary matters.[7] No correspondence from Graham to Conrad has been discovered. The NLS also holds the papers of Roland Eugene Muirhead, a major promoter of the second Scottish Home Rule Association and the National Party of Scotland, which contains Muirhead's correspondence with Graham, carried on over fourteen years, which provides us with an insight into Graham's later life in nationalist politics.

Notes

1. This extensive collection, donated to his *alma mater* in 1928, also contains an album of professional photographs of the shabby splendour of Gartmore House, commissioned by Graham in 1898, two years before the house was sold to pay his debts.

2. Anne Taylor, *The People's Laird: A Life of Robert Bontine Cunninghame Graham* (Edinburgh: Tobias Press, 2005), p. 327.

3. 'Following directions, he had already destroyed letters which, in a money sense would have been very valuable – letters by famous men to Cunninghame Graham; and he had to do this although it almost made him weep.' Aimé Felix Tschiffely, 'Reminiscences: Letters Destroyed', *Scotsman*, 19 October 1936, p. 11.

4. Richard Curle, ed., *W. H. Hudson's Letters to R. B. Cunninghame Graham* (London: Golden Cockerel Press, 1941). William Henry Hudson (1841–1922) Argentine-born naturalist and ornithologist. Author of *Green Mansions* (1904).

5. Edward Thomas, ed., *A Selection of Letters to Edward Garnett* (Edinburgh: Tragara Press, 1981).

6. Cedric Watts, ed., *Joseph Conrad's Letters to R. B. Cunninghame Graham* (Cambridge University Press, 1969).

7. Graham was instrumental in Conrad's literary success, and supported him morally and, it is hinted, financially. Conrad wrote to him: 'When I think of you I feel as tho' I had lived all my life in a dark hole without ever seeing or knowing anything.' Letter dated 14 January 1898. Watts, *Joseph Conrad's Letters*, p. 64.

Prologue: The Gentleman Adventurer

Robert Bontine Cunninghame Graham (1852–1936) was born in London to Anne Elizabeth Elphinstone Fleeming (1828–1925),[1] and Major William Cunningham Bontine [sic] (1825–83), scions of Scotland's landed patriciate. His principal family inheritance had come through his great-great-grandfather, Robert Graham of Gartmore (1735–97),[2] who had made his fortune in Jamaica, and who owned the estates of Gartmore, Ardoch, and Finlaystone.[3] Through various advantageous marriages he was related to several important naval, political, and commercial families, but as a result of inheritances and entails, his family was subject to an array of seemingly interchangeable surnames.

Graham's father, William, who had received a severe head injury during military service in Ireland, slowly became more disturbed, and by the summer of 1866, after attacking his wife with a sword, he had been put under restraint, but not before he had run up enormous debts. In 1870, at the age of seventeen, Robert, who had been educated at Harrow School and in Brussels, sailed for Argentina in an attempt to rescue his family's fortunes by cattle ranching, and found himself in the midst of a revolution. This was the first of three abortive business ventures in South America. The second, in 1873, found him in Paraguay, where he sought opportunities in cultivating the yerba-maté plant, the ingredient of a popular local infusion, but his explorations into the interior led to the discovery of abandoned Jesuit missions, which he described in his book *A Vanished Arcadia* (1901).

After his return to Europe in 1874, and further travels, in 1876 Graham sailed to Uruguay, with the intention of buying horses and selling them to the Brazilian Army, described in his novella *Cruz Alta* (1900).[4] This enterprise also came to nothing, but subsequently, back in Europe, he met a young woman who styled herself 'Gabriela de la

Balmondière', a Chilean poetess. They married in London and sailed for the United States in an attempt to set up a mule-breeding enterprise, but after a perilous journey into Mexico by wagon train, their Texan ranch was apparently burned down by Apaches. They returned to Europe in 1881, and lived quietly in Spain and Hampshire, prior to inheriting the family seat of Gartmore on William's death in 1883.

Like other Victorian gentleman-adventurers, throughout his varied career, Graham remained a restless traveller, drawn particularly to Hispanic regions, and to Morocco. In 1897, along with Syrian and Moorish companions, he undertook a perilous reconnaissance mission to the forbidden city of Taroudant in southern Morocco, disguised as a Turkish doctor, but was captured and imprisoned. His adventurers were recorded in his most celebrated book, *Mogreb-El-Acksa* (1898).[5]

Graham's early experiences in wild and dangerous places, while failing to bring financial security, provided him with a wealth of material for his future literary career, but it also imbued him with a particularly egalitarian and ecologically conscious world-view, a strong constitution, and an apparently impervious hide. This, combined with strong moral convictions and a predilection for fearless outspokenness, motivated him to become an unpaid Member of Parliament, when his time might have been better employed managing the family debts. However, it might also be considered, that at the age of thirty-three, apart from farming and estate management, which bored him, he was too old for military service, and unqualified for anything else.

Despite being blessed with great charm, eloquence, and wit, which otherwise could have propelled him to high political office, Graham's brief time as an MP was marked by anger and frustration, when, for the first time, he was confronted with the realities of the lives of working people, and parliament's stubborn opposition to change. Oblivious to his own political future, his erratic behaviour, and his campaigns on behalf of labour, within and without the House of Commons, quickly brought him to wide public attention, but his attempts to change it, by the election of working men, would end in disillusionment.

While remaining politically active throughout his life, campaigning on behalf of the poor and the disadvantaged, for women's rights, animal welfare, and Irish and Scottish home rule, Graham, who was a highly original political propagandist, increasingly turned to the written word as his principal form of expression. This would be his most substantial legacy – a unique and stylish interweaving of his two major drives – his nostalgic evocation of vanishing exotic locales and eccentric

characters, and his unstinting critiques of human greed, hubris, hypocrisy, and folly.

~

To date there have been nine dedicated biographies of Graham in English, and one in Spanish, all of which are out of print. The first was
published in his lifetime by an American, Herbert Faulkner West: *A
Modern Conquistador: Robert Bontine Cunninghame Graham: His Life
and Works* (1932).[6] The second, and the best known, *Don Roberto:
Being the Account of the Life and Works of R. B. Cunninghame
Graham, 1852–1936*, was published in 1937, a year after his death,[7] by
his friend, the Swiss horseman Aimé Félix Tschiffely. We have to wait
thirty years for the third, by another American, Richard E. Haymaker's
*Prince-Errant and Evocator of Horizons: A Reading of R. B. Cunning-
hame Graham* (1967).[8] In 1978, Alicia Jurado published her *El Escocés
Errante: R. B. Cunninghame Graham*, in Buenos Aires,[9] and a year later,
Cedric Watts and Laurence Davies published *Cunninghame Graham: A
Critical Biography*.[10] Professor Watts published his own biography, *R. B.
Cunninghame Graham*, in 1983, as did Alexander Maitland, in a book
entitled *Robert and Gabriela Cunninghame Graham*.[11] The eighth, *R. B.
Cunninghame Graham: Fighter For Justice*, was published privately by
the Reverend Ian Fraser in 2002, and two years later, Graham's great-
niece, Jean Cunninghame Graham, published her *Gaucho Laird: The
Life of R. B. 'Don Roberto' Cunninghame Graham*.[12] The tenth, *The
People's Laird: A Life of Robert Bontine Cunninghame Graham*, was
published in 2005 by Anne Taylor.[13]

The first four biographies, written by foreign nationals, can be dismissed as semi-fantasies that focused on the romantic life of their subject. Tschiffely's book, for example, was severely compromised by what
he himself candidly described as 'the conflict between truth and affection',[14] and it showed signs of being published in a hurry, soon after
his subject's death. Graham had asked Tschiffely to undertake the task,
apparently because he found Faulkner West's biography dull,[15] but more
likely because he wished to exert more control over how he would be
remembered. Taylor exposed much of it as romantic fabrication,[16] adding, that after publication, Graham dead became instantly more famous
than Graham alive.[17] Hugh MacDiarmid claimed that Tschiffely regarded
himself as the editor of an autobiography for which Graham supplied the
material.[18]

Watts and Davies's *Critical Biography* took a much more analytical
and pragmatic approach to its subject, confining Graham's early and less

verifiable life to a mere forty-eight pages. Watts had already produced a spirited critical profile of Graham in the introduction to his *Joseph Conrad's Letters to Cunninghame Graham*,[19] which showed an interest in untangling the Graham legend, and that motivation continued here. The book came into its own, however, when Graham's writings were systematically examined, at the point when he began to marshal his talents in more subtle ways to challenge prevailing orthodoxies, demonstrating a particular abhorrence of the 'Kailyard School' of Scottish writing. Graham's unsettling dialectic style is discussed in some detail, making this work the only worthy companion for anyone approaching his writings for the first time.

Watts's own biography of Graham, *R. B. Cunninghame Graham*, was published four years later in the United States. This book had a more general intent than his more critical collaboration with Davies, and in the beginning at least, there is a strong heroic element in recounting Graham's life, and his political beliefs and activities were confined to the opening biographical chapter. The major focus was on Graham's later literary sketches, and these were dealt with in a perceptive, amusing, and sympathetic manner, although Watts concluded that Graham was not a major author.[20]

Robert and Gabriela Cunninghame Graham, by Alexander Maitland, was potentially a doubly romantic homage, redeemed by Maitland's tactful scepticism and his awareness of the many inconsistencies in Gabrielle's history, which 'appears to be strikingly, even unreasonably obscure'.[21] Maitland was as yet unaware that it had been entirely invented.

The Reverend Ian Fraser's *R. B. Cunninghame Graham Fighter For Justice: An Appreciation of His Social and Religious Outlook*, was derived from his PhD thesis (1955), and is the nearest we get to what Tschiffely described as 'the Freudian dissecting table'.[22] However, Fraser made no concerted attempt to speculate on his subject's psychology in any real depth, claiming that insights into his character were rare,[23] although he failed to include any reminiscences from Graham's friends and colleagues. Fraser also concluded that Graham could not have been a genuine socialist.[24]

The work of Graham's great-niece and literary executrix Jean Cunninghame Graham, *Gaucho Laird*, was a family-style biography, containing letters and personal anecdotes. Three-quarters of the book is taken up with her great-uncle 'Bob's' boyhood and his adventures in the Americas, presumably to satisfy her obscure publisher's equine interests. Nonetheless, it was not entirely without some academic relevance, as it offered valuable connections to real characters and events that Graham incorporated into his works, validating the idea that he wrote only from his own experiences. Startlingly, she revealed his wife's real name,[25] and her origins as the daughter of a Yorkshire doctor, not a Chilean poetess, as they both claimed. This fact alone, must, by necessity, colour perceptions of Graham's presentation of self, while also undermining the conclusions of previous biographies where 'Gabrielle' played a significant part.

Distance lent disenchantment to the final biography, Anne Taylor's *The People's Laird*, a work that added a new level of detail and understanding to Graham's life, and on occasions, his psychology, when much of the mythology was removed, and the two earliest biographies debunked as being fabricated by Graham himself. At once intimate and matter of fact, it is the most comprehensive, detailed, explicit, and brave biography, extensively researched and referenced, with the judicious use of reports from Hansard and local newspapers. Taylor also tackled Graham's father's severe mental condition, the fiction that in childhood he was educated by his Spanish grandmother and that his first language was Spanish; his reputation as a youthful philanderer; his dubious experiences as a 'gaucho', and his morganatic marriage to a woman who had invented an exotic *alter ego*. These were subjects that the other biographers were either unaware of, or treated as taboo. It is difficult to see how this biography could be improved upon as a factual record of events, and an objective commentary on Graham's life. It was, however, badly let down by poor production values.

Apart from Taylor, all of Graham's biographers have more or less swallowed his myth whole, particularly the early biographers, who simply eulogised his slanted recollections and vanities, aimed at keeping his own memory alive. Deeper investigations reveal an altogether more complex picture, involving many failures and disappointments. Watts and Davies's works were the first serious attempt to get at the truth, but they too seemed in awe of their subject, and were written to help resuscitate Graham's name and reputation. Overall, this has resulted in a disjuncture between Graham's political and his literary life, which this study will argue were inseparable.

Notes

1. Daughter of Vice-Admiral the Honourable Charles Elphinstone Fleeming of Cumbernauld (1774–1840), and *Doña* Catalina Paulina Alesandro de Jiminez of Cadiz (1800–80).

2. Graham wrote a biography of Robert Graham, entitled *Doughty Deeds* (1925).

3. The Gartmore estate, which stretched from Aberfoyle to Kippen, had been in the family for 300 years. The other two estates faced each other across the River Clyde. Finlaystone was sold in the 1860s, and Graham bought back Ardoch, after Gartmore was sold in 1900 to pay off the family debts.

4. Anthologised in Cunninghame Graham, *Thirteen Stories* (London: Heinemann, 1900), pp. 1–84.

5. Cunninghame Graham, *Mogreb-El-Acksa* (1898) (London: Century, 1988).

6. Herbert Faulkner West, *Cunninghame Graham: His Life and Works* (London: Cranley & Day, 1932).

7. Aimé Félix Tschiffely, *Don Roberto: Being the Account of the Life and Works of R. B. Cunninghame Graham, 1852–1936* (London: Heinemann, 1937). Tschiffely also published an abridged version, entitled *Tornado Cavalier* (London: Harrap, 1950).

8. Richard E. Haymaker, *Prince-Errant and Evocator of Horizons: A Reading of R. B. Cunninghame Graham* (printed privately, 1967).

9. Alicia Jurado, *El Escocés Errante: R. B. Cunninghame Graham* (Buenos Aires: Emecé Editores, 1978).

10. Cedric Watts and Laurence Davies, *Cunninghame Graham: A Critical Biography* (Cambridge University Press, 1979).

11. Alexander Maitland, *Robert and Gabriela Cunninghame Graham* (Edinburgh: William Blackwood, 1983).

12. Jean Cunninghame Graham, *Gaucho Laird: The Life of R. B. 'Don Roberto' Cunninghame Graham* (Long Riders' Guild Press, 2004).

13. Taylor, *The People's Laird*.

14. Tschiffely, *Don Roberto*, p. xix. In a review of this biography, the critic V. S. Pritchett described Tschiffely as having 'a capacity for hero-worship'. V. S. Pritchett, 'New Literature', *London Mercury*, Vol. XXXVII, January 1938, p. 339.

15. Taylor, *The People's Laird*, p. 238. T. E. Lawrence described it as 'a disappointing book. Anything about the old Don should have been written with swagger.' David Garnett, ed., *The Selected Letters of T. E. Lawrence* (London: World Books, 1941), p. 341.

16. Taylor, *The People's Laird*, p. 237.

17. Ibid., p. 331.

18. Hugh MacDiarmid, *Cunninghame Graham: A Centenary Study* (Glasgow: Caledonian Press, 1952), p. 22.

19. Cedric Watts, ed., *Joseph Conrad's Letters to R. B. Cunninghame Graham* (Cambridge University Press, 1969).

20. Cedric Watts, *R. B. Cunninghame Graham* (Boston: Twaynes English Authors, 1983), p. 114.

21. Maitland, *Robert and Gabriela Cunninghame Graham*, p. 21.

22. Tschiffely, *Don Roberto*, p. xix.

23. Ian M. Fraser, *R. B. Cunninghame, Graham, Fighter for Justice: An Appreciation of his Social and Religious Outlook* (self-published, 2002), p. 8.

24. Ibid., p. 51.

25. Caroline Horsfall. This fiction, exposed by a member of the Horsfall family in 1986, had apparently been contrived and maintained because Graham's mother did not approve of her.

Introduction: The Periodic Legend

CUNNINGHAME GRAHAM'S CAREER IN the public eye demonstrated a remarkable longevity, spanning over fifty years: from an aristocratic 'cowboy-dandy' and radical *enfant terrible* of the British political establishment, he moved to a state of near veneration amongst every class in society. In 1927, the gossip columnist of the popular *Sunday Post* reported, 'There are few men nowadays so well known as Mr R. B. Cunninghame Graham',[1] and on his death in 1936 his early biographer Tschiffely believed that 'his name will surely grow'.[2] However, he quickly faded from both the academic and the public consciousness, and a mere sixteen years later, on his centenary, the cultural revivalist Hamish Henderson asked the question, 'Who Remembers Cunninghame Graham?'[3]

There have been brief episodes of reawakened interest in Graham. These were stimulated by occasional biographies and new anthologies of his writings, references by writers and academics who portrayed him as a visionary or a quaint anomaly, and more recently by exaggerated or simplistic claims, often sponsored by those who wished to promote or justify their own political agendas. There have also been periodic attempts to reignite interest by those whom Wendell Harris dubbed 'eager champions',[4] but Graham's name and reputation have stubbornly refused rehabilitation, and his many literary works, which were never commercially popular in his lifetime, remain little read. Consequently, his champions have focused on the romantic aspects of his life. Foremost among these were his part-Spanish ancestry, his early adventures among the gauchos and natives of South America, and his travels in Morocco; his radicalism and erratic behaviour as a Liberal Member of Parliament and the first declared 'socialist' there, and the formation of an early Labour party; his large literary output,[5] and his role as an inspirational Scottish patriot. These have, however, obscured rather than illuminated Graham's life, and aggregated, they have left us with a unique simulacrum of a romantic idealist, aesthete, and dilettante – portrayals and perceptions that this study will challenge.

The reasons for Graham's eclipse were complex, but part of the explanation is that his career appeared both disparate and contradictory, bifurcated between the radical political campaigner and ardent polemicist, and a nostalgic essayist; a nationalist and an internationalist; a Justice of the Peace and a disturber of the peace. Graham's legend also fed off disparate and contradictory elements in his character; great charm and charisma, a powerful and deep-rooted morality and philanthropy that frequently militated against his own best interests, and a personal vanity, coupled with a surprising humility about his own literary talents. These were counterpoised by elitism, and the instincts of an adventurous and incautious showman, complex combinations outwith normal human experience. This study will, however, propose that despite occasional impulsive acts and injudicious remarks throughout his life, Graham, driven by strong moral impulses, and a sometimes overpowering vehemency, demonstrated remarkable consistency of thought, and his proposed solutions to perceived political and social disparities, despite occasionally being wildly idealistic for their time, were, for the most part, practical.[6]

Of his literary abilities, opinion was also extraordinarily divided, ranging from the author and journalist William Power's assessment that Graham was 'perhaps the finest literary artist alive in Europe today',[7] to an obituary a year later in *The Times*, in which he was described as 'neither an essayist nor a historian'.[8] In 1910, a critic in *The Observer* wrote of his sketches, 'Judged upon their style, they rank among the best things ever written in this country . . . little works of art that place the writer by the side of the great story-tellers of France and Russia',[9] while a biographer of Graham's great friend Joseph Conrad believed that Graham was never primarily a writer, let alone an artist.[10]

In an attempt to de-'mistify' Graham's controversial beliefs and achievements, this study has set aside, where possible, the more colourful aspects of his life, including his nostalgic overseas memoirs, and has focused on his contributions to the political and cultural life of Scotland. However, Graham's foreign experiences cannot be ignored entirely, for they were a very significant influence on his political outlook, and there were strong thematic parallels with his Scottish works, which consolidated rather than dissipated these nostalgic preoccupations. It was also his international and cross-cultural perspectives that fitfully broadened out the Scottish experience onto the world stage, and remain a significant factor in the position he now occupies in the pantheon of notable Scots.

Graham's literary reputation has fared badly in the academic world, and he was not regarded as a major author in his own lifetime, nor subsequently. What has distinguished Graham was his ability to divide opinion both as a politician and as a writer. Certainly, most of his high-profile supporters who admired his writings knew him personally, or were Scots of a similar political persuasion. Political persuasion has also influenced Graham's reputation in Labour history, where his profile did not fit the standard model of the working-class hero. However, the evidence of his role in the creation of the first party of labour, and the later nationalist parties, has hitherto been thin and speculative, a situation that this book intends to clarify.

~

This analysis has divided Graham's public presence into three chronological periods, representing distinctive boundaries between major liminal phases. Part I, from 1885 to 1892, appraises Graham's activities in and outwith parliament, and also examines his early political views. Although he kept no journal,[11] and his handwriting was notoriously opaque (see Appendix I), many of his early speeches were reported verbatim in local newspapers, including audience reactions.[12] This part is therefore obliged to rely heavily on these reports, and letters to the press, as it attempts to identify and abstract common political themes or causes, and contextualise them in the turbulent political climate of his times. Later, when Graham pursued his campaigns through political journalism, his opinions were more fully expressed, but these, hitherto, have not been analysed. This part of the book also explores his early social and political influences, where there is documentary evidence, or tangible philosophical links.

Despite being the first declared socialist MP, and hailed in some quarters as a 'founder' of the Labour party, in most histories of the early socialist movements in Britain, Graham occupies a minor and incongruous position. From fragmentary evidence, and first-hand accounts, his role in the creation of Britain's first party of labour, the Scottish Parliamentary Labour Party (SPLP), and his subsequent relationship with it and Keir Hardie are examined for the first time.

Part II examines the period from 1893 to 1913. During this time, out of parliament, Graham remained politically active, while also pursuing a career as an essayist for mainstream literary publications. Although he was now obliged to frame his views more discreetly for a politically conservative readership, it proposes that the common themes explored in his early campaigns and journalism fed obliquely into his more literary works. Despite an increasing tendency towards nostalgic reminiscences of South America, North Africa, and Scotland, it also asserts that his preoccupations did not fundamentally alter, but continued to reflect his political, social, and cultural concerns. It also conjectures on Graham's choice of literary form, and questions the conclusions of previous commentators.

PART III covers the period from 1914 until Graham's death in 1936, the chronologically longest, but least active period. It examines the considerable impact of the First World War on his political outlook and his later Scottish writings, in an attempt to set them in a contemporary milieu, and questions whether they can be seen as part of any literary or cultural movement peculiar to Scotland. From memoirs, correspondence, and newspaper reports, it also examines Graham's role in the foundation of the Scottish National Party (SNP).

~

These 'parts' are divided further into what the author perceives as common themes in Graham's utterances and writings throughout his career, which although not exclusively 'Scottish', gave voice to beliefs that were diametrically opposed to Victorian shibboleths on morality, power, class, and the wider world, and marked Graham out as the most contentious, controversial, and contradictory Scot of his generation.

The first of these themes or causes, the one that formed the basis of Graham's early disquiet, was exclusivity in *land*, particularly in Scotland and Ireland. But after his first-hand experiences of working and living conditions of the poor, this was quickly subsumed into his campaigns on behalf of *labour* and against capitalism, which would dominate his early political career. By the beginning of 1887, land, as a campaigning issue at home, had all but disappeared, although it persisted as an underlying factor in Graham's attitude towards Britain's *empire*, which he equated with capitalist exploitation, and in which the Scots were not only eager participants, but also unconscious victims.

In the wake of imperial conquest and expansion, came empire's more enduring aftermath, the detrimental effects of *colonialism*, and Graham's concerns over ethnic, cultural, and environmental loss, which he ironically described as 'progress'. Colonialism, however, was not restricted in his mind to foreign intrusion, but also to the creeping imposition of what he considered pernicious political, economic, and cultural attitudes everywhere, including Scotland. Finally, Graham's involvement in the politics of both Ireland and Scotland would encompass all the aforementioned themes, culminating, near the end of his life, in his support for Scottish independence.

Notes

1. *Sunday Post*, 13 November 1927, p. 15.
2. Aimé Felix Tschiffely, *Fortnightly Review*, May 1936, p. 559.
3. Hamish Henderson, 'Who Remembers Cunninghame Graham?' *Daily Worker*, November 1952. Reprinted in *Alias, MacAlias: Writing on Songs, Folk and Literature* (London: Polygon 1992), pp. 319–20.
4. Wendell V. Harris, 'R. B. Cunninghame Graham', in *English Literature in Transition, 1880–1920*, Vol. 3, 1987, p. 221.
5. These eventually comprised thirty-four published volumes, divided equally between histories and anthologies of his sketches, which originally appeared in literary journals; over one hundred polemical essays for small left-wing publications, five pamphlets, and fifty prefaces, forewords, and introductions to the works of others.
6. Graham described himself as 'a practical man'. *Airdrie Advertiser*, 19 September 1885, p. 6. Later he wrote, 'All imaginative men are also practical, whereas the men who think that they are practical pass their lives in a dream.' Cunninghame Graham, 'Futurism', *Justice: The Organ of Social Democracy*, 30 April 1914, p. 9.
7. William Power, *Literature and Oatmeal* (London: Routledge, 1935), p. 168. William Power (1873–1951), journalist and socialist, leader of the SNP, 1942–5.
8. *The Times*, 23 March 1936, p. 18.
9. *The Observer*, 16 October 1910, p. 5.
10. Jocelyn Baines, *Joseph Conrad* (London: Weidenfeld & Nicolson, 1960), p. 203.
11. 'I never took a note on any subject under heaven, nor kept a diary.' Quoted in C. Lewis Hind, 'R. B. Cunninghame Graham', in *More Authors and I* (London: John Lane, 1922), p. 76.
12. 'It is very difficult for a man to sit and hear himself being praised. It is a far easier thing to face a hostile meeting with interruptions, jeers, sneers, and insults – so long as they throw no loose building material about.' Cunninghame Graham, *Scotsman*, 3 June 1929, p. 7.

PART I

'THE PRENTICE POLITICIAN', 1885–92

Part I Introduction

A s THE NEW LAIRD of the 12,000-acre Gartmore Estate in southern Perthshire, Graham, whose family had a long history of radicalism[1] and support for the Liberal Party,[2] either applied, or was approached, to become a Liberal candidate in the upcoming general election of 1885. The Liberals had seemed like his natural home, and notwithstanding William Ewart Gladstone's dominance of party and policies, he believed that they considered the interests of others more highly than their own, stating: 'If this is the case, I am proud, and you all may be proud of belonging to that party, as, what higher morality is there in the world than to do to others as you would they should unto you.'[3]

Despite going on to represent an industrial seat, it was from a distinctly rural tradition that Graham's political potential would emerge.[4] J. P. Cornford called it:

> 'The charmed circle' [which] existed to the extent at least that these men came from a hereditary ruling class, that they took for granted that they would play a pre-eminent part in politics, and that almost everyone else did too.[5]

Graham's attempt to become a Member of Parliament occurred during a period of political disarray for the Liberals, with major divisions within the party over landownership, church disestablishment, and Irish home rule. In addition, there were ongoing disputes over party structures and organisation, a growing sense of unease among moderates over the party's future direction, and resistance to change from the party executive.[6] Graham's candidacy for an industrial seat would, however, have been particularly attractive to party managers (the 'wire-pullers'), where any radical appeal would be more palatable coming from the lips of someone of his pedigree, on the basis that:

> If a workman votes for a man with a carriage and pair it is because he believes that his views will be more adequately and effectively represented by him than his opponent, who may have to do his business on foot.[7]

After declining to stand in another Glasgow seat, Graham was selected to stand in the constituency of Camlachie, a deprived area in the East End of the city.

Graham's early speeches, prior to his entry onto the national stage, provide us with a window into his views, unalloyed by his later political experiences, but from the beginning, he placed himself at the radical end of the party.[8] The influence of his family inevitably impacted on Graham's attitudes; moreover, it appears that his experiences living and working among local populations in South America instilled in him a more egalitarian spirit than would normally be encountered in someone from a similar social background.

Notes

1. Despite part of the family fortune being built on the use of slave labour in Jamaica.

2. The colonial administrator W. P. Adam, twice Commissioner for Works under Gladstone, had been MP for Clackmannan and Kinross, and the Liberal Party's Chief Whip, was a cousin and close friend of Graham's mother. Graham's first cousin, Sir Edmond Fitzmaurice, had had a distinguished career as Under-Secretary of State for Foreign Affairs in Gladstone's administrations. In addition, the Lord Provost of Glasgow, William McOnie, who had chaired Graham's 'complimentary dinner' on becoming the new laird, was a Gartmore man, and had voiced his enthusiasm for recruiting Graham to the Liberal cause. 'Complimentary Dinner to R. C. Graham Bontine [sic] of Gartmore and Ardoch.' *Stirling Observer*, 28 August 1884, p. 3.

3. *Airdrie Advertiser*, 19 September 1885, p. 6.

4. I. G. C. Hutchison, *A Political History of Scotland, 1832–1924* (Edinburgh: John Donald, 1986), pp. 221–2. Also, I. G. C. Hutchison, *Scottish Politics in the Twentieth Century* (Basingstoke: Palgrave, 2001), p. 13.

5. J. P. Cornford, 'The Parliamentary Foundations of the Hotel Cecil', in *Ideas and Institutions of Victorian Britain*, ed. by Robert Robson (London: G. Bell, 1967), p. 269. Hutchison related how that in some parts of Scotland, the power and influence of county families persisted until well into the twentieth century. Hutchison, *A Political History of Scotland*, pp. 221–2.

6. James Kellas, 'The Liberal Party in Scotland 1876–1895', *Scottish Historical Review*, Vol. XLIV, No. 37, 1965, p. 5.

7. Quoted in P. F. Clarke, *Lancashire and the New Liberalism* (Cambridge University Press, 1971), p. 85.

8. Heyck and Klecka defined radicals in this specific context as 'persons devoted to the destruction of privilege in landowning, church, and state'. T. W. Heyck and William Klecka, 'British Radical M.P.s, 1874–1895: New Evidence From Discriminant Analysis', *Journal of Interdisciplinary History*, Vol. 4, No. 2, 1973, p. 179.

1

Land and Labour: Words Adorned by Reason

L AND OWNERSHIP AND IRISH home rule were fiercely debated topics during this period, and they were particularly relevant in the constituency that Graham wished to represent, which contained significant Irish and Highland populations, and these became fundamental and recurring themes of his early campaigns. Land ownership in particular became a political entry point for many reformers and proto-socialists, at a time when the Scottish Land Restoration League was contesting seats at the upcoming election[1] and encouraging land raids on Tiree, which were regularly reported in Scotland's industrial heartland. David Lowe, who ran the office of Keir Hardie's *Labour Leader* publication, related how Graham had declined to stand for his initial choice of seat at Blackfriars in Glasgow when he heard the Crofters' Party candidate, James Shaw Maxwell, speak: 'Graham did not go to the platform, but from the front seat he followed the speeches with great eagerness. The ideas which had long been simmering in his head were being clothed in words and adorned by reason.'[2]

Graham's first recorded political speech was on 11 August 1885, when he was a guest speaker at Coatbridge in the contiguous constituency of North-West Lanarkshire, which, like Camlachie, was an industrial black-spot with significant Irish and Highland populations.[3] As a large landowner himself, he began diffidently on the subject of the speed of social and political reform, but unexpectedly, as if to distance himself from his own social position, he launched into an attack on the British upper classes, and their monopoly of the land:

> Here, and here almost alone, has the existence of enormous territorial possessions continued, and whilst in other civilised countries we find the land almost exclusively cultivated by the peasants or agricultural labourers themselves, in Great Britain is still to be found a class of feudal magnates who still enjoy privileges such as no class should enjoy to the exclusion of the rest in a civilised country.[4]

With these words, we can discern the first indication of the source of Graham's general disquiet and perturbation: that there were glaring disparities and imbalances at the very foundations of society, which were deforming it for the benefit of the few but to the disadvantage of the many. These were common, but deeply moral, aesthetic, and social impulses,[5] acting upon someone who was already predisposed to strong feelings of compassion and a sense of justice. At this stage, this disparity was most obvious in the ownership and distribution of land, particularly in Ireland and Scotland.

According to Graham, these monopolies had led to the extinction of 'our ancient class of sturdy yeomen', and in the Highlands, the population was 'constrained to live on the salvage of the land . . . situated between the devil and the deep sea'.[6] His proposed solution was the abolition of the inheritance laws and free trade in land, but he would also support a land tax.[7] These views, which were closer to the doctrines of H. M. Hyndman's quasi-Marxist Social Democratic Federation (SDF), in which William Morris had previously been active, would already have placed Graham among the supporters of advanced Scottish Liberalism, and they were met with an enthusiastic response from the floor. The speech, however, bore all the hallmarks of a probationary sermon, and the chairman assured the audience that the local association would proceed with the selection of a candidate with great vigour. A week later, Graham was invited to stand, which the Liberals in Camlachie did not oppose.

Land reform had been a highly contentious political issue for several years; John Stuart Mill had fervently attacked the landlord class in his *Principles of Political Economy* (1848), and he founded the Land Tenure Reform Association in 1868. The Irish National Land League was established in 1879, and in that year, one of its leading lights, Michael Davitt, proposed land nationalisation at a mass meeting in Glasgow. This issue was also part of a growing political and cultural awareness in both Ireland and Scotland, and a dissatisfaction with their place in the Union. In Scotland's case, dissatisfaction had initially grown over the treatment of Scottish legislation in parliament, and the issue of absentee landlords, particularly English owners of Scottish estates, referred to as 'holiday Celtic chiefs',[8] which W. L. Renwick cannily described as 'only half consciously, the native's resentment of the smug outsider who intrudes on his emotional territory'.[9] Vociferous objectors to this state of affairs included men like the classicist and Scottish patriot Professor John Stuart Blackie (1809–95),[10] the campaigning and disruptive Free Church of Scotland minister, James Begg (1808–83), the novelist James Grant (1822–87),[11] and through his newspaper *The Highlander*, John

Murdoch (1818–1903), who had worked in Ireland and associated with Irish nationalists. Employing Irish Land League methods, rent strikes began in Skye, followed by riots and arrests, which spread to other communities. James Hunter described parts of the Highlands and Islands, in the first weeks of 1883, as passing 'out of the United Kingdom's jurisdiction'.[12] By the spring of 1881, parliament had begun debating an Irish Land Bill, which gave rights to Irish tenants that were not available to Highland crofters.

The creation of the Scottish Land Restoration League in 1884, and increased civil disobedience in Ireland and Scotland, had also been inspired by the American Henry George's book *Progress and Poverty* (1879),[13] and by George's popular speaking tours in Britain and Ireland in the 1880s. Although he had developed revolutionary theories of land ownership, capital, and trade, George declared himself not to be a socialist,[14] but his works – rather than the writings of Karl Marx – are considered by many to be the major catalysts for the new breed of British radicals. The Labour politician, Philip Snowden, recalled, 'Keir Hardie told me that it was *Progress and Poverty* which gave him his first ideas of socialism. No book ever written on the social problem made so many converts',[15] and according to Peter Jones, Graham was more strongly influenced by George than any other writer,[16] although he did not substantiate this. Hardie would write of George's influence thus:

> Some years later, Henry George came to Scotland and I read *Progress and Poverty*, which unlocked many of the industrial and economic difficulties which beset the mind of the worker trying to take an intelligent interest in his own affairs and led me, much to George's horror in later life when he met me, into Communism.[17]

George's fundamental economic tenet was that restricted land ownership had driven the working population into poverty, by reducing farmers to tenants and labourers,[18] and had forced the rural population into the slums and sweatshops of the cities. He concluded:

> The wide-spreading social evils which everywhere oppress men amid an advancing civilisation spring from *a great primary wrong* – the appropriation, as the exclusive property of some men, of the land on which and from which all must live.[19]

His solution was not to confiscate the land, but to nationalise rents through taxation, and in consequence, '[t]o abolish all taxation save that upon land values',[20] thereby obliging large landowners to dispose of their property in small lots. Graham had only hinted at this solution in this first speech, but he had proposed giving powers to municipal councils for the compulsory purchase of land around county towns and villages, to be let out as crofts to labourers desirous of farming on a small scale,[21] with the aim of re-establishing strong local communities. Many years later, William Power wrote of Graham's belief in 'the Scotland of his dreams, which he is valiantly helping to create, is a Scotland nobly self-reliant and bravely idealistic, worthy of her own finest social and cultural traditions'.[22] Nor was Graham alone in this optimistic hope. W. H. Fraser contended that books like William Morris's *Earthly Paradise* (1870) and *News from Nowhere* (1890), particularly appealed in Scotland with their hankering for a rural past,[23] and this would also become a recurring theme in Graham's future literary output.

George's 'single tax' proposals had many adherents,[24] and it remained a political issue well into the twentieth century. The Liberal Government adopted such a scheme in their 1909 'People's Budget', as did the Labour government in 1931, but they were never implemented. However, it became increasingly challenged, particularly by socialists, who saw it as a distraction from the real cause of poverty – capitalism – and later, Graham himself became a vociferous opponent.[25]

Graham's election campaign gathered pace during the autumn of 1885, attracting larger and more enthusiastic audiences, and his statements became more extreme. Whereas in his first speech he had emphasised the huge inequalities of class, in his second, for the first time, in what would be a major theme of his campaigns, he passionately specified the consequences of such disparities:

> The Dukes of Westminster with £1000 a day and match makers in the East End of London, who after a hard day's toil, go to bed hungry – if the agricultural labourers of the Midland Counties of England, divorced from all connection with the soil of his native country, starving on 9s or 10s a week, and herded into one room with his male and female relatives of several generations, is a spectacle for much congratulation, then, certainly we are capable of no improvement.[26]

In a more radical departure, Graham then attacked 'the grasping capitalist class', and condemned 'the reduction of the great bulk of the population to the position of mere wage slaves'. Nevertheless, he refused to condemn capital and commerce outright, stating only that capital should be more equally distributed back to the labouring classes[27] – a particularly 'Georgist' philosophy. He proposed the payment of MPs,[28] which, he would subsequently state, would attract working-class members to an institution currently made up of 'landowners, capitalists, and lawyers, and far too few miners and masons'.[29] This was the first hint of what would become his fundamental political campaign, to have working men sent to parliament. He also stated that, since he advocated the abolition of primogeniture and entail, he supported the abolition of the House of Lords. Moreover, in an even more controversial statement, which separated him from the Liberals, Georgists, and the 'single-taxers', for the first time, he proposed the nationalisation of land, although the local newspaper report of his speech did not elucidate.[30] However, the radical nature of this proposal was unexceptional amongst the more dissident sections of society. The influential Scottish Liberal, R. B. Haldane, wrote: 'Nationalisation of land makes its appearance in the list of many a London Working Men's Club. Nationalisation of ordinary capital and State-regulation of wages appear hardly less frequently.'[31]

At this juncture, prior to entering the House of Commons, Graham's proposals were an assortment of radical influences, some of which had an old pedigree. Some echoed the Chartists' demands of almost fifty years earlier, and the rest were by no means unique. What was unique was that a major landowner and landlord, such as Graham, could put forward such proposals, which were controversial in Liberal circles at this time.[32] This would lead to accusations, both at public meetings and in the press, of hypocrisy, and place him in a paradoxical position of which he was very conscious. In 1887, *The Scotsman* suggested that Graham should put his faith in his socialist gospel by distributing his property among the poor.[33] In 1892, during his campaign to win Camlachie as a 'Labour' candidate, an elector asked, 'Seeing Mr Graham had stated that he was in favour of land nationalisation without compensation, would he show a good example and throw up his own land?' Graham replied that he would not; he was in favour of land nationalisation – not charity, but justice: '*If he threw up his land he would be shutting his mouth.*'[34] Herein lay the double paradox in which Graham now found himself. In an era of deference to power and money, particularly 'old' money, it had been his landed inheritance that had propelled him into a position of influence, where he could condemn the very system that had put him there, knowing full well that expressing such controversial views without his privileged position, he would have been ignored as a crank.

Until the 1885 general election, the land and Irish home rule questions were Graham's key issues, but growing in importance was the social question, and what he saw as the Liberal Party's responsibility:

I should suppose that the ultimate object of every Liberal worth the name is to endeavour to ameliorate the existing social conditions and to strive as far as possible to render the lives of the poor more bearable to them. Then by a wise and carefully considered legislation so to adjust the incidence of taxation that the heaviest burdens may be laid on those fittest to bear them, and lastly to endeavour so to reform our social system as to induce a greater division of wealth.[35]

He would find this a misplaced supposition, leading to increasing criticism and disputes with his party.

Graham's chances of success in the seat looked encouraging, but immediately before the election, Charles Stewart Parnell, leader of the Irish Parliamentary Party, issued an order to the newly enfranchised Irish voters in Britain, that in seats where a Conservative was opposed by a Liberal or a radical, they were to cast their votes in favour of the Conservative Party, since they now offered the best hope of progress towards Irish home rule. This was announced locally in the *Coatbridge Express*,[36] and it would prove fatal to Graham's campaign, as the Irish vote[37] swung solidly behind his opponent, John Baird,[38] himself a Highland landowner, and a nephew of ironmaster Alexander Baird of Lochwood,[39] the founder of Coatbridge's industrial wealth.

General Election Result, North-West Lanarkshire, *4 December 1885*

John Baird (Conservative)	4,543
R. B. Cunninghame Graham (Liberal)	3,442
Majority	1,103

Gladstone scraped back into power, with the support of the Irish MPs, on the basis that he would introduce an Irish Home Rule Bill. When this was defeated on 8 June 1886, he resigned. A second election was called for 9 July 1886, and Graham was again selected as the candidate for North-West Lanarkshire.

The Irish Question would dominate this 'Home Rule Election',[40] and formed the almost exclusive focus of Graham's speeches during the brief campaign. What also marked out this speeches was his apparent adherence to Gladstone, perhaps following criticism within the Liberal ranks during his previous campaign.[41] Despite this, he soon felt confident enough, while still appearing to support his leader, to openly criticise members of his own party, referring to them as 'galvanized corpses', and 'electroplated Liberals'.[42] This was no doubt intended to appeal to the radical elements who increasingly comprised his audiences, but it was a precursor of much more trenchant criticism once he was elected.

General Election Result, North-West Lanarkshire, *9 July 1886*

R. B. Cunninghame Graham (Ministerialist)	4032
John Baird (Conservative)	3698
Majority	334

Later, Graham would claim that it was the swing in the Irish vote that had won him the seat,[43] and not unexpectedly, the *Glasgow Herald* lamented his victory as 'both a surprise and a disappointment'.[44]

When he eventually took his seat, Graham declined to sit amongst his fellow Liberals, who were now in opposition, but, in what was an obvious statement, he sat between the Irish members and the newly elected MPs of Scotland's Crofters' Party. Considering his avowed support for Gladstone, which had helped him win, this was an act of open rebellion, and an indication that he had already decided to act independently.[45] The first opportunity for him to do this, and to 'lose his political virginity' as he termed it, was his maiden speech delivered in response to 'Her Majesty's Most Gracious Speech' on 1 February 1887, which was regarded by many as a satirical tour de force. This witty and blistering attack focused mostly on international affairs, and Ireland (dealt with below), but, appropriate to this analysis, both reflected on the consequences for the poor, and demonstrated an increasing concern for the pay and conditions of the British working classes. (For full text, see Appendix II.)

Graham's confidence and audacity quickly brought him to the attention of the political establishment, and he would remain a highly controversial figure during his brief parliamentary career. But here we can discern, for the first time, an outspoken freedom and sophistication of expression that would have been inappropriate within the confines of local party hustings, where he was often obliged to dissemble, or play to the sympathies of particular interest groups. Here also, his liberal use of quotes and references from many other sources would become a distinctive feature of his later political journalism, and mark him out as a highly original communicator. Watts and Davies raised an important point, which in retrospect we may also discern in his earlier pronouncements: 'There is the voice of the aesthete and wit.'[46] They also commented on another early parliamentary speech by Graham on the Ambleside Railway Bill, which combined 'social and aesthetic themes'.[47]

Graham's views, and his behaviour in parliament, were polarising opinion back in his constituency, as witnessed by a letter to the *Coatbridge Express*, signed 'Gladstonian':

> Will no candid friend risk the approbation of Mr Graham's worshippers, by giving the hon. gentleman's coat-tail a figurative pull, in the shape of an outspoken remonstrance when he exceeds the bounds of common-sense in his speeches and general conduct, as he has done lately in a most inordinate degree?[48]

These words point to a divergence in sympathies between the traditional Liberal members (in what we might call the 'Whig' and 'Moderate' traditions), and the enthusiasm of the party's new, perhaps younger supporters and newly enfranchised voters.

Although he was an MP for one political party, and would be a key figure in helping found two others, Graham freely admitted that he was not a party politician,[49] and in the following year, at a meeting of miners in Kilwinning, 'he reminded his hearers *that he belonged to no political party*'.[50] Convinced, moreover, that none of the political parties was in earnest, having no intention to fulfil any of the pledges they had given to the electors at the election times,[51] his increasing frustrations led to frenetic interruptions and incendiary language in the House. These were adversely reported in the *Airdrie Advertiser* under the title 'Mr. Graham's Eccentricities',[52] and on three occasions he was expelled from the Chamber for unparliamentary behaviour.

A remarkable feature of Graham's speeches, before and after entering parliament, was his willingness to express increasingly contentious and uncompromising opinions. He seemed oblivious to criticism, and even ridicule, which would be interpreted as a dismissive elitism. As the *Scottish Leader* reported, 'Mr Graham draws criticism upon himself from all sides – and the sternest form of it sometimes from those who are largely in sympathy with him'.[53] This illustrated not only a growing frustration, but also a careless attitude to the views of others, or, as *The Scotsman* put it, 'He has a great contempt for those who differ from him, and a great contempt for matters that stand in the way of the adoption of his principles'.[54] The English press wholeheartedly agreed:

> He is above all things a 'misanthropic professional philanthropist', whose love for his fellow man in the abstract is compatible with a limitless capacity for making himself objectionable to individuals in the concrete . . . He is unquestionably the most unpopular man in the House of Commons.[55]

Graham's condemnations became even more strident. In 1889, he described 'the odious bourgeois tyranny of the Gladstonian Liberals [who were] just as tyrannical to the working classes, and ten times more hypocritical than the Tories'.[56] By 1890 he considered that the Liberals be treated more severely than the Tories since they professed to be friends of the people, but were 'hypocritical Gladstonian bourgeois capitalists in disguise'.[57] Earlier that month he wrote:

> Take a biscuit, ascend to the upper galleries of the House of Commons, drop it . . . it shall have bounced from the bald head of a millionaire and rolled onto the paunch of a Capitalist, no matter from which side of the House you dispatch it.[58]

Graham's growing frustration and moral outrage with parliamentary politics was succinctly summed up in his article for the *People's Press*:

In the meantime all goes on as usual, the Devil's Dance we know so well, the drinking, drabbing, cheating, praying, stealing, the children crying for bread, the parents working at starvation pay for hideous hours (12 hours the average working day in England), the sweater piling up his wealth, the worker getting leaner and the idler fatter, the hatred growing deeper day by day, Liberals and Tories being leagued, by any means, by force or fraud, or both, to stop the working classes passing any legislation helpful to them, capital and labour being each day more fiercely antagonistic than the day before.[59]

If the land issue and Irish home rule had been predominant in trying to win his seat, on entering the House, they became less so, being quickly overtaken by the labour question, and parliament's inability or unwillingness to tackle social issues.

Notes

1. Kellas wrote that 'the Highland land reformers played an important part in the establishment of the Scottish Labour Party'. James Kellas, 'The Mid Lanark Election and The Scottish Labour Party (1888–1894)', *Parliamentary Affairs*, No. 18, 1964, p. 318.
2. David Lowe, *Forward*, 9 April 1910, p. 3.
3. Since 1883, there had been large and active Highland Association in Coatbridge, where land ownership was hotly discussed. *Coatbridge Express*, 11 November 1885, p. 2.
4. *Airdrie Advertiser*, 15 August 1885, p. 6.
5. Raymond Williams asserted that this concept was 'essentially, a product of the intellectual history of the nineteenth century'. Raymond Williams, *Culture and Society, 1780–1950* (London: Chatto & Windus, 1967), p. 130.
6. *Airdrie Advertiser*, 15 August 1885, p. 6.
7. Ibid.
8. H. J. Hanham, 'Mid-Century Scottish Nationalism: Romantic and Radical', in *Ideas and Institutions of Victorian Britain*, ed. by Robert Robson (London: G. Bell, 1967), p. 156.
9. W. L. Renwick, 'Introduction' to *W. E. Aytoun: Stories & Verse* (Edinburgh University Press, 1964), p. xiv.
10. As a direct influence on Graham's stance on the land issue, it may have been no coincidence that in the same year, Professor Blackie had published his book *The Scottish Highlanders and the Land Laws* (London: Chapman & Hall, 1885), which contained what he described as 'harrowing narratives' of Highland evictions. Blackie put the blame squarely on the shoulders of the English landlord, who has 'a right to do what he chooses with his own', p. 60, and he also deprecated the draining of the Highland population into the large industrial towns, p. 67. Graham, however, did not go so far in his specific 'national' accusations at this early stage of his career. As Vice-President of the SHRA, Graham would have known the Association's President, Blackie. A meeting, which both men attended, was reported in the *South London*

Gazette, 9 June 1888, p. 7, but so far, there are no other strong evidential links between them.

11. A second cousin of Sir Walter Scott, Grant was a founder and joint secretary of the earliest Scottish 'nationalist' organisation, the National Association for the Vindication of Scottish Rights (NAVSR).

12. James Hunter, *The Last of the Free* (Edinburgh: Mainstream Publishing, 1999), p. 313.

13. Henry George, *Progress and Poverty* (New York: Doubleday & Page, 1879. Reprinted in London: The Henry George Foundation of Great Britain, 1931). The book is estimated to have sold 3 million copies.

14. Henry George, *Protection and Free Trade* (London: Kegan Paul, 1886). Notes to Chapter XXVIII.

15. Philip Snowden, *An Autobiography* (London: Ivor, Nicholson & Watson, 1934), p. 49. Another noted convert was the erstwhile stockbroker, H. M. Hyndman, leader of the SDF.

16. Peter d'A. Jones, 'Henry George and British Labor Politics', *American Journal of Economics and Sociology*, Vol. 46, No. 2, 1987, p. 250.

17. James Keir Hardie, in *Review of Reviews*, June 1906, p. 57. George's unexpected second place in the New York City mayoral election of 2 November 1886, on behalf of the United Labor Party, which had come as a shock to many, also gave great encouragement to British socialists. The *Glasgow Herald* reported, 'The majority of his followers are ignorant labourers who flocked to him from the idea that he would do something to ameliorate their condition . . . The solid mass of 68,000 voters so led constitute a menace to social stability which is serious.' *Glasgow Herald*, 4 November 1886, p. 7.

18. Henry George, *Social Problems* (London: Kegan Paul, 1884), p. 56.

19. George, *Progress and Poverty*, p. 241. My italics.

20. Ibid., p. 288. George's proposals had a predecessor in Thomas Spence's book *Property in Land: Every One's Right* (1775), which Hyndman republished as *The Nationalization of the Land*, in 1882. Also, John Morrison Davidson's work, *Concerning Four Precursors of Henry George and the Single Tax* (1902), in which he asserted that the Scots, William Ogilvie (*An Essay on the Right of Property in Land*, 1781), and Patrick Edward Dove (*The Theory of Human Progression*, 1850), among others, had preceded George's proposals. Davidson himself had campaigned against landowners within the Liberal party (which at that time would have included Graham) for thirty years. In 1904, Graham wrote an introduction to Davidson's book *Scotland for the Scots*, which demonstrated Graham's own nationalist instincts. (For full text, see Appendix VI.)

21. Such a bill for compulsory purchase was proposed in the House of Commons by young progressive Liberals in 1891 and 1892, aided by the Fabian, Sidney Webb, but was unsuccessful.

22. Power, *Literature and Oatmeal*, p. 169.

23. W. Hamish Fraser, *Scottish Popular Politics: From Radicalism to Labour* (Edinburgh University Press, 2000), p. 119.

24. George's ideas had many supporters in Scotland, particularly in Glasgow. Elwood P. Lawrence, *Henry George in the British Isles* (Michigan State University Press, 1957), p. 117. Hutchison stated that for many Liberals the single tax 'became very attractive'. Hutchison, *Scottish Politics*, p. 6.

25. Between 13 October 1906 and 2 February 1907, Thomas Johnston's *Forward* denounced George as a defender of capitalism, under headlines such as 'False and Misleading Statements' and 'Popular Fallacies – Henry George Exposed'. In 1912, Graham claimed that Socialism had left George's ideas 'half a century behind'. *Glasgow Herald*, 27 September 1912, p. 8.

26. *Airdrie Advertiser*, 19 September 1885, p. 6.

27. Ibid.

28. This had been a fundamental demand of the Chartist movement which had been active in the early part of the century.

29. *Coatbridge Express*, 11 November 1885, p. 3.

30. Ibid.

31. R. B. Haldane, 'The Liberal Party and its Prospects', *Contemporary Review*, January 1888, p. 149.

32. After 1889, the taxing of land was increasingly taken up by Liberal and radical politicians.

33. *Scotsman*, 6 December 1887, p. 4.

34. *Glasgow Evening News*, 25 June 1892, p. 5. My italics.

35. *Coatbridge Express*, 4 November 1885, p. 1.

36. *Coatbridge Express*, 25 November 1885, p. 1, and 2 December 1885, p. 2.

37. Most Irish males in the constituency still did not meet the extended franchise criteria set out in the Third Reform Act of 1884.

38. *Coatbridge Express*, 2 December 1885, p. 2. Baird had sensationally displayed his feudal instincts in front of the Napier Commission in 1883. Graham and Baird, however, remained on cordial terms, having attended Harrow School together. Graham later stated, 'two men more profoundly ignorant of every political question than Mr. Baird and myself you could not possibly have found'. *Coatbridge Express*, 8 June 1889, p. 4.

39. Another estate once owned by Graham's great-great-grandfather, Robert Graham of Gartmore. Cunninghame Graham, *Doughty Deeds* (London: Heinemann, 1925), p. 162.

40. Hutchison, *A Political History of Scotland*, p. 169.

41. *Airdrie Advertiser*, 3 July 1886, p. 5.

42. *Coatbridge Express*, 7 July 1886, p. 2.

43. *Airdrie Advertiser*, 2 November 1889, p. 5. At least one Irish political activist had been encouraging his compatriots to vote for Graham. On 2 July 1886, at a largely attended meeting of Irish electors in Whifflet, the speaker (Mr Kierney, National League Organiser) encouraged them to 'vote solid for Mr Cunninghame Graham (*Cheers.*)'. *Airdrie Advertiser*, 3 July 1886, p. 5.

44. *Glasgow Herald*, 10 July 1886, p. 4.

45. This is perplexing. Heyck and Klecka, through their use of the statistical procedure of 'discriminant analysis', calculated that with the loss of Whig

and 'moderate' Liberals over the Irish Home Rule crisis by 1886, the Radicals formed the majority of Liberal MPs in Parliament. Heyck and Klecka, 'British Radical M.P.s, 1874–1895', p. 179.

46. Watts and Davies, *Cunninghame Graham*, p. 58.

47. Ibid., p. 59. Graham made this speech a month after meeting William Morris. It may not be a coincidence that Morris was a disciple of John Ruskin, and in 1876, Ruskin had supported a protest against the proposed extension of the railway, organised by his St George's Company. It is likely that Graham was giving voice to Morris's own long-held objections.

48. *Coatbridge Express*, 3 August 1887, p. 3.

49. *Airdrie Advertiser*, 21 April 1888, p. 5. As early as November 1885 Graham had told prospective constituents at Calderbank that 'no man should follow his party so blindly as to entirely divest himself of his own free will'. *Airdrie Advertiser*, 21 November 1885, p. 5. In 1908, he stated that 'he had always held that the party system had been the curse of the country'. *Glasgow Herald*, 20 October 1908, p. 7.

50. *Coatbridge Express*, 27 November 1889, p. 2 My italics.

51. *Coatbridge Express*, 8 June 1889, p. 4.

52. *Coatbridge Express*, 20 August 1887, p. 4.

53. Reported in *Coatbridge Express*, 6 March 1889, p. 2, after Graham was 'pilled' (his membership rescinded) at the Reform Club in London.

54. *Scotsman*, 20 April 1892, p. 6.

55. *Observer*, 20 June 1889, p. 4.

56. Cunninghame Graham, letter to *The Scotsman*, 14 October 1889, p. 8.

57. Cunninghame Graham, letter to *People's Press*, 31 May 1890, pp. 4–5.

58. *People's Press*, 3 May 1890, p. 18.

59. Cunninghame Graham, 'Joined to Their Idols', *People's Press*, 22 November 1890, p. 7.

2

Political Influences: Metamorphosis

B EFORE PROCEEDING TO WHAT would be a major crossroads in
Graham's political career, it is worth considering the influence of
other political and social thinkers who would inspire him. Like his influence on Keir Hardie and many others, Henry George's impact on Graham
was that of a medium, between the land issue, and his later full-blown
socialism, a step that George himself did not take. An earlier influence,
however, one who may have underpinned his early political attitudes,
appears to have been the Welsh philanthropist and social reformer
Robert Owen (1771–1858), but the only clue to this was a reference in
William Morris's diary of 27 April 1887, where he recorded a speech
that he, Morris, had made in Glasgow:

> Cunninghame Graham M.P. took the chair for me . . . he declared himself
> not to be a socialist *because* he agreed with the Owenite doctrine of man
> being made by circumstances; which seemed strange, & I rather took him up
> on that point.[1]

It is not clear what Graham meant by this statement, or if his knowledge
of, or interest in Owen, was recent or longer term, but certainly, there
are strong resonances of Owen's theories in Graham's political and social
outlook.[2]

Owen was another practical idealist whose ideas Graham may have
been drawn to, and another man, like George, who offered readily
understood solutions to societal ills, believing that man's character was
moulded by his cultural and physical environment. Through his social
experiments, Owen had attempted 'to make the workplace "rational,"
thus to bring "harmony" to the community, to make it a place where
social peace would reign'.[3] This was essentially an aesthetic argument,
which would have undoubtedly resonated with Graham's search for
political enlightenment.[4] It also chimed with Joseph Conrad's assertion

that, fundamentally, it was human nature that Graham wished to see changed.[5] Moreover, according to Owen, changes to the environment, and thus man's character, could be instigated only by 'those who have influence in the affairs of men'.[6] Whether this idea influenced Graham to become a man of affairs himself can only be conjectured, certainly, it carried a subtext with which Graham undoubtedly agreed – elitism.[7] Also, Owen's solution was a rural one, wherein the bulk of the population would labour on the land to secure their sustenance:

> [A] whole population engaged in agriculture, with manufactures *as an appendage*, will, in a given district, support many more, and in a much higher degree of comfort, than the same district could do with its agricultural separate from its manufacturing population.[8]

This would also have been highly appropriate to the Scotland of his dreams, but by Graham's time, in an increasingly industrialised country, with a huge and expanding imperial market for its manufactured goods, it was extraordinarily unrealistic. Notwithstanding, it is an idea that finds echoes in Graham's equally unrealistic desire to recapture his idealised rural past, which would constantly recur in his Scottish writings.

Here then, we have two almost certain influences on Graham's early political thought. The first, Georgist, was that from time immemorial, the appropriation and exclusive property in land was the direct cause of poverty, both in the countryside and the cities, and since this was a fundamental anomaly, its continuation would only exacerbate the lot of the poor. Thus, we have Graham's commitment to radically alter the terms of land ownership and distribution. The second, Owenite, was that from birth, the human mind was a *tabula rasa*, but since time immemorial, people had been conditioned by circumstances into certain modes of thought and types of behaviour.[9] Thus we witness Graham's campaigns for a shorter working day (as a starting point for a more extensive improvement in working and living conditions), free education, and a more nebulous attack on class divisions (not yet class politics). According to Owen, however, these reforms could only be instigated from above, and since men of influence and power were by and large landowning or capitalist politicians, as things stood, it was inevitable that any attempt by men like Graham to change society through parliamentary action was doomed to failure, unless parliament itself, controlled by such men, was radically changed. Thus we have Graham's later but overarching campaign to get working men elected. However, this change could only be instigated by an intelligentsia. For Graham, perhaps, Owen and George's proposals were complementary, and combining them would mean a return to the land in a more sustainable way than before, for a more self-sufficient population, while manufacturing would be carried out along more rational lines, without dispute, for the benefit of all. Graham's early agenda can be viewed as being idealistic and unrealisable – utopian; it is an aesthetic ideal, but there was unquestionably a logical, practical, but perhaps reductive mind at work.

Graham's words and behaviour had attracted the attention of prominent socialists, and he was soon embraced by the denizens of London's radical demi-monde, rubbing shoulders with Marx's daughter Eleanor, and her husband, Edward Aveling, the anarchist Prince Pyotr Kropotkin, and Henry Hyndman; activists such as Annie Besant,[10] and the trade unionists John Burns, Ben Tillet, and Tom Mann. Withal, on 26 January 1887, five days before his maiden speech, Graham sought out his most direct and powerful influence, the English textile designer, poet, author, socialist, and Victorian one-man industry, William Morris (1834–96), a central figure in the Arts and Crafts Movement. However, it was not until after Graham's maiden speech that Morris considered it worth recording their meeting in his diary:

> I ought to have noted that on the day that Parliament met, a young and new M.P., Cunninghame Graham by name, called on me by appointment to pump me on the subject of Socialism. A brisk sort of young man; the other day he makes his maiden speech and produced quite an impression by its brilliancy & socialistic hints.[11]

Graham's political and literary career was characterised by fortuitous if unintended consequences, and Morris's biographer, A. C. Rickett, wrote:

> It was the remarkable maiden speech of Mr Cunninghame Graham in the House of Commons that first drew him [Morris] towards the speaker. He recognised at once a man of rare courage, combined with an eloquence and intellectual power seldom found in the arena of modern politics.[12]

The three scholarly biographies of Graham place Morris as the foremost influence on his early political development. In Watts and Davies's *Cunninghame Graham: A Critical Biography*, two reflective comments stand out. The first was Morris's assertion that he had been 'forced by the study of history and the love and practice of art into a hatred of civilisation which, if things were to stop as they are, would turn history into inconsequent nonsense',[13] which they believed might equally have applied to Graham himself.[14] The second was their reference to Graham's 'Morris-like instinct to relate the political to the aesthetic and cultural'.[15] The authors did not develop this idea, but it is a highly significant factor in understanding Graham's uniqueness and legacy.

Anne Taylor speculated that Graham was attracted to Morris's denunciation of what he called 'the filth of civilisation':[16]

> whereby the acts of selfish industrialists and greedy tradesmen threaten to destroy everything of beauty and traditional worth. Later it confronted him each time, on returning home from some far distant country as yet untouched by industry, his ship traversed the riverside slums of Liverpool or Glasgow.[17]

Taylor further believed that it was Morris who consolidated Graham's metamorphosis into a socialist,[18] or as Watts recorded:

> [Morris] helped to convert into socialism his freelance radicalism and to divert into political channels his aristocratic contempt for the bourgeoisie, his chivalrous sympathy for the underdog, and his aesthetic revulsion against the grime and squalor of industrial Victorian Britain.[19]

James Redmond wrote that Morris's socialism had a compassionate rather than an ideological basis, which in no way mitigated the seriousness, even violence of his conviction.[20] Hyndman's description of Morris might be more pertinent: 'What was inartistic and untrue jarred upon him so acutely that he was driven to try and put it right all at once.'[21] Both of these analyses, including the elements of impulsive vehemency and manic drive, could equally be applied to Graham.

Graham would refer to Morris as 'a dear friend of mine',[22] and in 1919, writing to the dramatist Henry Arthur Jones, he stated, 'I became a socialist . . . largely owing to Morris.'[23] Morris, for his part, at least at the beginning of their acquaintance, found Graham an enigma. In a letter to Bruce Glasier, Morris wrote, 'Cunninghame Graham is a very queer creature and I can't easily make him out', adding, 'I am almost afraid that a man who writes such preposterous illegible scrawl as he does must have a screw loose in him'.[24] It appears, moreover, that Graham and his wife were regular attendees and speakers at talks in Morris's house in Hammersmith,[25] where they would have mixed with the leading socialists of the day, including H. G. Wells,[26] and Graham would become a regular contributor to Morris's journal, *Commonweal*.

Morris, in turn, had been deeply influenced by the writings and philosophy of two 'Scots',[27] Thomas Carlyle and John Ruskin,[28] but Ruskin more than Carlyle,[29] for, like Ruskin, he had come to the study of social problems by the way of art.[30] Ernest Barker wrote:

> Ruskin combined the artist's longing for beauty with the moralist's passion for social justice, integrated into what he described as 'Vital Beauty, [the] felicitous fulfillment of function in living things, more especially the joyful and right exertion of perfect life in man'.[31]

Raymond Williams wrote that in Ruskin's thinking, the transition from artistic criticism to social criticism was quite natural,[32] and Redmond declared that it was 'very common in the nineteenth century, to consider ethical and social problems in aesthetic terms, and to see aesthetic questions as being inseparable from moral and political considerations'.[33]

In his introduction to Ruskin's most influential treatise on the 'disorderly habits' of labour, *Unto This Last*,[34] Clive Wilmer described Ruskin's objections to the principles set out in economic theories that pervaded Victorian society, and described the book as 'first and foremost a cry of anger against injustice and inhumanity; the theories of the Political Economists had outraged his strongest moral convictions'.[35] In this work, Ruskin clearly set out his beliefs:

> It is verily this degradation of the operative into a machine, which, more than any other evil of the times, is leading the mass of the nations everywhere into vain, incoherent, destructive struggling for a freedom of which they cannot explain the nature to themselves . . . It is not that men are ill fed, but that they have no pleasure in the work by which they make their bread, and therefore look to wealth as the only means of pleasure. It is not that men are pained by the scorn of the upper classes, but they cannot endure their own; for they feel that the kind of labor to which they are condemned is verily a degrading one, and makes them less than men.[36]

Morris, who was a central figure in the Aesthetic Movement, was a direct inheritor of Ruskin's aesthetic vision. This was not the intellectualised concept that it later became in literary theory, but simply, to quote Stephen Regan, 'the aesthetic came to represent the idealised form of *value*, beyond the actual values of competitiveness, exploitation, and possessiveness – a realm of order and harmony'.[37] It was the world's dis-harmony, which Morris described as 'this sordid, aimless, ugly confusion',[38] particularly the huge social and economic inequalities, and what he saw as the consequent perversion of values, that angered and frustrated him, and for which socialism appeared to provide both logical and practical solutions. Morris defined his own political faith as 'Socialism seen through the eye of an artist',[39] and later he expanded on this idea:

> Socialism is an all-embracing theory of life, and that as it has an ethic and a religion of its own, so also it has an aesthetic: so that to every one who wishes to study Socialism duly it is necessary to look on it from the aesthetic point of view. And, secondly, I assert that inequality of condition, whatever may have been the case in former ages of the world, has now become incompatible with the existence of a healthy art.[40]

Williams believed, however, that Ruskin's aesthetic ideas of *'design and function'* did not support a socialist idea of society, but an authoritarian one, which included a very emphatic hierarchy of classes.[41] Ruskin also displayed a typical mid-Victorian conviction that hard work and application were the foundations of moral virtue, and that indolence was an indication of moral and social degeneracy, which must be discouraged at all costs: 'First, it ["old" Communism] means that everyone must work in common, and do common or simple work for his dinner; and that if any man will not do it, he must not have his dinner.'[42] Morris certainly agreed, and according to Shaw, he regarded himself fundamentally as a 'communist', on the basis that:

> he knew that the essential term, etymologically, historically, and artistically, was Communist; and it was the only word he was comfortable with. Going straight to the root of Communism he held that people who do not do their fair share of social work are 'damned thieves,' and that neither a stable society, a happy life, nor a healthy art can come from honoring such thieving as the mainspring of industrial activity.[43]

Graham also shared this superior moral attitude, vividly demonstrated in his political journalism, which marked him out as radically different from those whose lives he sought to improve, leading inevitably to schism.

What distinguished Morris from Ruskin was that Ruskin advocated individual rather than public effort to achieve what he termed 'true felicity',[44] whereas Morris, according to Williams, sought to attach Ruskin's values 'to an actual and growing social force – that of the organised working class. This was the most remarkable attempt that had so far been made to break the general deadlock.'[45] However, neither Morris's Socialist League nor Hyndman's Social Democratic Federation (SDF) believed in parliamentary representation,[46] whereas Graham still believed, at this early stage, that it was possible to change the Liberal Party from within by the election of working-class members to Parliament, and, as a man of honour, since he was elected as a Liberal, and still had supporters in his constituency, that he should fulfil his duty to them.

Morris may also have influenced Graham's future literary output, which, although quite distinctive from Morris's, until the end of his life resounded with echoes of the older man's nostalgic idealism, and his disdain for so-called civilisation and progress. Morris may indeed have exerted an even wider influence on Graham's thought. It is worth noting that Morris had come under the influence of the Oxford Movement in his youth, and although, like Graham, he was an atheist, he had developed what he called 'anti-Puritanism and anti-Protestantism', which he

associated with a rigid and hypocritical morality.[47] This was also apparent in Graham's later literary works, in his aversion to Calvinism, for
similar reasons. To escape these strictures, Morris had embraced late
Victorian Romanticism and Medievalism, while Graham would look to
a pre-Reformation Scottish past, and the pre-industrial societies that he
had experienced overseas.

What, in turn, distinguished Graham from Morris, against the
received wisdom that Graham was an idealist and a Utopian, was his
distaste for speculation or fantasy, or, as he called it, 'invention',[48] showing much more interest in practical means than romantic ends. Morris
had tried to represent a higher civilisation in his futuristic novel *News
from Nowhere* (1890), but that was not something that Graham tried to
emulate. Graham agreed with his friend, the naturalist W. H. Hudson:
'Nothing was more intolerable to Hudson than a Utopia, as it must ever
be to all artistic minds. Better the freedom of the wilds than a society
where there is no folly, sorrow, or no crime.'[49] It is likely that Morris was
simply another catalyst for ideas that had already been formulating in
Graham's mind, stimulated by Owen, George, and perhaps Ruskin, but
unlike most other Scottish proto-socialists, Graham had direct and close
contact and dialogue with Ruskin's famous protégé.

Neither Morris nor Graham were political philosophers or dogma-
tists *per se*, Morris admitting that he 'suffered agonies of confusion of the
brain' trying to understand Marx's economic theories,[50] and that 'political economy is not my line, and much of it appears to me to be dreary
rubbish'.[51] Similarly, Graham wrote, 'I am a believer in the theories of
Karl Marx to a great extent, but, both as regards Christianity and Socialism, I care more for works than faith.'[52] Friedrich Engels had initially
believed Graham to be 'a Communist, Marxian, advocating the nationalisation of all means of production',[53] but changed his mind, describing
him to Eleanor 'Tussy' Marx as 'an English Blanquist'.[54] This was another
hallmark of Graham's political activities, for although a renowned orator and literary polemicist, he was fundamentally a practical man of
action, who became frustrated by endless discussions and debates with
no practical outcome, a situation that dogged the early socialist factions.
There is no question, however, that Graham was attracted to Marx's
theories, as they too offered what seemed like practical solutions to previously intractable social problems, becoming the fourth major influence
on Graham's thought, and it is likely that Morris helped Graham along
that path. By 1889, Graham described himself as 'a follower of Marx',[55]
although, shrewdly, Malcolm Muggeridge wrote: 'Marx was as antipathetic to him [Graham] as Samuel Smiles,[56] and as boring.'[57]

The most significant factor in Graham's initial discussions with Morris, however, was timing, and we now come to the next pivotal moment in his political development, where social theories encountered social reality, which had the combined effect of galvanising him into a dogmatic socialistic crusader.

Notes

1. 'William Morris's Socialist Diary', 27 April 1887, ed. by Florence Boos, *History Workshop Journal*, Issue 13, Spring 1982, p. 48.
2. Owen's influence had not entirely disappeared since his death almost thirty years earlier. The Scottish socialist, Bruce Glasier recalled that a few of the older attendees at early socialist meetings in Glasgow were 'Owenites', who had heard Owen and the Chartist Henry Hetherington speak, and 'who had not wholly lost the faith and hopes of their younger days'. James Bruce Glasier, *William Morris and the Early Socialist Movement* (London: Longman's, 1921), p. 28.
3. V. A. C. Gatrell, 'Introduction' to Robert Owen's *A New View of Society: Report to the County of Lanark* (London: Penguin, 1969), p. 9.
4. Arthur Koestler postulated that such revelations constituted 'spontaneous illumination', the perception of a familiar event in a new, significant, light. It also had an emotional aspect: 'The two together – intellectual illumination and emotional catharsis – are the essence of the aesthetic experience.' Arthur Koestler, *The Act of Creation* (London: Hutchinson, 1969), p. 328.
5. 'You are misguided by the desire of the impossible – and I envy you. Alas! What you want to reform are not institutions – it is human nature. Your faith will never move that mountain.' Watts, *Joseph Conrad's Letters*, p. 68. Letter dated 'February' 1898.
6. Gatrell, 'Introduction', p. 101.
7. '"Give me but polish," says the pebble, "and I should be even as is a diamond." But the pebble polished is still a pebble, and the diamond still sparkles in a higher planet.' Cunninghame Graham, 'Heather Jock', *Saturday Review*, 30 January 1897, p. 110.
8. Robert Owen, *A New View of Society: Report to the County of Lanark* (1821) (London: Penguin, 1969), p. 228. My italics.
9. This was a challenge to the concept of class. Gatrell believed that 'the doctrine Owen was playing with was potentially subversive of the social and political hierarchy which at one level of consciousness he wished to preserve'. Gatrell, 'Introduction', p. 29. Gatrell also believed that Owen's thought was 'derived from a strictly paternalistic, anti-democratic, and retrospective social ideal that was ill-attuned to the part it was called upon to play in the history of men, and that is one reason why "Owenism" was an ideology which did not survive mid-century' (p. 21).

10. Annie Besant (1847–1933). An English socialist, writer, and orator, theosophist, women's rights activist, birth-control pioneer, and supporter of Irish and Indian independence.

11. Boos, ed., 'William Morris's Socialist Diary', p. 26.

12. A. C. Rickett, *William Morris* (London: Herbert Jenkins, 1913), p. 246.

13. William Morris, *How I Became a Socialist* (London: Twentieth Century Press, 1896), p. 12. This view of history's function was particularly 'Hegelian', but was more likely an echo of Hegel's young disciple, Karl Marx.

14. Watts and Davies, *Cunninghame Graham*, p. 59.

15. Ibid., p. 247. Watts described the 1890s as 'the era of Aestheticism'. Watts, *R. B Cunninghame Graham*, p. 2. In an obituary in *The Glasgow Herald*, the writer believed that the basis of Graham's political faith 'was artistic rather than economic'. *Glasgow Herald*, 21 March 1936, p. 11.

16. Morris, *How I Became a Socialist*, p. 12.

17. Taylor, *The People's Laird*, p. 67.

18. Taylor, *The People's Laird*, p. 197.

19. Watts, *Joseph Conrad's Letters*, pp. 10–11.

20. James Redmond, 'Introduction' to Morris's *The News from Nowhere* (London: Routledge & Kegan Paul, 1977), p. xi. Also Glasier, *William Morris and the Early Socialist Movement*, p. 32.

21. H. M. Hyndman, 'Introduction' to William Morris's *How I Became a Socialist*, p. 6.

22. Graham, letter to *Glasgow Herald*, 23 May 1908, p. 12. Graham had broken down and was unable to continue addressing a memorial meeting a week after Morris's funeral. E. P. Thompson, *William Morris: Romantic and Revolutionary* (London: Pantheon Books, 1976), p. 63. Graham also wrote a moving description of Morris's funeral, 'With the North-West Wind', *Saturday Review*, 10 October 1896, p. 81, reprinted in the *Labour Leader* as 'The Dirge of the North Wind', 17 October 1896, p. 361, and anthologised in *The Ipané* (1899), pp. 156–63.

23. Doris Arthur Jones, ed., *Taking the Curtain Call: The Life and Letters of Henry Arthur Jones* (London: Victor Gollancz, 1930), p. 304.

24. May Morris, ed., *The Collected Works of William Morris*, Vol. II (London: Longman's, 1910), p. 210.

25. *Chiswick Gazette*, 15 September 1906, p. 5, and 'The People's M.P.'. *People's Press*, 26 April 1890, p. 3. 'Gabrielle' also wrote on political/aesthetic matters such as 'Art & Commercialism', in *To-day*, June 1889, pp. 42–7, 'The Best Scenery I Know', *Saturday Review*, 4 September 1897, pp. 256–7, and 'Family Portraits', in *Outlook*, 7 January 1899, p. 724.

26. Walter Crane, *An Artist's Reminiscences* (London: Macmillan, 1907), p. 262.

27. Clive Wilmer wrote, 'like so many of those who sought to explain the laws of economics, he [Ruskin] was of Scottish descent'. Clive Wilmer, ed., 'Introduction' to John Ruskin's *Unto This Last and Other Writings* (London: Penguin, 1997), p. 8. As the son and protégé of the Scottish philosopher,

economist, and historian, James Mill, a.k.a. Milne (1773–1836), John Stuart
Mill's name might also tentatively be added to this list. Graham's views on
land taxation, women's rights, and empire, were similar to Mill's.

28. Ernest Barker, *Political Thought in England From Herbert Spencer the Present Day* (London: Williams & Norgate, 1915), p. 190. Barker also described
Ruskin as 'a foster-father of many English Socialists', p. 196. Joan Abse
added, 'not a parent of direct lineage, be it noted, but a supportive inspiration
along the way'. Joan Abse, *John Ruskin: The Passionate Moralist* (London:
Quartet Books, 1980), p. 238. Kenneth Morgan wrote that Ruskin's essays,
entitled *Unto This Last*, 'provided something of a moral framework for [Keir]
Hardie's shadowy political philosophy'. Kenneth O. Morgan, *Keir Hardie:
Radical and Socialist* (London: Phoenix, 1988), p. 126.

29. Peter Stansky, *William Morris* (Oxford University Press, 1987), p. 12.
Apparently, Carlyle's novel *Sartor Resartus* (1836) had had a profound
effect on the young Hardie.

30. Ibid., p. 190. Ruskin also wrote on the morality (or otherwise) of empire.
John Ruskin, 'Traffic', lecture delivered in Bradford Town Hall on 21 April
1864.

31. Ruskin, *Modern Painters*, Vol. II (London: George Allen, 1906), p. 31.

32. Raymond Williams, *Culture and Society*, p. 138.

33. Redmond, 'Introduction', p. xvii.

34. According to J. W. Mackail, it was this book that directly influenced Morris
to embrace socialism. J. W. Mackail, *The Life of William Morris*, Vol. II
(1899) (New York: Dover Books, 1995), p. 201.

35. Wilmer, 'Introduction', p. 21.

36. Ruskin, 'On the Nature of the Gothic', in *The Stones of Venice* (1853) (New
York: The National Library Association, 2009), p. 163.

37. Stephen Regan, 'Introduction: The Return of the Aesthetic', in *The Politics
of Pleasure* (Open University Press, 1992), p. 3. My italics. The concept of
'harmony', of course, also pervaded Robert Owen's works.

38. Morris, *How I Became a Socialist*, p. 12.

39. Philip Henderson, ed., *The Letters of William Morris to His Family and
Friends* (London: Longman's, 1950), p. 187.

40. Morris, 'The Socialist Ideal: Art', *New Review*, January 1891, p. 87.

41. Raymond Williams, *Culture and Society*, p. 140, original italics. Robert
Hewison confirmed that despite his move towards social radicalism in the
mid-1850s, Ruskin 'continued to deny the possibility of equality, and never
abandoned his authoritarianism'. Robert Hewison, *Ruskin and His Contemporaries* (London: Pallas Athene, 2018), p. 88.

42. Ruskin, 'Charitas', in *Unto This Last*, p. 295.

43. George Bernard Shaw, *Morris As I Knew Him* (New York: Dodd & Mead,
1936), p. 11.

44. Ruskin, *Unto This Last*, p. 226.

45. Raymond Williams, *Culture and Society*, p. 148.

46. According to Shaw, the real business of Morris's Socialist League was 'that of making Socialists'. Shaw, *Morris As I Knew Him*, p. 18. In 1885, Morris had written to Fred Pickles, a pioneer of the Bradford Branch of the Socialist League: 'If you send members to parliament they must be sent with the express purpose of overthrowing it as it exists at present; for it exists for the definite purpose of continuing the present evil state of things.' Norman Kelvin, ed., *The Collected Letters of William Morris*, Vol. II (Princeton University Press, 1987), p. 462.

47. May Morris, *Collected Works of William Morris*, p. 59.

48. Cunninghame Graham, *Faith* (London: Duckworth, 1909), pp. xi–xii. Graham would have been described in the philosophy of T. E. Hulme as 'a romantic', repudiating 'fancy' for 'imagination'. T. E. Hulme, 'Romanticism and Classicism', in *The Collected Writings of T. E. Hulme*, ed. by Karen Csengeri (Oxford: Clarendon Press, 1994), p. 59.

49. Curle, *Hudson's Letters*, p. 80.

50. Morris, *How I Became a Socialist*, p. 10.

51. Glasier, *William Morris and the Early Socialist Movement*, p. 32.

52. Cunninghame Graham, letter to the *Christian Socialist*, 6 January 1888, p. 13.

53. Wilhelm Liebknecht, *Briefwechsel mit Karl Marx und Friedrich Engels*, ed. by George Eckert (The Hague: Mouton, 1963), p. 304.

54. Émile Bottogelli, ed., *Friedrich Engels: Correspondence*, Vol. II (London: Lawrence & Wishart, 1959), p. 183. 'Blanquist' = A follower of the French revolutionary socialist, Louis Auguste Blanqui (1805–81).

55. Cunninghame Graham, letter to *The Star*, 5 June 1889, p. 4.

56. Samuel Smiles (1812–1904). Scottish author and reformer. His book *Self Help*, published in 1859, sold an estimated quarter of a million copies, which were widely circulated.

57. Malcolm Muggeridge, 'Cunninghame Graham', *Time and Tide*, Vol. XVII, 28 March 1936, p. 440.

3

Parliament: The Practical Idealist

ALMOST IMMEDIATELY AFTER HIS maiden speech, on 4 February 1887, Graham was back in his constituency following disturbances and arrests in the Lanarkshire coalfields, and the looting of food shops in Blantyre and Coatbridge by striking miners.[1] From his own words, this was the first time he had come into direct contact with the unemployed,[2] and had his first experience of the miners' working and living conditions. This was also when he first met Keir Hardie,[3] a miner and journalist who had come to prominence in the previous year. Graham spent most of February attending and addressing miners' meetings, of which he claimed he addressed '63 or 64' (where he could hardly have failed to meet Hardie), and encouraged them to unite, and to put pressure on their MPs.[4] However, with the miners and their families in deep distress, a motion to resume work was passed at a meeting of the Scottish Miners Federation on 21 February, but Graham promised to champion their cause in parliament.[5] It was reported soon afterwards that Graham had addressed fellow Liberals at Coatbridge:

> When I bought my ticket at Euston [station] and came here, I knew I was leaving behind me every chance of rising in political life. What had I, a landlord, to gain by championing the working class? I had everything to lose, but I found the miners in a worse position than I could have believed. Would you have me say to those poor starving fellows that I could do nothing for them?[6]

It is from this point that we witness, if not exactly class politics in Graham's utterances, then the emergence of a more direct and visceral awareness of class divisions and their consequences.

By the middle of 1887, the land issue had all but disappeared from Graham's speeches, although Irish home rule was still occasionally mentioned.[7] His focus now became the plight of the miners, but increasingly, the idea of labour representation in the House of Commons. The first opportunity we have to witness any consolidation of his views came on 15 August 1887, during the marathon Coal Mines Regulation Bill, which contained over fifty clauses dealing with the miners' working conditions. This was a bill introduced by the Liberals (who were now in opposition), supported by Irish MPs. Graham now pursued his promise to his mining constituents, and was active throughout the long hours of debate, speaking nineteen times in support of various clauses.[8] His own amendment, which proposed the restriction of miners' working hours to eight, was tabled on 3 September, which would eventually form the basis of a much wider agenda, during his time in parliament and after. This proposal had apparently been prompted, not only by Morris's influence, but also by a dramatic revelation while walking through Trafalgar Square in the summer of 1887, where he had witnessed large numbers of destitute men and women camped there.[9] As Graham later recalled, 'It immediately struck me that the most tangible common-sense reform that could be applied was one that would induce the capitalist to employ more labour, and absorb the unemployed into the ranks of the employed.'[10] This, he believed, could be accomplished by shortening working hours, sharing work more equally to prevent the accumulation of large fortunes, and distributing the fruits more equally.[11] To Graham, this would cease to be simply a means of alleviating unemployment and the harshness of the miners' working lives, it would become the first step on the road to the final emancipation of labour.[12] Moreover, he added that it would be 'the battle ground on which the first real skirmish of Capital and Labour (in our time) will be fought'.[13] In the meantime, his proposal had already been incorporated into his amendment to the Bill:

> I wish Parliament to step in and give them that protection by giving them an eight hours day. It has been said that we would be opening the gate to other questions of a vastly wider scope by accepting this Amendment. If we did so, I for one would be glad, because I wish to see this principle applied to every trade in the country.[14]

Aware that his motion was falling on deaf or hostile ears, Graham concluded with the words:

> I can tell [the Home Secretary] the miners look forward to the time when the Government will take over the mines and machinery and work them for the benefit of the people and not for the selfish ends of a few capitalists.

His amendment was doomed from the outset, and was greeted with jeers and laughter from both sides of the House, although Taylor wrote, 'in all probability [this] was the first time nationalisation of the coal mining industry was taken seriously by anyone in the House of Commons'.[15] Greater disappointment and anger were to follow when the amended Bill came back from the Lords on 12 September, minus several of the clauses that Graham had campaigned for. He interrupted the proceedings several times, concluding with the words, 'it does seem a curious thing that an Assembly which is not elected by popular vote should dare to dictate to us, who are elected',[16] and was asked by the Speaker to withdraw.

It should be noted at this point that campaigns for a shorter working day had a long history. Sidney Webb and Harold Cox, in their book *The Eight Hours Day* (1891) called it 'the legitimate descendant of the agitation which resulted in the Ten Hours Bill of 1847',[17] and they believed that it would be 'the most important industrial movement of the close of the century'.[18] Calls for such a reduction had been a fundamental demand at the International Working Men's Association in Geneva in August 1866, repeated by Marx in *Das Kapital* in 1867, and it was a founding principle of Hyndman's SDF from its inception in 1884. In Scotland, the demand for shorter hours was first raised in 1858 at the Glasgow Trades Council, but nothing was done.[19]

By now, the Lords' dismissal of these grievances seems to have triggered a more militant response in Graham, who continued speaking at miners' meetings throughout Central Scotland. At Broxburn on 7 October 1887, following the forced eviction of mining families, *The Scotsman* reported that Graham had guardedly advised the use of intimidation against 'black-nebs',[20] but he was careful to urge them not to be so foolish as to break the law, adding, 'Short of this, anything might be done.'[21] This, however, would not be the last time that he hinted at, or took direct action, to further political goals, and on 26 June 1889, the *Coatbridge Express* reported the threat of prosecution over an inflammatory speech in Leith.[22] Indeed, in May 1891, he was arrested and expelled from France for 'the violent character of his speech'.[23]

The most egregious event in Graham's political career occurred on 13 November 1887 when he took part in a violent confrontation in Trafalgar Square, leading a charge against police lines with John Burns and Hyndman, where he was badly beaten, arrested, and sentenced to six weeks' imprisonment.[24] (See Appendix III.) His arrest immediately elicited support from Morris and Oscar Wilde, both of whom rushed to Bow Street Magistrate's court. Morris later wrote, 'His conduct will long be remembered, one would hope, by lovers of freedom; but he must expect for some time to come to be a pariah among MPs. To do him justice he is not likely to care much about that.'[25]

By 7 December, a London correspondent for the *Coatbridge Express* noted that:

> One of the most popular men in London at the present hour is Mr Cunninghame Graham. Any one who doubted it would have done well to go to the Clerkenwell meeting of the unemployed. He was cheered to the echo by the landless and labourless.[26]

There were profiles of Graham in the press, including in a new left-leaning populist newspaper called *The Star*, which the *Coatbridge Express* reprinted under the title 'Romantic Career of Mr Graham M.P.'.[27] The conservative press was, however, less flattering: *The Spectator*, for example, described him as a 'political mountebank'.[28] This view was shared by many in the Liberal establishment, witnessed by a letter to the *Coatbridge Express* from an unnamed 'Chairman of a Liberal Association', opposing a resolution at the Scottish Liberal Conference that protested against Graham's imprisonment: 'The above individual is not a political martyr, he has been imprisoned like any disorderly person, and like many sound Liberals, I regret his locks have not been cut, as it might help to cool his ardour.'[29]

Graham in prison uniform. This portrait occupied a prominent position in the billiard room of Gartmore House.

Throughout his election campaigns, Graham, while critical of British political institutions, had still paid occasional lip-service to the Liberal leader, Gladstone, whom (his friend and biographer, Tschiffely, informs us) Graham despised 'with all his heart and soul'.[30] The reason for this antipathy is clear. At a time when allegiance to old authorities was breaking down, Gladstone's position within the Liberals remained unassailable, particularly in Scotland. And whereas Graham believed that the instigation of legislation on conditions and hours of work, and the improvement of the lot of the poor, were entirely within any government's purview, Gladstone did not. During his Midlothian Campaign of 1879, Gladstone had stated that the government's role was not to lead, but to 'soothe and tranquilise . . . to produce and maintain a temper so calm and so deliberate in the public opinion of the country that none shall be able to disturb it'.[31] Such a policy, in the face of what he perceived as glaring poverty, inequalities and abuses, would be anathema to an increasingly impatient man of action like Graham, who was now enjoying some celebrity.[32] His distancing from the Liberals was further increased by the publication (while in prison) of an article entitled 'Has the Liberal Party a Future?',[33] which questioned the very *raison d'être* of his party, and was an angry riposte to the placatory article in the same journal of the previous month by the MP for Haddingtonshire (East Lothian), R. B. Haldane.[34] In Graham's opinion, the Liberals were concerned solely with achieving and retaining power, and he concluded that it was only Gladstone's skill and personality that held the party together:

> His very shortcomings they condone, but nothing but the deepest scorn is manifest for those timorous, miserable, invertebrate animals who, whilst posing as Liberal leaders, are really Tories at heart; who have seen the poor bludgeoned and outraged in London, the crofters driven to desperation, the Welsh farmers infuriated, and have said not a word; too timorous to risk a newspaper reviling, too utterly empty to be able to face the pin-prick of public opinion, so that an immediate collapse brings about one thing only – at any price and at any cost return to Downing Street, and a fat salary – incompetent leaders, as useful to a democracy as a blind dog to a blind beggar. No, if the Liberal party has a future, it must get rid of these nobodies, and show that it has no fear of modern thought; it must pledge itself to an Eight Hours Bill, institute a municipality for London, nationalise the land, and commence public works for the unemployed; and then, if it has good luck, it may regain the confidence of the democracy that is to say, *if some other party has not been beforehand in the field.*[35]

Hutchison concurs that the Liberals had been preoccupied with 'faddist' issues and were indifferent to economic and social questions:

> [T]ypified by the general hostility to the demand for an eight-hour day in the coalfields – resulted in the growing alienation of the working class voters [which gave] an impression of circumstances being highly propitious for the movement towards independent working class representation.[36]

After 1886, there was a gradual abandonment of the Liberal Party by politically conscious working men. Heyck and Klecka attributed this to the fact that with the Radicals in control, they could no longer blame their shortcomings on Whigs and moderates:

> Working men could see that Radicalism, by the late Victorian years, was essentially a middle-class Nonconformist movement, and after nearly 150 years of tenuous cooperation with middle-class radicals their interests would not be adequately served by the Radical elite.[37]

In Laybourn's assessment, 'In the end, the lack of positive response from the Liberal party drove the working men to look towards the Labour party not for socialism as much as for the representation of its own sectional interests'.[38] Graham's ambition for a party of labour was thus extremely prescient, and by September 1887 we can witness the first signs of his desire to see 'labour' candidates stand under the Liberal banner. In a somewhat disingenuous speech at a mass meeting of Ayrshire miners in support of Hardie, Graham said:

> When they talked about labour candidates they simply meant to add a battalion to the Liberal army, a battalion of light skirmishers, who, when the main army went a little slow, were always in the lead. If they had some of these men who were real democrats in Parliament they would strengthen the Grand Old Man's hands, and set him where he ought to be, at the head of the Government. (*Applause.*)[39]

However, in what appears to be a major development of his ideas, this speech was followed by another, to miners in Tranent, reported by *The Scotsman*: 'Mr Graham then related to the meeting a dream which he had recently. He dreamed that all the working classes of Scotland, England, and Wales, being united together and running their own candidates for Parliament.'[40] At almost exactly the same time, J. L. Mahon, who was often in Graham's company, wrote in Morris's *Commonweal*, 'As appearances go at present, there may soon be a Scottish Labour Party of which Mr. Cunninghame Graham will be the chief.'[41] Mahon obviously looked to Graham to lead such an enterprise, but despite his enthusiastic predictions, it is apparent that as an upper-class landowner, it was not a role that Graham saw himself filling. In Graham's mind, this new movement had to come from the grass roots to have any credibility. In August 1888, he had written, 'No man like myself, however much he may sympathise can ever properly represent them',[42] and again he made it perfectly clear that he had no such ambitions in a speech to the Liberals in Coatbridge in November 1889. It had been put to him that he wished to see a Labour party with himself as leader as 'a sort of Parnell (*Laughter.*), but what he really wanted was to see working men like [John] Burns, Hardie, and [Tom] Mann' enter parliament to demand reforms, 'and he would be content to retire to a quiet country life at Gartmore'.[43]

Graham seemed content to take a supporting role, but determined to push a working-class leader forward, and it was Hardie whom he saw as the ideal candidate. His difficulty was that Hardie remained a committed Liberal, and was reluctant to break with them, so it appears that a compromise was reached, whereby they would create a labour pressure group within the Liberal fold.[44] However, sending men to the Commons from a particular class went against mainstream Liberal thought,[45] and in 1888, Hardie was rejected by the Liberals as a candidate for the constituency of Mid-Lanark, and stood as an 'Independent Labour' candidate. *The Scotsman* reported:

> Mr Cunninghame Graham thinks Mr Hardie a fit candidate for Mid Lanark, and Mr Hardie himself comes forward, he is snubbed and flouted and has injurious accusations brought against him . . . Men whose mouths are filled with declarations of the greatness of the masses as against the classes will have nothing to do with Mr Hardie. They set up a sort of political hierarchy, and, under cover of the so-called Liberal Association, look down with contempt on Mr Hardie and labour candidates.[46]

This report confirmed that Graham was seen as actively promoting Hardie within the Liberal Party caucus, and to Hardie's biographers, his rejection was the beginning of his disillusionment with the Liberals. However, not untypically, Hardie eulogists have subsequently diminished or omitted Graham's role. In his essay, 'Keir Hardie's Conversion to Socialism',[47] Fred Reid suggested that Hardie's candidature was on his initiative alone, and disingenuously claimed that he had planned for his own defeat:

> [T]he Mid-Lanark by-election should be seen as the test of a strategy fully worked out in Hardie's mind by the middle of 1887, rather than a spontaneous gesture of stubborn independence against the 'unexpected' resistance of the local Liberal Association to Hardie's nomination.[48]

On 27 April 1888, against concerted Liberal and Irish nationalist opposition[49] and with only half-hearted support, Hardie was badly defeated, garnering a mere 8.4 per cent of the votes cast.[50]

By-Election Result, Mid-Lanark, *27 April 1888*

John Philips (Liberal)	3,847
William Bousfield Graham (Conservative)	2,017
James Keir Hardie (Independent Labour)	617

It has long been maintained among certain interest groups that Graham was *the* founder of 'Labour' as a political entity, but his exact role and significance has been difficult to establish. Most likely this is because the party's foundation had been tentative, involving many unrecorded discussions, doubts, disputes, and compromises. Lowe, who was directly involved in its formation, wrote:

> The origins of an unpopular movement are not easily collected. Early events of importance passed unrecorded, and successes which gave heart to the pioneers were received in silence by the newspaper press.[51]

Robert Smillie,[52] the secretary of the Larkhall Miners' Association and a close colleague of Hardie's, was the only member present at what appears to have been the party's conception, who wrote a first-hand account of the mood of the meeting, and of Graham's inspiration. This contradicted Reid's slanted analysis that it was anything other than a bitter disappointment:

> On the day after this historic election [Hardie's defeat at Mid-Lanark] a number of Keir Hardie's supporters met in Hamilton to mingle their tears together. It could not be said that the gathering was a joyful one – although, looking back on it after all these years, I do not think that we were absolutely downhearted. In fact, my opinion is that the result of this election acted as a stimulus to many of us to go forward. Mr. R. B. Cunninghame Graham was present at this meeting, but he was not downcast. Instead he took the view that we should go on with the forming of a new and independent party. The meeting adopted this view, and it was decided that we should start out on a new line independent of the other two political parties.[53]

Having displayed unaccustomed forbearance in the face of Hardie's reticence, with this defeat, Graham had seized his opportunity, and their party within a party, which would be known as the Scottish Parliamentary Labour Party (SPLP), was first convened on 19 May, but it was not constituted until 25 August. *The Scotsman* reported:

> On Glasgow Green, Mr Cunninghame Graham and Mr Keir Hardie appeared as the apostles of Labour – with a big L. There is no evidence that labour with a small initial has any greater fascination for them or their handful of followers than it has for ordinary mortals.[54]

Another man who was at the centre of developments at this time was Robert Smillie's close colleague, 'Sandy' Haddow, who insisted that it was only after his defeat at Mid-Lanark that Hardie 'came over to the Socialist side. He and Cunninghame Graham formed the Scottish Labour Party.'[55]

The membership diploma of the SPLP, which carried the images of both Hardie and Graham, and bore Scotland's Royal Stuart motto, 'Nemo Me Impune Lacessit' ('No one challenges me with impunity'), and the legends, 'No Noble Task Was Ever Easy,' 'No Monopoly,' and 'No Privilege.' This tattered example belonged to the Edinburgh-born socialist and Irish nationalist, James Connolly.

Despite his key role in the formation of the SPLP, Graham remains on the fringes of subsequent Labour history in Britain, although Reid grudgingly acknowledged his contribution:

> One final contact arising out of the London visits needs to be noted. This was R. B. Cunninghame Graham. Graham's even-handed attacks upon both the Conservative government and the Liberal front bench for ignoring the condition of the working class attracted Hardie's admiration. Indeed, it would not be too much to say that Graham offered Hardie a model for parliamentary agitation.[56]

As a Hardie eulogist, Reid's account was not untypical, dismissing Graham as one of Hardie's 'contacts', and failing to acknowledge their partnership. Glasier, for instance, wrote that Hardie and Graham were close companions for six years, and that they 'went about in harness'.[57] Caroline Benn, in contrast to other Hardie biographers, wrote that Hardie needed a mentor, to help him make the transition from regional to national stage,[58] and while Hardie offered Graham an understanding of working-class life and needs, Graham offered Hardie 'an inside knowledge of how the governing classes really worked, and the courage to stand up to them'.[59] Thus, Graham had guided Hardie in his way of thinking and acting, and was certainly, if Smillie's account was correct, an instrumental facilitator in the creation of the SPLP, which, even though it remained a small pressure group rather than an effective political force, was the precursor and test-bed for the far more successful Independent Labour Party (ILP). Once Hardie was fully engaged, however, Graham then seems to have welcomed the mixed role of midwife, propagandist, and patron in the party's early development. He took the honorary position as president, as he had done in the early SHRA, and would do much later in the National Party of Scotland (NPS) and the SNP.

Pelling insisted that the new party was not committed to socialism, but 'was composed of men who recognised the necessity of building a labour party first and making it socialist at a later stage in its development'.[60] At their first conference they passed resolutions on full adult suffrage, triennial parliaments, payment of MPs and expenses, 'home rule all round',[61] the abolition of the House of Lords, state insurance, opposition to state control of the hours of labour, the abolition of primogeniture and entail, and the Georgist programme of taxing land. All of these were policies on which Graham and others had campaigned (except Graham wished to nationalise land), but we can only conjecture to what extent he directed these proposals. Henry Champion, the Honorary Secretary of the SDF, and editor of the *Labour Elector*, although happy that at last a party of labour had been formed, was in no doubt about what lay ahead:

> Although I am in some degree an outsider, and my opinions can have no binding force upon you, I venture to claim that I speak not altogether without some experience of the difficulties you will have to encounter, and the opposition you will have to face.[62]

The extent of the new party's support is also difficult to unearth. It was rumoured (no doubt humorously) that the executive were careful not to appear together in case they were photographed as representing the party's full strength.[63] According to the political activist and publisher, James Leatham, who knew both Graham and Hardie, Hardie was unknown to the public nationally, but Graham's nationwide celebrity, and popularity among the workers, sustained a higher profile for the party than it would otherwise have received[64] (or perhaps warranted). A reporter from the *Daily News* was certain that Graham's role in the SPLP's formation was significant. In an interview two months after Graham's release from prison, and a week before Hardie's defeat, the newspaper reported, 'The subject of conversation was the position and prospects of the Labour Party which Mr Cunninghame Graham is a large part.'[65] Graham then spoke of the formation of the party, which he did not envisage being composed exclusively of working men. He believed that many of them were not men of affairs and could not take a statesman-like view of any subject, but enough members should be elected to hold the balance of power, and to hold the other parties to account.[66] This seems to confirm that his thoughts on the new party were well advanced before its inception, and it would also apparently hold true for the next stage of its development. Moreover, it also demonstrated Graham's belief that 'the middle classes are, as a rule, far better political manipulators than are the working classes'.[67] Here was another illustration (if so far, somewhat weak) of another feature of his personality, which would have longer-term repercussions – his elitism.

In June 1889, Champion wrote that Graham was 'speaking out clearly and persistently in favour of the formation of a distinct, and independent Labour Party'.[68] Nonetheless, progress for the new party remained slow. As Lowe intimated, the press boycotted their meetings,[69] and *The Scotsman* reported:

> Despite great efforts being put forth by the Scottish promoters of what is called the Labour Party to secure adhesion to their ranks, the idea of Labour representation has not taken any firm hold of the public mind . . . the objects of the Labour Party, as put forth by Mr Cunninghame Graham and his friends, have rather alarmed than pleased the public.[70]

Nor had the idea taken a firm hold among labour propagandists. For example, as late as March 1892, John Trevor,[71] the editor of the *Labour Prophet* wrote, under the heading 'An Independent Labour Party?':

> I have weighed the matter well. The cause of Labour is to me a sacred cause . . . I have, however, come to the conclusion that the formation of an independent Labour party is the most impractical of proposals and the forlornest of hopes. To begin with, the men who must compose such a party must be taken to be such men as could only be properly described as Socialists.[72]

The formation of the SPLP, and the possibility of a nationwide successor, was also not welcomed by the working-class establishment. Graham and Hardie faced not only apathy from the workers themselves, but outright antagonism from large sections of the trade union movement. W. H. Fraser devoted considerable space to describing the reluctance of the trade unions in Scotland to support them,[73] and Clayton wrote:

> The well-established Trade Unions of skilled workmen regarded the preaching of Socialism in the 'eighties with cold indifference; their elected officials were mildly contemptuous of the new gospel; in many cases frankly hostile. No political faith was required of the members of these Unions, but the leading spirits were Liberals; in religion Methodists or freethinkers.[74]

Despite this antagonism, Graham and Hardie forged ahead, and with Glasier, they represented their new party at the Marxist International Socialist Labour Congress (which initiated the Second International) in Paris in July 1889. Hardie addressed the Congress several times, and Graham presided over the final day, addressing the delegates in English, French, and Spanish.[75]

At the Trade Union Congress conference in Dundee in September 1889, Hardie, Graham, and their new party were roundly abused by many of the delegates, who regarded them as upstarts and ingrates who were disrupting what had already been established. One delegate stated, 'We have by slow means built up a position for the working classes; and it is by such proper means that we mean to work in the future',[76] and their Eight Hours proposal was defeated by almost two to one.[77] Graham was accused of associating with questionable politicians, and another delegate reminded his comrades that 'able as Mr Graham might be, there were men in the Labour movement before Mr Cunninghame Graham was heard of'.[78] There is no doubt, however, that Hardie recognised Graham's contribution:

> If you went out on the streets and asked the first hundred men you met who was the leader of the Labour party in Parliament what name would be mentioned in answer? (Voices, 'Broadhurst' and 'Keir Hardie,' and laughter.) – not Keir Hardie – (*Laughter.*) – but a man who was in this hall, and not even honoured with a place on the platform – Mr Cunninghame Graham.[79]

The Fabian, Beatrice Webb, who was present at the conference, noted the antagonism, almost hatred, among the TUC leadership who were trying to keep out 'wolves in sheep's clothing'.[80] Even the Labour Electoral Conference, whose aim was to get working men elected to parliament, was antipathetic to Graham and Hardie on the basis that they were socialists.[81] This also applied to the Parliamentary Committee of the TUC (a wing of the Liberals). Their Local Option Eight Hours Bill stated 'This only is certain, the committee will have nothing more to do with Mr Cunninghame Graham, and the opponents of state intervention on the committee felt that this year [1891] they are free of a great incubus',[82] confirming that Graham was regarded by many as a danger and an inconvenient nuisance, and that he would not be re-elected. Graham lost no time in publishing his own views, stating that the workers should:

> repudiate the reactionary doctrines advanced in the antediluvian Congress of respectables at Dundee. The reason for the enslavement of men, whose leaders are Shipton[83] and Broadhurst,[84] and whose god is broadcloth, is not far to seek.[85]

Graham's 'labour' activities were also causing problems in parts of his constituency where some believed he was not representing them or their opinions. For example, open warfare, carried on through correspondence between Graham and the Tollcross Liberal Association, appeared in the *Glasgow Herald* in early November 1889:

We, the members of Tollcross Liberal Association, at our annual general meeting, herby condemn the conduct of Cunninghame Graham, M.P., as pursued by him at the recent by-election in Dundee and in the previous elections for Mid-Lanark and Govan; we consider he was entirely out of place as a Liberal representative in trying to stir up strife amongst the Liberals of these constituencies, and thereby endangering the seat to the Liberal party; we rejoice that the Liberal electors of these constituencies put a true value on the utterances of our M.P. by ignoring them and proving true to the Liberal party and its great leader, Mr Gladstone; we would recommend that Mr Graham in future, if unable to support the candidate of the Liberal Association of any constituency where an election may take place, that he at least refrain from opposing him, leaving that work to be performed by the Tories, to whom it properly belongs.[86]

Graham's reply was typically robust and dismissive: he supported the nationalisation of capital and land, the disestablishment of the English and Scottish national churches; *adult* ('not manhood') suffrage; that he was a Republican, and that he had endeavoured to get men into parliament, from impoverished backgrounds, who would help these aims. He continued:

What I will not do is act against what I believe to be right, *either* for Mr Gladstone or any other man. Now what I believe to be wrong is a state of society in which the vast bulk of the people are very poor, work long hours, and have no property, and in which two political parties pass their time in quarrelling with one another, and not in seeking to remedy the above mentioned state of matters.[87]

Here was Graham in full-blown, uncompromisingly moralistic mode. The antipathy of the Tollcross Liberals, however, was in stark contrast to packed meetings held throughout his constituency in the previous month, where at Coatbridge for example, he was cheered throughout.[88] At a meeting in Shettleston a week later, a vote of confidence was carried by acclamation.[89] What we appear to be witnessing is Graham's recurring ability to divide opinion, garnering popular support among certain sections of the working-class electorate, to whom he was a hero, but the reverse among the Liberal members and officials, to whom he was a dangerous threat.

Rumours began to circulate that Graham did not intend to stand for re-election.[90] On 8 March 1889, *The Scotsman*'s political correspondent reported: 'I am informed on very good authority Mr Cunninghame Graham has in contemplation his early retirement from parliament, and a complete withdrawal from politics.'[91] At a special meeting in February 1889, the North-West Lanarkshire Liberals pressed him to give them a definite answer about his future, but he requested a delay until Easter.[92] On 23 April, a letter from Graham appeared in the *Evening Citizen* refuting the charge from the Liberals that he had been evasive in his answers, and that 'one should wash one's linen in private', but, despite this assertion, he was extremely frank about his financial position:

> I have repeatedly stated my great penury and the sacrifice I was making to obtain the money to fight the seat again. On top of this, and at a period when an election is still remote, I am now asked to say whether my means are such as in three years I am again to undertake a very expensive campaign. After having been severely restricted in order to enter Parliament, I would have thought it hardly necessary [words illegible] force from me the avowal of the only crime that is never pardoned in this country, that of being poor.[93]

Eleven months later, on 1 March 1890, the *Airdrie Advertiser* announced that Graham planned to contest Greenock (another constituency with large Irish and Highland populations) as a Labour candidate,[94] and on 14 March, he wrote to the North-West Lanarkshire Liberal Association, severing his connection, and thanking them for their support as 'one whose views were not always in accord with theirs.'[95]

It is apparent that cutting ties with the Liberals, who still enjoyed large support in Scotland, was proving difficult, and Graham and Hardie attempted to find a compromise, and also to pressure the Liberals into accepting working-class candidates, by threatening to split the vote in marginal constituencies. On 20 December 1894, Andrew Provand, MP for Glasgow Blackfriars, wrote to Lord Rosebery[96] discussing a meeting held the previous summer between the Liberal Chief Whip, Edward Marjoribanks,[97] and the 'Labour Party', to discuss an accommodation over parliamentary seats, and that a similar meeting had taken place three or four years earlier (presumably 1890), between Graham, Hardie, and Marjoribanks. As a reflection of the attitudes within the Liberal party, Provand considered that any deal with the 'socialists' would be deeply unpopular among most Glasgow Liberals, and that '[i]t would create a split in the Party as pronounced as the [Irish] Home Rule Bill did'.[98] Nevertheless, Graham seems to have believed that at this meeting an accord had been reached, that if his SPLP declined to fight the Partick Division of Glasgow and supported the Liberal candidate, then Marjoribanks would concede them Greenock and two other constituencies on the understanding that 'the Labour candidates gave adhesion to the political programmes of the Liberal party on other than labour questions'.[99] This was undoubtedly seen as a great opportunity for the new party (or in reality, faction), for, simultaneous with Graham's letter of resignation, Hardie and Shaw Maxwell approached the North-West

Lanarkshire Liberal Association with a resolution that they should put forward a Labour candidate:

> This, it seems to us, would be putting into practice the spirit of the agreement recently come to by Mr Marjoribanks M.P., the Liberal Whip, on the one hand, and the representatives of the Scottish Labour party on the other, and a means whereby unnecessary friction could be avoided.[100]

With two years still to run in this parliament, it appeared that the SPLP were trying to force the issue by striking while the iron was hot, and gaining enough time to campaign under a new banner. However, the Association rejected the right of any other organisation to interfere with their choice,[101] and it was reported that they had invited two mainstream Liberals to seek selection.[102] The Greenock Association also rejected any such arrangement, and *The Scotsman* reported:

> It was only the other day that the Greenock seat was placed in a curiously unique position among all the seats in Scotland. Mr Marjoribanks sold it under the ingenious reservations, to The Scottish Labour Party for the price they could give in the shape of votes for Sir Charles Tennant[103] in Partick. Before the election took place it became evident that he had sold what was not his, and that he had attempted to traffic the Greenock seat without even the leave of the Greenock Gladstonians. The latter at once began to look for a candidate for themselves.[104]

The editorial went on to conjecture that Marjoribanks ('the sagacious whip') 'had arranged a pretty little plot and as was likely – there would be the great consolation that one of the most troublesome of Mr Marjoribanks' thorns in the flesh would be removed'.[105] The *Labour Elector* announced that Marjoribanks had denied ever making such an agreement with Graham or anyone else, and its editor, Champion, could hardly conceal his elation when writing:

> We hope Mr. Graham still retains his original high opinion of the character of Liberal Whips, and that they will not seriously think of breaking finally with the Liberal Party. It is such an honourable Party, and so devoted to the cause of Labour that Mr. Graham really mustn't, he mustn't indeed.[106]

This apparent duplicitousness (or self-delusion) must have been a great disappointment to Graham, who, having indicated his intention not to stand again in North-West Lanarkshire, had now burned his boats. However, there was no obvious demonstration of this in his letters to the press or in his journalism, and as usual, he continued to vigorously lambast 'Liberal sham' and 'Tory cheat'.[107]

Despite this setback, Graham continued to campaign feverishly in parliament, and toured the country speaking in support of various groups of striking workers, continuing his involvement with the Scottish home rule movement,[108] and trying to organise Labour in Ireland.[109] In August 1890, he restated his policies in *The Star*:

> No kings but a republic. A president with a modest salary. No rampant race of princes and princesses to be provided for out of the hedger's toil, the miner's sweat. An eight hour day; overwork for none, continuous employment for the entire population; few or none unemployed. State control of land and mines. Free access to the soil and mineral wealth for all. Railways and tramways owned by the state. A minimum wage. Five shillings at least for all who do an honest day's work.[110]

Lastly, in accordance with what has been argued was his underlying aesthetic sense, national aid to art: 'Art and culture brought home in manufacture and in every phase of life to the poorest.'[111] His split with the Liberals had, however, left him politically exposed, and in a letter to John Burns he wrote, 'The House is beginning to find out that there is nothing and nobody behind me. Anyone but the idiots in Parliament would have seen this long ago.'[112] Prior to this, by April 1890, Tom Mann was convinced of his political impotence.[113]

According to Taylor, 'At some time in the summer of 1891 an offer from a friend to pay his election expenses determined Graham to accept an invitation from the Liberals of Camlachie to be their candidate at the 1892 general election'.[114] At his first address, on 11 November 1891, he received the sort of reception he had been used to from the mainly appreciative audience, and his nomination was accepted. Considering his extreme views, previous attacks on the Liberals, and the formation of a new party, this was rather extraordinary, and may attest to his continuing celebrity. However, as soon as his campaign started in the following year, Graham abandoned any pretence of supporting the Liberals; he openly attacked them again, and was dropped as their candidate. An editorial in *The Scotsman* opined:

> In the exercise of his independent judgment [Graham] thought the right thing to do was to attack in the most bitter way the leaders of the Liberal party, and to dissociate himself practically from the main body of the party on various points. Under such circumstances, it was not surprising that the Association should have come to the conclusion that Mr Cunninghame Graham had failed to satisfy the first conditions of a Liberal candidate, that they should have settled on Mr McCulloch [Gladstonian] and chosen him.[115]

On 4 June 1892, a public meeting was held in the constituency at Bridgeton, where Graham put himself forward as an 'Independent Labour Party' candidate,[116] and the Eight Hours Bill and land nationalisation were his main platforms. The meeting was constantly disrupted by rival supporters, and could not begin until two members of the audience were ejected. A motion was carried supporting his candidature, as it was next day at a meeting of the Irish National League in the Gallowgate.[117] A public meeting for the official Liberal candidate, John McCulloch, on 3 July, turned into a riot, led by 'Sandy' Haddow and other Labour supporters. The *Glasgow Observer* believed that Graham was behind the disruptive behaviour, adding:

> He fostered treason to Liberalism wherever he found opportunity and then cried out like an injured innocent when the Liberals turned on him and rent him . . . refusing all approach to amicable arrangement.[118]

Graham had campaigned vigorously, although he was not in the constituency during the last week of the campaign, choosing instead to help Hardie win West Ham. In his absence, he had enlisted the support of his wife 'Gabrielle', who made an inflammatory speech in which she described the Liberals as 'miserable piddling party hacks, dull heavy beery-brained dullards who would sell their souls if they had any'.[119] The *Glasgow Herald* wrote of her, 'Mrs. Cunninghame Graham is an exceptional woman, and it may be as well that her performance of last Sunday should remain exceptional.'[120] Despite well-attended meetings, but with little help from his supporters and the Irish vote cleaving to the official Liberal candidate after Parnell's disgrace over his divorce proceedings, Graham lost badly, polling only 11.9 per cent of the vote.[121]

General Election Result, Camlachie, *6 July 1892*

Alexander Cross (Liberal Unionist)	3455
John McCulloch (Liberal)	3084
Cunninghame Graham (Scottish Labour)	906
Hugh Watt (Independent Liberal)	179

The news of Graham's defeat was received by the Labour supporters in London with a good deal of regret, and hopes were expressed that he would re-enter parliament.[122] At a meeting in Newcastle shortly afterwards, Hardie proposed that Graham, 'as the most brilliant man in the Labour party out of Parliament', should stand there in the future,[123] but Graham's defeat was the end of his parliamentary career. Despite the drift of the tide towards Unionism in Scotland, Gladstone now led a minority Liberal Government, but three Independent Labour MPs had been elected, including Hardie. Writing of Graham's defeat, Watts and Davies commented:

Edward Aveling and Eleanor Marx wrote that the labour representation movement had lost 'something more than a head – their heart.' It was meant as a tribute, but it raises a question – was the political Graham all heart and no head?[124]

Taylor wrote of the event:

> In the circumstances prevailing at the time – his low state of health, his urgent need for money, the damaged prospects for the Scottish Labour Party – his first reaction to his dismissal probably was relief; now he had time to rest, to reflect; time to decide whether he was pleased or sorry.[125]

Ironically, on 2 October 1892, three months after Graham's defeat, a report was issued at the National Liberal Federation's annual meeting at Newcastle, known as 'The Newcastle Programme'[126] which, according to Peter Weller, was a response to the loss of middle-class support and enlarged working-class franchise and 'made it clear that some gesture had to be made to labour'.[127] The programme endorsed many of the issues that Graham had begun campaigning for five years earlier, including giving compulsory powers to local authorities to acquire lands for allotments, smallholdings, and labourers' dwellings, which was a policy to turn agricultural workers into small-scale tenants. It also sought home rule, church disestablishment in Scotland and Wales, triennial parliaments, fair taxation of land values and ground rents, repeal of the laws of primogeniture and entail, and freedom for tenants to sell or transfer their interest. Employers' liability insurance was also proposed, and there was reference to the reduction of the hours of labour, and recognition of the principle of the payment of MPs. Weller added, '[T]he Newcastle Programme mainly represented the radicalism of the previous decade, not a new departure in Liberal policy.'[128] However, it was indicative that at last, significant elements within the party were aware that progressive policies were required to counter increasing calls for change.

The question might then justifiably be asked: if Graham had not resigned his seat, and if he had behaved more consensually within the Liberal caucus, could he have achieved some measure of change, which, during his brief time in parliament, he had not? Inevitably, to avoid alienating middle-class supporters, a major stumbling block remained the Liberals' position on adopting working-class candidates in working-class districts, and it is difficult to envisage Graham accepting this.

At the Newcastle meeting, Gladstone created the impression that the programme would be binding on the party, but this was not the case, and Peter Stansky concluded, 'In short, whatever else may be said about the Newcastle Programme, it proved of no value to the Liberal party as a cohesive force.'[129] Furthermore, according to Hutchison, 'In the administration of 1892, Gladstone readily acceded to Marjoribanks's recommendation that the institution of a Scottish Grand Committee was sufficient to meet the needs of Scottish legislation. Scottish Home Rule was thus effectively shunted aside.'[130] All this gives justifiable credence to Graham's continuing disillusionment with the Liberal party in general, and Gladstone in particular.

Notes

1. *Airdrie Advertiser*, 12 February 1887, p. 3. Troops had been called out to protect property.
2. Cunninghame Graham, 'Aspects of the Social Question' *English Review*, December 1908, p. 165.
3. Morgan, *Keir Hardie*, p.18. When they met is disputed. David Lowe contradicted himself, saying that they both descended a pit at New Cumnock together, in early 1887 (*Glasgow Evening Times*, 4 February 1938, p. 3), and also that they met for the first time during Hardie's election campaign in Mid-Lanark in 1888 (*Glasgow Evening Times*, 29 October 1937, p. 3). Graham himself was equally uncertain, stating that it was 'about the year 1887 or 1888'. William Stewart, *J. Keir Hardie* (London: Cassell, 1921), p. 51.
4. *Coatbridge Express*, 8 June 1887, p. 2.
5. *Airdrie Advertiser*, 26 February 1887, p. 5.
6. Ibid.
7. *Coatbridge Express*, 2 March 1887, p. 2.
8. In reply to accusations that Graham was acting on his own authority, Hardie wrote to *The Scotsman* to say that Graham 'has acted not only with the consent, but under the direct instructions of the miners' representatives'. *Scotsman*, 20 August 1887, p. 10.
9. The summer of 1887 was unusually hot, and hundreds of unemployed people were living in Trafalgar Square, where the fountains offered some relief from the heat, and it became a focus for protest. Fear of a socialist revolution led to the outlawing of public meetings in the square, which precipitated the 'Bloody Sunday' riot. (See Appendix III.)
10. *Airdrie Advertiser*, 8 June 1889, p. 4. The English trade unionist, Tom Mann, wrote that Graham was actively recruited to the Eight Hours League (an offshoot of the SDF), soon after entering Parliament. Tom Mann, *Memoirs* (London: MacGibbon & Kee, 1923), p. 44.
11. *Labour Elector*, 8 February 1890, p. 93.
12. Ibid., p. 71.
13. Ibid., p. 93.
14. PP. Coal Mines Regulation Bill, Consideration, 3 September 1887, Hansard, Vol. 320, cc 1088.

15. Taylor, *The People's Laird*, p. 159.
16. PP. Coal Mines Regulation Bill: Consideration of Lords Amendments, 12 September 1887, Hansard, Vol. 321, cc 435.
17. Sidney Webb and Harold Cox, *The Eight Hours Day* (London: W. Scott, 1891), p. 12.
18. Ibid., Preface (no page number).
19. W. Hamish Fraser, 'Trades Councils in the Labour Movement in Nineteenth-Century Scotland', in *Essays in Scottish Labour History*, ed. by Ian MacDougall (Edinburgh: John Donald, 1978), p. 10.
20. A derogatory working-class reference to strike-breakers, although its original meaning was the opposite, being someone of democratic and anti-government sympathies.
21. *Scotsman*, 8 October 1887, p. 8. The report continued: 'He expects everybody to walk on the edge of the precipice as skilfully as he does; and while they are making the experiment he retires to the shelter of his hotel.'
22. *Coatbridge Express*, 26 June 1889, p. 2.
23. *Coatbridge Express*, 13 May 1891, p. 2.
24. It is estimated that 400 people were arrested, and seventy-five badly injured. The police action, under the direction of Commissioner Sir Charles Warren, would be Graham's *cause célèbre* for several months, which he pursued through Parliament and the press, proclaiming his innocence and victimhood, and he was still writing about it twenty years later. Warren resigned less than a year after 'Bloody Sunday', over the police force's inability to solve the 'Jack the Ripper' murders.
25. *The Commonweal*, 26 November 1887, p. 377. Morris had witnessed the scene, as did George Bernard Shaw.
26. *Coatbridge Express*, 7 December 1887, p. 1.
27. *Coatbridge Express*, 25 January 1888, p. 1.
28. *The Spectator*, 28 January 1888, p. 8.
29. *Coatbridge Express*, 22 February 1888, p. 1.
30. Tschiffely, *Don Roberto*, p. 195. Graham also reputedly said, 'I sometimes wish I could believe in religion, for if I did I could be sure that Gladstone was in hell.' Quoted in David Daiches, *A Companion to Scottish Literature* (London: Edward Arnold, 1981), p. 89.
31. *The Times*, 26 November 1879, p. 6.
32. Graham's return to Scotland directly after his trial was greeted by an estimated eight thousand supporters in Glasgow, and 'the scene was one of the wildest enthusiasm'. *Airdrie Advertiser*, 26 November 1887, p. 3.
33. Cunninghame Graham, 'Has the Liberal Party a Future?' *Contemporary Review*, February 1888.
34. Haldane, 'The Liberal Party and its Prospects', pp. 145–60. At this time, Haldane had been lecturing in working men's clubs against the theories of Marx, Henry George, and against Graham himself. In a letter to his mother, dated 25 October 1887, Haldane wrote that Graham's speeches were 'doing

a great deal of mischief all over Scotland'. Haldane of Cloan Papers, NLS. MSS 5940, f.101. Despite their opposing views, however, Graham referred to Haldane as 'a personal friend'. *Scotsman*, 13 October 1887, p. 6. Haldane for his part had stood bail for Graham following his arrest, and given evidence in Graham's favour at the subsequent trial, which putatively set back his own legal career. Haldane joined the Labour party in 1923, and served as Lord Chancellor in Ramsay MacDonald's government in 1924.

35. Cunninghame Graham 'Has the Liberal Party a Future?', p. 300. My italics. At this stage, Graham had obviously been contemplating a socialist alternative.

36. Hutchison, *A Political History of Scotland*, p. 179.

37. Heyck and Klecka, 'British Radical M.P.s, 1874–1895', p. 183.

38. Keith Laybourn, *The Rise of Labour* (Polytechnic of Huddersfield, 1990), p. 6.

39. *Coatbridge Express*, 21 September 1887, p. 2.

40. *Scotsman*, 24 October 1887, p. 8.

41. *The Commonweal*, 22 October 1887, p. 87. E. P. Thompson described Mahon as 'a floating agitator'. Thompson, *William Morris*, p. 351.

42. *The Miner*, August 1888, p. 86.

43. *Airdrie Advertiser*, 3 November 1889, p. 5.

44. The idea of a party within a party was by no means unique among the Liberals. The most significant precedent was Joseph Chamberlain's National Liberal Federation, formed in 1877, plus the many divisions in the Liberal ranks, including double candidatures over church disestablishment, and Irish home rule at the 1885 and 1886 general elections. Hardie apparently still felt a strong affinity with the Liberals, and clung to the forlorn hope of working within the party for much longer than Graham. In his election manifesto of 1892 he stated, 'Generally I am in agreement with the present programme of the Liberal Party'.

45. *Manchester Guardian*, 24 March 1888, p. 5. Even by 1914, when the Labour Party was firmly established, Lloyd George, addressing the National Reform Union proclaimed, '[I]t is better that we should have a party which combines every section and shade of opinion, taken from all classes in the community, rather than a party that represents one shade of opinion alone or one class of community alone.'

46. *Scotsman*, 18 April 1888, p. 6. Although not yet officially founded, the name 'Labour Party' was already in common use.

47. Fred Reid. Derived from his doctoral thesis 'The Early Life and Political Development of James Keir Hardie, 1856–92', DPhil, Oxford University, 1969.

48. Ibid., p. 19.

49. *Labour Elector*, 22 June 1889, p. 4.

50. *Labour Tribune* described Hardie's campaign as 'hard and well organised', supported by 'that Goliath of politics – Mr Cunninghame Graham', but

concluded that 'the Labour Party was not as strong in Scotland as its voice is loud'. *Labour Tribune*, 12 May 1888, p. 5.

51. David Lowe, *Souvenirs of Scottish Labour* (Glasgow: W. R. Holmes, 1919), p. v. Much of this work was reprinted from Lowe's writings for Thomas Johnston's *Forward* newspaper, published ten years previously.

52. Robert Smillie (1857–1940). Later, President of the Lanarkshire Miners' Federation, President of the Miners' Federation of Great Britain, and MP for Morpeth, among many other positions.

53. Robert Smillie, *My Life For Labour* (London: Mills & Boon, 1924), p. 293.

54. *Scotsman*, 28 August 1888, p. 4.

55. Alexander 'Sandy' Haddow, 'Reminiscences of the Early Socialist Movement in Scotland', *Forward*, 8 May 1909, p. 6.

56. Fred Reid, 'Early Life and Political Development of James Keir Hardie', p. 45. Hardie's formative experience of the House of Commons under Graham's direction was discussed at length in Emrys Hughes, *Keir Hardie* (London: George Allen & Unwin, 1956).

57. James Bruce Glasier, *James Keir Hardie: A Memorial* (Manchester: The National Labour Press, 1919), p. 20. Stewart praised Glasier's intimate knowledge of the early Labour and Socialist movement 'in all its phases and aspects', and 'his long and close intimacy with Hardie both in public and private life'. Stewart, *J. Keir Hardie*, p. vii.

58. Caroline Benn, *Keir Hardie* (London: Hutchison, 1992), p. 45.

59. Ibid., p. 49.

60. Henry Pelling, *Origins of the Labour Party, 1880–1900* (Oxford University Press, 1965), p. 70.

61. The SHRA's main propagandist, Charles Waddie, apparently first coined this popular expression. See 'Obituary', *Glasgow Herald*, 6 February 1912, p. 7.

62. *Labour Elector*, 21 September 1888, p. 4.

63. William Martin Haddow, *My Seventy Years* (Glasgow: Robert Gibson, 1943), p. 34. According to 'Sandy' Haddow, the first socialist meeting that Hardie addressed was at Parkhead Hall (no date), and after posting two hundred bills, it attracted an audience of thirteen. Haddow, 'Reminiscences', p. 6.

64. James Leatham, *60 Years of World Mending* (1940) (Turriff: Deveron Press, 2016), p. 154.

65. 'Mr Cunninghame Graham Interviewed', reprinted in the *Airdrie Advertiser*, 21 April 1888, p. 5.

66. Ibid.

67. Cunninghame Graham, letter to *Forward*, 1 May 1909, p. 2.

68. *Labour Elector*, 22 June 1889, p. 4.

69. *The Labour Prophet: The Organ of the Labour Church*, March 1892, p. 18.

70. *Scotsman*, 6 June 1889, p. 4.

71. John Trevor (1855–1930). A Unitarian minister who founded the Labour Church in Manchester in 1891.

72. *Labour Prophet*, March 1892, p. 18.

73. Fraser, *Scottish Popular Politics*, pp. 125–8.

74. Clayton, *Rise & Decline of Socialism*, p. 54.

75. Graham's reports on the Congress appeared in the *Labour Elector* on 27 July 1889, pp. 54–5, and 3 August, p. 71.

76. *Scotsman*, 5 September 1889, p. 6. With the influx of new societies, by 1891, the TUC voted in favour of an eight-hour working day.

77. Ibid.

78. Ibid.

79. Ibid.

80. Norman Mackenzie, ed., *The Letters of Sidney and Beatrice Webb* (Cambridge University Press, 1978), pp. 69–70. Beatrice Webb converted to socialism in 1890.

81. *Scotsman*, 9 April 1890, p. 6.

82. *Scotsman*, 15 October 1891, p. 5.

83. George Shipton (1839–1911) was a prominent trade unionist.

84. Henry Broadhurst (1840–1911) was a leading early trade unionist and a Lib–Lab MP.

85. *Labour Elector*, 7 September 1889, p. 153.

86. *Glasgow Herald*, 7 November 1889, p. 10.

87. Ibid.

88. *Scotsman*, 25 October 1889, p. 6.

89. *Airdrie Advertiser*, 2 November 1889, p. 3.

90. *Coatbridge Express*, 20 February 1889, p. 2.

91. *Scotsman*, 8 March 1889, p. 5.

92. *Airdrie Advertiser*, 23 February 1889, p. 4.

93. *Evening Citizen*, 23 April 1889, p. 5. Graham had inherited over £100,000 worth of debts from his father. At the end of July that year, the *Coatbridge Express* published news that Graham's estate at Ardoch had been put up for sale in lots, totalling over £50,000, but '[a]t the sale, no offers were made, and the proceedings were adjourned'. *Coatbridge Express*, 31 July 1889, p. 2.

94. *Airdrie Advertiser*, 1 March 1890, p. 3.

95. *Coatbridge Express*, 19 March 1890, p. 2.

96. Archibald Philip Primrose, 5th Earl of Rosebery, 1st Earl of Midlothian (1847–1929). A senior Liberal politician who served as Prime Minister from March 1894 to June 1895. Rosebery described himself to Joseph Chamberlain as 'a Scottish home-ruler'. Robert Crewe, *Life of Rosebery*, Vol. 1 (London: John Donald, 1931), p. 174. He also supported an eight-hour working day and, as a major landowner, the abolition of the law of primogeniture, and the creation of more allotments for the working class.

97. Pronounced 'Marshbanks'. Graham had been Marjoribanks's 'fag' at Harrow School, where he had been bullied by him. Jean Cunninghame Graham, *Gaucho Laird*, pp. 55–6.

98. Andrew Provand MP, letter to Lord Rosebery, 20 December 1894. Rosebery Papers, NLS. MS 10100. My thanks to Dr Catriona MacDonald for this information.
99. *Airdrie Advertiser*, 1 March 1890, p. 3.
100. *Coatbridge Express*, 19 March 1890, p. 2.
101. Ibid., p. 1.
102. Ibid., p. 2.
103. Sir Charles Tennant, 1st Baronet (1823–1906). Scottish industrialist, Liberal politician, and father-in-law of future Prime Minister Herbert Asquith, who had been Graham's legal counsel during his trial. See *passim*.
104. *Scotsman*, 28 February 1890, p. 4.
105. Ibid.
106. *Labour Elector*, 22 March 1890, p. 185.
107. Cunninghame Graham, letter to *The Star*, 25 August 1890, p. 3.
108. *Scotsman*, 31 March 1890, p. 6.
109. *Scotsman*, 15 September 1890, p. 8.
110. *The Star*, 25 August 1890, p. 4.
111. Ibid.
112. Cunninghame Graham, letter to John Burns, 24 October 1891. John Burns Library, University of Warwick, MSS 259.
113. Tom Mann, letter to Burns, 30 April 1890. Ibid.
114. Taylor, *The People's Laird*, p. 222.
115. *Scotsman*, 2 July 1892, p. 11. On the eve of poll, McCulloch, who would come second, described Graham as an 'insane and impractical politician'. *Glasgow Evening News*, 6 July 1892, p. 4.
116. Taylor wrote that Graham had 'popped up with a new label – that of the Independent Labour Party'. The ILP was not formally inaugurated until 1893 (Taylor, *The People's Laird*, p. 223), and it is possible that Graham, rather than jumping the gun, was forcing the issue that a nationwide organisation was required.
117. *Scotsman*, 6 June 1892, p. 8.
118. *Glasgow Observer*, 9 July 1892, p. 5. Founded in 1885 as Scotland's Roman Catholic newspaper, it was a strong supporter of Gladstonian Liberalism, which it believed offered the best chance of Irish home rule. It later became the *Scottish Catholic Observer*.
119. Ibid.
120. *Glasgow Herald*, 7 July 1892, p. 8.
121. Graham again put himself forward as a socialist candidate in Camlachie in 1900, but was rejected in favour of A. E. Fletcher, the editor of *New Age*, which in 1908 printed four of Graham's political essays, including 'The Real Equality of the Sexes'.
122. *Glasgow Herald*, 10 July 1892, p. 7.
123. *Scotsman*, 16 July 1892, p. 6.
124. Watts and Davies, *Cunninghame Graham*, p. 96.

125. Taylor, *The People's Laird*, p. 225.
126. *The Spectator* described it as 'a document which, though bearing traces of having been concocted in the offices of a clique of political wire-pullers, is nevertheless the official pronouncement of the attitude of the party in regard to the various items of the Liberal programme'. *The Spectator*, 3 October 1891, p. 8. Hutchison described it as a reiteration of an 'assorted collection of sectional demands'. Hutchison, *A Political History of Scotland*, p. 179.
127. Peter Weller, *The New Liberalism: Liberal Social Theory in Great Britain, 1889–1914* (1982) (London: Routledge, 2016), p. 61.
128. Ibid.
129. Peter Stansky, *Ambitions and Strategies: The Struggle for the Leadership of the Liberal Party in the 1890s* (Oxford: Clarendon Press, 1964), p. xii.
130. Hutchison, *A Political History of Scotland*, p. 173.

4

Political Journalism: Confidence and Impunity

Graham had long harboured ambitions to become a writer,[1] but in 1887, he had written to a friend, 'I am at last forced back on *Justice* again,[2] as no paper will take anything from me. Fancy the *Yellow Book* refusing a thing of mine on the grounds that it was immoral. Cretins, liars, etc.'[3] However, after 'Bloody Sunday', things changed dramatically. His article 'Has the Liberal Party a Future?' had displayed passion and style, but in a busy political year, in which he continued his campaigns against the government, and the police, and his attempts to bring the conditions of Britain's poor to the attention of his parliamentary colleagues,[4] Graham was slow to take up his pen again. It was the working conditions of the nail and chainmakers of Cradley Heath in the Black Country, particularly for the women workers, that spurred him to write in their defence, and in early December 1888, he contributed an introduction to a pamphlet entitled 'The Nail & Chainmakers'. Here, for the first time, while still polemical, was an eloquent and absorbing piece of descriptive prose, foreshadowing the 'sketch' style that would be the hallmark of his later literary output, and a new career as a social commentator. Its often short, stabbing sentences painted a vivid and disturbing picture of Dickensian squalor and degradation, 'Mud, dirt, desolation, unpaved street, filthy courts, narrow reeking alleys, thin unkempt women, listless men with open shirts showing their hairy chests. Mud, dirt; dirt and more mud.'[5] This was a festering sore of exploitation and profiteering, recognised, but ignored.[6] The essay was an indictment of the use of sweated labour, and failures at every level of capitalist society and the social system. But readers might also recognise strong similarities in content and style with passages in Engels's *The Condition of the Working-Class in England* (1845).

An almost contemporaneous piece was Graham's introduction to, and adumbration of, a booklet entitled *A Labour Programme*,[7] by Mahon, in which Mahon set out his theories, and potentially incendiary proposals for the reorganisation of society. However, what marked out Graham's commentary was its restrained style in comparison to his 'Plea For the Chainmakers'. Also, for the first time in print, his attempted something altogether more literary and reflective, incorporating what would become a hallmark of his political journalism: frequent literary references, particularly from Shakespeare. Champion criticised the programme for being impractical, but of Graham he wrote 'In his half dozen pages Mr. Graham contrives to write some true and pointed sentences but, as is his wont . . . to wrap them up in sayings which, to adopt his own trick of Shakespearian quotation will be "caviar to the general".'[8] Since this work was presumably aimed at ordinary working people, Graham had made no concessions in his writing to the uneducated, and frequently displayed an aristocratic disdain for mass readership. An observer might be forgiven for concluding that here, and in his upcoming works for socialist journals, he was flexing his literary muscles and playing to his strengths as a well-read, urbane gentleman, or, as Champion hinted, his tendency to show off. It should be noted that after 1895, when he began his long career writing for literary publications read by a more educated public, these affectations all but disappeared.

To date, Graham's journalistic contributions had been mostly to the work of others, but from early September 1888 until August 1891, while still an MP, he embraced political journalism as a vehicle for his campaigns for social justice. The first of these publications was Champion's *Labour Elector* (which Graham partly owned), and whose campaigns chimed with his own, particularly its exposure of inhuman work practices, and its support of New Unionism and the eight-hour day. The biographies by both Watts and Davies, and by Taylor emphasised the importance of the *Labour Elector*, and Taylor confirmed that it was Graham's 'first taste of regular campaigning journalism'.[9] In addition, his speeches were frequently featured as news items. Henceforth, in his work for the *Labour Elector*, the *People's Press*, and others, to which he contributed almost one article per week, his themes would fall into five main categories: *reportage*; the impotence, indifference, and corruption of parliament; worker's rights and the eight-hour day; the evils of capitalism and the plight of the poor; and public versus private morality. Only some of these will be addressed here.

Stirring the working classes into concerted action would be *the* common theme that united all of Graham's writing during this early period.

In his essay 'Working Class Politics', Hutchison described the early difficulties of establishing a thriving socialist presence in Glasgow prior to the establishment of the ILP in 1893.[10] The Irish nationalists, for example, pursued their own home rule agenda, while the land reformers, mostly of Highland origin, remained within the Liberal fold.[11] This lack of cohesion and militancy within the working class prevailed to a lesser or greater extent throughout Britain; all of Graham's journalism during the period was thus hortative political propaganda in some form, encouraging the workers to assume their rights. His *reportage* was the most obvious means of encouraging support, by reporting on strikes and conferences, 'The Marxist Congress',[12] 'The Dundee Congress',[13] or 'Our View of the Strike'[14] being early examples. These were attempts to 'talk up' the labour cause, demonstrating, where possible, workers' solidarity and the effectiveness of militancy, and at times exaggerating the movement's strength and momentum. His confident assertions were nonetheless belied by the indifference, passivity, and often downright hostility he found among the workers themselves, and his frustration over their inability to look after what he considered to be their own best interests. At a meeting in Dundee in September 1889, for example, Graham displayed his elitist instincts by storming out after telling those assembled that they were only fit to be represented by capitalists, and offering a few epigrams on the stupidity of the working classes.[15]

Political apathy was something that many political thinkers, before and after Graham, had considered problematic, if not intractable. In the year Graham was born, the radical philosopher, John Stuart Mill, had written of 'the extreme unfitness of the laboring classes for any order of things which make any considerable demand on either their intellect or their virtue',[16] while Ruskin, as we have seen, saw the workers as having been degraded into a confused and hopeless passivity. Hyndman was convinced that 'the slave-class cannot be freed by the slaves themselves. The leadership, the initiative, the teaching, the organisation, must come from those who were born into a different position.'[17] Despite his impatient outbursts, Graham, at this period at least, seemed to understand the huge cultural and generational shift required to counteract the years of passivity and obedience, believing, as he wrote in *A Labour Programme*, that the working classes would in time seize the day. In a piece entitled 'If Cock Robin is Dead – Who Will Kill King Capital?', he criticised an article by Sidney Webb, believing that Webb took a patronising view and had too low an opinion of the capabilities of the working classes. Graham blamed religion and commerce ('chapel and till') for their passivity, and their misplaced belief in the Liberal Party as the only vehicle for change.

Equally, he did not wish to see the workers corrupted by their advancement. For Graham, the only solution was purely 'labour' politics to avoid the mistakes of the past, and no collaboration with the middle classes:

> Better by far the workman in his club, caring for naught (as Webb says) but his beer and skittles, than transmutated [sic] to a smug, cheating bourgeois, or led by him and deserted on the post as heretofore.[18]

Graham was all too aware, however, that once a working man had improved his position, he was just as liable to turn on his fellows and betray his class, stepping on his comrades instead of helping raise them up. In a piece entitled 'China Dogs', he humorously put the blame for these misplaced aspirations on the cosy symbols of Victorian domesticity that ornamented the mantle-shelves of many working-class homes, the 'wally-dugs', which to him were a sign of bourgeois ambitions: 'Then the black coat appears and all that implies. The men who worked with him declare that Jack or Jim has become a toff, the fact being really that he is a mixture of a skunk and fool.'[19] This was another particularly elitist and idealistic perspective. Graham's fundamental hope was that human nature could be changed so that material considerations, among a population that had hitherto suffered deprivation, could be made subordinate to a desire for independence and the sort of non-materialistic self-improvement promulgated by Smiles and others, which could be considered extremely patronising. However, the Reverend David Summers believed that 'Cunninghame Graham's "sermon" on China Dogs appealed to and was remembered by ILP and SDF members alike'.[20]

Graham, nevertheless, was not above using working-class material ambitions as a counter-argument when it suited him. In his 'An Open Letter to Prince Kropotkin',[21] he wrote about the abolition of property:

> It would not be from the propertied class, believe me, that the outcry against Communism would come . . . No, but the poor, who, never having enjoyed property, at present in the main look at all social reforms as merely an opportunity to acquire, and would resent bitterly when they found they were to call nothing their own.[22]

Both of these opposing sentiments reflected Graham's disdain for bourgeois attitudes and his own 'heroic-élitism': 'Respectability is England's curse, and Scotland's bane',[23] or again, 'Respectability! I hate respectability . . . What did respectability mean? Why, when respectability shut the door of its snug villa it showed humanity out.'[24] This view was undoubtedly developed from Graham's colonial or at least foreign experiences, and they were by no means unique. Hugh MacDiarmid, for example, would write: 'I have, in short, no use for anything between genius and the working man'.[25] Even John Buchan, whose political views were diametrically opposed to both Graham and MacDiarmid's, had his Scottish hero, Richard Hannay, say:

> A man of my sort, who has travelled about the world in rough places, gets on perfectly well with two classes, what you may call the upper and the lower. He understands them and they understand him. I was at home with herds and tramps and roadmen, and I was sufficiently at ease with Sir Walter. I can't explain why, but it is a fact. But what fellows like me don't understand is the great comfortable, satisfied middleclass world, the folk that live in villas in suburbs. He doesn't know how they look at things, he doesn't understand their conventions, and he is as shy of them as of a black mamba.[26]

We might suspect that these sentiments reflected Buchan's colonial experiences in southern Africa, where class structures were less rigid, but perhaps more polarised, where both upper and lower classes shared the same deprivations and existential challenges, and where strength of character and strength of arm were as important as social status. These attitudes were also elitist, or at least exclusive, exclusive of the bourgeoisie, and may characterise a certain type of Scot. This indeed may be the clue to Graham's whole political philosophy and eventual literary output, missed by his biographers, that poor working people had authenticity and individual, intrinsic worth because they had not (yet) been corrupted by materialism. Moreover, this worth, rather than being developed for their own betterment, and the betterment of society as a whole, had been exploited and abused for the profit of the base and the greedy, who were themselves less worthy in every way. Certainly, Graham's political campaigns were on behalf of the working class, but his later Scottish 'portraits' dealt only with these the upper and lower classes, the bourgeoisie being entirely absent.

The theme of parliamentary corruption and indifference would become a regular feature in Graham's work for the *Labour Elector*, and later the *People's Press*, under the ironic title 'The People's Parliament'. At the beginning, these purported to be reportage, but soon, they reverted to political broadsides with the common theme 'Nothing will change until we have real Labour Members to discuss Labour and Domestic matters, from the standpoint of the working classes'.[27] The second regular feature in both the *Labour Elector* and the *People's Press* was written under the heading 'Foreign Notes', in which Graham reported on labour disputes abroad, almost exclusively in parts of the Hispanic-speaking world. Many were from direct experience of his continuing travels, but they were the first examples of what, in later life, would distinguish his 'aesthetic' in the public perception: depictions of exotic locales, curious customs, freedoms, and dangers. It was in one of these foreign notes entitled 'Lisbon Revisited'[28] that Taylor discerned the birth of a new form of expression that would dominate Graham's later career:

> Here, suddenly, after years of arid polemic, was a brief glimpse of a new kind of writing that was beginning to come more often and more easily to him: to say what he saw; to describe what he, and others, did, he discovered was intensely satisfying.[29]

It was hardly years – Graham's journalism proper had begun exactly eight months previously, and to describe his early political writings as 'arid polemic' is misleading. Graham's works stood out from the standard reports in socialist journals as highly individual expressive declarations that dealt with social problems and deprivation at a very human level, and attacked or ridiculed the institutions and attitudes that he believed created and sustained them. This, as we have seen, included criticism of the attitudes of the working class themselves which, perhaps, only a man of Graham's background, in an age where deference to class still pertained, could write with confidence and impunity. However, although aimed at this readership, a typical piece might wander off in any direction, crossing continents if necessary to make some point, and decorated with his beloved literary allusions. Again, we might be forgiven for suspecting that Graham was engaged in learning a different trade, or releasing pent-up literary urges. Certainly, 'Lisbon Revisited' was the first time he had let some 'sunshine' into his work, and this was quickly followed up with 'Life in Tangiers',[30] which was a much freer, imaginative, and revelatory expression. This is a very marked departure from what had gone before, and it seems that writing about exotic, warm locations, freed the reflective, abstract dreaming hitherto concealed. Tangiers for example, despite its barbaric laws and corruption, offered a more egalitarian, 'harmonious' lifestyle:

> And if they do occasionally cut off a man's head, they do not crush out his life with hard work and stupid hypocrisy, as in England. Is not a country in which each man cultivates his own little plot, sits in his own little shop, works at his own loom, wields his own hammer in his own forge, nearer to Socialism than in England. There is no great machine industry; no public opinion; no roads; no railways; no standing army; and little or no education. Are men, therefore the happier? Yes, I think so.[31]

This was also the first appearance of what would become another common theme in many of Graham's subsequent writings, an 'anti-statism', a belief that so-called less developed societies represented a freer, more natural and harmonious existence than that enjoyed by more advanced societies. This was not socialism as we understand it; it was commonality based on individualism and respect rather than collectivism, community rather than central planning, a preindustrial society that did not need regulation nor (more importantly) strict conformity, or even much government. It was, nonetheless, a particularly Manichaean world view; Britain was dark, unnatural, mechanistic, materialistic, 'this bleak grey town, with its cold winds, its electric light, and all the concomitant horrors of civilization'.[32] At home, the people were degraded either by poverty or by wealth, while sunnier climes appeared to retain a classless spontaneity due to a common lack of material possessions, and this too would develop into a recurring theme. Graham was aware of the many negative aspects of such less developed societies, but these were offset by equality, self-reliance, and other personal freedoms, as expressed in many of his later works:

> They esteem a man by virtue of his being, and no one sinks himself in his profession or forgets for an instant that God created firstly men, and that the state of politician, soldier, pimp, king, priest and tide-waiter is secondary, and can be laid aside or altered, if fortune changes or the occasion serves.[33]

Watts described this as Graham's 'anti-rational primitivism (I mean a form of nostalgia for a relatively primitive state of being)',[34] which would be illustrated in Graham's most celebrated work, *Mogreb-el-Acksa* (1898).[35] In this account of his attempted journey across the Atlas Mountains in Morocco in 1897 disguised as a Turkish doctor, Graham asked whether, if people were democratically governed and 'tamed', they would really be 'happier than the unregenerate Moors, who lie and steal, fight, fornicate, and generally behave themselves as if blood circulated in their veins and not sour whey?'[36] Watts also used this term to describe Conrad's works: 'the view that a limitation of the individual's consciousness or reflective and ratiocinative abilities may best equip him for life.'[37] This primitivism threads through Graham's works, including his earliest semi-tale *Evolution of a Village*, and would be a recurring motif in his sketches of lowborn Scottish characters.

Here, then, in these early 'political' works, we can distinguish not only a means by which he could express himself artistically, but equally important, in his works set overseas, his future preoccupations with personal freedoms that were under attack from encroaching 'progress'. As such, they are a direct linkage between his early polemics, and his later career as an impressionistic 'sketch' writer. Graham's articles were thus quite unique in early socialist literature, such as Hardie's *The Miner*, or much later, Thomas Johnston's *Forward*, which usually confined themselves to news of disputes and strikes, and the finer points of socialist doctrine. Even though roughly half of his pieces reported on industrial action and agitation (and small unattributed news items that betrayed his style), half were reflective, attacking the institutions that opposed change, and from his perspective, held the working classes in their place. Of these, his 'People's Parliament', 'Public Opinion', 'Bloody City', and 'Reptile Press' were the finest examples. His style also became more fluid and conversational, as if he was liberating his sometimes nostalgic, and sometimes febrile imagination, although the less regimented and less stenographic style of the *People's Press* might also have been a contributing factor. This turned him into what would be termed today a feature-writer, in pieces such as 'If Cock Robin is Dead – Who Will Kill King Capital?' 'Utopia', and 'China Dogs' (discussed above).

It may be said, from reading these, that Graham's political ideas, up to this point, were now fully developed. He had adopted and adapted the ideas of others, combining them with his life experiences, predispositions, and education into a personal philosophy that he believed was the antidote to a deformed society, the inequalities of which he found offensive, but he had now had a satisfying medium in which to express them. Also, from the outset of his journalistic career, we find a wry or ironic humour. It had already been reported that his jokes from the platform helped attract large crowds, but the page offered more scope to develop a mocking style, particularly when he wrote about the House of Commons and fellow politicians.

With the closure of the *Labour Elector*, Graham immediately started contributing to the new publication, the *People's Press*, a weekly journal 'devoted to the interests of labour', writing thirty-seven pieces in the publication's year-long existence. However, ten days prior to his first article, a short piece by Graham, entitled 'Parable of the Paitans'[38] appeared in the American publication *The Knights of Labor*. Here, for the first time, we can witness an attempt at storytelling to make a political point (although what the point is, is not easily descried), and in what would become common in much of his later works his parable was set in southern America. Slowly then, despite his continuing campaigns, we can witness his development as a writer, in which his earlier life experiences, his wide reading, and his natural gifts of humour would play an increasingly important role, often suffused among serious political points. Again, his readership's educational attainments were ignored, as a wide knowledge of history, political economy, and literature (particularly the classics) was displayed, decorated with his beloved literary allusions, all tumbled together with panache and a carefree showmanship, as if pent up for many years.

Moreover, what also distinguished Graham's early journalism was much more fundamental. Whereas he encouraged the workers to unite and fight for better wages and conditions, both from the platform and on the page, what separated him from his left-wing contemporaries in the nascent labour movement was an aesthetic sensibility that obliged him to disdain industrialism as a whole, as a corrupting and evil influence, of which exploitation, poverty, and social ills were merely symptoms. This placed him firmly in the tradition of men like Carlyle, Owen, Ruskin, Morris, and D. H. Lawrence.

With the closure of the *People's Press* in February 1891, Graham lost a major platform for his opinions and literary ambitions, and his unique literary output was considerably curtailed just before he was obliged to leave parliament, with only an occasional article for the *Worker's Cry*, the *Labour Leader*, the *Labour Prophet*, and the *Workman's Times*, up until March 1894. It would not be until 1895, that Graham's literary career was reinvigorated, but this time in an entirely new direction.

Notes

1. 'His main interest is, however, in literature.' 'Mr Cunninghame Graham Interviewed', *Airdrie Advertiser*, 21 April 1888, p. 5.
2. *Justice: The Organ of Social-Democracy*, published by the SDF.
3. Tschiffely, *Don Roberto*, p. 264.
4. PP. Motions and Question, 11 August 1888, Hansard, Vol. 330, cc 416–19.
5. Cunninghame Graham, 'A Plea for the Chainmakers', in *The Nail and Chainmakers*, Labour Platform Series, No. 2, 1888, p. 103.
6. 'The condition of the people at Cradley Heath has been well known for the last fifty years to the public. Disraeli called it Hell-Hole. Royal Commissions not a few have reported on it. Radicals have questioned about it. Philanthropists have sighed and passed on. Clergymen of various denominations have passed lives of modest usefulness endeavouring to divert the minds of the people from the ills they endure in this world, to the prospective happiness they may enjoy in the next. But nothing has, so far as I am aware, ever been attempted in a practical way to improve their condition.' Cunninghame Graham, 'Plea For the Chainmakers', p. 101.
7. Cunninghame Graham, 'Introduction' to *A Labour Programme*, by J. L. Mahon, Labour Platform Series, No. 1, 1888, pp. 1–7.
8. *Labour Elector*, 12 January 1889, p. 8.
9. Taylor, *The People's Laird*, p. 203.
10. Hardie wrote, 'it is the slum vote which the socialist candidate fears most'. James Keir Hardie, *From Serfdom to Socialism* (London: G. Allen, 1907), p. 26.
11. I. G. C. Hutchison in *The Working Class in Glasgow, 1750–1914*, ed. by R. A. Cage (London: Croom Helm, 1987), pp. 113–14.

12. Cunninghame Graham, 'The Marxist Congress', *Labour Elector*, 27 July 1889, pp. 54–5.
13. Cunninghame Graham, 'The Dundee Congress', *Labour Elector*, 7 September 1889, pp. 152–3.
14. Cunninghame Graham, 'Our View of the Strike', *Labour Elector*, 21 September 1889, p. 181.
15. Lowe, *Souvenirs of Scottish Labour*, p. 36.
16. John Stuart Mill, *Principles of Political Economy*, Preface to 3rd edition (London: John W. Parker, 1852), p. 9.
17. H. M. Hyndman, *The Record of An Adventurous Life* (London: Macmillan, 1911), p. 397.
18. Cunninghame Graham, 'If Cock Robin is Dead – Who Will Kill King Capital?' *People's Press*, 5 July 1890, p. 3.
19. Cunninghame Graham, 'China Dogs', *Labour Prophet*, May 1892, pp. 33–4
20. David F. Summers, 'The Labour Church and Allied Movements of the Late 19th and Early 20th Centuries', DPhil, University of Glasgow, 1958, p. 115.
21. Pyotr Alexeyevich Kropotkin (1842–1921), a Russian philosopher and prolific author, who lived in London. Kropotkin preached anarcho-communism and co-founded the anarchist journal *Freedom*.
22. Cunninghame Graham, 'An Open Letter to Prince Kropotkin', *Labour Elector*, 8 February 1890, p. 109.
23. Cunninghame Graham, 'Ca' Canny', *People's Press*, 29 November 1890, p. 7.
24. *Edinburgh Evening News*, 18 March 1887, p. 3.
25. MacDiarmid, *Lucky Poet: A Self Study* (London: Methuen, 1943), p. 402.
26. John Buchan, *The Thirty-Nine Steps* (1915) (Ware: Wordsworth Classics, 1994), p. 92.
27. Cunninghame Graham, 'The People's Parliament', *Labour Elector*, 13 July 1889, p. 13.
28. Cunninghame Graham, 'Lisbon Revisited', *Labour Elector*, 21 December 1889, p. 396.
29. Taylor, *The People's Laird*, p. 218.
30. Cunninghame Graham, 'Life in Tangiers', *Labour Elector*, 11 January 1890.
31. Ibid., p. 28.
32. Ibid.
33. Cunninghame Graham, 'Introduction' to *Companions in the Sierra* by Charles Ruddy (London: John Lane, 1907), p. 12.
34. Watts, *R. B. Cunninghame Graham*, p. 47.
35. Cunninghame Graham, *Mogreb-El-Acksa*. Conrad eulogised it (letter dated 9 December 1898, Watts, *Joseph Conrad's Letters*), p. 111, and MacDiarmid called it 'one of the best books on travel ever written'. MacDiarmid, *Centenary Study*, p. 28.
36. *Mogreb-el-Acksa* (1898) (London: Century, 1988), p. 69.
37. Watts, *Joseph Conrad's Letters*, p. 55.
38. Cunninghame Graham, 'Parable of the Paitans', *Journal of the Knights of Labor*, 13 March 1890, p. 4.

5

Empire: Imperial Sceptic

As we have seen, Graham's time in parliament was preoccupied by what he saw, fundamentally, as the chronic results of industrialisation at home. More significantly, he would stand out from most of his political contemporaries as a man who had first-hand experience of the deleterious effects of capitalism and empire on developing countries. He would also stand out among the vast bulk of the British population, at a time of imperial expansion and pride, as an imperial sceptic, and later, as a vociferous anti-imperialist.[1] This chapter considers Graham's early moral concerns over the acquisition and expansion of this empire, before moving on to the effects of colonialism and capitalism on indigenous peoples, however, his anti-imperial and anti-racist writings would not reach a vitriolic crescendo until 1896 and 1897, described in Chapter 10.

Britain's imperial justification and hubris found no better expression than in the works of two authors, Brooke Foss Westcott, Bishop of Durham, and John Robert Seeley. Westcott, who wrote extensively on religious and imperial matters, believed that it was the spiritual duty to spread 'the spirit of England',[2] and he extolled Seeley's 1883 book, *The Expansion of England*. In this, Seeley set out the equivalent of a manifest destiny for Britain, justifying imperialism as a benefit to the world with the words, 'The English State then, in what direction and towards what goal has that been advancing? The words which jump to our lips are Liberty, Democracy.'[3] Duncan Bell reminded us that Seeley's book had been an instant success, 'helping to set the terms of late Victorian debate about empire and remaining a standard reference point for decades to come. It remained in print until 1956, the year of Suez.'[4] It was the ideas expressed by Seeley that typified much of late nineteenth-century thinking on empire, so that the radical Liberal, and arch-imperialist, Joseph Chamberlain could say in 1897, 'We feel now that our rule over their territories can only be justified if we can show that it adds to the happiness and prospects of the people.'[5] Bell commented, however, that 'the professed principles and the grubby reality were very different'.[6]

In his early speeches, any extreme sentiments that Graham may have harboured against the empire were necessarily mitigated by the prevailing national mood and his desire to become a Member of Parliament. His reluctance notwithstanding, in his first speech at Coatbridge, as a visiting speaker, Graham suggested to his audience that 'I would call on you to resist the glare and tinsel of a *meretricious* Imperialism'.[7] More controversially, a month later, at Shettleston, he asserted that imperial conquest was merely an opportunity for rich merchants to dispose of their shoddy goods. He also questioned whether the possession of enormous wealth 'conduces much to love of country', but that the finer patriotic virtues were more commonly found among the poorer classes. More controversially, he continued, in what would be a very significant trope in his later writings on empire and colonisation:

> There is also a question to be asked – and it is a very serious one, involving far greater interests than mere national ones – Does British rule always conduce to the wellbeing and comfort of the nations of the absorbed territories? Very often it does not. It is very doubtful whether, on the contrary, it does not very often tend to their speedy degradation, misery, and final extinction.[8]

Graham then referred to 'useless wars', particularly in South Africa, by which 'a most effectual preventative check has been put to the increase of population in that country', adding 'We have tried to win the affections of the natives of Afghanistan by advancing into their country and killing large quantities of them.'[9] Also, controversially, coming from a newly selected Liberal candidate, he believed that this would be the case, whichever government was in power, the first evidence of his cynicism about his own party. It also indicated that at the very start of his political career, Graham had already formed his attitude to matters imperial and to Britain's place in the world, although Watts and Davies remind us that his father, Major Bontine, had also campaigned against overseas military adventures.[10]

Graham's first election address expressed a more balanced view of his stance on foreign affairs in the first edition of a new local newspaper:

> I am opposed to an aggressive foreign policy, and am of the opinion that the interest as well as the dignity of the country will be better secured by exhibiting a consistent regard to the just rights of other nations than by any assertion of lordly domination. I do not favour the idea of a large military class, or excessive expenditure in National defences, believing that the true defence of a country is to be found in its inhabitants.[11]

It was thus at his maiden speech, away from the necessity to circumscribe his statements to satisfy local sectarian interests and populist sentiments (although the speech was fully reported in the local press), that Graham began to express himself more trenchantly on imperial matters:

> It is not to be expected that Her Majesty's Government would vouchsafe to the House any idea of when the British troops might be withdrawn from Egypt. That is expecting far too much. But, surely, it would be wise to let the House know when it was intended to withdraw those troops from their inactivity in that pestilential region, and from playing the ungrateful role of oppressors of an already down-trodden nationality. (*Radical cheers.*) But no. The bondholders must have their pound of flesh. We must also protect the so-called high road to India by the Suez Canal, in order that the very last straw might be laid on the unfortunate fellaheen.[12]

He then moved onto the subject of British involvement in Burma, where:

> the misguided people, who, in their pig-headed way, were endeavouring to defend their own country. Surely, it can be no great matter of self-congratulation for Britons with arms of precision to shoot down naked savages.

Then, after criticising the expense of finding places for the younger sons of plutocrats and autocrats, he moved on to the world stage: 'I deprecate spending the money of this country to forward the ambition of soldiers and diplomats who made the name of Britain execrated in the four corners of the globe. (*Irish cheers.*)'[13]

Undoubtedly, Graham's fundamental objections to the empire were again moral: that it was wrong to take possession of the land and the person of others, with the concomitant threat of coercion, exploitation, and corruption of the natives, and the exportation of the ugliness that he increasingly saw around him. He also believed that the 'glory' of the empire was a standing insult to the poverty and deprivation he encountered at home, stating at a meeting in Edinburgh: 'I contrast the boasted greatness of the Empire with the fact that last evening I attended a meeting of Glasgow tramway men to protest against a working day of sixteen or seventeen hours and ask for the boon of a twelve hour day!'[14] The need to sustain such an empire, and to exploit its markets, was simply sucking more of the British population into sweatshops, and was a distraction from what he considered to be more pressing and immediate concerns, as set out in a speech he made to miners in Tranent on 22 October 1887, anticipating a new political force:

> If we had forty, or fifty, or even thirty candidates pledged to represent Labour in Parliament, and when Government came in with its bill for armies and navies and foreign politics and all that sort of humbug, these men would put down their feet and say: 'The men we represent are not interested in foreign

politics one atom. They don't care a farthing whether the French, the Germans, or the Japanese occupy Egypt. Let them manage their affairs, as we want to manage ours.'[15]

Graham drew little distinction between the poor of Britain, and the poor of Britain's colonies – both were the result of exploitation, which turned local populations into wage slaves. India, he believed, was run on the basis of a vast system of extortion and tyranny, which was crushing the life out of millions in order to provide salaries for a body of European officials, whose places could just as well be filled at a quarter of the expense by men of the various Indian races.[16] It would not be until he left parliament, however, that his most outspoken criticism of imperialism and racism would be expressed.

As we have seen, from the start of his political career, Graham had attacked the class system as being no better than feudalism,[17] and as he grew to believe that the House of Commons was a sham, an institution that maintained a corrupt status quo, there only to 'bolster up their kings and queens', he made a direct attack on the very symbols of empire:

> How can the veriest Tory get up any enthusiasm about a set of beings who have nothing Royal about them either in appearance, habits, or in reality. The fact is, they are not real kings or queens, but merely official puppets, and created by Parliament. Who but a fool could excite himself at the spectacle of that stout, bald-headed German gentleman, the Prince of Wales? Excellent, if you like, performing all the offices an unconscious automaton would perform as well, but oh, how uninteresting. Can anyone contemplate the hideous Hanoverian tribe of foreign princes without being moved to disgust at the creatures themselves, and to pity for the nation that tamely submitted to be ruled by them?[18]

And again, in his essay entitled 'Notions', 'A king for instance is a notion, and a very foolish one'.[19] He had publicly declared that he believed in a Republic,[20] but this attack on the monarchy was extraordinary for its outspokenness, particularly a mere two years after Queen Victoria's Golden Jubilee, ongoing imperial conflicts, and expansion of empire in southern Africa. There would be more subtle criticisms of monarchy, albeit in more prestigious and more widely circulated publications, particularly his poignantly mocking sketch of Victoria's funeral procession in 'Might Majesty & Dominion', published in 1901.[21]

Notes

1. The Scottish writer, George Blake, summed it up: 'Britannia ruled the waves, and nobody took much account of rebellious Zulus, Boers, Fuzzy-Wuzzies and such. All the British people had good reason to be content with their

international status at least; and such a man as Keir Hardie was obviously mad.' George Blake, *Barrie and the Kailyard School* (London: Arthur Barker, 1951), p. 21.

2. B. F. Westcott, 'The Empire', in *Lessons from Work* (New York: Macmillan, 1901), pp. 377–8.

3. John Robert Seeley, *The Expansion of England* (1883) (Cambridge University Press, 2010), p. 7. In this book, Seeley made the famous comment that the empire had been 'acquired in a fit of absence of mind', p. 8. He also omitted any reference to Scotland, and throughout, referred to 'the English Empire'.

4. Duncan Bell, *Reordering the World: Essays on Liberalism and Empire* (Princeton University Press, 2016), p. 265.

5. Joseph Chamberlain, 'True Conception of Empire' (1897) in *Mr Chamberlain's Speeches*, ed. by C. W. Boyd (London: Constable, 1914), p. 23. The Liberal Party did not fully accept itself as the so-called Liberal Imperialist Party until 1892 (the year Graham left parliament), under the guidance of an influential faction of young Liberal politicians, among whom the Scots R. B. Haldane, Lord Rosebery, and Ronald Munro Ferguson were the most prominent.

6. Bell, *Reordering the World*, p. 53.

7. *Airdrie Advertiser*, 15 August 1885, p. 6. My italics.

8. *Airdrie Advertiser*, 12 September 1885, p. 3.

9. Ibid.

10. Watts and Davies, *Cunninghame Graham*, p. 50.

11. *Coatbridge Express*, 14 October 1885, p. 3.

12. PP. 'Her Majesty's Most Gracious Speech (Adjourned Debate)', 1 February 1887, Hansard, Vol. 310, cc 444–5. (For full text, see Appendix II.)

13. Ibid.

14. *Scotsman*, 11 June 1889, p. 6.

15. *Scotsman*, 24 October 1887, p. 8.

16. Cunninghame Graham, 'The People's Parliament', *Labour Elector*, 24 August 1889, p. 92.

17. *Airdrie Advertiser*, 15 August 1885, p. 6.

18. Cunninghame Graham, 'The People's Parliament', *Labour Elector*, 10 August 1889, p. 92.

19. Cunninghame Graham, 'Notions', *People's Press*, 15 November 1890, p. 7.

20. *Glasgow Herald*, 7 November 1889, p. 10.

21. Cunninghame Graham, 'Might Majesty & Dominion', *Saturday Review*, 2 February 1901, p. 168. Anthologised in *Success* (1902), pp. 81–5.

6

Colonialism: The Hand of Man

To Graham, the more insidious consequence of imperialism was its impact on indigenous peoples and the environment through colonisation, not simply by foreign settlement, but by the imposition of foreign ideas, lifestyles, and economics. During his early political career he rarely looked overseas, but this would change after his electoral defeat in 1892, when his writings would become dominated by the destructive impact of the hand of man, and what he ironically termed 'progress'.

His first reference to this encroachment appeared in the *Labour Elector* in January 1890, where he wrote about the emigration scandals and corruption in Argentina, which already had 2,700 miles of railway, and was experiencing a huge influx of poor European immigrants, who were being confined in ever-expanding cities:[1]

> I, for one, would rather have seen the country in the possession of the *gauchos*, and the Spanish provinces now depopulated inhabited by the poor creatures who, to escape taxes and sweaters in Spain, have been made the unwilling instruments both of their own ruin and the destruction of both Indians and *gauchos*. I cannot see why, until Europe is cultivated like China, there is a necessity for emigration at all.[2]

As a precursor to this, between leaving the *Labour Elector*, and just prior to contributing to the *People's Press*, Graham had a story published in a short-lived journal called *Time*, edited by Belfort Bax, entitled 'Horses of the Pampas'. In his own words, 'these rambling and incoherent reminiscences' were prompted by a letter from a friend in Argentina, which caused his thoughts on the Eight Hours Bill to become 'vaguer and dimmer'.[3] Here is the first occasion on which he wrote nostalgically of his earlier life in South America, which could hardly be more different than his current circumstances. The piece was described by Watts and Davies as:

an essay which, while recalling affectionately the way of life that Graham had seen in South America, lamented its inevitable demise. Perhaps his attack on the ugliness of industrial civilization does have a tenuous connection with the Eight Hour Bill . . . but it is clear that for the first but certainly not the last time, Graham's memories have taken control. His career as a writer, indeed, is the story of an irrepressible rememberer trying to discipline his reminiscences without sacrificing their subversive power.[4]

We can compare this march of progress, which was inexorably destroying natural habitat and traditional lifestyles, with what he regarded as deliberate ethnic cleansing of Native Americans. Reacting to reports coming from the United States, on what was called 'the Ghost Dance craze'[5] at the end of 1890, and the beginning of 1891, Graham published three pieces in the *Daily Graphic*, described by John Walker as 'an anguished cry from the heart against the cruel treatment of the American Indian'.[6] All three pieces could be read as one, as they followed the same argument. The Indians were more sinned against than sinning, they had been robbed, cheated, and killed, and those who survived could stand it no longer. Graham blamed those who were in pursuit of money, whisky sellers, Bible peddlers, and land speculators. He also blamed the press for deluding their readers.[7]

Nearer home, Graham's notable work, which blurred the borders between imperialism and cultural destruction, took the form of an anticapitalist, dystopian fable set in northern Ireland,[8] a microcosm of what had already befallen many of the rural inhabitants of mainland Britain. It first appeared as a pamphlet entitled 'Economic Evolution', published in 1891 by the socialist James Leatham's Deveron Press, then, in the following year in *The Albemarle*, as 'Evolution of a Village',[9] and later published by the Socialist Party of Ireland as 'An Irish Economic Revival'.[10] This unsubtle moral tale concerned a village where life was unhurried, and although starvation was never far away, the people enjoyed a contented, natural lifestyle, where 'Prostitution, Respectability, Morality and Immorality, and all the other curses of progressive life, with them had little place'. Then a mill was built:

> Capital had come . . . It banished idleness, peace, beauty, and content; it made the people slaves. No more they breathed the scent of the fields and lanes, but stifled in the mill. There was a gain, for savages who did not need them purchased, at the bayonet's point, the goods the people made.[11]

At last, Graham had linked what he considered capitalist exploitation at home with imperial and colonial exploitation overseas, whereby both populations had, in reality, been enslaved. As early as 1888, a reviewer wrote of him, 'He labours under the settled conviction that civilisation is a failure',[12] which was undoubtedly correct.

Notes

1. Edwin Williamson, 'Argentina: The Long Decline', in *The Penguin History of Latin America* (London: Penguin, 2009), p. 459.
2. Cunninghame Graham, 'Foreign Notes', *Labour Elector*, 25 January 1890, p. 54.
3. Cunninghame Graham, 'Horses of the Pampas', *Time* (London), 1 April 1890, p. 378. Reprinted in his first anthology, *Father Archangel of Scotland* (London: Adam & Charles Black, 1896).
4. Watts and Davies, *Cunninghame Graham*, p. 155.
5. George Tindall and David Shi, *America: A Narrative History* (New York: W. W. Norton, 1999), p. 870. These events culminated in the Massacre of Wounded Knee on 29 December 1890.
6. John Walker, ed., *The North American Sketches of R. B. Cunninghame Graham* (Edinburgh: Scottish Academic Press, 1986), p. 25.
7. Cunninghame Graham, 'The American Indians: Ghost Dancing', *Daily Graphic*, 29 November 1890, p. 14.
8. It was not entirely fanciful. Through a reference to a famous greyhound, Graham deliberately placed it in the vicinity of Lurgan, near the shores of Lough Neagh. According to Leatham, Graham had got his background information from the Glasgow-based Irish socialist, John Ferguson. James Leatham, 'The Passing of "Don Roberto"', *The Gateway*, March 1936, p. 13.
9. Cunninghame Graham, 'The Evolution of a Village', *The Albemarle*, June 1892, pp. 204–7. Anthologised in *Success* (1902), pp. 177–86.
10. Published in both journals without permission. Leatham, *60 Years*, p. 165.
11. Cunninghame Graham, 'Evolution of a Village', p. 207. The theme of a mill destroying a community, this time an Arab one, appeared in another sketch-tale of Graham's entitled 'El Babor', published in *Father Archangel of Scotland*, pp. 131–45.
12. *Vanity Fair*, 25 August 1888, p. 145.

7

Ireland and Scotland: A Patient Realist

WITH A LARGE IRISH constituency, Graham's views on home rule and land reform shaped his pronouncements prior to entering parliament. His first major statement on Ireland was given at Shettleston on 7 September 1885, where he insisted that its inhabitants:

> were the same clay as ourselves (*hear, hear.*) . . . We should at once endeavour to remove all distinction of treatment between English, Irish, and Scottish men. Justice should be made absolutely impartial, without reference to race, creed, or locality, local self-government in its fullest sense should at once be accorded to Ireland, and the rule of the Castle swept away.[1]

At his next speech, given on 17 September in Coatbridge, while conceding that Ireland was 'difficult to touch on, and so kittle when touched', he believed that the history of Ireland had been 'a history of oppression, misconception, tyranny, and folly, such as the world has hardly ever seen, and such as may well make us blush for the Anglo-Saxon race.'[2] If the land question was paramount throughout Britain, in Ireland it had been intensified by the evil of absenteeism, whereby the greater portion of the revenue of the kingdom was spent outside, by a small privileged class. His solution was to abolish what he referred to as 'the puerile vice-regal system', to stop treating the population of Ireland as children, but to treat them as we would treat ourselves, to impartially accord them their rights and justice, and to grant them full powers to manage all their internal affairs.

These views no doubt appealed to the Irish home rule elements in his audiences, but over 80 per cent of Irish immigration into Scotland's Central Belt came from Ulster;[3] and the majority were neither nationalists nor Roman Catholics, but many were Orangemen and sectarian incidents were common in the constituency.[4] Graham's views on Ireland were thus as likely to alienate as attract support, which, added to Parnell's command that Irish home rule supporters should vote Tory, undoubtedly lost him the 1885 election. In fact, the local newspaper noted the unique sight, at the end of the tumultuous election campaign, of joyous Roman Catholic and Protestant electors, amicably celebrating the announcement of Graham's defeat – together.[5]

During the brief Home Rule Election campaign of 1886, Graham now tailored his views to his audiences, and trod a fine line between the religious divides. At his first speech back at Coatbridge, he asked if Britain had been wrong, and if an Irish Parliament should be restored, the 'withdrawal of which formed so black and so base a page in our national history', creating a state of anarchy, agrarian outrage and disturbance, with the prohibition of public meetings, censorship of the press, 'and a thousand and one fictitious annoyances which were incidental to governing Ireland according to English ideas. (*Cheers.*)' He continued, 'Had these annoyances been imposed upon Scotland, they would have resulted in civil war – aye, and would have deluged the country in blood from John o' Groats to the Solway. (*Cheers.*)'[6] However, very conscious that the prospect of Irish home rule was seen by many as a threat to the integrity of the Union and the Empire, at his next meeting, at predominantly Protestant Calderbank,[7] Graham attempted to put the minds of his audience at ease by saying that any devolved powers would deal only with purely Irish affairs, and that Westminster would retain the power of veto.[8]

After his electoral success, Graham no longer needed to dissimulate. In his maiden speech, recent events in Ireland were a central theme, particularly the evictions at Glenbeigh in County Kerry. After rent increases of 50 per cent, seventy families on the estate of Rowland Winn (later Lord Headley), who could not pay, were ruthlessly evicted in January 1887, and their houses levelled or burned.[9] It was also a situation that gave him the opportunity to exercise his ironic wit, stating:

> It is the pride and the privilege of the Irish landlord to look after the interests, creature as well as spiritual, of his tenants; and, such is the relation of class to class that, so far from turning them out on a bleak, cold winter's night, the landlord has provided his dependents with a fire to warm their hands; only, through a pardonable inadvertence, it was their houses that had furnished the blaze.[10]

Following this, although he still campaigned vigorously for Irish home rule on the platform, Graham rarely mentioned Ireland in parliament as there were 'many more able speakers than myself to deal exclusively with that question and were returned exclusively by Irish electors for that purpose'.[11] In fact, following his new adherence to socialism, he increasingly believed that filibustering by Irish MPs, under Parnell's direction, designed to grind parliament to a halt, was holding back legislation on labour and social issues. Ireland in his view had become a convenient political football for both the Tories and the Liberals to slow down change, and 'a Dutch auction' in the purchase of Irish votes.[12] At a St Patrick's Day rally in Glasgow, Graham stated:

> The Irish question was a godsend to the present Government. They did not want it settled; they wanted to have it hanging on for ever, because they knew when it was settled the attention of the democracy of this country would be directed to much more pressing social questions. They knew that the separation with which they were always charging the Liberals was their trump card.[13]

And again, as he wrote in the *People's Press* in 1890, 'It was convenient, very, to be able to close the mouths of those who asked for labour legislation, with the Home Rule plug',[14] and that all that was currently going on in Ireland under the Conservative Government was abetted 'by the secret connivance of the Liberals'.[15]

His home rule sentiments applied equally to Scotland, as Graham believed 'their interests were identical'.[16] He believed further that the Irish electors themselves, particularly in Britain, should be fighting for social justice as well as home rule. At the St Patrick's Day gathering in in Glasgow City Hall in March 1888, he reminded his audience that there was not one labour representative in Scotland, and appealed to them to send to parliament a man from the working class (at this time, Hardie).[17] Like his pronouncements on Scotland, home rule by itself, without fundamental changes in the social order, was not enough; home rule in Ireland would make no difference to the people unless they themselves took the reins of Government:

> If the Irish nation want political rather than social freedom, if they want the Pope to rule their country, if they want to protect their industries, to set up a Republic, if they want all or none of these things, they should have to power to choose them. At present they may be said to be a race apart, caring for naught but national affairs. It may be, when they have weighed their 'patriots' up and found them merely bourgeois after all, they will tire of them, and try something better.[18]

It was at Graham's first speech in Coatbridge, as a visiting speaker, that he had made his first public utterance on Scottish Home Rule. Here, however, he presented it as a matter of equality:

> Being all part and parcel of one kingdom, I can see no reason why English and Scottish men should enjoy privileges that Irishmen do not, nor, on the other hand, do I perceive the reason why Irishmen should have privileges that

are denied to the English and Scotch. Therefore, I may begin by stating that I can see no valid reason why Home Rule should be extended to Ireland unless at the same time it is extended to England and Scotland.[19]

These utterances were concurrent with a growing national mood in some parts of Scottish society. In the opinion of the historian of empire Sir Reginald Coupland, modern Scottish nationalism had made its first appearance in 1853, not as an offshoot of the revolutions of 1848, or as a result of the Church Disestablishment question, but simply from the growing feeling that 'the operation of the political system, established by the Union, was unfair and inefficient',[20] resulting in the creation of the short-lived National Association for the Vindication of Scottish Rights (NAVSR).[21]

By 1879, Gladstone had come round to the idea of some form of devolution of local issues to overcome the Irish *impasse*, as long as the supremacy of the Imperial Parliament was maintained.[22] Gladstone's only concession in Scotland, however, had been the establishment of the Scottish Office in 1885, but further concessions on home rule for Scotland were inevitably subservient to his objective of home rule for Ireland, and were to suffer the same fate. Kellas wrote:

> The impotence of Scottish Liberalism within the British party system contributed to the emergence of a Scottish Home Rule movement at this time, which was as much an expression of dissatisfaction with the place of the Scottish Liberal Party in the Liberal Party as a whole, as with the place of Scotland in the United Kingdom. Most Scottish nationalists were strong Liberals.[23]

Scottish home rule was, in consequence, a topic of discussion in political and cultural circles in Scotland, and, according to Hutchison, 'it was extremely and spontaneously popular, generating real enthusiasm'.[24] This was also true in North-West Lanarkshire, as witnessed in the *Airdrie Advertiser*, which reprinted an extensive manifesto from the *Scottish Review*, outlining how a Scottish Parliament might be organised and what powers it might have.[25]

Increasingly for Graham, Scottish home rule was not just a matter of equality of political representation, but potentially, a means by which social legislation could be more speedily enacted, and in a report in the *Edinburgh Evening News*, he made a connection between home rule, socialism, and the land question:

> It seemed to him that that what their aristocratic and plutocratic friends were afraid of was that should Home Rule be carried it would be but one step towards the taking of the fortress of property; because the experience of

modern thought pointed conclusively to the argument that the soil should be owned by the cultivator.[26]

This also contained the seed of a 'national' question, whereby the livelihoods of the peasantry, who were to him the custodians of Scotland's individuality, could be preserved. It is thus impossible to disassociate land from Graham's early engagements with issues of Scottish identity and heritage, and his desire for Scottish home rule, and from the beginning, his parliamentary campaigns contained an emotive patriotic element:

> As a politician, and a Scotchman, and a practical man, I cannot but look with regret on the falsely so-called principle that has tended to depopulate the most picturesque, patriarchal, curious, and old-world district of our native country. Therefore, it is to the new electors that I turn in behalf of the Highland crofters, and to ask them to make an absolute stand against further evictions, and against the further extension of the deer forests, and to protest against all the Highlands being turned into a sort of new forest [sic] for the delectation of the London stockbroker and the Hebrew financier. (Loud applause.)[27]

This 'blood and soil' animus was further reinforced in Graham's mind by history. At an election address at Coatbridge during his 1886 campaign, he recalled (rather fancifully) that in the Highlands there had been no absolute property in land, the land had belonged to the clan, and the chieftain and clansman had equal rights, 'And thus they found, owing to this patriarchal system, a freer, a nobler, and a more manly [heroic] style of manners and customs prevailed than there did among the Normans in England.' He wished that this relationship still existed, and that 'the soil of the country be used for the cultivation of food, not the cultivation of rents'.[28]

A month later, back in Coatbridge, he made a particularly nationalistic speech in which he stated his belief that this independent Scottish spirit existed not only in the Highlands, and among people of the soil but also among the working poor:

> Though the upper classes had become Anglified, yet he was glad to know that the working men had remained intensely Scottish, and he knew that this name would be received with joy by them, and that they would not see the name of Scotland merged with England. (Cheers.)[29]

This more patriotic declaration followed closely on the formation in May 1886 of the first Scottish Home Rule Association (SHRA),[30] which Graham had immediately joined, and he appeared to be playing to the gallery, displaying for the first time a growing strain of 'identity nationalism', as he continued:

We have to bear in mind that we want no Englishman to represent Scottish seats. (*Cheers.*) We want none of their fine fellows coming down in the Pullman car from London (*Laughter and cheers.*) – giving a club address and talking in their fine English, and then, like swallows, flying away and leaving us and never coming near until the next election. We want good hard-headed Scotchmen to represent us (*Cheers.*) I will never believe for a moment that there was any necessity for Liberal Associations writing up to London and saying 'Send us a candidate as per invoice.' (*Laughter.*) Surely it is an insult to the Scottish people to have a candidate sent down bottled, preserved, and labeled in that way. (*Cheers, and a voice – 'That's a good yin', and laughter.*) Scotchmen should never elect an Englishman, no matter of what party or how well qualified he was for an English seat. I think we should again take a lesson from the Irish, who would rather elect an Irish lamp-post than an English duke. (*Laughter.*)[31]

This rhetoric reflected an unspoken, or at least an unspecified belief, that Scotland, as a stateless nation, was in fact a marginalised internal colony of England,[32] but it is an underlying theme that ran through political utterances on Scotland, particularly, at the beginning, on land ownership issues, but would not find full voice until his overtly nationalist speeches of the 1920s.[33]

At Graham's second public meeting, at Shettleston on 7 September 1885, having been selected as the prospective MP, a new issue appeared on his agenda, that of local self-government, particularly in the rural districts, which he believed everyone favoured. The main thrust of this was that revenues raised in these areas could be better spent there. The idealised past again provided an example of more local self-government, a government closer to the people:

Among the ancient Celts, every district, however small, enjoyed the most complete autonomy. One of the first things that every district should have the power of inquiring into is as to how the revenue raised in that district is spent – (*Applause.*) – and to completely convince itself that the revenue raised (in Shettleston for example) is not expended, so to speak, in keeping up the railings in Hyde Park.[34]

This localism, was apparently based on an unsentimental accountability, but he saw the more pressing demands in Ireland taking precedence:

As Scotchmen, they should help the Irish with all their heart to gain Home Rule. (*Hear, hear.*) They should never forget that the idea of Home Rule originated with the Irish, and they should never lose sight of it till they see a Parliament legislating for matters in purely Scottish in Edinburgh or Linlithgow. (*Loud cheers.*)[35]

Again, while asserting his support for Gladstone at a meeting of the Glasgow Central Liberal Association, and declaring in favour of a parliament in Dublin, he believed that the time had now come for Scotland to have a parliament of her own.[36] This belief was being expressed elsewhere in his constituency, and during the miners' strike, which had been occupying Graham's time. William Small, the miners' organiser and an original member of the SPLP and ILP, told the striking workers (among mentions of dynamite and revolution), 'They needed Home Rule in Scotland, and the sooner they had it, the better for all concerned',[37] which indicated that it was seen by others in the labour movement as a means of dealing more directly with economic and social problems.

Taylor wrote that Graham, along with Keir Hardie, was the principal begetter of the SHRA,[38] but offered no proof of this, and if it was so, it was just prior to his reselection as candidate for North-West Lanarkshire in June 1886, and prior to his meeting and close association with Hardie, which almost certainly occurred a year later. Coupland stated that it was the SHRA's president, Dr Gavin Clark, MP for Caithness[39] who became 'a leading Scottish Home Ruler, and presently the cause began to spread among the people at large',[40] although he added that in Scotland ardent nationalists were a small minority.[41] This opinion, however, runs contrary to Hutchison's view of its popularity, expressed above, but it seems that this enthusiasm was relatively brief, and Chris Harvie believed that 'it became part of the repertory of party "faddists" and socialists'.[42] Harvie added that there could never be a Scottish Parnell, since the Liberals 'massively endorsed the Union', and that 'by 1906 over half the Scots M.P.s were English'.[43]

In his essay 'The First Home Rule Movement in Scotland, 1886–1918', Graham Morton wrote at some length on the lack of parliamentary time given to Scottish legislation and the perceived financial loss suffered by Scotland, which were the main concerns of the SHRA, but he made no mention of Graham or Hardie as key figures,[44] nor did Naomi Lloyd Jones.[45] R. E. Muirhead, writing to Graham in 1927, mentioned only his titular position:

> In view of the fact that you were a Vice-President in the old Home Rule Association which was established by the late Mr. Charles Waddie in 1886, it is quite in keeping that you should now occupy the position of President of the present Scottish Home Rule Association.[46]

The SHRA itself claimed that its founder and driving force was Waddie, an Edinburgh printer,[47] who remained a relentless campaigner and lobbyist on the home rule issue until his death in 1912. Watts and Davies also made no mention of Graham's founding role, only that he and Hardie were 'original members',[48] nor did his early biographers, Faulkner West and Tschiffely. Faulkner West (who, like Tschiffely, was a confidante of Graham) wrote only: 'He always believed in the autonomy of states and has always been a foe of English Imperialism.'[49] Certainly, Graham was in attendance at a meeting of the SHRA on Tuesday 5 June 1888, in Fleet Street, London, where he and various speakers, including Waddie and Professor John Stuart Blackie, addressed the audience.[50] At this meeting, fundamental divisions on policy demonstrated the association's inherent weakness as a potent political force. Waddie desired a form of federalism, while Blackie's stated aim was that Edinburgh should be the seat of a separate and independent government. Graham's priority was a Scottish Parliament that 'would do justice to their crofters and keep them at home, to pass an Eight Hours Bill for the miners, to settle the liquor laws, and to nationalise the land'.[51] The leading figures were nevertheless agreed that a Convention should be held in Scotland at the earliest date. This meeting was the SHRA's first annual conference in Glasgow on 18 September 1888, but there is no record of Graham's attendance; however, Hardie was there, questioning why the Association had regretted supporting his candidature in Mid-Lanark.[52] There is a distinct lack of evidence for Taylor's assertion that Graham was 'the principal begetter' of the SHRA and that he was deeply involved in its development. In 1952, Muirhead, the founder and sponsor of the second SHRA, wrote:

> Although Graham had been a member of the earlier Scottish Home Rule Association which had been established in 1886, it was not until he joined the second Scottish Home Rule Association that he took an active interest in the movement for Scottish self-government.[53]

It is worth noting that the SHRA membership agreed at this conference that although Scotland's voice should be heard in the national parliament, a legislature should be established in Scotland to have full control of Scottish affairs, including civil servants and judges, but the integrity of the empire was to be maintained.[54] On the land issue, its policy remained identical to Graham's, as reported in the *New York Tribune* on 5 September 1888:

> They [the SHRA] want to abolish the Law of primogeniture and entail; they want to secure the land for the poor people, who do all the work upon it, they want to abolish the system of royalties, whereby the man who owns the land gets for every ton of coal mined as much as the poor fellow who digs it out of the ground; they want to put a stop to the practice of turning large tracts of country into deer farms.[55]

Graham's first opportunity to make a practical contribution to the Scottish home rule debate was when he spoke in the House of Commons on 9 April 1889 in support of the first Scottish Home Rule Bill, presented by Clark, and William Hunter, MP for Aberdeen North.[56] Clark's speech began by emphasising that the Bill would in no way endanger the Union, but although it was presented for 'practical considerations, there is a sentimental basis for the growing Home Rule movement in Scotland', and that in parliament, and elsewhere, Scottish nationality was deliberately ignored, and the use of 'English' in place of 'British' was widespread. Moreover, he argued that Scottish business in the House was neglected, or blocked by English members, and he cited several examples. He also recited a list of other grievances such as unfair taxes, lower pay rates for officials, and other financial irregularities. His solution was to introduce 'devolution upon lines of nationality', but the Imperial Parliament would still remain the High Court of Final Appeal.[57]

While appearing to speak in support of the motion,[58] Graham said that he did so on very different grounds from either Clark or Hunter. Although he agreed that there had been a growing feeling in favour of home rule in Scotland, in his opinion, it was not on sentimental grounds, but from the extreme misery of a certain section of the Scottish population, who demanded legislation that would relieve that misery. Members from Scotland were fond of representing Scotland as a sort of Arcadia, but:

> in face of the misery existing in the Highlands and Islands, that we have women in Aberdeen to-day toiling for 6s. or 7s. a week; that we have 30,000 people in Glasgow who herd together in one room; and in face of the fact that we have a Socialistic agitation on foot in the East and West of Scotland, I must say I do not think the condition of the poor in that country is one very much to be envied.

Despite this, Graham believed that democratic ideas were much further advanced in Scotland than in England, especially on the eight hours debate, free education, and other matters, and he also believed that parliament would soon be called on to face the demand for a legislature for Scotland. He concluded his speech with a recapitulation that there must be working-class representation in any such body:

> It has been said that in the event of the institution of a Scottish Legislature we should largely be represented by the merchants of the country. To that statement I say, God forbid! I believe I speak the feelings of a large section of the Scotch people when I emphatically state that, were such a Legislature ever created, we should find the working classes much more represented than is the case here.

After further speakers, including Gladstone himself, the House divided: Ayes 79; Noes 200. Later, Hardie wrote:

> Dr. Clark deserves credit for pushing on his Scottish Home Rule resolution to a division in Parliament. True, the only member who showed any true appreciation of what Home Rule would ultimately lead to was Cunninghame Graham. Dr. Hunter's nice picture of a Scottish Parliament composed of smug, bald, pot-bellied shopkeepers is too laughable to be taken seriously. With Mr. Graham we say in all seriousness, 'God Forbid.' Of course the G.O.M. [the Grand Old Man] was cautious, and threw the onus on the people of Scotland. In this he is perfectly right. I believe the people of Scotland desire a Parliament of their own, and it will be for them to send to the next House of Commons a body of men pledged to obtain it.[59]

Hardie made the point, with some justification, that although in some quarters there had been growing enthusiasm for home rule in Scotland, there had been no groundswell of public opinion in favour of it, and, unlike Ireland, there was no political bloc of MPs dedicated to its achievement. Certainly, there was no political leader around whom such a movement could cohere, of the status or fiery determination of a Parnell, whose purposefulness was described in Graham's subsequent memoir of him.[60]

As we have witnessed from the beginning of Graham's entry into the House of Commons, land ownership – despite his rhetoric, historical precedents, demands for local democracy, and 'identity nationalism' – had been entirely subsumed into the wider social question. His position was in fact more clearly stated a month after his home rule speech in parliament, when he addressed the London Branch of the SHRA:

> Mr Cunninghame Graham, M.P., said he was for Home Rule for Scotland because of the neglect of certain social questions by the Imperial Parliament – the bread and butter questions: the question whether the crofters and cottars should be sent to Canada or remain at home: whether the miners should work ten or twelve hours a day in the pits, to pile up wealth for greedy capitalists, while they themselves remained poor; and above all, the question whether the poor in the East End of Glasgow, Edinburgh, and Dundee should be allowed to remain in the degraded and neglected condition that he, speaking as a Scottish member of Parliament, undoubtedly would say they were at present. These were the questions which induced him personally to be in favour of Home Rule for Scotland.[61]

This was reinforced at a speech in Edinburgh in the following month:

One of these questions is the institution of a Scottish Parliament, because without it we should experience the very greatest difficulty in introducing labour legislation for Scotland. Owing to this question not having been put forward at election times, members of the present House of Commons can turn round and say that they had no mandate from their constituents to advance labour legislation.[62]

The twin barriers to Scottish home rule, Graham believed, were the same as the barriers to social change, the greed and self-interest of the middle and upper classes and the apathy or intransigence of the poor. Among the higher echelons in Scotland there were what he called 'the English factions', who knew that 'hopes of social advancement, of connection with rich men, and all the rest of it, lay for [them] in a parliament in London, not in parliament in Edinburgh'.[63] However, like the workers whom he had attempted to stir into action on their own behalf, there was little sign of a proud and independent peasantry rising to meet his aspirations. In an article for the *People's Press*, Graham lamented their passivity, this lack of 'heroic virtue', foreshadowing a common theme in his later writings, that Scotland had been diminished, made meek and compliant, by the twin curses of Calvinism and capitalism, a process that Graham wished to stem, and reverse:

> Where is the Scot who as Froissart said is so 'cunning on his horse?' Where is he of adventure and devilment? It looked as if Knox and all his whey-faced chiels had set it at rest for ever ... He has his minister, his fear of hell, his wish to be respectable, all of these things that the capitalist can play. What wonder, therefore, that in Scotland, where all these causes operate in a way incredible to a stranger, where men are still 'religious,' where strong bearded fellows, who have been deceived for years with parties, still go on drinking in the same old lies, what wonder that the modern Scottish workman should have become, by force of circumstances, an exceeding slave. Slave of the hopeless sort, who thinks he is free, and hugs his party chains, and chains of kirk, and of respectability, and says 'look at me and see how free I am.'[64]

Notes

1. *Airdrie Advertiser*, 12 September 1885, p. 3.
2. *Airdrie Advertiser*, 19 September 1885, p. 3. Kittle: Scots = Ticklish.
3. Hutchison specified 82.3 per cent. Hutchison, *The Working Class in Glasgow*, p. 129.
4. These had reached a peak with serious riots in Coatbridge during August 1883.
5. *Airdrie Advertiser*, 5 December 1885, p. 5.

6. *Coatbridge Express*, 30 June 1886, p. 2.
7. Mining communities had become ghettoised, as the mines were segregated by the owners along religious lines, to avoid sectarian trouble.
8. *Coatbridge Express*, 7 July 1886, p. 2.
9. These events had already been brought to the attention of the House of Commons on 28 January 1887.
10. Hansard, Her Majesty's Most Gracious Speech. Adjourned Debate. 1 February 1887.
11. *Airdrie Express*, 25 November 1889, p. 5.
12. Cunninghame Graham, Reports, *Labour Elector*, 22 June 1889, p. 4.
13. *Edinburgh Evening News*, 1 March 1887, p. 4.
14. Cunninghame Graham, 'Home Rule', *People's Press*, 20 December 1890, p. 7.
15. Cunninghame Graham, letter to the *People's Press*, 31 May 1890, p. 5. The Fabian George Cole wrote that Gladstone and the Liberals' preoccupation with Irish home rule was one of the main reasons for the loss of working-class support, and the formation of the Labour party. G. D. H. Cole, *British Working Class Politics, 1832–1914* (London: Routledge, 1941), pp. 82–3.
16. *Airdrie Advertiser*, 15 October 1887, p. 5.
17. *Coatbridge Express*, 21 March 1888, p. 2.
18. Cunninghame Graham, 'Home Rule', p. 7.
19. *Airdrie Advertiser*, 15 August 1885, p. 6.
20. Reginald Coupland, *Welsh & Scottish Nationalism* (London: Collins, 1954), p. 281. Although he did not believe that the church Disruption of 1843 had a direct effect on 'national' sentiment, Hanham wrote that the new Free Church of Scotland had produced outspoken critics of the relationship between Scotland and England: 'The first clear statement of the Scottish national case was made by a Free Church minister, the brilliant, flamboyant, and erratic James Begg, in January 1850.' Hanham, 'Mid-Century Scottish Nationalism', pp. 153–4.
21. Colin Kidd described the NAVSR as 'the eccentric grandparent of the modern [Scottish] nationalist movement'. Colin Kidd, 'Sentiment, Race and Revival: Scottish Identity in the Aftermath of the Enlightenment', in *A Union of Multiple Identities: The British Isles, c 1750–1850*, ed. by Lawrence Brockliss and David Eastwood (Manchester University Press, 1997), p. 121.
22. *The Times*, 27 November 1879. p. 6.
23. Kellas, 'The Liberal Party in Scotland', p. 15.
24. Hutchinson, *A Political History of Scotland*, p. 171.
25. *Airdrie Advertiser* (Supplement), 22 August 1885, p. 5.
26. *Edinburgh Evening News*, 1 March 1887, p. 3.
27. *Edinburgh Evening News*, 19 September 1885, p. 6.
28. *Coatbridge Express*, 30 June 1886, p. 2.
29. *Coatbridge Express*, 28 July 1886, p. 2.

30. This was the first substantive 'nationalist' movement since the demise of the NAVSR, which had ceased its campaigns in January 1855 owing to British reverses in the Crimean War. *Caledonian Mercury*, 5 February 1855, p. 3.
31. *Coatbridge Express*, 28 July 1886, p. 2.
32. This political situation is discussed at length in Michael Hechter's *Internal Colonisation: The Celtic Fringe in British National Development, 1536–1966* (London: Routledge & Kegan Paul, 1975).
33. Any early reticence to spell this out may have been based on the fact that as someone who was born in London, educated at Harrow School, and maintained a residence in the most fashionable areas of London's West End, where, in later years he spent about half of his time, he might again stand accused of hypocrisy.
34. *Airdrie Advertiser*, 12 September 1885, p. 3.
35. *Coatbridge Express*, 28 July 1886, p. 2.
36. *Coatbridge Express*, 2 March 1887, p. 2.
37. *Airdrie Advertiser*, 19 February 1887, p. 5.
38. Taylor, *The People's Laird*, p. 317.
39. Dr Gavin Brown Clark (1846–1930), a social-reforming medical doctor. He was the Honorary Secretary of the Transvaal Independence Committee, and was an unsuccessful Labour candidate in the general election in Glasgow in 1918.
40. Coupland, *Welsh & Scottish Nationalism*, p. 298.
41. Ibid., p. 301.
42. Harvie, *Scotland and Nationalism*, p. 22.
43. Ibid., p. 21.
44. Graham Morton, 'The First Home Rule Movement in Scotland, 1886–1918', in *The Challenge to Westminster*, ed. by H. T. Dickinson and Michael Lynch (East Linton: Tuckwell Press, 2000), pp. 113–22.
45. Naomi Lloyd Jones, 'Liberalism, Scottish Nationalism and the Home Rule Crisis, c. 1886–93', *English Historical Review*, Vol. 129, 1 August 2014, pp. 862–87.
46. R. E. Muirhead, letter to Cunninghame Graham, 2 May 1927. R. E. Muirhead Papers, NLS. Acc.3721. Box 7.
47. W. Mitchell, *Is Scotland to Be Sold Again?* (Edinburgh: Scottish Home Rule Association, 1892), p. 8.
48. Watts and Davies, *Cunninghame Graham*, p. 249.
49. Faulkner West, *Cunninghame Graham*, p. 58.
50. 'Home Rule For Scotland', *South London Chronicle*, 9 June 1888, p. 7.
51. Ibid.
52. *Freeman's Journal*, 19 September 1888, p. 5.
53. Muirhead, 'Foreword' to MacDiarmid's *Centenary Study*, p. 5.
54. W. Mitchell, *Is Scotland to Be Sold Again?*, pp. 8–9.
55. Reprinted in *Coatbridge Express*, 19 September 1888, p. 1.

56. PP. Motions: Home Rule For Scotland, 9 April 1889, Hansard, Vol. 335, cc 68–124.

57. PP. Motions: Home Rule For Scotland, Hansard, Vol. 335, cc 68–74. (For full text, see Appendix V.) This was a restatement of the NAVSR's policies of thirty-six years earlier.

58. He in fact undermined their more consensual, conciliatory statements, demonstrating the gulf that now existed between Graham and his Liberal friends and colleagues.

59. *Labour Leader*, April 1889, p. 3.

60. Cunninghame Graham, '*An Tighearna*: A Memory of Parnell' *Dana* (Dublin), November 1904. Anthologised in *His People* (1906), pp. 274–87.

61. *Coatbridge Express*, 8 May 1889, p. 2.

62. *Scotsman*, 11 May 1889, p. 6.

63. *Scotsman*, 28 January 1890, p. 7.

64. Cunninghame Graham, 'The Scotch Strike', *People's Press*, 17 January 1891, p. 7.

Part I Conclusion

THE TRUE DRIVES OF men and women are often hidden from them, and from others, and with such huge family debts, why Graham chose a career as an MP, to the further detriment of his financial position, can only be conjectured.[1] It appears, however, that at the beginning of his political career, he was motivated by a fundamental but nebulous humanitarianism, combined with a powerful moral indignation and a careless spontaneity, which prompted him to behave like a late Victorian evangelical preacher and crusader, with the religion missing. However, contrary to the belief that he was a romantic idealist, Graham, at this stage, was a somewhat simplistic rationalist, who experienced a spontaneous illumination that there were easily understood solutions to what had previously been considered intractable social problems.

Graham eventually won his parliamentary seat by a skilful blend of personal charm, bravura oration, and occasional dissembling, aided by propitious timing. When he entered the House, however, he quickly came to believe that it was an oligarchy in which MPs who claimed to have the interests of the nation and its people at heart, habitually put their party first, and strove for political dominance; his frustrations became more acute, resulting in what looks like a deliberate suicidal act of defiance. This led to unexpected and probably undeserved consequences, propelling him into the public eye, whereby he became a political martyr and celebrity overnight, who was lauded and derided in equal measure, establishing a revolutionary reputation among the chattering socialist elites.

Coming from a rural background, Graham initially saw exclusivity of land ownership as paramount, and it remains an issue that blights Scotland to this day. But after witnessing the more immediate consequences of unemployment and poverty at first hand, and what Engels described as 'social murder',[2] whereby the lower orders were condemned by the ruling elites to lives that were nasty, brutish, and often short, he passionately pursued a desire for more fundamental and universal political change. This, via Morris, developed into an adherence to socialism, including, apparently, Marxism. Morris, inspired in his turn by Ruskin, had proposed, rather vaguely, mass class action, but Graham took Morris's ideas to the next stage by envisaging a distinctive party of labour that could change legislation, and thus society, at its source. It would be no exaggeration to claim that there was a direct philosophical lineage from Ruskin, through Morris, to Graham himself, and then to Hardie, and if that were the case, the consequences, even in embryo, were far-reaching and profound.

Like much of Graham's life, his adherence to socialism was con-tradictory. Also, it would become increasingly apparent that his elit-ist, altruistic socialism was of a very different complexion from that of the future rank-and-file Labour members, which would lead to schism. Will Rothenstein wrote: 'Conrad knew that Cunninghame Graham was more cynic than idealist and was by nature an aristocrat, whose social-ism was *a symbol* of his contempt for a feeble aristocracy and a blatant plutocracy.'[3] Nevertheless, he pursued his new convictions relentlessly, inadvertently following John Stuart Mill's advice: 'If it is not fully, fre-quently, and fearlessly discussed, it will be held as a dead dogma, not a living truth.'[4]

Graham's new-found celebrity and continuing campaigns on behalf of the poor and the unemployed led to a brief flowering as a political commentator for small socialist newspapers. What differentiated his essays from conventional political journalism was their eloquence, their untrammelled idiosyncratic humour, and their wide-ranging expressive-ness, which made them not only propaganda, but entertainment. Also, despite his impatient outbursts, he revealed an understanding of human foibles, something that other socialist writers rarely, if ever, dwelt upon. Moreover, his apparently careless attitude to the tastes, attainments, and interests of those for whom he wrote fuels the speculation that he was primarily indulging his experiences, education, and anger in print, simply because he needed to, and could, and in the longer term, it was only a testing ground for his later literary career. However, despite his artistic bravado, Graham harboured a deep insecurity about his literary talents, and in the prefaces to his later anthologies he constantly cast doubt on his appeal as a writer. Nor did he know or understand those for whom he wrote, which perhaps explains the often random, sometimes chaotic nature of the works. This finds echoes in the self-doubts expressed by Carlyle, when he wrote to Ralph Waldo Emerson: 'I never know or can even guess what or who my audience is, or whether I have any audience: thus too naturally I adjust myself to the Devil-may-care principle.'[5]

Making an assessment of Graham's contribution to social change through his parliamentary activities has proved difficult for his biographers. Taylor made no attempt to sum up any impact, and according to Watts and Davies, 'with someone in his solitary position, the question is one of influence and example rather than direct political effect'.[6] His first biographer, Faulkner West, wrote, 'It would be stupid, no doubt, to claim for Cunninghame Graham any great success in Parliament',[7] but that missed the point. Graham's lasting legacy, as Watts and Davies suggested, was predicated on the effect that parliament had on him, not the effect he had on it. His hopeless attempts to get labour legislation enacted convinced him that any change could come only from working-class empowerment, and greater autonomy for both Ireland and Scotland, and he was quick to realise that this was impossible within the Liberal fold.

The creation of a party of labour would prove difficult in the face of concerted opposition from all sides, including the working-class establishment and the indifference and lack of political experience of the workers themselves. Unlike the autocratic Hyndman, Graham understood that his position and his temperament disqualified him from leadership. Nor did he possess the patience or the application to perform the role of a party functionary, involved in day-to-day organisation, essential to the development of any new political entity. Fortuitously, he recognised these skills in Hardie, and he set about grooming him to take up the role. Graham's early relationship with Hardie was one of mutual validation, whereby Graham, now with some experience, initiated Hardie into the esoteric rituals of the House of Commons, and with a high political visibility, raised Hardie's profile in the eyes of the public and the press. For his part, Hardie, who had experience of grass-roots activism, and the working conditions and demands of the workers, validated Graham in the eyes of those he wished to serve and inspire, and allowed him to speak on their behalf with confidence. However, the reluctant Hardie still cleaved to the Liberals, and as a compromise, both men attempted to push forward their agenda within the Liberal party, as a staging post, by the proposed selection of working-class candidates, and to find an accommodation. Through a combination of naivety and duplicity, this backfired. However, it was the Liberals' rejection of this proposal, and their rejection of Hardie as a parliamentary candidate – apparently insignificant acts – that set in motion the catena that led to the Liberal Party's eventual decline. Graham and Hardie now felt roused, against concerted opposition, to establish an independent party, the development of which, after many setbacks, would eventually displace the Liberals as the main opposition in the House of Commons.

If we seek Graham's earliest contribution to the political life of Scotland, while a Scottish home rule movement was still in its infancy and as yet a faddist issue, it remains his role in promoting and encouraging the formation of the SPLP. First-hand accounts of its inception were, however, rare and fragmentary, comprising personal reminiscences and assumptions by the press. In all probability, its foundation was not considered significant at the time, and only became important when seen in retrospect, as the first step in presaging something more lasting that extended to the whole of Britain. However, despite early reverses, the timing of such a party was propitious. Since the Liberals were unable or unwilling to adapt to the changes that the broader franchise would bring, and within proliferating Radical and Working Men's clubs, and the growth of New Unionism, the recently enfranchised workers recognised the Liberals' inability to serve their interests. It was Graham, inspired by Morris, who had the earliest and clearest vision of this independent party of labour within parliament, and it was Graham who manoeuvred Hardie to take up the reins. His uniqueness in the world of Scottish politics, at this stage, was the outsider's clarity of vision, unhampered by the prejudices, caution, and inhibitions of a local habitué, the innate confidence of his class, and an admiration for the primal virtues drawn from his overseas experiences. Graham's appeal to the radical elements was his social position and high profile, which gave exposure and some credibility to their minority views, but it was particularly in his inspirational influence on others to act decisively that his real contribution lay.

Although described in *The Scotsman* as 'the head' of the Labour Party,[8] Graham preferred to oversee, agitate, inspire, and promote, a stance repeated throughout his life, that of the 'insider outsider'. This distance, his lack of personal ambition, and an aristocratic *de haut en bas*, would soon create misunderstandings and strains among his Labour colleagues, leading, according to Lowe, to personal abuse. However, there was also a misunderstanding by many labour historians of his role as an early midwife of what would become profound social and political change. Nonetheless, it was also this impatient bloody-minded idealism that was largely responsible for creating a political entity that would eventually achieve most of his aims. Joseph Conrad's biographer, Jocelyn Baines, claimed: 'Cunninghame Graham championed causes because he was roused to do so, not because he expected them to triumph (if he had he probably would not have bothered).'[9] This was an over-romantic view that failed to appreciate that the causes Graham chose were *premature* of fruition, as all causes must be. Graham *did* expect them to eventually triumph, and his career was replete with examples of crusades and campaigns that, in time, came to some sort of realisation, albeit by the hands of others. That, perhaps, did not bother him, but the reality of these successes rarely lived up to his idealistic moral vision, which would lead to disappointment and disillusionment.

Notes

1. Boredom was undoubtedly a factor.
2. Friedrich Engels, *The Condition of the Working-Class in England* (1845) (Oxford University Press, 1993), pp. 106–43.
3. William Rothenstein, *Men and Memories* (London: Faber & Faber, 1931), p. 165. My italics.
4. Mill, *On Liberty* (1859) (Cambridge University Press, 2004), p. 157.
5. Joseph Slater, ed., *The Correspondence of Emerson and Carlyle* (New York: Columbia University Press, 1964), p. 98. Emrys Hughes related how Carlyle had taken Emerson to parliament, and after half an hour listening to a debate, whispered to the American, "Do you no believe in the Devil now?" Hughes, *Keir Hardie*, p. 34.
6. Watts and Davies, *Cunninghame Graham*, p. 98.
7. Faulkner West, *Cunninghame Graham*, p. 96.
8. *Scotsman*, 5 July 1890, p. 6.
9. Baines, *Joseph Conrad*, p. 198.

PART II

'THE FOUNTAIN OF HIS BRAIN', 1893–1913

Part II Introduction

WITH HIS FAILURE TO be elected as an 'Independent Labour' candidate,[1] the cuckoo had fallen out of the nest, and Graham, still only forty, was now faced with the potential demise of his political and literary ambitions, and the continuing burden of huge debts. Pritchett wrote that he had been squeezed out of politics by overwhelming, dull conformity:

> The English love of convention, their worship of the whole ritual of self-restraint, is often laughed at for its dullness and as if it were only dull. But it is more than that. It is pervasive, systematic, overwhelming. It wins in the end.

He was thus labelled 'an aristocratic minority, a nuisance who, in due process of English tolerance, would shortly graduate and become legend, as a pelted [sic] crank gets a knighthood or ascends to the Lords'.[2]

This was undoubtedly a major low point in Graham's life, but virtually nothing has been written about it. The two men who had his ear in later life, and who might have given an insight into his state of mind, his biographers – Faulkner West and Tschiffely – remained silent. After describing Graham's defeat, Faulkner West moved on to his friendships and literary output, while Tschiffely glossed over the entire period and simply recorded: 'Time often hung a little heavily on Don Roberto's hands, especially in the long spells of rain which visit the District of Menteith.'[3] However, Graham and his wife suffered considerable hardships trying to keep their home,[4] and the painter John Lavery recorded a particularly revealing incident:

> When I knew him at this time [1896] his finances were in a shocking state and things were getting unbearable down at Gartmore. Suddenly he wrote to say that he could stand it no longer. Would I come down at once and see him end it all with Pampa [Graham's horse] in a spot where I had painted a view of the Rob Roy country that he loved.[5]

While Tschiffely only conceded Graham's tendency towards the morose,[6] Benn wrote that along with Hardie, Graham and his wife were unrecognised manic-depressives,[7] although she did not substantiate this. Nonetheless, in a letter to Garnett, dated 1 March 1899, Graham wrote, 'My view of life is almost the same as yours. It is a joke, a black joke of course, but we must laugh at our own efforts',[8] and Conrad had commiserated with Graham on his depression in a letter dated 9 December 1898.[9] Depression might well explain Graham's erratic behaviour, and his need for ceaseless action to stave it off. Indeed, another 'cowboy-colonel' who admired Graham's adventurous tales, and who himself suffered from depression, future United States President 'Teddy' Roosevelt, succinctly summed this up: 'Black care rarely sits behind a rider whose pace is fast enough.'[10]

It might have been expected that for someone who, through temperament and experience, was deeply disillusioned with parliament, frustrated by the working classes and their representatives, and continually berated by the press and fellow politicians, a withdrawal from politics would have been an attractive option. Indeed, most historians have written that Graham now retired from political activity for the next thirty-five years, and this became the general impression and consensus. However, he quickly became re-engaged. In fact, he would re-emerge as an even more outspoken political activist, social commentator, and propagandist, but outwith mainstream politics, and he would develop into a respected literary artist. This period of his life would thus be the most challenging to his political and journalistic careers, as his earlier experiences and preoccupations were now obliged to find new outlets for expression, away from the frenetic life of a Member of Parliament and a party agitator.

Almost immediately after performing so poorly at Camlachie, Graham went abroad. The *Aberdeen Evening Express* reported that he was leaving for Spain en route to Morocco, with the caveat, 'If he carries out a notion which he has been thinking over, his absence from us may take a somewhat permanent form',[11] which sounds like pique, or as Watts and Davies, described him, 'a zealot disillusioned'.[12] This was followed by a period of adjustment, during which time his foreign travels increased, but he was also forced to face the real danger of losing his home. Leatham wrote that Graham had confided in him that he took less than £100 a year from his estates, and that '"I tremble in the presence of my poorest tenant."[13] This I took to mean that he was afraid the tenant might ask for repairs or improvements which he could not afford.'[14] Lowe was in no doubt that financial pressures were a major factor in Graham's withdrawal from parliamentary politics, adding: 'Within a few months thereafter he realised with painful clearness that the debt which he had inherited along with his estate was too burdensome to be borne much longer.'[15]

Despite these challenges, however, it soon became apparent that Graham had lost none of his drive, and that his political and moral views had not been vitiated. However, the very nature of his new position meant that he was now isolated from day-to-day political life and political interest groups. Thus, the emphases on the major topics discussed in Part I significantly alter, as Graham was obliged to accept a more distanced stance, and to express himself increasingly through the written word.

Notes

1. Despite the fact that the ILP was not founded until the following year, Graham, apparently, already had the name in mind.
2. V. S. Pritchett, 'New Literature', p. 340. Leatham wrote that after Camlachie, Graham was so embittered that he carried a walking stick with a grotesque handle, which he said represented 'the head of the intelligent elector'. Leatham, 60 Years, p. 153.
3. Tschiffely, Don Roberto, p. 269.
4. Taylor, The People's Laird, pp. 229–33.
5. John Lavery, The Life of a Painter (London: Cassell, 1940), p. 89.
6. Tschiffely, Don Roberto, p. 24.
7. Benn, Keir Hardie, p. 46.
8. Cunninghame Graham, letter to Edward Garnett, 1 March 1899 (MS: University of Texas).
9. Watts, Joseph Conrad's Letters, p. 111.
10. Theodore Roosevelt, Ranch Life and The Hunting Trail (1888) (New York: Century, 1911), p. 59. Roosevelt's son, Kermit, wrote an 'Introductory Note' to Graham's sketch 'Long Wolf': 'My father had been for many years an eager reader of all that Cunninghame Graham wrote . . . I thought at the time that here was a writer that could make Buffalo Bill and his era live and speak and act for our children, and our children's children.' Cunninghame Graham, Rodeo (London: Heinemann, 1936), pp. 1–3. Graham claimed to have first met William 'Buffalo Bill' Cody in San Antonio, Texas, in 1880. Cunninghame Graham, letter to Theodore Roosevelt, 27 March 1917. Reprinted in Cunninghame Graham, Rodeo, p. 2. Graham entertained Cody at the Glasgow Art Club during his 'Wild West' show's second visit to the city between 1 and 6 August 1904.
11. Aberdeen Evening Express, 16 September 1892, p. 5.
12. Watts and Davies, Cunninghame Graham, p. 118. In 1893, Graham again visited Spain and Morocco, this time with the naturalist W. H. Hudson, to research a book, and in 1894 he was back in Spain, prospecting for gold.

13. According to Maitland, the estate made an annual profit of £660, p. 53. However, much of this was taken up by annuities to older relatives, and house maintenance.
14. Leatham, *60 Years*, pp. 162–3. This, not untypically, stands in contrast to his obituary in *The Scotsman* in which it was stated, 'he soon became recognised as the best farmer in the district'. *Scotsman*, 23 March 1936, p. 10.
15. Lowe, 'The Old Scottish Labour Party', *Glasgow Evening Times*, 18 February 1938, p. 3.

8

Labour: An Aristocratic Minority

ON 11 FEBRUARY 1893, Graham's first letter to a newspaper since June of the previous year appeared, and he was again addressing meetings, and promoting the ILP.[1] Notably, in September of that year, he made an impassioned speech at Featherstone in West Yorkshire, condemning police action in which two miners had been shot dead, in what became known as the Featherstone Massacre, attacking both 'hypocritical Liberals' and 'Tory tyrant.'[2] He also continued to write sporadically for socialist publications such as the *Social Democrat* until 1897, and *Justice* until 1902. However, he no longer made references to land ownership, or to those who made their living from the land, or to Ireland.

Opportunities for political office still presented themselves, but he showed no interest. In 1894 the socialist and Irish nationalist, James Connolly, offered to support him as a Labour candidate in Edinburgh, to which Graham replied, 'Many thanks for asking me to stand. However, I have no money, I am sorry to say, and this is the third or fourth offer I have been obliged to decline.'[3] Even with his financial position secure, in 1905 he turned down an invitation to stand as a socialist candidate for the Leith Burghs,[4] and again in South Aberdeen in 1910, with the words that he would 'not re-enter [the] gas-works for £5000 a year'.[5]

His financial tribulations continued, and in October 1895, it was reported that another farm around Gartmore had been sold, and that Graham had been disposing of the estate in portions.[6] It was also around this time that he began a consistent literary career as an unpaid memoirist and social commentator, and by 1896, as the author of virulent attacks on British imperialism and racism. It is impossible to tell, what, if any, the effect these personal pressures and distractions had had on his renewed political activism,[7] but there is a growing awareness of his disillusionment with the party that he was so instrumental in founding. Watts and Davies conjectured:

> There is a case for saying that Graham was disillusioned by success. He was, legend claims, a lover of lost causes; one might therefore argue that he became bored with a cause that appeared to be winning after all. But one might also argue that the success of the ILP was not enough, and that the progress of the Left had been too slow for him to tolerate.[8]

The latter part of this argument carries more weight; Graham remained desperate for political change, but this was proving elusive, and Labour's ranks began to fill with people whom he now believed put themselves before the cause. No doubt repeating his patron's words, Tschiffely put it thus:

> When the Labour Party became strong, and a number of 'big' men joined its rapidly growing ranks, he characterised the leaders as 'p[iss]pot Socialists, a lot of disillusioned Lords and Baronets, surrounded by the most bigoted bunch of bourgeois and social climbers.'[9]

Perhaps Paul Bloomfield got nearer the truth when he described Graham's attitude as being similar to the scepticism of the poet John Milton, when Milton wrote: 'the new presbyter is but old priest writ large.'[10] Significantly, Bloomfield did not agree with Tschiffely that Graham was only a socialist until he thought the movement might succeed, but because he saw in this success the inevitable consequence: 'the existence in all of us of that "new presbyter," biding his time.'[11]

Graham was not the only original SPLP member to become disillusioned with the ILP. In 1909, 'Sandy' Haddow recalled the excitement of earlier days, but then his disappointments:

> And so the ball rolled on into the ILP for better or worse, and district councils, federations, executive councils, and sharks grew more plentiful . . . aggressive fighting force gone. It was no place for me . . . I now plough a lonely furrow with pleasure.[12]

At this juncture, it is worth commenting on the fundamental personality and class differences between Graham and his Labour colleagues. Tschiffely, again undoubtedly quoting from Graham, conceded that his socialist companions considered him 'different from themselves',[13] and Sam Mavor wrote that Graham was not taken seriously by his fellow-socialists.[14] Graham's privileged upbringing had encouraged a manner that Compton Mackenzie would later describe as 'polite *hauteur* [which] kept everybody at a distance',[15] or as Garnett described him, 'Like the prince in the fairy tales he was accessible to all men yet stood aloof from them'.[16] This would no doubt have riled many of those with whom he worked, but those whom he addressed from the platform would not have felt it, and he enjoyed continued popularity for his oratory and his stylish demeanour throughout his life.

Of his elitism, MacDiarmid wrote that among his Labour colleagues, Graham was considered to be 'anti-democratic',[17] and compared him in this to Carlyle, whom he argued was 'an anti-democrat of the most pronounced and uncompromising type', asserting, typically, that it was not democracy that the people wanted, but that their deeper will was 'good government by competent rulers'.[18] MacDiarmid went further in saying that Graham would have agreed with Carlyle that the people were 'mostly fools', to the extent of being 'mere mesmerized cattle' under the malign influence of the political cant and claptrap abundantly poured forth by 'stump orators of every denomination, all intent on getting their votes'.[19] If Graham agreed with this, he did not say it so bluntly, although there were frequent examples of a patrician attitude in his writings. In his tale 'Snaekoll's Saga', for example, he let loose a diatribe on those who ordered society, in a particularly cynical fashion:

> The world is to the weak. The weak are the majority. The weak of brain, of body, the knock-kneed and flatfooted, muddle minded, loose-jointed, ill-put-together, baboon faced, the white eye-lashed, slow of wit, the practical, the unimaginative, forgetful, selfish, dense, the stupid, fatuous, the 'candle-moulded,' give us our laws, impose their standards on us, their ethics, their philosophy, canon of art, literary style, their false morality, their supplemented morganatic marriage, social injustice done to women; legal injustice that men endure, making them fearful of the law . . . in sum, the monstrous ineptitude of modern life, with all its inequalities, its meanness, its petty miseries, contagious diseases, its drink, its gambling, and terror of itself, we owe to this pug-nosed brothers in the Lord, under whose rule we live.[20]

This was artistic exaggeration, but it undoubtedly reflected Graham's general feelings towards humanity of 'the naughty nineties', one critic describing his sketches as having a style that was 'unassuming and conspicuous, like a well-bred man in a room full of rich clowns'.[21] This reached a crescendo in a vitriolic attack on public hubris, low appetites, morals, and tastes, in a *reductio ad absurdum* entitled 'The Pyramid',[22] published in 1900. Here, barely able to contain his repugnance, he recorded his impressions of a music-hall-cum-circus, where 'the great, the generous public, were represented in all its phases, of alcoholic, of bestial, brutal, lustful, stupid, and commonplace'. In 1902, a critic in *The Athenaeum* wrote of him, 'this writer betrays himself as a born and instinctive Tory',[23] and after Graham's death, the American writer, philanthropist and horseman

Edward Larocque Tinker wrote, '[H]e was interested in his fellow man for whom he felt compassion balanced by contempt.'[24]

The incongruity of Graham's position was exacerbated by a sea-change in political and social attitudes within the labour movement itself. Benn wrote of this period of rapid and stark transition, 'The cloth cap man, once derided, was now exalted; Hyndman, the wealthy Oxbridge graduate, became a villain.'[25] Leatham put it thus: 'The political fashion changed so completely in the mining areas that the new Labour label counted for everything, and past services, ability, and actual political principles did not, for a time, seem to matter.'[26] MacDiarmid named some men with whom Graham might have worked:

> But the future of the Labour and Socialist Movement lay with a very differ-ent type with whom he could not have worked and from whom he could not have disguised his contempt . . . They knew, and could know nothing of his writings; their pabulum was of a very different kind – and these two were mutually exclusive.[27]

There may also have been a consensus among Labour's new adherents that they wished to achieve success on their own terms, without the help of a class renegade like Graham. Moreover, Lowe wrote that Graham, who had also stood aloof from the cabals and dissensions, pettiness, and arguments that plagued Scottish Labour, had finally resigned his presi-dency and membership because Hardie refused to support his demand for an apology from two party officials who had grossly insulted him.[28]

Unlike the vast majority of Labour's adherents, Graham's livelihood and his lifestyle were not dependent on physical labour or political change, but on his own personal fulfilment. Watts and Davies quoted from a letter that Graham wrote to Garnett in 1899, in which they saw a remarkable paradox:

> Writing on politics is rot. But politics are good in themselves, this way. A man spends all his life for an idea (I speak of your Parnells etc.), is spat upon, reviled, & laughed at, for a fool, dies broken hearted, hated by those he fought against, half understood (at most) by those he strove for, & most likely not thoroughly believing in the cause, for which he gave his life. The last is the thing, & politics *that* way understood leaves literature millions of leagues behind, even from an artistic standpoint.[29]

They added, 'Even from an artistic standpoint. A man who does not thoroughly believe in his own cause may yet choose to campaign untir-ingly for others, and in doing so he reconciles the moral and the aes-thetic.' If this was indeed the case, ambitions that were less than this, or based purely on self-interest, no matter of what social class, would have strained Graham the moralist's sympathy and patience, but to some of his colleagues, this demeanour would have smacked of artificiality.[30] Watts wrote:

> Graham was an affectionate connoisseur of the absurdities of human nature; and to him, both a skeptic and an idealist, there was something ludicrous yet heroic about men who strive arduously and give their lives for beliefs that defy reason.[31]

Graham's writings were full of heroic failures who fitted this description – the sun-bleached skeletal remains of a long-dead general seated in a chair on a beach in Cuba, 'an archetype of those who fail'.[32] Or the socialist pamphleteer, Betterton,[33] who, despite his eccentricities, poverty, and unswerving idealism, was, we might imagine, more deserving of Graham's admiration, despite, or maybe because of, his lowly social position.

As Hardie's profile increased, Graham maintained an enigmatic distance, and by 1894 their relationship had fractured. Lowe referred to the bad feeling between them in his report of a rally held in Coatbridge in 1898, in which Hardie hoped Graham would stand for parliament again, this time as a *bona fide* Labour candidate:

> It was a huge meeting and might have achieved its purpose, but, unfortunately, Keir Hardie was in the chair. The Irish element raised obscure personalities, those same dark rumours which had ended with estrangement of Graham and Hardie, with the result that by a small majority, our mission was defeated. Graham did not appear on the scene at all; the meeting was tentative.[34]

Through disillusionment or personal slight, Graham was losing faith in Labour as a political instrument, and as early as 1905 he was openly criticising it: 'Had the party been called a Socialist party I would gladly have come forward, but so long as "Labour" is attached to the question it made a farce of the whole proceedings.'[35] As a leading figure in the Men's League of Women's Suffrage in 1907, in front of a large audience in Glasgow, including the militant suffragettes Charlotte Despard, Mrs Philip Snowden, and Christabel Pankhurst, he stated that 'the eminently respectable Labour party were insignificant. Lions roaring in the desert. Heroes on the platforms when there is no danger, and dumb dogs in the House of Commons.'[36] Subsequently, his 'socialist' views became more extreme. Watts and Davies described him as '[a] mobile freelance well to the left of the working-class movement, joining forces with the most prominent or notorious militants . . . Graham did much to precipitate that unrest.'[37] In September 1908 during an unemployment crisis in

Scotland, following an impassioned speech on behalf of the unemployed in George Square, Glasgow, *The Scotsman* described him as 'the chief spokesman of the deputation', and 'a fanatical philanthropist',[38] accusing him of encouraging violence and crime:

> The meaning of such language is perfectly unmistakable. Mr. Graham protests his sense of responsibility; but nobody who recalls his career would attach any high value to that . . . his speech is calculated to promote a resort to crime by people who are not habitual criminals.[39]

Later, at 'a great socialist demonstration' chaired by Graham on 2 November 1908, at which Hardie was the principal speaker, Graham expressed his doubts about the party's direction and effectiveness.[40] In the following month, at the Guildhall Conference on 'Law and the Right to Work', he stated that he disliked the words 'Labour politics or Labour Party, as they are merely red herrings drawn across the trail', and that despite the very best intentions, the forty Labour MPs, placed there by the self-sacrifice of their brothers in the mines, in the factory, had failed in their missions, perhaps by no fault of their own. He added:

> There is an old proverb that you can't touch pitch without being defiled, and it has proved true again. They have become, perhaps unwittingly, statesmen, not revolutionaries. I stand for Socialism. I want a direct line of cleavage. (*Applause*.)[41]

He then alluded to the formation of a small Socialist party in the next parliament, which he hoped would be able to take up the cause of the unemployed. (*Applause*.)[42]

By 1910, even Lowe accused the Labour Party of impotence,[43] and there was also a general suspicion, expressed by Smillie, that 'In the mind of the Englishman[,] Scotland was merely a province of England', and that the ILP 'wire-pullers' had been 'working for the demise of the Scottish section'.[44] In 1912, Leatham, wrote:

> The Labour Movement has got into some very bad hands, and initiates nothing, devises nothing, is not aggressive, shows no courage, lets one occasion slip by after another without anything done or even said that is at all to the purpose.[45]

There were strong parallels here with Graham's previous relationship. He had very quickly become disillusioned with the Liberals when he came to believe, through his experiences in parliament, that they had no intention of fulfilling the role they had proclaimed. Now, having focused so much time and effort in promoting working men as MPs, the same disillusionment had reappeared.

Notes

1. *Scotsman*, 16 February 1893, p. 6, 27 January, 1894, p. 6, 28 August 1894, p. 6, and *Manchester Guardian*, 20 March 1893, p. 8.

2. 'Mr Cunninghame Graham and the Featherstone Riots', *Manchester Guardian*, 12 September 1893, p. 7. His 'impression' of the aftermath was anthologised as 'A Yorkshire Tragedy', in *Progress and Other Sketches* (1905), pp. 187–98.

3. Donal Nevin, ed., *Between Comrades, James Connolly, Letters and Correspondence, 1889–1916* (Dublin: Gill & Macmillan, 2007), p. 8. Edinburgh-born Connolly was executed by the British in 1916 for his part in Dublin's Easter Rising.

4. *Scotsman*, 4 October 1905, p. 12.

5. *Scotsman*, 7 January 1910, p. 9.

6. *Scotsman*, 1 October 1895, p. 5.

7. The ILP was established at a meeting in Bradford in January 1893, but there is no record of Graham attending.

8. Watts and Davies, *Cunninghame Graham*, p. 118.

9. Tschiffely, *Don Roberto*, p. 260. Stephen Graham wrote, 'aristocrats often become revolutionaries through loathing of parvenus and parvenu culture', and like Tolstoy, Graham had 'a true aristocratic hate of the bourgeoisie and of upstart officialdom'. Stephen Graham, *The Death of Yesterday* (London: Ernest Benn, 1930), p. 46.

10. John Milton, 'On the New Forcers of Conscience Under the Long Parliament' (poem, 1646).

11. Paul Bloomfield, *The Essential Cunninghame Graham* (London: Cape, 1952), p. 23.

12. 'Sandy' Haddow, 'Reminiscences', p. 6. Following his death, Graham paid tribute, and unveiled a memorial to Haddow. *Glasgow Herald*, 14 August 1922, p. 10.

13. Tschiffely, *Don Roberto*, p. 213.

14. Sam Mavor, *The M&C Apprentices' Magazine*, Vol. XX, Summer 1936, p. 56.

15. Compton Mackenzie, 'Don Roberto: On the Centenary', *The Listener*, 29 May 1952, p. 868.

16. Edward Garnett, 'R. B. Cunninghame Graham', p. 128.

17. MacDiarmid, *Centenary Study*, p. 12.

18. Ibid., p. 13.

19. Ibid., p. 14.

20. Cunninghame Graham, 'Snaekoll's Saga', *Saturday Review*, 18 December 1897, p. 709. Anthologised in *The Ipané* (1899), pp. 141–56.

21. *Observer*, 17 March 1912, p. 5.

22. Cunninghame Graham, 'The Pyramid', *Justice*, 1 May 1900, pp. 6–7. Anthologised in *Success* (1902), pp. 100–8.

23. *Athenaeum*, 15 November 1902, p. 645.

24. Edward Larocque Tinker, 'New Editions, First and Otherwise', *New York Times Book Review*, 29 November 1936, p. 20.

25. Benn, *Keir Hardie*, p. xvii.

26. Leatham, *60 Years*, p. 159.

27. MacDiarmid, *Centenary Study*, p. 9. MacDiarmid went on to assert that the Labour movement, as its membership and power increased, 'involved a progressive deterioration of mind and spirit', while 'the majority of the M.P.s it returned to Westminster were mentally negligible'. Ibid., p. 10. As to the attitude of Scotland, MacDiarmid wrote: 'Cunninghame Graham's attributes were no asset among his countrymen but were generally resented as a sort of insult to their own irremediable mediocrity and lack of *panache*.' Ibid., p. 16.

28. Lowe 'The First Time It Has Been Told: Why Cunninghame Graham Left the Labour Party', *Glasgow Evening Times*, 11 February 1938, p. 3.

29. Cunninghame Graham, letter to Edward Garnett, 28 January 1899, quoted in Watts and Davies, *Cunninghame Graham*, p. 290–1.

30. Jeffrey Meyers wrote, '[T]his artificiality and egoism combined with disdain and contempt combined to explain Graham's failure in both politics and art.' Jeffrey Meyers, *Fever at the Core: Six Studies of Idealists in Politics* (London Magazine Editions, 1976), p. 44.

31. Watts, *R. B. Cunninghame Graham*, p. 42. Graham's personality did not appeal to everyone of his own class. Edward Garnett's son, David, wrote that Graham was 'a visitor who impressed my imagination rather than won my heart . . . But when he made a speech or wrote a book he adopted a pose, and his vanity overcame him.' David Garnett, *The Golden Echo* (London: Chatto & Windus, 1953), p. 68. David also wrote that his father tolerated Graham's vanity, which assisted in the expression of his personality. Ibid., p. 69. David 'Bunnie' Garnett would in his turn become a noted writer and publisher, a prominent member of the Bloomsbury Group, and co-founder of the Nonesuch Press.

32. Cunninghame Graham, 'The Failure of Success, *Saturday Review*, 17 May 1902, p. 631.

33. Cunninghame Graham, 'An Idealist', *Saturday Review*, 25 August 1906, pp. 232–3. Betterton was the thinly disguised Dan Chatterton (1820–95), London slum-dweller, atheist, communist, anti-monarchist, radical pamphleteer, and publisher of *Chatterton's Commune, the Atheistic Communistic Scorcher*.

34. Lowe, *Glasgow Evening Times*, 4 March 1938, p. 3. These dark rumours may have been a reference to Graham's position on the board of management of the *Labour Elector*, and its association with Scottish political activist Maltman Barrie, 'the purveyor of Tory Gold', and the *éminence bleue* of early labour politics.

35. *Scotsman*, 23 December 1905, p. 10. The name 'Labour Party' was not adopted until 1906. In 1908, the English socialist and trade union activist Ben Tillett published a savage attack on Labour: 'The House of Commons

and the country, which respected and feared the Labour Party, are now fast approaching a condition of contempt towards its parliamentary representatives.' Ben Tillett, *Is the Parliamentary Labour Party a Failure?* (London: Twentieth Century Press, 1908), p. 11.

36. 'Women's Suffrage: Demonstration in Glasgow: Speech by Mr Cunninghame Graham', *Glasgow Herald*, 5 October 1907, p. 8. The reporter believed: 'The fact that Mr. R. B. Cunninghame Graham was in the chair doubtless accounted in some measure for the dimensions of the audience.' Typically, Graham's speech as chairman was reported in full, while the eminent lady guests were given only a few lines each.

37. Watts and Davies, *Cunninghame Graham*, p. 221.

38. *Scotsman*, 25 September 1908, p. 6.

39. *Scotsman*, p. 4.

40. *Glasgow Herald*, 3 November 1908, p. 7.

41. *Manchester Guardian*, 7 December 1908, p. 9. In a diary entry for 12 March 1908, Wilfred Scawen Blunt recorded Graham's low opinion of the new Labour MPs: '[B]ut he [Graham] tells me they are a useless lot. When they get into Parliament they are at once bitten with the absurd idea that they are no longer working men, but statesmen, and they try to behave as such ... they would do more good if they came to the House in a body drunk and tumbling about on the floor.'
Wilfred Scawen Blunt, *My Diaries*, Vol. II (1908) (New York: Alfred A Knopf, 1921), pp. 196–7.

42. This may have been a reference to a nascent British Socialist Party (see below).

43. Lowe, *Forward*, 9 April 1910, p. 3.

44. Robert Smillie, *Forward*, 6 February 1910, p. 2.

45. Leatham, 'Barren Labourism', *Gateway*, July 1912, p. 17.

9

Literary Career: A Queer Potency

GRAHAM'S URGE TO WRITE had not abated, and his first literary attempts in print after leaving parliament were his essays *Father Archangel of Scotland* (1893),[1] and 'In the Tarumensian Woods' (1894).[2] His major long-term literary breakthrough, however, was precipitated in 1895 with the publication of a guidebook entitled *Notes on the District of Menteith*.[3] Taylor believed that due to Graham's notoriety as hero/villain, his slim volume was widely reviewed,[4] and it ran to three reprints. Most significantly, the *Saturday Review* extolled it as:

> The wittiest little book to come out in a long time. Mr. Graham has found his vocation. We hope that he will cease to 'fash' himself with politics and give us many another book small or great but, like this, discursive, poetical, full of ingenious reflection and pleasant distortion of history.[5]

Taylor added that as a direct consequence of this piece, Graham had been recruited to the *Saturday Review* by the new owner and editor, Frank Harris,[6] who had purchased the periodical after *Notes* was published, and that his first article was 'Salvagia', published in September 1896. Taylor's assertions were, however, incorrect. Harris purchased the *Saturday Review* in December 1894, and Graham made his first contribution to it in early August 1895,[7] the same month as his *Notes* appeared in print, and a month before it was reviewed. Graham continued his association with the journal long after Harris sold it in 1898, and contributed sketches and book reviews up until 1913, with occasional articles between 1924 and 1926, and a final article in 1931. It had been by a stroke of luck and personal contact[8] that he became a regular contributor, and it was the prestige of the *Saturday Review* that made and sustained his literary reputation, for, as Taylor wrote:

> While his political articles had much of the force and style of his later work, very few of his contemporaries, and fewer still of what have to be termed his

social equals, took the *Labour Elector*, *Justice*, or *The People's Press*. *The Saturday Review* was a different matter: discussed in the London clubs and, if not always read, at least laid out on the table in the library of every country house in Britain.[9]

Hitherto, Graham's literary output had been marginal, and somewhat chaotic. Now, writing for a prestigious periodical, which was described by the *Manchester Guardian* as 'soaked in eighteenth-century Toryism',[10] undoubtedly lent a new kudos and respectability that he had lacked in the eyes of the public and his peers. It was, nevertheless, an odd partnership, the fiery communistic iconoclast, writing for the sedate country house journal, but it seems that his writing talents, plus his larger-than-life personality, could compensate for much. In 1899, a reviewer for the *Saturday Review* wrote of him:

> Many heresies may be forgiven or at least ignored for the sake of brilliant individuality in a humdrum age, and though we do not take the man seriously, we owe homage to the master of style. Indeed, were we invited to recommend a model of graceful, vigorous and eloquent English, we could mention few modern examples better calculated to instruct and inspire.[11]

These condescending words probably summed up the thoughts of many reviewers and readers, who chose to separate what they considered Graham's controversial, and to them, eccentric views, from his persona and his literary talents.

Notes

1. Cunninghame Graham, 'Father Archangel of Scotland', *Nineteenth Century*, September 1893, pp. 384–9.
2. Cunninghame Graham, 'In the Tarumensian Woods', *Nineteenth Century*, August 1894, pp. 244–25. Anthologised in *Father Archangel of Scotland* (1896), pp. 79–102.
3. Published in August 1895. The *Aberdeen Journal* proffered that it was 'not a guide book in the ordinary sense at all', but 'a delightful monograph on Menteith', and went on to describe it as 'this bright, attractive, and sparkling little volume'. *Aberdeen Journal*, 2 September 1895, p. 6.
4. Taylor, *The People's Laird*, p. 225.
5. *Saturday Review*, 21 September 1895, p. 437. Fash: Scots = Bother, annoy.
6. Harris wrote: 'What a crew of talent to get together on one paper before they were appreciated elsewhere – [H. G.] Wells and [Bernard] Shaw, Chalmers Mitchell, D. S. McColl, and Cunninghame Graham.' Frank Harris, *Contemporary Portraits*. Third Series (privately printed, 1920), p. 47. Harris was another adventuring outsider, a maverick in the sedate publishing world, who would have found Graham's unconventionality attractive.

7. Cunninghame Graham, 'A Jesuit', *Saturday Review*, 3 August 1885, pp. 135–6.

8. At this time, Graham and Harris socialised in the same London circles, and occasionally rode together in Hyde Park.

9. Taylor, *The People's Laird*, p. 235. When Harris purchased it, it had a circulation of 5,600, and he had offered £1 per reader in payment.

10. *Manchester Guardian*, 'Miscellany', 23 February 1914, p. 7.

11. *Saturday Review*, 29 April 1899, p. 533. In 1910, Graham was attacked in *The Academy* in response to his letter entitled 'Patriotism': '"the socialist descendant of kings," and red rag ranter, who rather than bestow his bits of copy upon their natural inheritor the Socialist *New Age* prefers to air himself in the high Tory *Saturday Review*.' *The Academy*, 5 February 1910, p. 124.

10

Empire: The Insidious Bacillus

Now constrained from writing socialist polemic, Graham had to find other less politically partisan themes. Two subjects that were not overtly socialist, but were analogous with his views on the conditions of the working poor, were his views on empire and colonialism. As we have seen, Graham had expressed imperial scepticism on the hustings and in parliament, but his early socialist journalism made little reference to imperialism. Now, between 1896 and early 1899, obviously driven by deep anger, he wrote four extraordinary explicit articles with an anti-racist, anti-imperialist, and anti-capitalist message.

Graham's new literary career was contemporaneous with the approach of Queen Victoria's Diamond Jubilee (1897), when a fevered imperial jingoism was nearing its height.[1] As previously acknowledged, he drew no distinction between capitalism and imperialism; indeed, as Bernard Porter observed in the wider context, there were 'signs towards the end of the century that the nation's policy was being shaped by capitalists to an extent unknown before, and with little concern for the interests of anyone but themselves'. He added, 'emotional accretions to the name of the Empire became thicker and more beguiling as the last thirty years of the century wore on'.[2] Thus, for Graham, the forthcoming hubristic celebrations provided a perfect excuse to attack capitalism and the powerful elites both directly and obliquely.

A key event that excited national passions, but also exacerbated moral qualms among certain sections of society, as well as international condemnation, was the botched Jameson Raid of 1895 to 1896, sponsored by Cecil Rhodes, which had been aimed at provoking conflict with the Boers. Porter agreed that the raid 'pointed a clear and unmistakable connection between empire and finance',[3] and it was an excellent opportunity for Graham to voice his anger.[4] Surprisingly, after publishing only two pieces in the *Saturday Review*, it was this conservative journal that published his first major anti-imperialist tirade, since it was also a direct attack on Rhodes (whom elsewhere he had called the 'Bulawayo Burglar'[5]), a man whom Harris knew and admired.[6] It was also an attack on British intrigues in southern Africa as a means of gaining access to the goldfields and diamond mines, published in two parts under the title 'Fraudesia Magna'.[7]

After tracing the advance of the Boers, and their destructive impact on the native inhabitants, Graham remarked that at least they were not 'money-grubbers', but added:

> Nothing excites our [British] wrath more fully than to see rich mineral lands in the hands of others. It seems to strike us as a sort of coming between the Lord and His anointed. We have a mission to perform, and to be free to follow it we must have gold and diamond mines in order to obtain a market for our sized cotton and our trash from Birmingham. Superior morality is not bound by treaties . . . Britons were never slaves to treaties when gold was found in adjoining countries.

Never reluctant to introduce Spanish or South American allusions, Graham then compared Rhodes to Cortez in his love of wealth and power, but there the resemblance ended. Rhodes was no warrior, he took no physical risks, but offered the British upper classes and industrialists huge profits, 'chances of wealth unsoiled by work'. For this, he had used others, like his friend, the Scot, Dr Leander Starr Jameson, to do his dirty work by goading the Boers into war in 'a sordid and tinpot affair . . . England, perhaps, is justified, if not by works, by her humiliation; for, once again, the whole world thinks us liars'.[8]

Graham was by no means alone in his scepticism; many on the left shared his views. For example, ten years earlier, Morris's *Commonweal* railed against it: 'this rhetoric about honour and glory, and law and justice simply means NEW MARKETS, and nothing more; that the whole bombastic business is just a glorification of commercialism.'[9] In 1886, the Marxist, Belfort Bax, wrote the following:

> We seem at the present time to have arrived at the acute stage of colonial fever which during the last three or four years has afflicted the various powers of Europe. Germany is vying with France, England with both, in the haste to seize upon 'unoccupied' countries, and to establish 'protectorates' – the cant diplomatic for incomplete annexation – over uncivilized peoples.[10]

Graham's next anti-imperialist diatribe, *The Imperial Kailyard: Being a Bitter Satire on English Colonisation*,[11] was a pamphlet the sentiments of which would have been unlikely to appear in a mainstream journal. Here he recalled how, in the naivety of youth, he had once believed that all the good and honourable virtues had been patented in England, that wherever the British flag floated all were free and equal before the law, irrespective of rank, position, or colour, and that:

> The sanctity of British soil, the superior virtue and chivalry of my coun-
> trymen, their justice, toleration, and fair dealing with all stronger than
> themselves, and their generous commercial attitude to weaker nations than
> themselves, grew to be my most serviceable creed.[12]

If some slight injustices had been done in extending these blessings, this was only natural – all change incurred some loss; the odds were so great.[13] Graham's anger was then loosed on 'the useless sons' and missionaries sent to administer and pacify these far-flung regions, degraded by their institu-tion, as were their 'niggers', and if on some rare occasion one (a coloniser) was killed, the corrupt press described it as 'a massacre'.[14] This was a bitter indictment indeed, a comprehensive attack on arrogance, brutality, hypoc-risy, and jingoism as Britain plundered its way around the world under the guise of a civilising mandate, sending armies of incompetents to rob and defile. His focus then turned to Britain's contemporaneous involvement by proxy in the Matabeleland Rebellion (1896–7):

> No one doubts that eventually the Matabele will be conquered, and that our
> flag will wave triumphantly over the remnant of them, in the same way as it
> waves triumphantly over the workhouse pauper and the sailor's poor whore
> in the east end of London. Let it wave on over an empire reaching from north
> to south, and still keep waving over Leicester Square, where music halls at
> night belch out their crowds of stout imperialists.[15]

The third piece, also an indignant biting satire, was 'Bloody Niggers',[16] published in the Marxist journal, the *Social Democrat*. This ironic dia-tribe was really an extension of *The Imperial Kailyard*, but a more specific assault on bigotry, describing the world, its resources, and its peoples as having been designed by an all-wise Creator exclusively for British use. Why had this Jahvé gone to the trouble of creating those other races, if not to be ruled by Englishmen:

> 'Niggers' who have no cannons, and cannot construct a reasonable torpedo,
> have no rights. Their land is ours, their cattle, fields, their houses, their poor
> utensils, arms, all that they have; their women, too, are ours to use as con-
> cubines, to beat, exchange, to barter for gunpowder and gin, ours to infect
> with syphilis, leave with child, outrage, torment, and make by consort with
> the vilest of our vile, more vile than beasts.[17]

Apart from the strong moral critique, it is worth noting in both of these tracts that to Graham, imperialism was not something that exclusively

occurred overseas, out of sight. It was all around, part of the same insti-
tutionalised system of greed and exploitation that the jingoistic public
swallowed, as part of their own enslavement:

> If they are poor, then woe betide them, let them paint their faces white with
> all the ceruse which ever Venice furnished, to the black favour they will
> come. A plague of pigments, blackness is in the heart, not in the face, and
> poverty, no matter how it washes, still is black.[18]

This extraordinary broadside concluded by asking if England was 'a vast
and seething mushroom bed of base hypocrisy', and God 'an anthropo-
morphous fool'.

As if to encapsulate all of his anger, the fourth anti-imperialist piece
was a breathless newspaper article entitled 'Expansion of Empire', published only eight days before the Jubilee, in which he ridiculed Britain's
imperial ambitions:

> In every corner of the world some epoch-making little man has been
> extending our national power on an insecure footing and building his own
> fortunes. Truly an age of expansion, national expansion and international
> expansion . . . Well, it is done, and hardly a corner of the known world
> remains in which the name of Britain is not mentioned with a curse.[19]

'Conscience', he satirically asserted, was a British product, and once
across the English Channel it withered and died; the British were the
chosen race, and had taken out a patent on the 'gentleman' to defend
themselves from the infringement of copyright by foreign counterfeits.
Thus, Britain reserved the right to reclaim the rest of the world from
barbarism and recast it in its own image,[20] and to illustrate the greed
and insidiousness of these empire-builders, Graham published a two-
part article on the machinations of British business interests in Morocco,
under the title 'The Voyage of the Tourmaline' (1898).[21]

The period 1896 to 1897 marked the high points of Graham's anti-
imperialist writings, but a final criticism was published in early 1899, in
a letter in the *Daily Chronicle* in which he again attacked the hypocrisy
of empire, pointing out the similar actions the British had taken to quell
or destroy native people as a patriotic right, while the Turks, who were
killing Armenians, were tyrants:

> We are the Turks, the oppressors, spoilers, and the patriots were the men
> who fell for those old-world ideals – love of their country and their faith? If
> not, surely there is one patriotism for the Whites, another for Arabs, and a
> third for blacks, all differing in degree, and each divided from the other by
> biothermal lines. So what is patriotism at Ashford-under-Lyne is rank rebel-
> lion in Darfur, and becomes Anarchism in Rhodesia; and so on of all the

virtues, vices and the like the whole gamut of the human farce . . . let us go on 'rugging and reiving' for the sake of Christ, or to obtain new markets, or for the sake of the great cause of human progress, or for some other reason never yet made plain.[22]

The satirical stridency of Graham's writing, and the expression of such uncompromising and controversial views, is worthy of note, for their courage if nothing else. This was particularly true when their publication coincided with the zenith of British nationalism, prior to the beginning of the Second Boer War,[23] and a period of paranoia that found voice in a popular literary fashion known as 'Imperial Gothic'. Works in this genre revealed underlying anxieties over matters of mysticism, miscegenation, degeneracy, contagion, irrationality, and the fragility of civilisation. Many people also felt threatened by the economic and technological rise of other European powers, which found expression in yet another popular literary form, 'Invasion Literature',[24] in which the outward thrust of imperialist adventure was reversed. Elleke Boehmer wrote of these concerns:

> Though fears and doubts about Empire only came fully into their own in the new century, expressions of anxiety about social regression and national decline were widespread. Movements that implied a loss of traditional authority – Irish nationalism, socialism, the New Woman – met with stern repression.[25]

It is worth noting that the topics that Boehmer selected were exactly the topics that occupied Graham's early crusades, and we might ask to what extent these formed a deliberate and comprehensive attempt, in his own small way, to undermine all aspects of British establishment authority. Perhaps the best example of this appeared in *Mogreb-El-Acksa*, where Graham attempted to present foreign incursions through the eyes of the inhabitants, and to understand local cultures on their own terms, without the strictures of foreign moralities.[26] It was in substance an attack on the attitudes of the travel books of the time, which took a superior position over the backwardness, the racial characteristics, and the practices of indigenous populations. In the words of Philip Healy, in his introduction (appended in 1988), 'Europeans have no proprietary claim on other countries because of some "higher" morality which they enjoy'.[27] A reviewer in *The Academy* regarded it 'as a satire on things done in Mayfair or Mincing Lane . . . a constant playing off of British character against the types of Morocco under a convention of social and political equality as between us and them'.[28]

Graham did not confine his criticism to British imperialism. In 1898, he condemned America's role in the ten-week Spanish-American War, and in 1900, in a letter to the *Saturday Review* he criticised Britain for betraying her old ally, Spain, to gain American favour.[29] Also, as a frequent visitor to, and writer on Morocco, for the months of April and May 1906, during the Moroccan Crisis, Graham was given the title of 'Special Correspondent' for the *Glasgow Herald*, the newspaper that had once campaigned against his election to parliament.

Graham's most controversial public utterance on the subject of empire took place at a conference entitled 'Nationalities and Subject Races', held in Caxton Hall, Westminster, between 28 and 30 June 1910, which attracted a large and enthusiastic international audience. Graham had his opportunity to share his uncompromising views during the fifth and final session, entitled 'Proposed Remedies'. Here he stated that he hated the idea of empire; he believed that, initially at least, Britain had sent great men to introduce civilisation to her overseas possessions, but little by little, 'the insidious bacillus of Imperialism' had undermined its high ideals, being corrosive both to the rulers and the ruled. Most controversially he stated, 'I am not one of those people whom the word assassination terrifies.'[30] Garnett witnessed this speech with his eighteen-year-old-son, David. Many years later, David recalled Graham's words in his memoirs:

> The only speech I heard, which was not completely boring, was delivered by Cunninghame Graham. He began his speech with the words: 'I am not one of those who tremble [*sic*] at the word – ASSASSINATION!' There was a storm of applause, which prevented his proceeding for some minutes, and it was obvious that all the delegates, whatever the colour of their skin, were consumed with the passionate longing to commit murder.[31]

Graham, of course, had associated with Kropotkin, and various other anarchists who were part of Morris and Garnett's inner circles that also included Sergey Stepnyak-Kravchinsky, the assassin of General Nikolai Mezentsov, Chief of the Tsar's secret police. He had also been closely associated with Michael Davitt, who had at one time promoted violence and served seven years in prison for gunrunning. In Graham's more sanguine (or rather sanguinary) moments, such direct action no doubt had its appeal. However, following the First World War, he took an entirely contrary view and reacted angrily to political assassination, particularly in Ireland.

If Ireland had slipped from Graham's agenda during this period, this was likely because it had been overtaken and subsumed by a growing and more general imperial clamour, and Ireland, in Graham's mind, was also a colony, ruled over by unwelcome foreigners and subject to the same misconceptions as other colonised peoples.

Notes

1. Or as Graham called it, 'Union Jackism'. Cunninghame Graham, 'The Voyage of The Tourmaline II', *Saturday Review*, 18 June 1898, p. 811.
2. Bernard Porter, *Critics of Empire: British Radicals and the Imperial Challenge* (1968) (London: I. B. Tauris, 2008), p. 36. Graham received the briefest of mentions in this book, as a note on p. 100.
3. Ibid., p. 41.
4. It may also have been Graham's response to the Poet Laureate, Alfred Austin's hastily written, and much-ridiculed poem, *Jameson's Ride*, printed in *The Times* on 11 January 1896, and Rudyard Kipling's hubristic and unapologetic *Hymn Before Action*, published there in the same month. Kipling's more famous poem 'If' (1895) was apparently inspired by Jameson. In a letter to Graham, dated 26 January 1899, Edward Garnett described Kipling as '*the* enemy'. Manuscript Collection of Admiral Sir Angus Cunninghame Graham, NLS.
5. Cunninghame Graham, 'With the North Wind', *Saturday Review*, 10 October 1896, p. 389.
6. Frank Harris, *My Life and Loves*, Vol. II (privately printed, 1925), p. 463.
7. Cunninghame Graham, 'Fraudesia Magna', *Saturday Review*, Part I, 21 March 1896, pp. 293–5; Part II, 4 April 1896, pp. 340–2.
8. Despite his attacks on British intrigues in South Africa, Graham saw the Boers as in many ways worse, as reported in a speech he gave in Edinburgh on 22 September 1899, *Scotsman*, 23 September 1899, p. 12.
9. *The Commonweal*, May 1885, p. 39.
10. Ernest Belfort Bax, *The Religion of Socialism* (1886) (Books for Libraries Press, 1972), p. 43.
11. Cunninghame Graham, *The Imperial Kailyard: Being a Bitter Satire on English Colonisation*, pamphlet (Twentieth Century Press, 1896), pp. 1–15.
12. Ibid., pp. 3–4.
13. Ibid., p. 7.
14. Ibid., p. 12.
15. Ibid., p. 15.
16. Cunninghame Graham, 'Bloody Niggers', *Social Democrat*, April 1897, pp. 104–9. Anthologised in *The Ipané* (1899), as 'Niggers', pp. 164–77. This was in the same year that Conrad published *The Nigger of the 'Narcissus'*.
17. Cunninghame Graham, 'Bloody Niggers', p. 108. Garnett believed that '*Niggers* should live by its pillorying of the Englishman's attitude to natives'. Garnett, 'Cunninghame Graham: Man and Writer', p. 129.
18. Cunninghame Graham, 'Bloody Niggers', p. 108. *Ceruse*: Latin/Old French = A lead-based cosmetic skin-whitener.
19. Cunninghame Graham, 'Expansion of Empire', *Sunday Chronicle*, 13 June 1897, p. 2.
20. Ibid.

21. Cunninghame Graham, 'The Voyage of the Tourmaline I', *Saturday Review*, 4 June 1898, pp. 739–40, and II, *Saturday Review*, 18 June 1898, pp. 810–12.

22. Cunninghame Graham, letter to *Daily Chronicle*, 11 January 1899, p. 3.

23. It is all the more perplexing that Graham published no critique of Britain's involvement in the Second Boer War (1899–1902), nor mentioned Emily Hobhouse's reports on the conditions in British concentration camps during the conflict. On the contrary, in a letter dated 14 December 1901, Graham almost condoned their use, or suggested they were no worse than recent American actions in the Philippines. Cunninghame Graham letter, 'Buncombe', *Saturday Review*, 14 December 1901, p. 740.

24. Classics of this genre were *The Invasion of Dorking* (1871), *The War of the Worlds* (1898), *The Riddle of the Sands* (1903), *The Invasion of 1910* (1906), and *The War in the Air* (1907).

25. Elleke Boehmer, *Colonial and Postcolonial Literature: Migrant Metaphors* (Oxford University Press, 1995), p. 22.

26. See Andrew C. Long, 'A Refusal and Traversal: Robert Cunninghame Graham's Engagement with Orientalism in *Mogreb-El-Acksa*', *Nineteenth-Century Literature*, Vol. 63, No. 3, 2008, pp. 376–410.

27. Philip Healy, 'Introduction' to Graham's *Mogreb-El-Acksa* (London: Century, 1988), p. xvi. This was also closely analogous with John Stuart Mill's views on empire:

> To suppose that the same international customs, and the same rules of international morality, can obtain between one civilized nation and another, and between civilized nations and barbarians, is a grave error . . . To characterize any conduct whatever towards a barbarous people as a violation of the law of nations, only shows that he who so speaks has never considered the subject.

Mill, *Dissertations and Discussions: Political, Philosophical, and Historical*, Vol. 3 (New York: 1874), pp. 252–3.

28. *The Academy*, 13 October 1900, p. 301.

29. Cunninghame Graham, letter to *Saturday Review*, 3 February 1900, p. 138.

30. 'Conference Report, Caxton Hall, Westminster', 28–30 June 1910 (London: P. S. King, 1910), pp. 142–6.

31. Garnett, *The Golden Echo*, p. 119. He continued, 'Although I was very uncritical at that age, it did strike me that Cunninghame Graham's remark was one of the silliest I had ever heard. He was in no danger of assassinating or being assassinated. He had no reason to tremble.' The economist and social scientist, J. A Hobson, who had chaired the meeting, in an obfuscatory response, denied that Graham had said anything that was 'a direct encouragement to murder'. While regretting Graham's words, he added: 'I did not think it necessary, by my intervention from the chair, to give additional prominence to Mr. Graham's language, which was not that of instigation, or, indeed, of particular condonation, but a rhetorical protest against the ruling out of violent methods.' *The Nation*, 16 July 1910, p. 563.

11

The Sketches: A Secondary Storyteller

IN 1924, LESLIE CHAUNDY, who compiled the first bibliography of Graham's writings, wrote that Graham had told him that his works were written largely for his own amusement, since he was not a professional writer,[1] and Graham admitted to Garnett, 'I am an essayist and an impressionist, and secondly a storyteller but have the story telling faculty very weakly. Therefore if you cut out my reflections, nothing remains.'[2] He also eschewed what he termed 'invention', stating:

> It is (I think) a general belief, that every writer draws his matter straight from the fountain of his brain, just as a spider weaves his web from his own belly. This may be so, especially with folk of much invention and no imaginative power. The makers of Utopias and the like, forecasters of society under socialism no doubt enjoy the gift. Peace and good luck to them. It may be that which I refer to as invention they style imagination.[3]

Thus, no longer able to write overtly polemical pieces, however unconventional, for his new, more conservative readership, and lacking, or unwilling to employ, a storytelling talent, he was now obliged to find another form. Fortuitously, he had already tentatively prototyped the hybrid 'sketch' form in his foreign reports for the *Labour Elector* and the *People's Press*, and this, by necessity, now became his medium.[4] These occasional contributions to the *Saturday Review* and other periodicals were known as 'middles',[5] vivid descriptions of locations that he had experienced at first hand, knew about, or was interested in, in South America, Morocco, and later, Scotland, which eventually comprised a unique literary legacy. Chris GoGwilt wrote:

> It is really the sketch that defines the genre of all of Graham's works, and his sketch artistry is the medium through which 'the adventure of being Cunninghame Graham'[6] links the battlefronts of socialist struggle and colonial politics.[7]

GoGwilt believed that these more literary offerings were in fact heavily disguised critiques of the advance of so-called civilisation, mediums for anger and nostalgia, which implicitly regretted the destruction of environments, lifestyles, and traditions. In other words, they were *political*, and this is how most of them should be interpreted.

Watts believed that it was in an early piece, 'A Jesuit',[8] that Graham developed the impressionistic sketch into the 'sketch-tale', first by the atmospheric evocation of place, and by what John Walker described as one of his recurring literary techniques, 'the story within the sketch'. Here, a doomed Jesuit, the 'tobacco priest', was pursuing his mission of bringing light to the heathen, facing the jungle and its horrors, and it was important in literary terms, because, for the first time, it was self-contained, and did not rely on verification from older recorded material. For Graham, at this stage of his career, it was also an admirable demonstration of restraint, as he allowed his reader's imaginations to conjure up the priest's fate, which made it all the more disturbing.[9] This sketch was a precursor to what would become Graham's standard format of a long, vivid description,[10] usually of some South American location, followed by the gist, short bursts of (sometimes violent) action, or a meditation, often switching between discourse and narration, and what Watts described as 'panorama terminating in close-up'.[11] Watts believed that 'his better tales are frequently those which employ the oblique narrative form, so that the comments are assimilated to the personality of the fictional teller of the tale-within-the-tale'.[12]

These works often carried a peremptory punch at the end, or simply stopped at the point where the protagonists walked or rode off the page – a snapshot of a continuum, as Graham himself recorded: 'I liked the manner of his going off the stage.'[13] This would become another feature of Graham's long writing career, leaving the reader to decipher a meaning or a moral. However, in most of his works there was no exact meaning or moral, other than his nostalgic regret for the passage of time and the loss of more natural and spontaneous lifestyles and populations, overcome by encroaching civilisation – political statements in their own right. The reader was thus often left with a feeling of incompleteness. James Steel Smith made probably the most comprehensive attempt to describe their uncomfortable uniqueness:

> Without themselves seeming accidental or incomplete, Graham's tales leave one with an aftersense of fragmentation, a feeling that the scene or episode or persons described were fragments of something not given and to be guessed at. They are bright, vivid pieces, but their very vividness somehow suggests chipping, a breaking-off in such a way that the ragged edges, clear and hard,

promise, without defining, a larger reality – which, too, might be just a large, jagged fragment.[14]

Smith believed that this incompleteness had two primary purposes. First, to make the core of his otherwise impressionistic story explosive, by illustrating 'un-rationalised, uncompensated loss', and second, to demonstrate a 'casual irrelevance and unreason' ('anti-rational primitivism') in the events described.[15] Smith, then, like other critics of Graham's works, had great difficulty in classifying them, but was conscious of what might be called a practised emotional detachment, as if the author was above and unmoved by the often violent or tragic scenes he had witnessed and was now describing, the stance of a superior and heroic witness. One critic wrote:

> Sketches, stories, studies, or what do you call them? Is Mr. Graham a novelist or an essayist; is he bent on picturesque reminiscence or on preaching? In truth we do not know, and do not believe Mr. Graham knows either.[16]

Wendell Harris acknowledged, 'The difficulty of knowing precisely what to call these brief pieces of prose is a reflection of Graham's uncertain appeal as a writer.'[17] Harris concluded that his perseverance in this chosen form was Quixotic; indeed, apart from his histories and travelogues, and a very few notable exceptions, Graham persevered in this form throughout his writing career, and seemed incapable of developing, or had no desire to develop further, despite encouragement from his great supporters Conrad and Garnett to do so.

Watts believed that in his young adulthood Graham had been influenced by the 'chronicler of frontier life', the popular American author, Bret Harte (1836–1902), whose Western tales, according to Watts, had been told with 'vernacular gusto and boldness, captured the democratic imagination by their combination of humour, realism, and sentimental pathos'.[18] Watts quoted from a letter from Graham to his mother in which he wrote, 'Decidedly it is reserved for me to be the Bret Harte of the South, but in Spanish or English.'[19] He was certainly an admirer of Harte, and his support for the Native American peoples, writing in 1891:

> I had hoped that the *matchless pen* of Bret Harte would have raised a protest against the doings in Dakota; if the protest had been made it would have run through the American press like wildfire, and surely must have produced some good.[20]

There were similarities in the writings of both men, particularly of course in Graham's South American work. Both had an eloquent writing style, and both dealt with life in primitive, and often hostile 'frontier' environments, where human life was arbitrary. Both used the short story length, and both employed 'the authorial silent finish'.[21] Unlike Graham, however, Harte was a storyteller, using the minimum of description. In its place, he employed the locations and character names to communicate the roughness, exoticism, and imminent danger of his settings, relying on his readers' already established knowledge of popular 'cowboy' literature. Graham, however, whose South American and North African names and cultures were more diverse, and far less well known, despite his economy in the handling of detail, had to rely more heavily on description. This, combined with his desire to recapture his experiences, may simply account for the impressionistic nature of his works, where the setting, by necessity, took inordinate precedence over the action.

It is safe to assume that Graham's anti-imperialist works had little or no effect on British public opinion; as Gregory Claeys wrote of the critics of empire, 'naysayers and doom-mongers were rudely brushed aside'.[22] Moreover, in another example of the fortuitous unintended consequences that occurred throughout his life, these works had a long-term effect on his literary career. Graham's impressions of the funeral of William Morris, for the *Saturday Review*,[23] had been read and retained by up-and-coming publisher's reader and editor at T. Fisher Unwin, Edward Garnett, mentioned above. Garnett, another imperial sceptic, was planning a series of books entitled the Overseas Library, which aimed at presenting a true picture of imperial expansion, and the challenges and thoughts of those involved, stating, '"The Overseas Library" makes no pretence at imperial drum-beating, or putting English before Colonial opinion. It aims instead at getting the atmosphere and outlook of the new peoples recorded, if such is possible.'[24] Garnett had also been impressed by Graham's anti-imperialist pieces, and wrote to him through Conrad (whom Graham had first befriended in 1897), 'I read your Sketches as they appeared in the *Saturday Review* and very much taken with them – the paper on Morris's funeral appearing to me the best thing of its kind I have met with.' This was the beginning of a friendship and collaboration that would span almost four decades, with Garnett constantly commenting on Graham's work, and offering advice.

Garnett had complimented Graham on his erotically charged sketch *Aurora La Cujini*,[25] to which Graham replied that it was 'an impression, nothing more, but that is all I can do'.[26] Nevertheless, Garnett persevered over several years, by a mixture of blandishments and gentle criticism, encouraging him to extend himself by becoming more emotionally expressive, and to develop his plots and characterisation into full-blown stories: 'I want you to think over what there is in yourself and life which you have shrunk from writing.'[27] It appears, however, that Graham lacked the confidence to push these boundaries, responding, 'Now you must understand that I am a man of action and have passed most of my life out of doors. I am really *pas de blanque*, extremely diffident in all I write.'[28] As Helen Smith wrote:

> Once again, what Garnett perceived a flaw was the result of a deeply personal and subjective element in Graham's writing; the 'man of action, the disdainful witness' gains the upper hand over the artist, despite his attempts to persuade Graham that it '[is] the artist that is the most important now.'[29]

Smith also perceived that both Graham and Garnett were similar in many ways, cosmopolitan and irreverent, and that they 'also shared a sardonic wit, coupled with a strong streak of melancholy, a fierce strain of anti-imperialism, and a love of the underdog'. She recognised too a 'mutual feeling of displacement',[30] similar perhaps to Watts and Davies's description: 'Cunninghame Graham observed Britain as a detached but easily-angered stranger might have done.'[31] Garnett also noted a lack of subtlety in Graham's work, in one instance, commenting on Graham's 'Evolution of A Village', he wrote, 'I think your account would be more likely to *live* if it had a little more wrist play and a little less battering blows; if its tone were quieter, more ironical, even congratulatory it would be more dangerous.'[32] Graham, it seems, certainly at this early stage of his writing career (pre-1900), remained first and foremost a polemicist, where the style, and even the subject, remained secondary to the broadly political message.

Notes

1. Leslie Chaundy, *A Bibliography of the First Editions of the Works of R. B. Cunninghame Graham* (London: Dulan, 1924), p. 3.
2. Cunninghame Graham, letter to Edward Garnett, 6 August 1898 (MS: University of Texas). Quoted in Helen Smith, *The Uncommon Reader: A Life of Edward Garnett* (New York: Farrar, Straus and Giroux, 2017), p. 107.
3. Cunninghame Graham, *His People* (London: Duckworth, 1906), p. ix. He expressed very similar sentiments in *Faith* (1909), pp. xi–xii.
4. In an attempt to differentiate between the short story and the sketch, George Scott Moncrieff wrote that there was never a satisfactory distinction, 'mainly depending on the individual's requirement for a plot'. George Scott Moncrieff, 'Cunninghame Graham and a Contemporary Critic', *Outlook & The Modern Scot*, May 1936, p. 27.
5. Infrequent literary essays placed between reviews and news items. Watts describes them as 'stories, essays reminiscences and descriptive pieces – particularly if, during this heyday of European imperialism, they dealt with remote and exotic regions'. Watts, *R. B. Cunninghame Graham*, p. 32.

A contemporary reviewer described Britain's fascination with travel: 'The spirit of vagabondage possesses the nation. Call it what you will, *Reiselust*, or go-fever, we are most of us subject to this malady.' *Outlook*, 6 May 1899, p. 455.

6. A reference borrowed from G. K. Chesterton's *Autobiography* (London: Hutchinson, 1936), p. 269.

7. Christopher GoGwilt, 'Broadcasting News from Nowhere: R. B. Cunninghame Graham and the Geography of Politics in the 1890s', in *High and Low: Moderns Literature and Culture 1889–1939*, ed. by Maria DiBattista and Lucy McDiarmid (Oxford University Press, 1996), p. 239.

8. Cunninghame Graham, 'A Jesuit', *Saturday Review*, 3 August 1895, pp. 135–6. Anthologised in *Father Archangel of Scotland* (1896), pp. 103–14.

9. Watts related that the story was based on Graham's own recollections of a steamboat journey in 1872. Watts, *R. B. Cunninghame Graham*, p. 43.

10. Gregory Smith perceived this as a common trait in Scottish literature, and described it as the 'Scots' zest for handling a multitude of details rather than seeking broad effects by suggestion is very persistent', and 'the tedious arithmetic of the Scottish mind'. G. Gregory Smith, *Scottish Literature* (London: Macmillan), p. 5, p. 19.

11. Watts, *R. B. Cunninghame Graham*, p. 50.

12. Watts, *Joseph Conrad's Letters*, p. 30.

13. Cunninghame Graham, Preface to *Brought Forward* (London: Duckworth, 1916), p. x.

14. James Steel Smith, 'R. B. Cunningham Graham as a Writer of Short Fiction', *English Literature in Transition*, Vol. XII, No. 2, 1969, pp. 61–2.

15. Ibid.

16. *Outlook*, 6 October 1900, p. 313.

17. Wendell V. Harris, 'R. B. Cunninghame Graham', pp. 221–4.

18. Watts, *R. B. Cunninghame Graham*, pp. 30–1.

19. Ibid. From 1880 to 1885, Harte had been the United States Consul in Glasgow.

20. Cunninghame Graham, 'The Redskin Problem: "But 'Twas a Famous Victory,"' *Daily Graphic*, 5 January 1891, p. 6. My italics.

21. Watts and Davies, *Cunninghame Graham*, p. 157. Neil Munro wrote of this device, 'I have learned to look for these conclusions in the minor key with expectancy', *The On-Looker*, p. 304.

22. Gregory Claeys, *Imperial Sceptics: British Critics of Empire, 1850–1920* (Cambridge University Press, 2010), p. 3. Claeys described the rather chequered response of British socialists towards the empire. Like Graham, some regarded it as an evil imposition, some saw it as a distraction from conditions at home, while others saw it as a democratic and liberating force. Claeys, p. 125. Claeys incorrectly confined Graham in the second category, as one who only lamented its deleterious effects at home.

23. Cunninghame Graham, 'With the North-West Wind', *Saturday Review*, 10 October 1896, p. 389. Anthologised in *The Ipané* (1899), pp. 156–64.

24. Edward Garnett, 'The Prospectus for the Overseas Library', reprinted in John Gaggin, *Among the Man-Eaters*, Vol. 8 (London: Unwin, 1900), no page number.

25. Cunninghame Graham, *Aurora La Cujini: A Realistic Sketch in Seville* (London: Leonard Smithers, 1898). Anthologised in *Charity* (1912), pp. 146–62. Rothenstein claimed that Graham's inspiration came from a print of a Spanish dancer with that name that they had seen in a shop window in Madrid. Rothenstein, *Men and Memories*, p. 224.

26. Cunninghame Graham, letter to Garnett, 27 August 1898. Quoted in Laurence Davies, 'R. B. Cunninghame Graham and the Concept of Impressionism', DPhil, University of Sussex, 1972, p. 64. Watts suggested that Graham's 'impressionism' was a deliberate decision to fit in with current artistic trends (Watts, *R. B. Cunninghame Graham*, pp. 57–8), but this statement belies that. Also, Graham persisted in his impressionistic style until his death in 1936, long after Impressionism was no longer in vogue.

27. Edward Garnett, letter to Graham, 28 December 1905. Cunninghame Graham Papers, NLS. Acc.11335/71.

28. Quoted by Taylor, *The People's Laird*, p. 276.

29. Helen Smith, *The Uncommon Reader*, p. 107.

30. Ibid., pp. 104–5.

31. Watts and Davies, *Cunninghame Graham*, p. 35.

32. Garnett, letter to Graham, 30 June 1898. Cunninghame Graham Papers.

12

Colonialism: Misdirected Labours

THE BULK OF GRAHAM'S most outspoken anti-imperial works were focused around 1895–6, where, apart from 'Fraudesia Magna', they were confined to small circulation periodicals, a pamphlet, and a provincial newspaper known for its radical opinions, where they would have been little read, and had no discernible influence other than to attract Garnett to him. There was, however, a more subtle but related canon of work that found a wider readership, sketches set in exotic locations, which gave him more scope to develop his impressionistic skills, and which were a more consistent conduit for his views on the lasting impact of imperialism's economic and cultural impositions.

Graham had been struggling with a history of the gauchos since 1894, when his friend, the naturalist and author, W. H. Hudson, encouraged him to write about his own experiences in South America in the form of vignettes, following the model of *La Pampa* (1890), by the French author, Alfred Ébélot:[1]

> If you could get up a book containing mainly your own impressions of Gaucho life and character, on the lines of the French work 'La Pampa,' and well illustrated (like that work), it would, I think, stand a better chance of success than a historical book.[2]

It appears that it was from Ébélot that Graham, at least at the beginning, derived his inspiration. He did indeed use his own memories as a means of celebration, of documentation, but, more often, like Ébélot's work, they were a means of communicating loss. If his anti-imperialist polemics dealt with the moral questions of conquest and annexation, these pieces would mourn the consequences of colonisation, and the advance of 'civilisation' and 'progress', and the subsequent passing of uniqueness, of customs, of whole populations, as well as the loss of habitat. An excellent example of this was his early sketch 'Un Angelito' (1899),[3] which described the gaucho custom of displaying the corpses of recently deceased infants:

> An 'Angelito' stored in a cool, dark room to keep him from the flies, and then brought out at night to grace a sort of Agapemone,[4] shows past and present linked together in a way that argues wonders, when they both make way for that unfathomable future, the fitting paradise for the unimaginative . . . one thing I know, that in the Pampa of Buenos Ayres it and all other customs of a like kind are doomed to disappear.

Jennifer Hayward wrote, 'Ultimately, the dead child becomes the absent centre of the story, standing in for the larger cultural loss that was taking place – unmourned and almost unnoticed – all around it.'[5] Graham was quite specific about what was responsible for this loss:

> A cultivated prairie cut into squares, riddled with railings and with the very sky shaped into patterns by the crossing lines of telegraphs, may be an evidence, for all I know, of progress; but of all that makes a Pampa what the Indians imagined it when they gave the plains the name – for Pampa in the Indian tongue signifies the 'space' – no traces will be left.[6]

Graham's great-niece, Jean, described his encounter with such an 'angelito' twenty years earlier, in 1876,[7] and it became increasingly apparent that he was drawing almost exclusively on his own experiences to illustrate these links between the past and the present that were being broken, the natural environment destroyed, and a rural society cast adrift from its physical and cultural roots. This was exactly the same situation, and economic and cultural consequences, that he had so vehemently attacked in the context of Scotland. Hayward believed that Graham was:

> to some extent an 'outsider', simultaneously within and outside imperial networks of power. His unique sensibility as a border-crossing Scot, strengthened by the cultural awareness he developed while travelling in South America, gave him an unusual perspective on the countries he visited.[8]

The subjugation of these populations, leading to the exclusivity of land ownership, became in some form or another his major preoccupation when dealing with natural and traditional habitats, or addressing racism and ethnic cleansing, or unconscious despoilment.

On this latter topic, Graham's first descriptive sketch, set in such an environment, had been 'In the Tarumensian Woods' (see *passim*), which was a confused and confusing piece, because it tried to combine two of his major themes of this period, 'religious enterprises pursued under disadvantageous circumstances',[9] and civilisation's baleful effects on native populations. Claiming to have been transcribed from an old manuscript, it began as a defence of the Jesuits and their selfless work among the

Guarani Indians in the eighteenth century. In this, Graham related a tale of a priest who brought three members of a native family into his township. They were soon afflicted by lethargy and pains, and one by one they wasted away and died. After praising the piety and sacrifice of this priest, he also called him 'muddlehead', and suggested that the baptisms he had carried out had resulted in death. The priest, however, believed that the deaths were due 'to the exceeding compassion of the Almighty', and Graham concluded that 'the Jesuits did much good, mixed with some folly, as is incidental to mankind'.[10] Consequently, this respect slowly disappeared, and we might contrast it with an uncompromising stance towards similar good works, written ten years later:

> Who does not feel as if a slug was crawling on his soul on reading in some missionary report of all their misdirected labours and their sufferings, and of the perils that they have endured, to turn some fine free race of savages . . . into bad copies of our lowest class, waddling about in ill-made clothes and claiming kindred with us as brother 'Klistians' in the Lord?[11]

This unconscious impact on native populations, due to arrogance and naivety, would become a constant theme in Graham's works.

Muggeridge believed that Graham admired the fearless and sensual in mankind, but 'Since they were not so, he had to comfort himself with dreams, and self-dramatisation, and heroic episodes'.[12] They were, however, undoubtedly also an attempt to share his experiences of unique landscapes and cultures with his readers. But, as the one who is sharing these experiences, describing exotic, lawless, and often dangerous locations, he was incidentally presenting himself as hero, or at least a witness, a role that can be heroic in its own right. Indeed, Shaw may have been slyly referring to this when he wrote, 'Cunninghame Graham is the hero of his own book.'[13] Thus, as discussed earlier, Graham the aesthete was slowly turning himself into a *frondeur*–dandy–adventurer–*literateur*. Watts wrote that Graham was 'mythogenic, he attracted and helped to generate myths about himself',[14] which should include his supposed capture by Indians and his capture by revolutionaries and being forced to fight on their side, neither of which was ever substantiated; his supposed time teaching fencing in Madrid,[15] and his wife Gabrielle's fabricated background. Tschiffely's assertion that he had been appointed a colonel in the British Army during the First World War was also inaccurate. In Pritchett's critique of Tschiffely's biography of Graham, he wrote:

> Spaniards understood him more truly. They were, those who knew him, inclined to soft pedal his Spanish grandmother; at the *gaucho* they raised their eyebrows a little; for them he was pure mad Scot and there is no doubt, I think that they were right.[16]

Not only were some things exaggerated, inconvenient facts that did not fit the legend also disappeared. This at first seems at odds with his desire to stay in the background as a politician, but it is self-romanticisation rather than self-aggrandisement. Graham's temperament was more suited to playing *el gran señor*, the speech-maker, the controversialist, the distant aesthete, the shepherd, content to lead his flock from behind.

Since his attacks and satires on British imperial attitudes were predicated on the commonly held acceptance of the right to conquest and colonisation, Graham next turned his attention to the exploiters and colonisers, but it was not until February 1898 that two significant sketch-tales appeared, dealing with two very different types of men. The first was another erotically charged sketch-tale entitled 'Bristol Fashion' after the words of a sea captain named 'Honest Tom Bilson', who plied his trading vessel along this Moroccan coast, 'a strange hell-broth of geography, ethnicity, flora and fauna'. Part I was a colourful evocation of this exotic world, of the unscrupulous practices of the captain, and of his treatment of his 'niggers', and it seems that we are in the territory, first of Herman Melville, or the nautical word-pictures of William Clark Russell. A contemporary reviewer wrote that it was a story 'which Mr. Conrad might have been proud to sign'.[17]

Bilson displayed in microcosm all that Graham despised about imperial commerce; he was one of thousands nibbling on the edges of empire, there to unscrupulously exploit the natives and imperial leftovers as quickly as possible. Bilson in Graham's eyes was simply common clay, incapable of any higher aspiration other than his own selfish needs; his 'anti-rational primitivism' was his defining characteristic:

> Men's minds are built in reason-tight compartments, and what they do but little influences them. Honest Tom Bilson cared not for speculations, but acted in a manner he called practical, that is, he tried to square his conscience with his life, except when personal interest, hate, love, and other human passion intervened.[18]

Thus, when he recaptured his escaped black 'Krooboys', he promptly sold them to cannibals, and when he was back in England, retired to church-going respectability, he regularly boasted about it. Again, Graham's great-niece, Jean, claimed that this tale was drawn from his own experience of a sea voyage in 1875, captained by the New Englander, Bilson,[19] showing again that he was, in most of his writings, using material from his past.

It should be noted that throughout these and other sketch-tales, along with an uncompromising directness of expression, there was also a strong thread of sardonic black humour, which threw the often grisly nature of his depictions into sharp relief. An early reviewer in *The Spectator* noted, 'Mr Cunninghame Graham is as plain in his language as he is independent in his opinions, and his readers who object to a spade being called a spade had better look elsewhere for their entertainment.'[20] In a letter to Graham about Graham's tale *Snaekoll's Saga*, in which he inferred that his Icelandic hero was eaten by his own horse, Conrad wrote, 'As to the Saga it confirms me in my conviction that you have a fiendish gift for showing the futility – the ghastly, jocular futility of life.'[21]

Graham's next piece in this anti-colonial group was a tale entitled *Higginson's Dream*, which concerned a trader who was similar to the sympathetic Jesuit, one who empathised with and befriended the natives, but to Graham, the influence of men like this was even more insidious and dangerous than that of transients like Bilson. Like the missionary in *In the Tarumensian Woods*, despite his altruism, Higginson's very presence and influence exerted baleful effects on the indigenous population, 'the strange anæmia which comes to wild peoples by the mere presence of a white man in their midst . . . the "modorra"[22] [which] exterminates the people whom he came to benefit'.[23] This peculiar malady was more fully explained in a letter to the *Saturday Review* in 1903, where Graham described how, during the Spanish conquest of the Canary Islands, natives simply sat down by the roadside and died. 'What caused it, probably was the mysterious influence induced by the presence of the whites. Usually, gin and rum . . . with small-pox, aid the civilizing rifle bullet.'[24] There is no evidence that Graham met a Higginson, but he became a means by which his apparent fascination with this mysterious wasting affliction and the baleful effects of civilisation could be communicated.[25]

Graham was by no means the first or only writer to deny the idea of progress in native societies. There were many precedents, including Herman Melville. In *Typee* (1846), Melville's most widely read novel up until the late 1930s, based partly on his own experiences, he regretted European penetration of the South Seas, particularly, like Graham, by those of a low moral character:

> Alas for the poor savages when exposed to the influence of these polluting examples! Unsophisticated and confiding, they are easily led into every vice, and humanity weeps over the ruin thus remorselessly inflicted upon them by their European civilizers. Thrice happy are they who, inhabiting yet undiscovered island in the midst of the ocean, have never been brought into contaminating contact with the white man.[26]

Living in the South Seas, another far-travelled Scot, and near contemporary, Robert Louis Stevenson, had also recognised, in the words of Professor Barry Menikoff, 'the irrevocable advance of European whites

throughout the Pacific, and the consequent decline of Polynesian culture'.[27] Later, Graham's great friend, Conrad, produced perhaps the finest examples of the genre, in his short story 'An Outpost of Progress'
(1897), and his novella *Heart of Darkness* (1899).

Many of Graham's reminiscences of life in South America, especially
among the lawless gauchos, were purely nostalgic, filled with images of
rough-hewn men living in un-hewn environments, where luxuries and
manners were few, and life was spontaneous, not a little dangerous,
and brief.[28] Even though some of his characters were not indigenous in
the true sense of the word, and may have been exploiters and abusers
in their own right, they were indigenous *then*. They were indigenous in
Graham's memories, a motley collection of pioneers and survivors, who,
unconsciously, had created a new aesthetic. They had a sort of riotous
harmony, one that contained a strong measure of mutuality, both of
which he was only too aware would be destroyed by the self-interest of
modern society. This ugliness and constriction were the fault of greedy
land-grabbers, and by what Augustine Friedl called 'lagging emulation',
peasant imitation of city fashions.[29] Graham opposed both physical
invasion and the stealthy imposition of cultural imperialism, and was
engaged, both politically and in his reflective writings, not just in reminiscence, but in what Michael Herzfeld called:

> *structural nostalgia*, the longing for an age before the state, for the primordial
> and self-regulating birthright . . . that citizens can turn against the authority
> of the state itself, along with all the other similarly vulnerable symbols of
> official fixity.[30]

In these words, which are redolent of Graham's attraction to anarchism,
we can unite his earlier political campaigns in Britain, particularly on
land ownership, poverty, social inequality, and a desire for Scottish home
rule or independence, for Herzfeld asserted that '[n]ostalgia for original
perfection is common to much nationalist historiography, as it is to religious narrative. Both explain the compromising of purity . . . in terms of
the corrosion of time.'[31]

The key issues in this structural nostalgia, according to Herzfeld, were,
what he referred to as (1) 'replicability in every succeeding generation',
of kindness, generosity, and hospitality, which each cohort reproduces
a few years or decades later, and (2), the converse, 'damaged reciprocity: the virtue that has allegedly decayed always entails some method of
mutuality, a mutuality that has been, perhaps irreversibly ruptured by the
self interest of modern times', losing its pristine perfection and in danger of disappearing altogether.[32] This is perhaps an accurate description
of Graham's deepest concerns (in both South America and Scotland),

reflected in his next meditation, which appeared in the anthology *A Vanishing Race*, where he opened with words that probably encapsulate a large part of his motivation: 'A melancholy interest attaches to anything about to go for ever. Especially so to a people who with their customs, superstitions, and mode of life, are doomed'.[33] This concerned the disappearance of the gauchos, as Graham knew them, 'still savage enough to know by a footprint if the horse that passed an hour ago was mounted or running loose. A strange compound of Indian and Spaniard, of ferocity and childishness, *a link between ourselves and the past.*'[34] It was these linkages that would increasingly dominate his work, particularly when he turned his attention to Scotland.

The new urban, constricted, regulated culture would replace the old gaucho way of life, but that, in its turn, had replaced an earlier, more natural form of existence: 'As the gaucho replaced the Indian, the European colonist will replace him, one more type will have faded from the world, one more step will have been made to universal ugliness.'[35] Now it seemed that a crisis point had been reached, for what Graham had experienced and remembered (idealised, perhaps), despite its being superimposed, had a unique quality of freedom and spontaneity of its own, which would vanish, never to return: a situation that he had already witnessed in Scotland. The cause was urbanisation and commerce: 'Commerce, that vivifying force, that bond of union between all the basest instincts of the basest of mankind, that touch of lower human nature which makes all the lowest natures of mankind akin.'[36] Graham died during a visit to Argentina, and in an obituary published there, the writer and diplomat Emilio Lascano Tegui wrote that he probably 'died of disillusionment when he saw the results of the new, improved, "civilised" country, with its railways, telegraph wires, tall buildings, etc., a country despoiled, its innocence and purity gone forever'.[37]

Notes

1. Alfred Ébélot (1837–1912). 'Ébélot who wrote of the rapid transformation of the Argentine gives these pages a melancholy interest and a sort of historical value'. *La Pampa: Mœurs Sud-Américaines* (Paris: Zulma, 1992), p. 20. Ébélot's book also contained a tale entitled *La Pulperia*, a title that Graham used in a similar sketch in the *Saturday Review*, 22 October 1898, pp. 529–30. Anthologised in *Thirteen Stories* (1900), pp. 163–75. In 1992, Sandra and Glenn Erikson repeated an accusation made by Frederick H. Garcia of 'blatant plagiarism' in Graham's *A Brazilian Mystic* (New York: Dodd, Mead, 1920), of Euclides da Cunha's 1902 book *Os Sertões* ('The Backlands'). Sandra S. Fernandes Erickson and Glenn W. Erickson, 'Cunninghame Graham's Plagiarism of da Cunha's *Os Sertões*, and Its Role

in Vargas Llosa's *La Guerra del Fin del Mundo*', *Luso-Brazilian Review*, Vol. 29, No. 2, 1992, pp. 67–8.

2. Curle, letter from Hudson to Graham, 17 April 1894. It appears, however, that it was in fact Graham who first mentioned 'a French book' to Hudson, and Hudson replied in a letter dated 10 March 1894 stating that he had not read it. None of Graham's letters to Hudson have survived.

3. Cunninghame Graham, 'Un Angelito', anthologised in *The Ipané* (1899), pp. 36–46.

4. Greek = Abode of love.

5. Jennifer Hayward, 'R. B. Cunninghame Graham and the Argentinian Angelito', in *Empires and Revolutions: Cunninghame Graham and His Contemporaries*, ed. by Carla Sassi and Silke Stroh (Scottish Literature International, 2017), p. 99. Hayward also pointed out the strong similarities between this sketch and Ébélot's 'El Velorio' ('The Wake'), published in 1890, p. 102.

6. Cunninghame Graham, 'Un Angelito', p. 45.

7. Jean Cunninghame Graham, *Gaucho Laird*, p. 158.

8. Hayward, 'R. B. Cunninghame Graham and the Argentinian Angelito', p. 102.

9. Cunninghame Graham, 'Father Archangel of Scotland', *Nineteenth Century*, October 1893, p. 385. Anthologised in *Father Archangel of Scotland* (1896), pp. 1–42.

10. Cunninghame Graham, 'In the Tarumensian Woods', p. 252.

11. Cunninghame Graham, *Progress and Other Sketches* (London: Duckworth, 1905), p. 4.

12. Muggeridge, 'Cunninghame Graham', p. 440.

13. George Bernard Shaw, 'Notes to *Captain Brassbound's Conversion*: Sources of the Play', in *Three Plays for Puritans* (1901) (London: Penguin, 2000), p. 341. In his autobiography, the painter 'Will' Rothenstein described his first meeting with Graham at a performance of Shaw's *Arms and the Man* in 1894. Graham's mother, who had been sitting nearby, introduced him to Graham at the interval with the words 'my son is a great friend of Mr Shaw'. Rothenstein, *Men and Memories*, pp. 179–80.

14. Cedric Watts, 'R. B. Cunninghame Graham: Janiform Genius', in *Empires and Revolutions: Cunninghame Graham & His Contemporaries* (Glasgow: Scottish Literature International, 2017), p. 12n18. (See Appendix VII.)

15. Watts and Davies, *Cunninghame Graham*, pp. 33–5.

16. Pritchett, 'New Literature', p. 340.

17. *The Academy*, 28 May 1898, p. 580.

18. Cunninghame Graham, 'Bristol Fashion', *Saturday Review*, 5 February 1898, pp. 431–2. Anthologised in *The Ipané* (1899), pp. 84–98.

19. Jean Cunninghame Graham, *Gaucho Laird*, pp. 139–43.

20. 'Current Literature', *The Spectator*, 24 June 1899, p. 887.

21. Conrad, letter to Graham, dated 7 January 1898. Watts, *Joseph Conrad's Letters*, p. 59.

22. Spanish = Torpor.

23. Cunninghame Graham, 'Higginson's Dream', *Saturday Review*, 1 October 1898, p. 431. Anthologised in *Thirteen Stories* (1900), pp. 177–87.

24. 'La Modorra De Uganda', Cunninghame Graham, letter to the *Saturday Review*, 3 January 1903, p. 15.

25. Bilson and Higginson were two sides of the same imperial coin, and were perhaps also typical of two types that Graham encountered in his political life. One, an *Untermensch*, only concerned with self, the other, a do-gooding fool, who believed that he was part of the solution, when in fact, he was the source of the malady.

26. Herman Melville, *Typee* (1846) (Ware: Wordsworth Classics, 1994), p. 12.

27. Barry Menikoff, *Robert Louis Stevenson and The Beach of Falesá* (Edinburgh University Press, 1984), pp. 3–4. Linda Dryden argued that 'Stevenson should be regarded as an imperial sceptic whose fictions prepared the way for the bleak vision of empire that Conrad espoused'. Linda Dryden, 'Literary Affinities and the Postcolonial in Robert Louis Stevenson and Joseph Conrad', in *Scottish Literature and Postcolonial Literature: Comparative Texts and Critical Perspectives*, ed. by Michael Gardiner and Graeme Macdonald (Edinburgh: Napier University, 2012), p. 88. Graham was an admirer of Stevenson's writings, and he left his collection of Stevenson's complete works to Gartmore Village Library in his will. *Scotsman*, 21 April 1936, p. 11.

28. This is particularly well realised in his sketch 'Un Pelado', *Saturday Review*, 15 May 1897, pp. 535–7. Anthologised in *The Ipané* (1899), pp. 26–35, it concerned the hanging of a Mexican, and 'La Pulperia', the evocation of a wild trading post (see *passim*).

29. Augustine Friedl, 'Lagging Emulation in Post-Peasant Society', *American Anthropologist*, June 1965, pp. 569–86. We might assume that 'fashions' also include social and cultural attitudes.

30. Michael Herzfeld, *Cultural Intimacy: Social Poetics and the Real Life of States, Societies, and Institutions* (London: Routledge, 2016), p. 28.

31. Ibid.

32. Ibid., p. 141.

33. Cunninghame Graham, 'A Vanishing Race', in *Father Archangel of Scotland*, p. 166.

34. Ibid., pp. 166–7. My italics.

35. Ibid.

36. Cunninghame Graham, 'Calvary', *Justice*, 1 May 1899, p. 5. Anthologised in *Thirteen Stories* (1900), pp. 188–99.

37. Vizconde de Lascano Tegui, 'Don Cunninghame Graham', *Nosotros*, 1 May 1936, p. 125 (translated from Spanish). Faulkner West wrote that W. H. Hudson 'never wished to return, for he knew the illusions that memory [he] created in *Far Away And Long Ago* would go crashing like a house of cards'. Faulkner West, *Cunninghame Graham*, p. 50.

13

Scotland: The Familiar Kail-yard

From its inception in May 1886, the SHRA had emphasised the comparative legislative neglect of Scotland. After its initial popularity, however, it went into decline, particularly after the death of John Stuart Blackie in 1895, and a resurgence of British 'national' sentiments, including the Conservative victory at the 'khaki election' of 1900. By 1902, the SHRA had, in Waddie's words, 'entered into a state of suspended animation'[1] due to Boer War jingoism. Nevertheless, between 1890 and 1914, measures proposing Scottish home rule were put forward no fewer than thirteen times in the House of Commons and were accepted in principle on eight occasions, yet none of the Bills succeeded in reaching Committee stage. According to Vernon Bogdanor this reflected the low priority attached to home rule even among parliamentarians sympathetic to the cause, and the appearance of Home Rule Bills was often part of a 'ritual gesture' by Labour and Liberal MPs.[2]

Out of the House of Commons, and to an extent, mainstream politics, during this period, Graham wrote nothing about Ireland except obliquely in an article entitled 'An Tighearna: A Memory of Parnell',[3] and nothing about the political situation in Scotland. His interest in Scottish home rule had mostly been pragmatic,[4] a means by which legislation, particularly on labour matters and social change, could be more speedily implemented; Scottish and Irish home rule could be a means of undermining the ossified power structures he had hopelessly attacked as an MP. It is also likely that he saw home rule as a means by which the empire could be eroded from within, expressed in a letter to the *Saturday Review*:

> Bulgaria, Roumania, Servia, Norway, have all seceded from Greater powers within the memory of man. Finland and Hungary, Poland and Ireland, with Bohemia and Macedonia, all mortally detest their union with great oppressive States. Nothing but force keeps any one of them a portion of the great empires to which respectively they all belong . . . the whole trend of modern

thought and economics is towards the evolution of small states, and every great unwieldy Power, our own included, is on the verge of a break-up and a return to its component parts.[5]

With Scotland in a state of national and cultural stasis, Graham began to display through his writings what might be described as 'reflective frustration', mixing anger with nostalgic reminiscence.

Having experimented with, and no doubt gained confidence from recording his South American experiences, it might have been assumed that Graham could have easily transferred these developing literary skills and his methodology to Scotland, but it would not be a simple transition. Although the heroic virtues of the Pampas were quickly disappearing, its dramatic incidents were still relatively fresh in his mind, which he could record, to demonstrate the vibrancy of the untamed. Scotland in contrast was an old country whose turbulent history and dramatic incidents were now in the distant past, that survived only in history books, folk memories and local traditions. Graham mourned the passing of the spontaneous life he had known in South America, but the life he had known in Scotland, and was witnessing again, was of an entirely different nature: domesticated, unheroic, often squalid; and conjuring up romance or excitement would not be an option, unless it lay in a remembered or imagined past. He was thus obliged to rely purely on nostalgia, seeking out links and echoes among the population and the landscape, and he may have been motivated to add spice to his early Scottish works by introducing South American memories and reflections.[6]

In his 1982 introduction to his anthology of Graham's *Scottish Sketches*, Graham's foremost 'eager champion' at the time, Professor John Walker, divided these infrequent writings into three periods. The first, around 1896–7, he described as 'bitter portrayals of the defects of the Scottish character somewhat in the naturalistic manner of George Douglas Brown's *The House with the Green Shutters* (1901)'.[7] The next two decades up to 1916 saw the bulk of Graham's Scottish works, in which Walker believed that he had settled into a more realistic portrayal of people and places, character types, customs, and events. In the third, near the end of his writing career, he believed that Graham was drawn into a dream world of mythology and sentimentality.[8] Walker, however, had chosen the sketches from Graham's own anthologies that were published during his lifetime, which Graham and his editor, Garnett, had selected and edited from articles, most of which had previously appeared in literary magazines. In many cases, these anthologies were published some time after the articles originally appeared, and Walker further distanced them by arranging them into themes, for example, 'Landscapes and Places', 'The Scottish Character', and 'The Scots Abroad', and so their essential historical and political chronology was often lost.

Walker's first and most distinctive group contained only three bitter portrayals, 'A Survival' (1896), 'Salvagia' (1896), and 'Heather Jock' (1897). Surprisingly, Walker failed to discern, or point out, that Graham had been quite explicit in each, that his motivations were revolts against, and subversions of, the popular literary genre of the time, the writings of 'The Kailyard School'. Thomas Knowles described this 'school' as 'characterised by the sentimental treatment of parochial Scottish scenes, often centred on the church community'.[9] Power assessed them as appealing to 'the amiable, respectable, slightly cosy church folk',[10] in whom Andrew Nash perceived 'a tendency to evade social and industrial issues'.[11]

The genre had many critics over the years, and criticism ranging from Brown's description of 'the sentimental slop of [J. M.] Barrie, and [S. R.] Crockett',[12] to George Blake's description of Crockett's works as 'sentimental sludge',[13] and to Kailyard literature in general, which 'presented the English and American reader with a picture of a country as a sort of collection of picturesque rural parishes peopled by "pawky" and/or "nippy" characters'.[14] Harvie categorised the literature as social escapism,[15] and Gillian Shepherd assessed the Kailyard works as parables that perfectly suited the mood and taste of the times: '[I]t is not far-fetched to claim that they were in a sense dictated by their readers. They are the product not only of three individuals but also of an era.'[16] That era was defined by Richard Cook as:

> The end-of-the-century bourgeois anxieties about the excesses of urbanisation, over-population, and moral decay, as well as New Woman politics and liberal municipalization of social programmes. The consumption of Kailyard literature outside Scotland – In England and even more so in The United States and Canada – suggests that the popularity of these narratives responds to anxieties that extended beyond the realities of Scotland.[17]

Cook continued to describe a bourgeois nostalgia for stability and traditional class structures, 'parish rule, and the strict control of deviant citizenry in the face of increasing economic disparities between the discontented lower classes and the triumphant middle classes',[18] a summation of everything Graham despised.

The first serious critic of the genre had been the novelist and literary critic Margaret Oliphant, who, in 1889, after praising the works of Barrie and his use of the Scots language, expressed her consternation at:

> the host of little books which are finding their way to immense popularity in Scotland with very little claim upon the attention beyond that which this

dialect brings . . . it is because we have so true a reverence for the language which Sir Walter Scott used, which was the mother tongue of Jeanie Deans and Edie Ochiltree, handled with the finest reticence, yet spontaneity, by our master in fiction, not because it was Scotch, but because it was the natural medium of speech to which many of his finest creations were born – that we regard the springing up of this literature which may justly be called provincial with dismay.[19]

These words preceded mounting criticism of those writers considered inferior to Barrie, particularly 'Ian MacLaren' and Crockett, some five years later in the national newspapers. For example, the *Glasgow Herald*'s criticism of MacLaren's *Beside the Bonnie Briar Bush* in 1894,[20] was followed by criticisms of Crockett's 'overpraised book', *The Stickit Minister*, in 1895.[21] Between these two critiques was the first use of the word 'kailyard' by J. H. Millar is his 1895 article 'The Literature of the Kailyard', in W. E. Henley's *New Review*.[22] In this piece, Millar reserved some praise for Barrie with the proviso that 'his writings are eagerly devoured in England by people who, on the most charitable hypothesis, may possibly understand one word in three of his dialogue'.[23] Millar went on to savage the works of MacLaren and Crockett, with a particular focus on Crockett's prose style, 'this slough of knowing archness, of bottomless vulgarity'.[24] It was not until later in 1896 that the word 'kailyard' became, and continued to be, a disparaging term for the genre.[25]

It was in this year that Graham started his own brief campaign against what he saw as a debasement of Scottish language and culture,[26] and there were three inextricably connected strands to his objections. Initially, like those of Oliphant and Millar, it appeared that his main concern was purely linguistic, as expressed in the preface to his first anthology, *Father Archangel of Scotland* (1896), where he referred to 'that all sufficient cloak of *kailyard* Scotch spoken by no one under heaven, which of late has plagued us'.[27] This was repeated in the first of Graham's 'bitter portrayals', a polemical piece entitled 'A Survival', also from 1896, half of which is taken up by an attack on the genre:

> It is in vain to plead that all our greatest writers in the past have written in what they hoped was English. Hume, Smollett, Thomson, and Sir Walter Scott, with Dugald Stewart and Adam Smith, endeavour to make themselves intelligible in English. Be all that as it may, the fact remains that the modern Scottish writer to be popular in England, must write in a dialect his readers cannot understand.[28]

Graham's second objection was that he believed that the settings, characters, and language of this literature was having the unwitting effect of mocking the Scots through stereotyping, and making a travesty of an ancient kingdom in the eyes of others. Millar later described this as 'this holding up of their fellow-countrymen to the ridicule and contempt of all sane and judicious human beings',[29] and also stated, 'The "Kailyard" writers, after all, have touched a mere fringe of the population.'[30] Graham continued:

> The fact remains that the modern Scottish writer to be popular in England must write in dialect. If he must live (and write) he has, I presume, to adopt the ruling fashion and write of weavers, idiots, elders of churches, small farmer's wives . . . I verily believe there is not a henwife, weaver, idiot, elder, or ploughman that would recognise himself in the dress in which the British public has been eager to welcome him.[31]

In his essay 'R. B. Cunninghame Graham: The Kailyard and After', Davies did not focus on Graham's disdain for the debasement of the language, but more on his second objection – the stereotyping of the Scots, and the 'narrow definition of Scottishness' presented to English and other readers that ignored Scotland's rapidly expanding industry and commerce[32] as a distortion of reality. However, he failed to follow through on why this would be so crucially important to Graham. Implicit in Graham's second objection lay a third, one that was entirely consistent with his political outlook. For a man who had spent the previous ten years fighting for the underdog and the industrial poor, Graham's experiences had shown him a grimy, industrial, impoverished, violent side of Scotland that cried out for reform, even revolution. Engels, for example, wrote that the poor of Edinburgh and Glasgow were worse off than any other part of the kingdom, 'and that the poorest were not Irish, but Scottish'.[33] Meanwhile, Kailyard literature was depicting a picturesque and harmonious continuity, disguising life's harsh realities, and ameliorating calls for social change.[34]

Blake claimed that the Industrial Revolution had:

> Knocked the old Scotland sideways, with a violence in both the process and the consequences unexampled. A really dramatic, often beastly, revolution was taking place. And what had the Scottish novelists to say about it? The answer is – nothing, or as nearly nothing as makes no matter. They might as well have been living in Illyria as in the agonized country of their birth.[35]

Harvie explained this, and the incongruity and popularity of the Kailyard writings, in the context of a modern industrial Scotland:

> A society beset by terrifying social problems was *threatened* by realism . . . exacerbated by the deep seated evils of poverty and overcrowding generated by Scotland's pell-mell industrialisation. To expose these would be revolutionary; it would also break the discipline of puritanism by mentioning the unmentionable. The Kirk enforced silence out of conviction, the middle class

out of fear. The bogus community of the Kailyard was an alternative to the horror of the real thing.[36]

Any revolutionary opportunity to subvert the genre would have been attractive to Graham, and so, in his three 'bitter portrayals', he attempted to inject a squalid reality into Scottish life in a manner that Watts described as 'tactical'.[37] However, any depiction of poverty, deprivation, and overcrowding in Scotland's industrial towns would have required vivid description, which, from his position as a rich landowner, would have appeared crass and patronising.[38] Instead, he chose the more available option of deconstructing the cosy bucolic lifestyle in his own familiar 'kail-yard' of Menteith, by holding up his fellow-countrymen to potential ridicule, but in a radically different way to the Kailyard writers.

In 'A Survival', the bulk of which was diatribe, Graham attacked the way Scotland was now perceived. He did this by undermining the concept of the Protestant work ethic, and the perceived passivity and orderliness of Scottish rural life, by introducing the reader to a more ancient past that was still present, in the form of a semi-drunken Highland crofter 'who cared but little for hard work', imported by an idealistic local landlord (most likely Graham himself),[39] who, in a short space of time, had reduced his farm to squalor. There is an unmistakable joy in his attempted sabotage, by what Watts and Davies referred to as 'his nostalgia for the pre-civilised'.[40] Finally, surveying the ramshackle, Graham, pursuing another common theme from his past, saw 'a picture of the old-world Scotland, which has almost disappeared. Sloth was not altogether lovely, but prating progress worse.'[41] Graham obviously revelled in this echo from the past:

> What I object to is the assumption that the 'douce' and Presbyterian, 'pawky' three-per-centlings of the kailyard men has quite eclipsed the pre-Culloden type. I say it lingers in spite of Butcher Cumberland, in spite of School Boards, education, kodaks, bicycles, excursion trains, cheap knowledge, magazines and Liberal politics; it lingers if only to disprove Darwinism.[42]

All of his Scottish 'portraits' would focus on those whom he regarded as 'pre-Culloden' types, from whichever strata of society, people he believed were a remnant of bygone days, who were principled, heroic, and had not been seduced by bourgeois ideas.

Graham's most direct attack on Kailyard cosiness was, however, reserved for his next piece, 'Salvagia',[43] published four months later, where again he made his target clear:

> Our reverend novelists,[44] 'tis true, have found out much about us, previously quite unexpected by ourselves; but then their works are not for home consumption, but sell in England and America, where, I understand, they

touch the cords of the great National Heart, and loose the strings of the great National Pocket.[45]

After a splenetic opening paragraph ranting at the god of Providence, Graham takes us to a country described on old Italian maps as Salvagia, and the reader is lulled into thinking that they are again in an exotic location. But with 'blear-eyed, knock-kneed young men' and 'red-haired and freckled, cow-houghed maidens', it is apparent that we are back in Scotland, and in a village ('"Gart-na-cloich" I think the name') that was his thinly disguised home village of Gartmore, with its 'jawbox at the door and midden at the back'.[46] It is a bucolic setting, but one that is a direct challenge to cosiness, and a direct assault on Kailyard mannered sentimentality:

> In every house a picture of Dr. Chalmers[47] flanked by one of Bunyan, and a Bible ever ready on a table for advertisement, as when a minister or charitable lady calls, and the cry is heard of 'Jeanie, rax the Bible doon, and pit the whisky-bottle in the aumrie.'[48] Two churches and two public houses, and a feud between the congregations of each church as bitter as that between the clients of the rival taverns ... No trees, no flowers, no industry, except the one of keeping idiots sent from Glasgow. Much faith and little charity, the tongue of every man wagging against his neighbour like a bell-buoy on a shoal. At the street corner groups of men standing spitting. Expectoration is a national sport throughout Salvagia ... Throughout Salvagia 'Thank you' and 'If you please' are unknown. In railway trains we spit upon the floor and wipe our boots upon the cushions, just to show our independence; in cars and omnibuses take the best seats; driving the weaker to the wall like cattle in a pen. In the streets we push the women into the gutters.

Any piety and respectability are false, a hypocritical veneer, which many contemporary readers would have instantly recognised. This is a graceless, vulgar kail-yard, neither dystopian nor lapsarian, but a satirical attempt at exaggerated social realism, in a location that he was familiar with. It is a parody of a Kailyard setting, a stony place, full of stony people, sterile, unmerciful, a place of Holy Willies, where the residents show little or no emotion, and any gentler qualities are well concealed.

Sardonic wit is at the centre of this piece, moreover, as the sketch turns into the 'sketch-tale', something else emerges: a remarkable stoicism in the face of tragedy when a village woman loses her four sons in a multiple drowning, but echoing a more ancient past:

> Passing the village, I heard the Coronach, which lingers to show us how our savage ancestors wailed for their dead, and to remind us that the step which separates us from the other animals is short. I asked a woman for whom the cry was raised. She answered, 'For the four sons of Lilias Campbell.' In the

stupid way one asks a question in the face of any shock, I said, 'What did she say or do when they were brought home dead?' 'Say?' said the woman; 'nothing; n'er a word. She just gaed oot and milked the kye.'[49]

This work was a very deliberate counter-blast against what Graham believed was emasculating and debasing Scotland into the picturesque, but there was something else at work. G. K. Chesterton had observed in Robert Louis Stevenson's Scottish novels that Stevenson, like many Scots, was proud of the extremities of Scottish landscape, character, and history, which others might have found harsh and cruel:

> Indeed, stories of this kind are told by Stevenson with a deliberate darkening of the Scottish landscape and exultation in the ferocity of the Scottish creed. But it would be quite a mistake to miss in this a certain genuine national pride running through all the abnormal artistry; and a sense that the strength of the tribal tragedy testifies in a manner to the strength of the tribe.[50]

There was more of a hint of this in Graham's first published anthology:

> Why is it that the races of English and Scotch have never really amalgamated? So close, so like, both wizened by the same east wind tormented more or less by the same Sunday, and yet unlike. St. George for Merrie England. No one in his wildest fits of patriotism ever talked of Merrie Scotland.[51]

This sketch was meant to shock, or at least discomfit the reader, to inject a note of harsh reality, to deliberately de-romanticise Scottish rural life. What effect this had on readers cannot be known, but the dark satire in 'Salvagia' failed to register with the few critics who commented upon it.

Throughout his literary career, it was entirely natural for Graham to cross frontiers, alternating not only his individual sketches between South America, North Africa, and Scotland, but also within the sketch itself. His *Notes on The District of Menteith*, for example, contains an incongruous paragraph on a dead gaucho, while his introduction to John Morrison Davidson's *Scotland for the Scots: Scotland Revisited* (1902)[52] is mostly set in Argentina. So it was with the third and final sketch-tale of this set, entitled 'Heather Jock' (1897), a flowing, self-confident, humorous description of a local eccentric, set in both Scotland and Argentina[53] that immediately displaces us from any cosy Scottish setting, and is the type of work that Pritchett praised: 'it freshened [the 'fug'] for a while and let the foreign air in.'[54] With these words, we are looking at a unique part of Graham's Scottish heritage, when the shutters are opened to reveal a wider world.

'Heather Jock' was an extraordinary, lyrical potage, confidently stirred together with black humour. But any consistent reader would be aware that although the subject matter and locations changed, Graham's themes, or rather his preoccupations, did not, and that his creative faculty was limited. Also, his range and depth of philosophical insights, no matter how well expressed, were now becoming wearisome, and the startling, dislocating juxtapositions were beginning to pall. Cedric Watts said of this, 'He is an idiosyncratic writer, but idiosyncrasies become predictable.'[55] Garnett nevertheless believed that despite the discords and lack of inventiveness, there was a central unity of purpose and expression:

> Everyday, commonplace, exceptional, or vanishing human figures, the Gaucho on the plains, mistress Campbell in Gart-na-Cloich, Heather Jock, or the Bristol skipper, all remote from each other, all part of the great ridiculous common Human Family! . . . that a volume of such Sketches lives *through its very diversity*, (& through the author's strong Central view) a really connected harmonious picture of life – the *sketches fall into harmony* & form an artistic whole. The wider the range, the more powerful artistically does the volume become – with each fresh atmosphere the reader yields more & more to the eyes that saw, to the spirit that interpreted.[56]

Like Millar, Graham believed that the Kailyard writers had reduced Scots to sad stereotypes that their English neighbours were all too ready to accept, another offence against Graham's wish to see the Scot depicted as hero, albeit these heroes now seemed confined to the past. The death of Heather Jock, even although he was a wild eccentric, was the loss of one more unique character. The old Scots had now been diminished, ruined by religion and industry, and in his sketch, *Father Archangel of Scotland*, he wrote of the hero:

> He, as a Scotchman, naturally turns to what is most natural in him . . . Take notice, of course, that the modern five-per-cent hypocritical shop-keeping Scotchman was unknown, so that the Scotchmen of that day, mostly warriors or theologians, were as different from the modern Scots as they were from Laplanders.[57]

These sentiments found a more comprehensive expression forty years later in MacDiarmid's book *Scottish Eccentrics*, which was a direct descendant of Graham's own sentiments and literary intentions. MacDiarmid noted in the Scots character a 'lightning-like zig-zag of temper [which] exists among us as frequently as ever and is perhaps more insidious and wide-spread in its influence behind the almost impenetrable concealment that has been imposed upon it, or assumed'.[58] Ultimately, however, the national spirit had been eroded until Scotland's survival was in doubt. MacDiarmid blamed this on Scottish acquiescence and indifference; their lack of historical awareness, Presbyterianism, English-controlled newspapers, and on the education system,[59] most of which figured largely in Graham's philosophy and writings. Again, as if echoing Graham's sentiments, Scott Lyall wrote of MacDiarmid:

> MacDiarmid's revolt against what he regarded as the provincialisation of not merely Scottish literature, but Scotland as a cultural and political entity, it is indicative of Scottish inferiorisation within a Britain controlled by the metropolitan elites . . . the Kailyard becomes for MacDiarmid an attitude of mind, one entirely at odds with his view of the Scots as fearless eccentrics.[60]

Herzfeld wrote that stereotypes serve the interest of power,[61] and the inward-looking, narrow, bucolic passivity of the Kailyard writers, in Graham's home rule agenda, would have suited the unitary state's agenda very well. Thus, Graham had set about debunking the mythology that had grown around Scotland by displaying a wide range of Scottish types who defied stereotyping, such as the semi-drunk Highlander, the population of 'Salvagia', and Heather Jock, by injecting a squalid reality and diversity, but also a stubborn independence into the Scottish character:

> Our northern wit runs ghastly and dwells on funerals; our men at drinking parties, dead but quite the gentleman still sitting at the table; sometimes on people drunk in churchyards; but always alternating, according to the fancy of the humourist, from one to the other of staple subjects for jesting, whisky or death.[62]

Neil Munro believed, however, that Graham had not taken his views on Scotland from real life, describing two old-fashioned stereotypes, the Celt who is always admirable, 'touched with old-time graces and courtesies', and the Lowlander, 'a religious bigot, prone to ardent waters', who Munro believed had not existed in Scotland for generations.[63] However, Graham often demonstrated a sympathy and a touching humanity when writing of low-born Scottish characters, particularly in sketches such as 'Beattock for Moffat',[64] and he continually exhibited a familiarity with Scottish dialect and a knowledge of the folk etymology.

Davies described Graham's Scottish sketches as 'bitter and cynical'[65] and Walker pointed out that 'nationalists of the 1930s . . . have tended to forget that in the early stages of his career . . . Graham had treated with a vitriolic realism the defects of the Scottish character and the abuses and vices of the national way of life'.[66] Stephen Graham fell into line with this view, when he wrote:

> For him, reality is Scotland; romance is South America. He is a bitter, sarcastic, even cynical, intellectual Scot, tearing and rending his own country when he thinks of it – but suddenly melted and sentimentalised by Spain. He writes of a decidedly real Scotland, but of an unreal, unearthly, romanticised, golden Spain. It is even touching, he cannot be critical of the Latin.[67]

However, these views could be interpreted quite differently. Graham's 'reality' (of which 'Salvagia' was the best example) was an exaggerated reality of Scotland *now*, while his realities of South America and Spain, were, by necessity, *then*, and distance, in Graham's imagination, always lent enchantment. When in his future works, Scotland is remembered *then*, his tone was quite different, and if not exactly 'golden', it has a benign and misty, ethereal quality, appropriate to its climate. Also, the only sketches that demonstrated this 'vitriolic realism' were the three discussed above, written at the height of Kailyard popularity, and neither Munro, (Stephen) Graham, Walker nor Davies, seem to have appreciated that in these works, Graham was undoubtedly parodying, or exaggerating for political effect. He would, however, continue to pursue the anti-stereotype agenda in his subsequent Scottish sketches and portraits, albeit in a less overtly polemical way.

According to MacDiarmid, Graham and his works were virtually unknown in Scotland,[68] and no contemporary review suggested that these sketches were attacks on Kailyardism. Much later, Nash described Graham as 'another important critic' of the Kailyard, but used only 'A Survival' as his example.[69] Watts wrote of Graham's continuing literary output:

> After 1899, he [Graham] showed little development as an essayist and short-story writer. The elegiac obituary study, the nostalgic traveller's anecdote, the remembered glimpse of life in a Spanish settlement, the brief character sketch of a soldier, a Spaniard, a Scot or a whore – these subjects recur, and so does the mood of pawky wistfulness and almost glib melancholy.[70]

However, neither Watts nor Walker had taken into account the next distinctive group of Scottish sketches that occupied the years immediately after 1900, which were entirely different in subject and character, and which, in their own more subtle way, were another antidote to Kailyard writing. This may be because they were spread out over many years, and never anthologised chronologically.

It may be a coincidence that Graham's more overt and stark anti-Kailyard texts ceased well before the publication of Brown's classic anti-Kailyard novel *The House With the Green Shutters*.[71] However, it was no coincidence that his subject matter changed sharply in 1900 immediately after the Gartmore Estate was sold to pay off his debts, perhaps reflecting ancestral guilt, but more importantly, his loss of mutuality with the neighbourhood and his past.[72] Power described them as 'sketches [of] a twilight Scotland, ennobled by tragedy and defeat'.[73] Munro, however, offered a different perspective. Munro doubted if, in his early years, Graham had much love for Scotland: 'But how unmistakably the soil of Scotland and his ancestry had dragged him back to affection became apparent to some of us after 1906.'[74] Munro was suggesting that it was not just the sale of his home, but the death of his wife that had stimulated patriotic feelings in Graham that would one day develop into a full-blown nationalism, adding enigmatically, 'On Inchmahome on the Lake of Menteith are always flowers.'[75]

The second of Walker's three groups of Scottish sketches were almost exclusively set in Scotland (or more particularly, Menteith) *then*, and were entirely nostalgic descriptions of landscapes that retained a tincture of the past, or portraits of old-world gentry ('pre-Culloden' types), types that were links to the past, but now, like Graham himself, had gone.[76] In his biography of Graham, Watts noted that:

> Graham throughout his life was profoundly troubled by the idea that just as an individual may be lost without trace in the jungle, so men of the past, leading worthy lives, may be lost to history by the force of oblivion, and so people of the present may be ignored and forgotten for want of a due memorialist. Thus Graham's socialism was linked, paradoxically, to a profound conservatism.[77]

Graham partly blamed the disappearance of this older world on the railway, which was the sworn enemy of such people, and was breaking the uniqueness and homogeneity of communities, while simultaneously increasing the uniformity and homogeneity of the nation. As Robin Gilmour described it:

> Railway travel made the metropolitan passenger aware of living in a land of regions, but it also accelerated the process by which those regions were in time standardized to a national norm . . . and more gradually in the loss or decline of regional customs and individuality.[78]

It had been the railway that had transformed the Highlands from a remote region into one that was accessible to the tourist and the sportsman. Large estates were now viable retreats for the wealthy, producing revenue for the entrepreneur, but speeding up depopulation, and harking back to Graham's early campaigns against absentee landlords and his campaigns for land reform.

This nostalgia for earlier times found expression in the first of these sketches entitled 'A Veteran' (1900), in which he wrote:

> But fifty years ago in windswept, ragged Scottish country houses not a few remnants of pre-railroad days still lingered on . . . Scotland alone could have produced, and perhaps only Scotch people could have appreciated such a survival of the youth of the nineteenth century.[79]

Here was the very distinctive community, remembered from Graham's childhood and young adulthood, that would be the theme of several of his works of this middle period, and it seems that his regrets and nostalgia for happy moments persisted for some time. Five years after leaving Gartmore, he returned to Menteith to unpack cases of pictures that a friend had kept for him. Later, he told Garnett, 'As they came out one by one, it seemed that they were alive, and that I was buried.' He continued:

> In the Autumn, I went to the Lake of Menteith to get some things I left there, to look at the graves of many of my people in an island there. By the side of the lake, there lived two old sisters, ancient retainers of my family their people had been. The last had died not long ago. The cottage was shut and the garden deserted. I sat down on the doorstep in the evening, and smoked a cigarette. The tobacco was too bitter. I am trying to write about it, and cannot.[80]

Sensing that at last here was a subject that Graham could use to express these deeper emotions, Garnett replied:

> Your words about Gartmore, and the island burying place give me all the feeling of the things inside you which you find it so impossible to express. *Write it*, my dear Amigo, in a journal as if you were communicating with yourself.[81]

Garnett believed that if Graham would allow freer access to his feelings and cast them in a more fluid form, then something beautiful and tender would emerge:

> You have a great deal in you which as yet you have not fully expressed . . . I want you to express yourself *fully* in literature . . . I want you to think over what there is in yourself and life which you have shrunk from writing. Perhaps you don't see my meaning – but there are always deeper selves within us than we *know*.[82]

He eventually wrote down this memory as 'Ha Til Mi Tuliadh'[83] ('I Will Return No More'), a title that held a double meaning, since it was reputedly the name of the song that Rob Roy MacGregor had requested on his death-bed, a fact that Graham undoubtedly knew, carrying as it did deeper historical resonances, and portents of death.[84] But he was aware that even in this piece, his most nostalgic so far for his ancestral home, he had failed to fully express his concealed emotions, and replied to Garnett, 'I see I have not done what I feel, but that is impossible.'[85] This reticence may have had several causes. First, it might simply have been fear of openly expressing feelings, a constraint that is not uncommon among men (and, it may be said, is common among Scottish men). It may also have been due to his upbringing, where any emotional display was frowned upon, or simply because he had no confidence in his abilities, as expressed in his preface to *The Ipané* where he wrote, 'Few men know why they write, and most men are ashamed of what they do when once it stares them in the face in moulded type.'[86] However, there may be a more tangible reason. Graham remained deeply political, and, as we have seen, certainly during this period, he was still fighting campaigns on and off the page, and no doubt adding new enemies to the old, or at least confirming the bad opinions of certain sections of society. This perhaps did not overly concern him, but displaying a softer side, or a suggestion of weakness, would have exposed a chink in his armour and undermined his reputation, and the myth that he had so carefully cultivated of the adventurous, fearless and incorruptible paladin, the 'Prince-Errant, and Evoker of Horizons', as his eulogist, Haymaker, called him.

This fear of emotional exposure eventually found voice in 1932 in the preface to his anthology *Writ In Sand*, where he wrote 'It is the natural instinct in the majority of men to keep a secret garden in their souls, a something that they do not care to talk about, still less to set down, for other members of the herd to trample on.'[87] However, it was in his final anthology that we can perhaps find the clue to Graham's reserve, and his aversion to narrative 'invention': that his imagination, which he considered 'the noblest faculty of the human mind',[88] was so vivid that he deliberately avoided dwelling upon it: 'To anybody cursed with imagination, the gift that makes life sometimes unbearable, it is infinitely sad.'[89] Here we can witness his reluctance to bare his soul in print, because, as a melancholic, he found his emotions too distressing to confront and brood upon. Many of his sketches, however, have real emotional heft, but it is the emotion of nostalgia, not of sentimentality, that he found much more fulfilling.

From 1900, Graham focused on plangent, atmospheric descriptions of landscape and eccentric relatives, links with an heroic past of a distinctly Scottish pattern, who occasionally still lingered from more gracious times.[90] They were echoes of a bygone age, descendants from ancient families, who had rank in their rural communities, and although as landlords they might sit uneasily in his ideal world, unlike the parvenu landowners, their lineage (like Graham's) was predicated on paternalism, not exclusivity in land. They represented the values of tradition, decency, and respect, a type rarely featured in contemporary Scottish writing. Graham was not only writing memoirs: these were documentaries, recording the disappearance of a way of life, to make a point about change and loss, and this applied to all his work, including his writings on South America and Spain, and to his Jesuits and Apaches, as much as to old-world Scots:

The people, too, I treat of, for the most part have disappeared; being born unfit for progress, it has passed over them, and their place is occupied by worthy men who cheat to better purpose, and more scientifically. Therefore, I, writing as a man who has not only seen but lived with ghosts, may perhaps find pardon for this preface, for who would run in heavily and dance a horn-pipe on the turf below which sleep the dead?[91]

In a rare detour from his local gentry, one particular sketch stood out among his Scottish portraits of the period, that admirably demonstrated the peculiar quality of life in Menteith, whereby Graham prematurely took the first tentative step into Walker's third category, 'the dream world of mythology'. 'Pollybaglan' (1903)[92] was a description of the landscape around a semi-derelict farm on Flanders Moss, and Graham's tenant who farmed it (in reality, Mr Mitchell of Polybaglot[93]):

Tall and shocked headed and freckled on the red patches of skin which a rough crop of beard and whiskers left exposed . . . The country people said that he was 'afu' soople for his years' . . . Withal a swimmer, an unusual thing amongst the older generation in Menteith.

There then followed a demonstration of Graham's ear for local dialect, as the farmer recounted diving into the River Forth:

Ye ken, man laird, whiles I just dive richt to the bottom of a linn, and set doon there; ye'd think it was the inside o' the Fairy Hill. Trooties ye ken, and saumon, and they awfu' pike, a' comin' round ye, and they bits of water weeds, waggin aboot like larich trees in the blast. I mind ae time I stoppit doon nigh aboot half an hour. Maybe no just sae much, ye ken, but time gaes awfu' quick when ye're at the bottom o' a linn.

This vernacular speech was by no means exaggerated, and as noted earlier, he seemed very familiar and at ease with not only the dialect but also its idioms, as beautifully demonstrated in such sketches as 'Beattock for Moffat', 'A Fisherman',[94] and 'Ha Til Mi Tulaidh'. However, notwithstanding the farmer's exaggerated claim, Graham was pointing to other hidden depths. The first, a small point, was the farmer's address to his landlord, which, although acknowledging Graham's status, revealed an intimacy and a freedom to speak. If one removed the word 'laird' it would be two friends having a conversation, perhaps his way of demonstrating an ancient demo-cratic spirit among the locals (and himself) that he admired.[95] The second depth was the very nature of the description, particularly the simile, expos-ing a sensitivity of perception that we might not expect to be exchanged between two Scottish men of differing social rank. The last was the most extraordinary feature, wherein the farmer described how time had become distended in this alien environment. It had become magical, other-worldly, which was analogous with the local legend of the seventeenth-century mystic, the Reverend Robert Kirk, inside Doon Hill (not two miles away). In this, Graham was of course suggesting another depth, the depth of folk belief, and if not actual belief, a spiritual connection to landscape and tradition, a desire to believe, to commune. As he recorded elsewhere, 'Faith it is said consists of the belief in something that we know to be untrue'.[96] In retrospect, the farmer was a mouthpiece for Graham's interest in the mystical, which was starting to find fuller expression. In 1933, he would write an Introduction to Kirk's *The Secret Commonwealth of Elves, Fauns and Fairies* in which he described the spirit of Menteith, a place that could engender such feelings: 'Even to-day, in the half-light of autumn evenings, the vale takes on once more an air of an older world.'[97]

Most of the people of whom Graham wrote were from his own class, who were not the subject matter of Kailyard novels – gentry who had retainers and butlers, but who conversed in Broad Scots – and, if he had not emphasised their Scottishness, could just as easily have fitted into English houses in England. Nevertheless, when added to the Heather Jocks, inebriated Highlanders, eccentric farmers, and village roughs, he had again broadened out the Scottish rural scene into a recognisable, eclectic, heterogeneous community, in a world lit only by fire, and when they died, they left the world 'poorer for a type'.[98]

Frederick Watson described, more succinctly than Graham himself, the old Scotland that Graham knew:

> Old things have not decayed – they have collapsed – as when an axe fells the oak in its prime. There still clung, amongst the aged, ancient prejudices whose roots were buried deep in the past. Those silent hills were still haunted by the dim echo of forgotten feuds. These were the days when drovers still lay wrapped in their plaids before a smoldering peat fire, when men of eighty spoke of the tales their grandfathers had quavered about Rob Roy, when the railroad was still struggling amongst the Northern hills. All this is not merely picturesque – it is important. I merely wish to emphasise the strange old world into which he [Graham] was born in the year 1852.[99]

Like Watson, Edwin Muir believed that Scotland's identity was in extreme danger, as he wrote in his *Scottish Journey*: 'Though Scotland has not been a nation for some time, it has possessed a distinctly marked style of life; and that is now falling to pieces, for there is no visible and effective power to hold it together.'[100] In 1904, the Scottish geologist Sir Archibald Geikie had noted 'a gradual decline in national peculiarities',[101] and in 1938, the

Scottish PEN met to discuss what was seen as a crisis in national identity.[102] This concern had a long pedigree, and even the Unionist, Walter
Scott, wrote in his Introduction to *The Minstrelsy of the Scottish Border*
of 'the peculiar features of whose manners and character are daily melting
and dissolving into those of her sister and ally'.[103] Muir believed that Scott
had been part of a process, whereby '[a] people who lose their nationality
create a legend to take its place',[104] but, since the mid-nineteenth century,
among certain individuals and groups, these fears were slowly becoming
politicised. Graham's nationalism, which had begun as a proposed remedy for social ills, was now developing into a more outspoken emotional
patriotism, an attempt to simultaneously return to, and proceed towards,
a more heroic existence, a means by which Scotland's distinctiveness
could be reclaimed and developed.[105]

T. E. Lawrence (of Arabia) described Graham's sketches of this period
as 'the rain-in-the-air-and-on-the-roof mournfulness of Scotch music in
his time-past style . . . snapshots – the best verbal snapshots ever taken
I believe',[106] but again, they were nostalgic rather than sentimental.[107]
Graham's Scottish portraits were typically set in grand, musty houses,
located in enclosed, shadowy landscapes. The contrast in atmosphere
between his South American and his Scottish settings could hardly be
greater; there was little 'sunshine' in the latter,[108] and many critics and
commentators have remarked on this contrast:

> He seems to belong by right to the red and yellow lands, where the sun
> marches in burning panoply all day through the brilliant expanse of heaven.
> But at the back of all this dazzle and heat, rise the wet hills and moor-
> lands which are his home, enshrouded in gleaming mist, or purified with
> snow. Between the fragrant wantonness of sunny lands and the frigid self-
> concealment of the North, his sympathies are always divided.[109]

But the chiaroscuro is deceptive; like his sketches of gaucho life, structural nostalgia was strongly in play. In addition, although the locations
were distinctly different, Graham's South American and his Scottish
portraits and sketches have something else in common – they depicted
'hybrid' cultures and locations that were never really pure in any sense.
His gauchos were descendants of European settlers who had bred with
and displaced the native population, and had become a distinctive group
in their own right. His 'old style' Scots were in fact incomers, like his
relative in 'A Veteran', whose inheritance had come from the world of
commerce, and who had displaced the Lowland Jacobite families who
had once dominated this part of Scotland.[110] In the same way, Menteith
had been deforested, drained, farmed, and managed by past generations.

Graham was only giving us a verbal snapshot of a continuum. Descendants of these semi-aristocratic incomers still discreetly occupy country houses in the Forth Valley and southern Perthshire today, just as working-class families have continued their tradition of poverty, rough types still wipe their boots on the cushions, and mists still rise from the Forth.

Menteith is itself a hybrid land, poised between the Highlands and the Lowlands, with strong characteristics and resonances of both. But, like many hybrids, it had, and still has, its own, distinctive and separate character,[111] particularly the preponderance of mist, to which Graham frequently referred, and in which his imagination was allowed freer rein. Another noticeable feature of these post-1900 Scottish sketches was that he was less inclined to interrupt his narratives by whisking the reader off to foreign climes, or going off at tangents, destroying the mood, and mood now became the central feature of all of his Scottish sketches, particularly when he turned increasingly to environment and landscape. Again, the hybrid nature of the area came into play, its frontier location, where, not far away, there were lonely lochans and ruined churches that allowed him to ponder on a deeper past, a past ignored by the Kailyard writers, a past where the Highlands and Lowlands were not so distinct, where 'broken' clansmen and caterans once made incursions, and drovers descended with their cattle on their way to market.[112] Even the present landscape, like the 'old style' people, assumed a mantle of the past and of loss, as in this quotation:

> Such was the place, one of the last examples of the old Scotland which has sunk below the waves of Time. Perhaps not an example to be followed, but yet to be observed, remembered, even regretted in the great drabness which overspreads the world.[113]

These were words that encapsulated Graham's documentary and political motivations. His Menteith was empty, lonely, haunted, or at least these were the places he sought out and recorded.

In such rural locations, however, was he in danger of falling into what Ian Campbell called 'kailyard traps'?[114] This question can be examined through Campbell's 'sketchy definitions' of what constituted the themes of Kailyard writing. Certainly, in his first example, Graham's Scottish works conformed to the 'rural' setting, what Campbell called 'limited environment'. However, Kailyard locations might better be described as parochial in the true sense of the word. In contrast, the only parochial setting for his sketches was in 'Salvagia', which was a deliberate parody on the Kailyard genre. Also, 'Transport is a prominent feature of kailyard – prominent, that is, by its absence', but, as we have seen,

Graham was very aware that the railway was in part responsible for the erosion of his old world. Things changed with Campbell's inclusion of 'Class', wherein the Kailyard characters 'have a narrow range of social experience, belonging to the comfortable working class'. Graham's portraits, on the other hand, oscillated between people further up the social scale, and those nearer the bottom, such as his description of mourners in his sombre sketch of a farming funeral, 'At Dalmary' (1909), and particularly, his affectionate portrait of his farm-servant in 'A Retainer' (1910).[115] As noted previously, Graham seemed at home with the lowly, unpretentious working classes, and the unpretentious upper classes, with no room in any of his works for the middle class, or the bourgeoisie, the very people at whom Kailyard literature was aimed, and who were lapping it up indiscriminately.

Things become more complex when we have to deal with 'Change', which Campbell believed could be tolerated in the Kailyard world, but within certain constraints; for instance, social mobility, or 'getting on'. However, these were individual efforts towards advancement; in rural environments there was no place for mass action to change social structures. Graham, who had fought for improved wages and work conditions, was all for the advancement of the working classes, but, as we have seen, he deprecated the potential for social climbing and bourgeoisie attitudes, which 'getting on' would most likely beget. As for women, Campbell believed that Kailyard writers commonly offered less: 'The distant cities provided domestic service – but they threatened Ruin. Far better the unchanging certainties of the Kailyard.'[116] This stood in stark contrast to Graham's views, particularly those expressed in his article 'The Real Equality of the Sexes',[117] and his lifelong commitment to women's suffrage and equal rights.

Campbell's next category was 'Christian values', which played an important part in the values of the Kailyard. Although describing himself early in his political career as 'a Protestant',[118] Graham was an atheist[119] who despised Calvinism, the central pillar of Kailyard writing, a creed that he blamed for the distortion of Scottish life.[120] In fact, his parody on Christianity in 'Salvagia' looked like a deliberate attempt to distance himself from this aspect of the Kailyard. Also, implicit in the Kailyard vision of 'Christian values' was the bourgeois idea of respectability, which, as we have witnessed, he also despised.

The major and overarching argument against Graham falling into these traps was what Campbell described as the passive instead of active nature of the Kailyard's highly selective depiction of Scottishness. This view ignored the reality of poverty, slums, drunkenness, and sweatshops, portraying instead a Scotland that was self-satisfied, complacent, and backward-looking: 'A gelling of attitude and myth, a freezing of the possibilities of change and redefinition.'[121] Theirs was a Scotland in aspic, which ignored a deeper past and a potential future. This, of course, was a denial of Graham's idealised vision of Scotland's heroic, ancient heritage, and a future that he hoped could reclaim it, and by which it could redefine itself in a better world. William Power described Graham's works as containing a 'vein of cynical humanism . . . as different as possible from the cosily insular sentiments of the Kailyarders',[122] and writing in *The Scotsman*, W. H. Hamilton stated, 'Cunninghame Graham's Scottish stories, with their frigid, decorous irony, owe nothing to it.'[123]

Graham's means of communicating diversification also found expression furth of Scotland, a diaspora of wandering Scots found in the colonies, crewing ships, or running factories in the Sahara, but his real fascination, was where he found the remnants of old Scotland, often surviving and harking back to the past, because they had been transplanted elsewhere, away from the despoliation of progress. The first such example was set in a monastery in Spain, where students (descendants of Scottish religious refugees) were training under the Rector:

> Only in *Redgauntlet* and in books of Jacobites does such a priest exist. I fancy the rector of the Scottish Castilian College is the last surviving type. *Scotissimus Scotorum*, a Scot of Scots. Over the Scottish College hangs an air of Scotland, but not of Scotland of to-day, but of that older Scotland that was poor and furnished soldiers and adventurers to the rest of Europe; that Scotland that vanished after Culloden, and has been replaced by factories and mines, progress and money, and an air of commonplace, exceeding all the world.[124]

However, the most border-crossing tale of hybrid cultures was entitled 'San Andrés',[125] which described Argentinian families whose ancestors had left Scotland after the 1745 Jacobite Rebellion. After five generations, they still maintained the traditions of their erstwhile homeland, a knowledge of English and a little Gaelic, and, of course, inevitably, 'a belief in the fairies and the second sight still lingered in men's minds, with many a superstition more consonant with mountains and with mists, than the keen atmosphere and the material life of the wild southern plains'. Although, now physically indistinguishable from their fellows, they had kept apart, joined by a common heritage:

> The patriarchal manners which their forefathers had brought from the Highlands, joined to the curious old-fashioned customs common in those day in Buenos Aires [province], had formed a race apart, in which Latin materialism strove with Celtic fervor, and neither gained the day.[126]

But tragedy and sudden death are never far away in Graham's sketches, and one of these descendants, 'Anacleto' (an amalgam of Scot and Argentine), returned from a cattle drive to find that his wife had died. This involved considerable grief and mourning, but the group retained a belief inherited from their forebears that mourning disturbed the sleep of the dead, and he muttered to himself:

> 'No, it would be cowardly to break her rest, Don Alejandro says so; he had it from his father, who spoke Gaelico,' he slowly lit a cigarette, and in the last rays of light, watched the smoke curl up in the air, blue and impalpable.[127]

Here was a beautiful rendering of Graham's abiding interest in the past intruding into the present through the transmission of values and tradition so that the past was kept alive.

Increasingly, peculiar local folk tales and superstitions would enter his mixture, fitting into Walker's third category, particularly during this later period, in a piece entitled 'The Beggar Earl' (1913),[128] along the infrequent Highland locations, and the use of the Gaelic language.[129] Walker made reference to 'the distant mists of Scotland'[130] in Graham's later works, and Tom Paulin referred to 'some fey Celtic mysticism, and sloppy romanticism',[131] but these are the only observations from any reviewer or biographer that somehow there is a connection between Graham's work and what was called the Celtic Revival. Whether these later works fit into that canon is hard to say; certainly, any definition of 'Celtic' in the context of Graham, and the setting of Menteith itself, throws up difficulties, unless 'Celtic' is interpreted and understood in the broadest sense. Graham was not a Celt, and historically (or as historically as is practical) Menteith, although once Gaelic-speaking, was now a frontier territory, a bastion against the Celt; Graham's local colonel in 'A Veteran' was no doubt typical among his neighbours in his hatred for 'a Free Churchman, a Tory, or a Highlander'.[132]

Culturally, Scotland lagged behind Ireland in its 'Celtic-consciousness', and behind other parts of Europe at this time in creating cultural and patriotic societies, but by the middle of the nineteenth century this was changing. Later, among certain groups of Scots, particularly in London, these began to develop a political hue as Scots began to realise that Scottish romanticism was not enough,[133] and anger became focused around the neglect of Scottish legislation in parliament, and absentee landlordism.

There was certainly a renewed interest in Highland culture, encouraged by the crofters bringing their lives to public attention, but there is doubt as to Scotland's significance in the Celtic Revival (1860–1930), and whether none but a very few Scots at that time saw Scotland or themselves as 'Celtic' at all. Ernest Renan's work, *Poetry of the Celtic Races*,[134] first published in English in 1896, hardly mentioned Scotland's Celtic inheritance, while Holbrook Jackson saw it largely as an Irish phenomenon, and traced the start of the movement to the publication of W. B. Yeats's first book of poems in Dublin in 1885.[135] Neil Munro, himself a Highlander, wrote that the 'Scottish Celtic Renaissance' was entirely Patrick Geddes's invention, 'originating in his Outlook Tower in Edinburgh, and ending there',[136] but there were certain historians, collectors, musicians, and artists who linked Scotland to a Celtic culture, including the folklorists John F. Campbell (1821–85) and John G. Campbell (1836–91), the historian William F. Skene (1809–92), and his critic Alexander MacBain (1855–1907). MacBain also co-edited the *Celtic Magazine*, which ran from 1875 to 1888 and featured scholarly historical essays and translations of Gaelic songs, but without any suggestion of feyness. The crofting activist, John Murdoch had published *The Highlander* between 1873 and 1881, and much later, Erskine of Marr published *Guth na Bliadhna*, which ran from 1904 until 1925 and which attempted to promote modern writing in Gaelic.

Curiously, while Highlanders were collecting and preserving their native history, folklore, and language, at the same time as Graham was embarking on his new literary career, his compatriot and close contemporary, the polymath Geddes (1854–1932), produced four editions of his review, *The Evergreen: A Northern Seasonal* (1895–6).[137] He was aided by a small coterie of fellow Lowlanders, 'the Geddes entourage',[138] which included the novelist S. R. Crockett, the artist John Duncan (1866–1945), and 'the mysterious personality' Fiona MacLeod,[139] who co-edited the works with Geddes. Jackson saw Macleod's work as significantly 'Celtic', however, it carried the proviso, 'The work of "Fiona MacLeod" possessed all the more pronounced characteristics of Celtic art, with its insistence on mystical aloofness so deliberate as to suggest *a determination to be Celtic at all costs*',[140] which might be said of the whole movement. Geddes's four seasonal volumes of *The Evergreen* were poetically and artistically inspired, 'Ossianic', and overflowing with mystical aloofness, and an other-worldly air; what Yeats referred to elsewhere as 'the very innermost voice of Celtic sadness, and that Celtic longing *for infinite things the world has never seen*'.[141]

A select few of Graham's more reflective Scottish sketches allude to a similar ambience, but his dream worlds were 'lost', *not* 'other'. Generally, his sketches were too detailed, too specific, too personal, and too likely to bring his readers back down to earth, as he undercut his own imaginings. Jackson wrote that Graham's personality could not be separated from his art; he was 'a raconteur, very much a realist'.[142] Walker described this third category of Graham's Scottish sketches, as being part of his 'dream world'; however, many of these works were more specific to the daydream, idealised reconstructions from his memories and subconscious emotions.[143] In his book *The Principles of Psychology*, Graham's contemporary, William James, unlike Freud, had surprisingly little to say about dreams, but there was one statement that seems particularly relevant: 'But if a dream haunts us and compels our attention during the day *it is very apt to remain* figuring in our consciousness as a sort of sub-universe alongside of the waking world.'[144] Graham's Scottish works have a strikingly similar oneiric atmosphere, particularly those set around his old home, as if drawn from such a sub-universe; and an other-worldly quality of an idealised landscape and of a past time, the accumulated products of powerful early memories, that he could not dispel.

Graham's imaginative faculty was usually confined to his experience, and his skill was the effective translation of this experience to the reader, which frequently took on a fantastical quality, but a real, not an invented one; a fantastical quality that is often found in the environs of Menteith. It is no accident that were we to seek one word that permeated his Scottish sketches and obscured the uncomfortable modern world, it would be 'mist', which he used frequently, and when he was aware that he was over-using it, he would find some other word combination to express it. 'Mist' is a word and phenomenon that not only cast an atmospheric pall over his sketches, it is also a device that provided him with a key to his subconscious, and was a realistic (non-invented) vehicle to express his imaginings to his readers,[145] because its presence blurred the difference between the present and the past, reality, and unreality.

The first sketch to use this device was 'The Grey Kirk' (1906), which described an unnamed ruined church and its environs,[146] 'shut out from all the world by mist and moors', but Graham was still not ready to abandon reality quite yet, and 'civilisation' had imposed itself on nature and on the past:

> Dark, geometrical plantations of black fir and spruce deface the hills, which nature evidently made to bear a coat of scrubby oak and birch. Wire fences gird them round, the posts well tarred against the weather, and the barbed wire so taut that the fierce winds might use them as Eolian harps, could they but lend themselves to song.[147]

Here of course, as in the Argentinian Pampas, man's presence had defaced nature, and even though the church itself had been built by the hands of men, its age had given it a venerable place in his idealised past.

Lochan Falloch (1908) was yet another evocation of place, this time a small lake to the west of Flanders Moss (again), 'an ancient sea [again], which even yet appears to roll in the white mist [again] of evening'. On this occasion, unreality was evoked further when the fairies made an appearance:

> If fairies still exist, they come, no doubt, from the Sith Bruach[148] which guards the Avon Dhu at Aberfoyle, and sail their boats of acorn-cups and leaves on the black lakelet. Upon the little beach they run their craft ashore and dance on the broad ribbon of smooth sand which rings the lake, as a black mezzotint is edged around with white. But if the fairies come, they come unseen, leaving no token of their passage but a few turned-up leaves which they have used for boats.[149]

The piece was the beginning of Graham's more consistent literary engagement with Walker's reference to mythology, and was concerned with 'the wondrous world of fairies',[150] but fairies that were very specific to the myths and legends of Menteith. If fairydom can be seen as a part of the Celtic Revival, then Graham had moved into this territory. The question remains, however, was it a conscious decision to be part of a popular genre, or was he simply reflecting on the folk traditions of his home?

Mist made no appearance in the next notable sketch. 'At Dalmary'[151] was the description of a ploughman's funeral worthy of Lewis Grassic Gibbon, and as usual, with all his pieces, roughly half was taken up with detailed descriptions of sights, sounds, and smells of the countryside, and where the fairies made their increasingly familiar appearance. The farmer-mourners were relative newcomers, 'holding their property but on suffrance [sic] from the old owners, who named every stone, *and left their impress even in the air*' (my italics). The awkward, abbreviated conversations between these men of the land about the weather, their crops, their beasts, the state of the market, and their hesitant platitudes about the deceased were expertly observed and related. Like Graham's observations on William Morris's cortege in 'With the North West Wind' (1896), and of Keir Hardie's funeral in 'With the North-East Wind' (1915),[152] a critic observed that 'he seems to have been everywhere and observed everything with the eye of a lynx and the memory of an elephant'.[153] Both of these tributes had political and social overtones, and some meditations on greatness, but 'At Dalmary' was an evocation of the ordinary, a scene without cynicism, a scene without sentimentality or tendentiousness.[154] What was missing from this sketch, however, and all of Graham's vivid observations, was any deeper reflection on a wider community of relationships, of mutuality, of social intercourse, which, if he was aware of such relationships, might have mitigated his generally pessimistic view of rural life. Perhaps it was because of his social position and distance that he was excluded from any such intimacies or participation, and that his sojourns in Scotland, particularly after the sale of Gartmore House, were increasingly episodic. Davies wrote that Graham was by nature 'a good observer but a poor participator',[155] and in consequence, he remained an outsider who has given us a very limited view of the reality of rural Scotland. Or was it the strategic expression of his observations and inner emotions, that he left the reader to interpret in their own way – a demo-cratic fallibility of iteration?

Mist can be obscuring and revelatory. Inside it, the normal world disappears; it blurs reality, both the physical and the temporal, and with our senses disarmed, we are thrown back on our own imaginings, and Graham's ghosts could assume a more substantial form as in 'At the Ward Toll' (1908).[156] But also in that sketch, the mist was a white board onto which he could project his visions. It is also revelatory when one is above it (as one often is at Gartmore); the vista is transformed into a sea (which he never tired of telling his readers it once was), or we might suspect, to his mind, a primordial landscape, where the marks of civili-sation were erased, and where the boundaries between past and present had been obliterated. Thus, the past could live again, and become more accessible. 'At the Ward Toll' is so typical of his work at this period that it could be a self-parody, opening with the words 'The mist had blot-ted out the moss, leaving the Easter Hill, Gartur, and the three fir trees above Sanochil, rising like islands out of a dead sea'. In this piece, set of course in his home territory, the word 'mist' is used five times, along with 'veil', 'a shroud of steam' (twice), 'billowy vapours', 'waves of vapour', 'gloom', and 'white dew'. In these mists (which give Menteith a 'double darkness'):

> The spirit of the north was in the air, intangible, haunting and vague, that make the dwellers of the north vague and intangible, poetic and averse to face the facts of life, yet leaves them practical in business, with a rind of hard-ness and a heart of sentiment.

As Graham rode through this miasma, he was surrounded by shadowy forms, people of the past, earls and warriors, 'Highlanders, driving their "creagh"[157] towards Balquhidder', appearing then vanishing, a caval-cade of history, like the one he imagined as he sat on the step of the dead spinster's house, while the 'spirits of the hills', long oppressed by man's dominance, 'had resumed their sway'. However, this would be no mere ghostly impression; it turned into a companion piece to his 'Introduc-tion' to Morrison Davidson's *Scotland and the Scots*.[158] In this, Graham meets a fellow Scot on the Argentinian pampa, and now, out of the mists (again perhaps to break the other-worldly spell), there is an even more remarkable encounter, with the sudden appearance a flesh-and blood Spaniard, who addresses him in Spanish, 'shivering in his light southern clothes'. The ensuing conversation (in Spanish), in these peculiar circumstances (to say the least), is as casual as the one on the plains. After a brief exchange, and a gift of cigarettes to 'Ildefonso', the Spaniard disappears off through the mists to '"walka Glasco" ... singing a tango in a high falsetto voice', a repeat of his common motif 'I liked the manner of his going off the stage'. Again, there is no explanation, but inevitably, nostalgia for place is present, as Graham reciprocates his own emotions and identity, and imagines that through the mists he is entering the Spaniard's home town of Vigo, where he lived with Gabrielle twenty-five years previously, just before returning to Britain. It concludes (predictably, in this fantastical, other-worldly, dislocating piece) with the words: 'I almost wondered whether Ildefonso Lopez had been a real man or but an emanation from the mist from which he issued out so suddenly, and which had swallowed him again almost as suddenly, upon his lonely way.'

We have to wait for five years until Graham revisits his fairy domain, and his mists, in a sketch referred to previously, entitled 'The Beggar Earl'. Based on a real eighteenth-century character, we are straight back to the Fairy Hill near Aberfoyle, with 'Pixies, trolls, and fairies, the men of peace',[159] but those humans, like the Reverend Kirk[160] and True Thomas,[161] 'remained as flies embedded in the amber of tradition', untouched by the pressures and traps of modern life. The Beggar Earl does not seek success, 'the most vulgar thing that a man can endure ... for men resent success and strive to stifle it under applause, lauding the result, the better to belittle all the means'.[162] This repeats the first words of his essay 'The Failure of Success': 'Success, which touches nothing that it does not vulgarise, should be its own reward. In fact, *rewards of any kind are but vulgarities.*'[163]

Despite this, the beggar had claimed to be, and had papers that he believed proved him to be, the rightful heir to the Earldom of Menteith, but the claim had been rejected, so he had published a pamphlet in which he wrote, 'there can be no true unity without religion and virtue in a State'. Graham commented, 'This marks him as a man designed by nature to be poor, for unity and virtue are not commodities that command a ready sale',[164] a comment that, despite his wealth, was undoubtedly self-referencing. Perhaps this was Graham's most complete 'Scottish' sketch, a touching portrait of eccentricity, without sentimentality set in Menteith, it was tangibly historical, without the fantastical (or most of it). Even the scenes and atmospheres that we are by now so used to feel like old friends, or at least, not out of place.

In April 1913, Graham published 'Mist in Menteith',[165] which draws us back into his mysterious realm, where the mists are again swirling, and transforming the landscape:

> When all is ready for them, the mists sweep down and cover everything . . . Inside the wreaths of mist another world seems to have come into existence, something distinct from and antagonistic to mankind. When the mist once descends, blotting out the familiar features of the landscape . . . So through our mists, a shepherd's dog barking a mile off, is heard as loudly as if it were a yard or two away, although the sound comes slowly to the ear, as when old-fashioned guns hung fire and the report appeared to reach one through a veil. Thus does the past, with its wild legends, the raiders from the north the Broken Men, the Saxon's Leap, the battles of the Grahams and the MacGregors, come down to us veiled by the mists of time.

This immersive quality, as we have seen, was a medium through which he could free his memories and desires. However, it was a device that was rarely used by the 'Celtic' writers. Graham seemed unable to break loose from the documentary form, unable to invoke the past, laden as it was with a supernatural atmosphere, without invoking some transformative medium. In her review of his anthology *Brought Forward* (1916), Amy Wellington wrote, 'His thought ends in a philosophical mist – in the poetic invocation of Mist in Menteith, a study in lyrical prose which reveals, above all others, the quality of his literary genius.'[166]

Politically, it may have been no coincidence that the popularity of the Kailyard genre was homologous with the Celtic Revival, occupying almost exactly the same timeframe, one that industrialised Scotland more readily found identification with, rather than the higher 'Celtic' form beloved by academics, poets, and dreamers. Harvie agreed that there had been an upswelling of localism during this period, including in England, due to growing centralisation, where:

> Patriotic agitation legitimised fringe groups – Jacobites, Gaelic enthusiasts, Catholics, even Tories – who could tap emotions which the ruling consensus neglected . . . which enabled the Scots to run with the ethnic hare and hunt with the imperial hounds.[167]

In their own way, the Kailyard novels were an attempt to stem loss of individuality and the decay of rural communities and traditions that Graham so cherished, and with the Celtic Revival, and agitation for home rule, were part of the same uncoordinated reaction. The difference was that the Celtic enthusiasts and the Kailyard authors (and their readers) were conservative and sentimental. Graham, on the other hand although nostalgic, was both a conservationist and a radical, who increasingly grew to believe that the only solution to stemming the decay of Scotland's individuality was political independence.

Nevertheless, the question remains: was Graham influenced by the resurgent interest in Celticism in these particular works, or were his themes and moods merely co-existent and coincidental to the prevailing fashion? Perhaps, Yeats's words might sum up Graham's impulses, as someone else who despised the encroachment of ugliness:

> I have desired, like every artist, to create a little world out of the beautiful, pleasant, and significant things of this marred and clumsy world. I have therefore written down accurately and candidly much that I have heard and seen, and, except by way of commentary, nothing that I have merely imagined.[168]

There were parallels between Graham and Yeats. Declan Kiberd pointed out that Yeats spent a large part of his boyhood in England, 'a fact which may have allowed him to reinvent his Irish childhood in a more pleasing pattern'. Kilberd then remarked on the number of commentators who had marvelled at just how many years Ireland's national poet managed to spend outside his native land, and that those who did so were more 'starry-eyed about the place than those living in it. So Yeats, too, is inventing Ireland, as he employs his autobiographer's art to remake his life.'[169] The quarter-Spanish Graham also spent much of his boyhood in England, and was educated at Harrow School and in Belgium,[170] before emigrating to Argentina at the age of seventeen. After 1900, he spent part of the year abroad, and divided his time in Britain between Scotland and London. This 'hybrid' Graham, who was continually reinventing himself, was also reinventing his hybrid countries, for, as Kiberd continued, 'the past is irrecoverable, that paradise is always by very definition lost', and has to be 'reborn as an idea'.[171] Graham's cosmopolitan and international experiences, and his periodic distancing both from Scotland and South America, lent a unique perspective on matters both political and cultural. As Hayward stated, above, the perspective of the outsider, who can at times see things more clearly and more distinctly, or at least differently, from those inhibited by commonly held perceptions, habituation, and familiarity. Kurt Wittig discussed this, referencing himself as an outsider who analysed Scottish literature, and describing his position thus:

> Somebody from outside enjoys a happy detachment. He has the advantage of seeing things from both outside and inside, so that he can distinguish between the typical (often, from inside, taken for granted) and the specific. And finally there is a better guarantee that he will be impartial, no matter how much he loves the country and its people.[172]

But Graham was neither happily detached nor impartial; he was passionately attached, but attached to what? Industrial Scotland, beset by poverty and enormous social problems, was something he had witnessed and railed against, and had attempted to find a remedy to it through the political process, but things were only getting worse. Now, his reflections were of a lost Scotland, a Scotland of the past, of his daydreams, which could still be re-invoked in the rural ambience of his erstwhile home.

Graham, at this stage, was moving towards a more nationalist position, both politically and culturally, but this was part of a growing zeitgeist, although only pursued politically by a small minority of the population, that would be temporarily interdicted by the First World War. However, this international nationalist still saw potential dangers, if the new nationalism was self-regarding and inward-looking, which he summed up in the following sentence:

> The rational pride of all men in their native land is praiseworthy, but he who sees only his native land, is blind or bourgeois, or at most a tyrant who has not come into his rights, by reason of the stronger tyrants who control the State.[173]

These sentiments were very prescient, considering what, ten years later, lay ahead for Scotland and the world.

Notes

1. 'The Vicissitudes of the Scottish Home Rule Association', *Edinburgh Evening News*, 17 April 1902, p. 3.
2. Vernon Bogdanor, *Devolution in the United Kingdom* (Oxford University Press, 1999), p. 120.
3. Cunninghame Graham, '*An Tighearna*', pp. 193–9.
4. Graham had said, 'They did not want a Parliament to sit and quote Burns or sing the praises of whisky or kilts.' *Glasgow Evening News*, 1 July 1892, p. 7.
5. Cunninghame Graham, 'Spain and Catalonia', letter to the *Saturday Review*, 30 June 1906, p. 819.
6. Graham liked to draw parallels between Scotland and foreign lands as disparate as Mexico, Morocco, and Afghanistan. A reviewer wrote: 'In *Notes on the District of Menteith* he talks pleasantly about atavism and things traditional and pantheistic.' 'The Stewartry of Menteith', *The Times Literary Supplement*, 5 March 1931, p. 166.
7. John Walker, ed., *The Scottish Sketches of Cunninghame Graham* (Edinburgh: Scottish Academic Press, 1982), p. 11.
8. Ibid. Watts believed that Graham's 'Middle Period' began in 1902, and ceased with the publication of *Brought Forward* in 1916. Watts, *R. B. Cunninghame Graham*, p. 82.

9. Thomas Knowles, *Ideology, Art & Commerce: Aspects of Literary Sociology in the Late Victorian Scottish Kailyard* (Gothenburg: Acta Universitatis Gothoburgensis, 1983), p. 13.
10. Power, *Literature and Oatmeal*, p. 161.
11. Andrew Nash, *Kailyard and Scottish Literature* (Amsterdam: Rodopi, 2007), p. 14.
12. Brown, letter to Ernest Barker, 24 October 1901. Quoted in James Veitch's *George Douglas Brown* (London: H. Jenkins, 1952), p. 153. Davies wrote that unlike Brown's novel, 'Graham's earlier attacks seem to have made little impression at the time'. Laurence Davies, 'R. B. Cunninghame Graham: The Kailyard and After', *Studies in Scottish Literature*, Vol. XI, No. 3, 1974, p. 157.
13. Blake, *Barrie and the Kailyard School*, p. 51. In 1895, the *Saturday Review* opined, 'Mr Crockett writes a kind of rheumatic English that is at times positively painful'. *Saturday Review*, 20 May 1895, p. 513.
14. Blake, *Barrie and the Kailyard School*, pp. 15–6.
15. Harvie, *Scotland and Nationalism*, p. 99.
16. Gillian Shepherd, 'The Kailyard', in *The History of Scottish Literature*, Vol. 3, ed. by Douglas Gifford (Aberdeen University Press, 1988), p. 311.
17. Richard Cook, 'The Home-Ly Nation: Nineteenth Century Narratives of the Highland Myth of Merrie Old Scotland', *Nineteenth Century*, Winter 1999, p. 1054.
18. Ibid.
19. Margaret Oliphant, 'The Window in Thrums', *Blackwood's Edinburgh Magazine*, August 1889, p. 265.
20. *Glasgow Herald*, 13 October 1894, p. 7.
21. *Glasgow Herald*, 26 September 1895, p. 7.
22. J. H. Millar, 'The Literature of the Kailyard', *New Review*, April 1895, p. 384.
23. Ibid.
24. Ibid., p. 393.
25. In his *A Literary History of Scotland*, Millar stated that the word 'Kailyard' was first coined by the Englishman W. E. Henley, 'and . . . no one else'. J. H. Millar, *A Literary History of Scotland* (London: T. Fisher Unwin, 1903), p. 511n. Henley had been a close friend of Robert Louis Stevenson, and was the model for 'Long John Silver'.
26. MacDiarmid testified to Graham's extensive knowledge of Scottish literature. *Centenary Study*, p. 20.
27. Cunninghame Graham, 'Preface' to *Father Archangel of Scotland*, p. ix. My italics.
28. Cunninghame Graham, 'A Survival' *Saturday Review*, 3 May 1896, p. 542. Anthologised in *The Ipané* (1899), pp. 107–19.
29. Millar, *Literary History of Scotland*, p. 659.
30. Ibid., p. 680.

31. Cunninghame Graham, 'A Survival', p. 542. In 1899, Graham experimented with his own version of colloquial Scots in two sketches written almost entirely in dialect. 'A Pakeha', *Westminster Gazette*, 31 January 1899, pp. 1–2. Anthologised in *Thirteen Stories* (1900), pp. 201–8, and 'Pax Vobiscum', *Westminster Gazette*, 25 February 1899, pp. 1–2.

32. Laurence Davies, 'R. B. Cunninghame Graham: The Kailyard and After', p. 159.

33. Engels, *Condition of the Working-Class*, p. 47.

34. In Cook's words, 'the Kailyard nation imagines its own legitimacy by naturalizing the hierarchies that sustain it'. Cook, 'The Home-Ly Nation', p. 1055.

35. Blake, *Barrie and the Kailyard School*, pp. 8–9.

36. Harvie, *Scotland and Nationalism*, p. 99, original italics. Power described social condition at that time in industrial Scotland as 'beyond the scope of realism'. Power, *Literature and Oatmeal*, p. 165.

37. Watts, *R. B. Cunninghame Graham*, p. 50.

38. A reviewer wrote of him, 'Mr. Graham is only a diver into the slums, not a dweller in them.' *Manchester Guardian*, 11 November 1902, p. 4. However, Graham was well acquainted with the conditions of the poor. During his Camlachie campaign in 1892, he conducted John Burns around the East End of Glasgow between 11pm and 2am, entering several tenements. A tearful Burns is reported to have exclaimed, 'No wonder these people drink', and 'My God, does Scotland stand where it did?' *Glasgow Evening News*, 13 June 1892, p. 3.

39. The location was 'Offerance' farm. Five farms in the district bore that name, all owned by Graham. *Valuation Roll*, Parish of Drymen, 1895–6.

40. Watts and Davies, *Cunninghame Graham*, p. 267. An alternative definition of 'structural nostalgia'.

41. Cunninghame Graham, 'A Survival', p. 544. Graham recycled this tale twenty years later in 'Transplanted In Vain', *Gateway*, September 1916, pp. 29–32.

42. Cunninghame Graham, 'A Survival', p. 543. Darwinism in this case probably did not refer to the theory itself, but to the belief that human progress necessarily followed a logical, smooth, and consistent evolutionary trajectory.

43. Cunninghame Graham, 'Salvagia', *Saturday Review*, 12 September 1896, p. 279. Anthologised in *The Ipané* (1899), pp. 130–40.

44. Undoubtedly a swipe at the Reverend John Watson, who wrote a strangulated Scots under the pseudonym Ian MacLaren.

45. Cunninghame Graham, 'Salvagia', p. 279. Here, the suggestion was that these writers were selling their birthright, and selling Scotland short in the eyes of foreigners, for personal enrichment.

46. Jawbox: Scots = A kitchen sink.

47. Dr Thomas Chalmers (1780–1847), was the first Moderator of the Free Church of Scotland and regarded as 'Scotland's greatest nineteenth-century

churchman'. Graham's father had funded the construction of the Free Church in Gartmore.

48. 'Jeanie, reach me down the Bible, and put the whisky bottle inside the medicine cabinet.' This sentence might be a deliberate subversion of Robert Burns' graciously pious poem 'The Cotter's Saturday Night', in which 'Jenny' is the daughter of the house.

49. Cunninghame Graham, 'Salvagia', p. 280. 'Nothing, not a word. She just went out and milked the cows.'

50. G. K. Chesterton, *Robert Louis Stevenson* (London: Hodder & Stoughton, 1927), p. 125.

51. Cunninghame Graham, 'De Heretico Comburendo', Anthologised in *Father Archangel of Scotland*, pp. 73–4.

52. Cunninghame Graham, 'Introduction' to John Morrison Davidson's *Scotland for the Scots: Scotland Revisited* (Edinburgh: F. R. Henderson, 1902), pages unnumbered. (For full text, see Appendix VI.)

53. Cunninghame Graham, 'Heather Jock', *Saturday Review*, 30 January 1897, pp. 110–12. Anthologised in *The Ipané* (1899), pp. 120–9. 'Heather Jock' was mocking nickname applied to several eccentric characters throughout Scotland, but this one was William Brodie (1802–84). In this sketch, Graham claimed to have received news of Brodie's death in Argentina, but by 1884, he was domicile in Scotland.

54. Pritchett, 'New Literature', p. 339.

55. Watts, *Joseph Conrad's Letters*, p. 30.

56. Garnett, letter to Graham, 19–24 May 1898. Watts, *Joseph Conrad's Letters*, p. 212. Original italics.

57. Cunninghame Graham, *Father Archangel of Scotland*, p. 12

58 Hugh MacDiarmid, 'The Caledonian Antisyzygy', in *Scottish Eccentrics* (London: Routledge, 1936), p. 284.

59. Ibid., p. 287.

60. Scott Lyall, 'Hugh MacDiarmid's Impossible Community', in *Community in Modern Scottish Literature* (Amsterdam: Rodop, 2016), p. 85.

61. Herzfeld, *Cultural Intimacy*, p. 181.

62. Cunninghame Graham, 'Heather Jock', p. 111. '[D]ead but quite the gentleman still sitting at the table' was taken from an event in the eighteenth century, when the Laird of Garscadden (now part of Glasgow), died during a drinking bout, but no one wished to interrupt the party by pointing it out. The expression 'Gash (ghastly looking) as Garscadden' subsequently entered popular parlance.

63. Neil Munro, 'A Group of Writing Men', *The On-Looker* (Edinburgh: Porpoise Press, 1933), p. 305.

64. Anthologised in *Success* (1902), pp. 139–54.

65. Davies, 'Concept of Impressionism', p. 3.

66. John Walker, 'Cunninghame Graham and the Critics', *Studies in Scottish Literature*, Vol. 19, 1984, p. 113.

67. Stephen Graham, *Death of Yesterday*, pp. 39–40.
68. *Selected Essays of Hugh MacDiarmid*, ed. by Duncan Glen (London: Jonathan Cape, 1952), p. 121.
69. Nash, *Kailyard and Scottish Literature*, p. 45.
70. Watts, *Joseph Conrad's Letters*, p. 30.
71. Ian Campbell wrote that Brown 'created a kailyard novel to subvert its values', which is exactly what Graham did in 'Salvagia' and possibly for the same reason, that it was 'the compliment the author of *The House with the Green Shutters* would have liked to pay his country'. Ian Campbell, *Kailyard: A New Assessment* (Edinburgh: Ramsay Head Press, 1981), pp. 11–12.
72. Lowe wrote of this period, 'In the turmoil of his impoverished condition, with the dark prospect ahead of having to sell part of his lands, his thoughts hovered lovingly over his ancestral environments.' David Lowe, 'The Old Scottish Labour Party', *Glasgow Evening Times*, 18 February 1938, p. 3.
73. Power, *Literature and Oatmeal*, p. 169.
74. Neil Munro, *The Brave Days: A Chronicle of the North* (Edinburgh: The Porpoise Press, 1931), p. 317.
75. Ibid. Graham's wife Gabrielle's, and later Graham's own burial place.
76. The pathos of Graham and his wife's departure from Gartmore in 1900 was captured in his sketch 'A Braw Day'. *English Review*, November 1911, pp. 609–14. Anthologised in *Charity* (1912), pp. 133–45.
77. Watts, *R. B. Cunninghame Graham*, p. 41.
78. Robin Gilmour, 'Regional and Provincial in Victorian Literature', in *The Literature of Region and Nation*, ed. by R. P. Draper (London: Macmillan, 1989), p. 52.
79. Cunninghame Graham, 'A Veteran', *Saturday Review*, 14 April 1900, p. 455. Anthologised as 'The Colonel' in *Hope* (1910), pp. 208–15. The elderly gentleman described was a senior cousin of Graham's named Alexander Speirs of Culcreuch (a castle and estate near the village of Fintry in Stirlingshire).
80. Cunninghame Graham, letter to Garnett, 26 December 1905 (MS: University of Texas). Quoted in Helen Smith, *The Uncommon Reader*, p. 108.
81. Garnett, letter to Cunninghame Graham, 2 December 1905. Cunninghame Graham Papers, NLS. Original italics.
82. Ibid.
83. Cunninghame Graham, 'Ha Til Mi Tualiadh', *The Speaker*, 17 February 1906, pp. 473–5. Anthologised in *His People* (1906), pp. 201–12. Gartmore Estate bordered MacGregor territory, and had been a victim of their frequent cattle raids.
84. Graham's wife, Gabrielle, who by this time was seriously ill, would die a few months later.
85. Cunninghame Graham, letter to Garnett, 9 January 1906 (MS: University of Texas). Quoted in Helen Smith, *The Uncommon Reader*, p. 108.

86. Cunninghame Graham, Preface to *The Ipané* (London: Fisher Unwin, 1899), p. vi.

87. Cunninghame Graham, Preface to *Writ In Sand* (London: Heinemann, 1932), p. xi.

88. Cunninghame Graham, *Thirteen Stories* (London: Heinemann, 1900), p. 130.

89. Cunninghame Graham, *Mirages* (London: Heinemann, 1936), p. 159. The reference was to the imagined fate of horses in the First World War, many of which he himself had purchased in South America.

90. Laird Wallace in Graham's 'Miss Christian Jean' is probably the best example of this. Anthologised in *His People* (1906), pp. 213–35.

91. Graham, *Thirteen Stories*, pp. x–xi.

92. Cunninghame Graham 'Polybaglan', *The Speaker*, 28 November 1903, pp. 214–15. Anthologised in *Progress & Other Sketches* (1905), pp. 251–9.

93. Gaelic: *poll-a-bagailt* = Stream with clusters of nut bushes.

94. 'A Fisherman', *Justice: The Organ of Social Democracy*, 3 May 1902. Anthologised in *Success* (1902), pp. 155–68.

95. Jean Cunninghame Graham wrote: 'Scottish lairds had nearly always been on friendly terms with their estate workers, feeling them to be equals; there was none of the English "feudal" relationship which produced the patronising breed of landowners that were sometimes found in the South.' Jean Cunninghame Graham, *Gaucho Laird*, p. 47.

96. Cunninghame Graham, 'Introduction' to Robert Kirk's *The Secret Commonwealth of Elves, Fauns and Fairies* (1933) (New York: Dover Books, 2008), p. 6.

97. Ibid., p. 7.

98. Cunninghame Graham, 'A Veteran', *Saturday Review*, 14 April 1900, p. 456.

99. Frederick Watson, 'R. B. Cunninghame Graham', *The Bookman*, March 1916, pp. 174–6.

100. Edwin Muir, *Scottish Journey* (1935) (London: Flamingo, 1985), p. 25. Muir envisaged the SNP as a vehicle for cultural salvation.

101. Archibald Geikie, *Scottish Reminiscences* (Glasgow: James MacLehose, 1904), p. 7.

102. 'Is There a Twilight of the Scots?: PEN Discussion at Stirling', *Scotsman*, 17 January, 1938, p. 14.

103. Walter Scott, *The Minstrelsy of the Scottish Border* (1802–3) (Edinburgh: Adam & Charles Black, 1873), p. cxxxviii.

104. Edwin Muir, *Scott and Scotland: The Predicament of the Scottish Writer* (New York: Speller, 1938), pp. 160–1.

105. '[T]he Southrons, who, impotent to conquer us in war, yet have filched from us our national character by the soft arts of peace.' Cunninghame Graham, 'The Beggar Earl', *English Review*, July 1913, pp. 569–70.

106. Garnett, *Selected Letters of T. E. Lawrence*, p. 341. Graham and Lawrence were acquainted, and according to David Garnett, Graham had written to

Lawrence: 'When, or if, you come to Scotland do not forget, this, *your* house.' David Garnett, 'Top People's Views of a Hero', *The Observer*, 15 July 1962, p. 18.

107. 'In dealing with Scotland and things Scotch, one should avoid sentiment, it destroyed those awful McCrocketts, and Larens, and is a snare to the pious chanting, hypocritical, hard, but at the same time sentimental, and whisky loving Scotchman. I am a Scotchman.' Letter from Graham to Garnett, 25 May 1898 (MS: University of Texas). Quoted by Laurence Davies in 'R. B. Cunninghame Graham: The Kailyard and After', pp. 157–8.

108. 'True, in the East there generally is sun, and every evil with the sun is less.' Cunninghame Graham, 'Heather Jock', p. 110.

109. 'My Heart's in the Pampas', *The Nation*, 30 March 1912, p. 1065.

110. Graham's cousin, 'The Colonel', was only the second generation to live in the house, in an estate originally bought by money from the American tobacco trade through Glasgow.

111. 'Perhaps the fact that the house stood just at the point where the Lowlands end and the great jumble of the Highland hills begins, and that the people were compounded of both simples, Saxon and Celtic mixed in equal parts, gave them all the place an interest such as clings to borderlands the whole world over, for even forty years ago one talked of "up above the pass" as of a land distinct from where we lived.' Cunninghame Graham, 'Miss Christian Jean', Anthologised in *His People* (1906), p. 217.

112. In a speech at Buchlyvie, Graham recalled the days when Highland cattle-drovers, on their way to Falkirk Tryst with their herds, slept by the road at night, leaving their dogs to watch over their charges. 'That would be as strange to the present generation as if a tribe of Indians came and camped by the roadside.' 'Modern Progress', *Scotsman* 31 July 1934, p. 13.

113. Cunninghame Graham, 'Caisteal-Na-Sithan' (Castle of the Elves), *Saturday Review*, 15 April 1911, p. 455. Anthologised in *Charity* (1912), pp. 81–93.

114. Campbell, *Kailyard*, p. 12.

115. Cunninghame Graham, 'A Retainer', *English Review*, July 1910, pp. 625–30. Anthologised in *Hope* (1910), pp. 175–85.

116. Campbell, *Kailyard*, p. 14.

117. Cunninghame Graham, 'The Real Equality of the Sexes', *New Age*, July 1908, p. 207.

118. *Coatbridge Express*, 7 July 1886, p. 4.

119. Tschiffely, *Don Roberto*, p. 435.

120. Faulkner West, *Cunninghame Graham*, p. 125.

121. Campbell, *Kailyard*, p. 10.

122. Power, *Literature and Oatmeal*, p. 169.

123. W. H. Hamilton, 'Trends in Recent Fiction', *Scotsman*, 8 March 1934, p. 2.

124. Cunninghame Graham, 'De Heretico Comburendo'. Anthologised in *Father Archangel of Scotland*, p. 69.

125. Cunninghame Graham, 'San Andrés', *English Review*, July 1911, pp. 602–9. Anthologised in *Charity* (1912), pp. 116–32.

126. Ibid., p. 604.

127. Ibid., p. 609.

128. Cunninghame Graham, 'The Beggar Earl', *English Review*, July 1913, pp. 569–74. Anthologised in *A Hatchment* (1913), pp. 183–94.

129. Particularly in Graham's final Scottish sketch, a misty-eyed piece entitled: 'Euphrasia', *Saturday Review*, 25 September 1926, p. 331. Anthologised in *Redeemed* (1927), pp. 172–6.

130. Walker, *Scottish Sketches*, p. 11.

131. Tom Paulin, 'Cunninghame Graham: A Critical Biography', in *New Statesman*, 24 August 1979, p. 274.

132. Cunninghame Graham, 'A Veteran', p. 455.

133. H. J. Hanham, *Scottish Nationalism* (London: Faber & Faber, 1969), p. 148.

134. Ernest Renan, *Poetry of the Celtic Races* (London: Walter Scott Publishing, 1896).

135. Holbrook Jackson, 'R. B. Cunninghame Graham: The Man and His Work', *To-day*, Vol. VII., March 1920, p. 148.

136. Munro, *The Brave Days*, p. 297.

137. Geddes also published a reprint of James Macpherson's *The Poems of Ossian* in 1896.

138. Philip Boardman, *The Worlds of Patrick Geddes* (London: Routledge & Kegan Paul, 1978), p. 150.

139. William Sharp (1850–1905).

140. Jackson, 'R. B. Cunninghame Graham: The Man and His Work', p. 150. My italics.

141. W. B. Yeats, 'A Visionary', *The Celtic Twilight: Faerie and Folklore* (1893) (London: Prism Press, 1990), p. 9. My italics.

142. Jackson, 'R. B. Cunninghame Graham: The Man and His Work', p. 4.

143. Arthur Symons wrote that Graham was '[a] dreamer with a passion for action, one whose dreams are action, yet whose actions are certainly for the most part dreams'. Arthur Symons, *Notes on Joseph Conrad and Some Unpublished Letters* (London: Myers, 1925), p. 32.

144. William James, *The Principles of Psychology II* (1890) (New York: Dover Books, 1950), p. 294. My italics.

145. Walter Scott alluded to mist many times while writing of Menteith in his novel *A Legend of Montrose* (1819).

146. Very obviously St Bride's fourteenth-century church in Douglas.

147. Cunninghame Graham, 'The Grey Kirk', *Guth na Bliadhna*, February 1906, p. 25. Anthologised in *His People* (1906), pp. 246–52.

148. Walter Scott's 'The Fairy-Knowe' (*Rob Roy*), which is Doon Hill, between Gartmore and Aberfoyle.

149. Cunninghame Graham, 'Lochan Falloch', *Saturday Review*, 4 January 1908, p. 11. Anthologised in *Faith* (1909), pp. 101–7.

150. It is perhaps relevant that Arthur Rackham's fairy illustrations were enjoying great popularity at this time, and 1906 was a particularly fruitful year for the genre, following J. M. Barrie's *Peter Pan* (1904).

151. Cunninghame Graham, 'At Dalmary', *Saturday Review*, 4 December 1909, pp. 687–9. Anthologised in *Hope* (1910), pp. 61–73.

152. This work was full of memories of more hopeful and inspiring times, as Graham gazed upon the mourners, many of whom had been at the forefront of the early socialist cause: 'They were all young and ardent, and as I mused upon them and their fate, and upon those of them who had gone down to the oblivion that waits for those who live before their time, I shivered in the wind.' Cunninghame Graham, 'With the North-East Wind', *The Nation*, 23 October 1915, p. 148.

153. *Saturday Review*, 29 April 1899, p. 533.

154. 'The author [Graham] is a realist of the realists. His subtle compassion for his fellow men, his indignant tenderness for the weak, and his utter lack of sentimentality is, however, at the root of his charm.' *Academy & Literature*, 25 October 1902, p. 437.

155. Davies, 'Concept of Impressionism', p. 3.

156. Cunninghame Graham, 'At the Ward Toll', *Saturday Review*, 7 November 1908, pp. 574–5. Anthologised in *Faith* (1909), pp. 108–17.

157. Gaelic = Pillage.

158. For full text, see Appendix VI.

159. A reference to the name of the fairies. When his characters pass this very hill, Walter Scott wrote in *Rob Roy*, 'They ca' them . . . Daoine Sith, quhilk signifies, as I understand, men of peace': an inaccurate translation.

160. The Reverend Robert Kirk (1644–92), minister at Aberfoyle, author of *Secret Commonwealth* (1692). He would undoubtedly have known Rob Roy MacGregor personally. In local folklore, Kirk did not die, but was held captive by the fairies inside Doon Hill for revealing their secrets.

161. Sir Thomas de Ercildoun, 'Thomas the Rhymer' (1220–98). Reputedly held captive by the Queen of the Fairies for seven years.

162. Cunninghame Graham, 'Beggar Earl', p. 570.

163. Cunninghame Graham, 'The Failure of Success', *Saturday Review*, 17 May 1902, p. 630. My italics.

164. Cunninghame Graham, 'The Beggar Earl', p. 571.

165. Cunninghame Graham, 'Mists in Menteith', *Saturday Review*, 5 April 1913, pp. 420–1. Anthologised in *A Hatchment* (1913), pp. 104–13.

166. Amy Wellington, 'An Artist-Fighter in English Prose: Cunninghame Graham', *The Bookman* (New York), April 1918, p. 157.

167. Harvie, *Scotland and Nationalism*, p. 24.

168. W. B. Yeats, *The Celtic Twilight: Faerie and Folklore*, p. 1. By Graham's definition, Yeats's 'imagined' would be his 'invented'. Graham and Yeats had a passing acquaintance; Frederick Niven recalled seeing them talking at the Court Theatre in London's Sloane Square. Frederick Niven, *Library*

Review, Winter 1932, p. iii. Yeats's published letters did not include any to Graham, nor was he mentioned, but Watts published one (undated, but between 1913 and 1916) concerning Graham's submission of a 'little Spanish play' (most likely Graham's translation of Santiago Rusinel's 'La Virgen del Mar') for consideration by the Abbey Theatre, which Yeats considered unsuitable. Cedric Watts, 'A Letter from W. B. Yeats to R. B. Cunninghame Graham', *Review of English Studies*, Vol. XVIII, 1967, pp. 292–3. One letter from Yeats did make a reference to meeting Graham's wife Gabrielle, 'a little bright American'. Allan Wade, ed., *The Letters of W. B. Yeats* (London: Hart-Davis, 1954), p. 62. Graham's translation was eventually performed at the Maddermarket Theatre in Norwich in 1958, for which his estate received royalties. My thanks to Professor Watts for this information.

169. Declan Kiberd, *Inventing Ireland: The Literature of a Modern Nation* (London: Jonathan Cape, 1995), p. 107. Kilberd added, '[B]ehind such an aphorism lies a familiar strategy of the Irish Protestant imagination, estranged from the community, yet anxious to identify itself with the new national sentiment', who, faced with 'a painful accusation against their own people . . . turned to geography in an attempt at patriotization.' Ibid.

170. Graham's mother lived permanently in London, and he maintained apartments in Mayfair and Belgravia throughout his later life.

171. Kiberd, *Inventing Ireland*, p. 108.

172. Kurt Wittig, *Scottish Tradition in Literature* (Edinburgh: Oliver & Boyd, 1958), p. 7.

173. Cunninghame Graham, 'Introduction' to Ida Taylor's, *Revolutionary Types* (London: Duckworth, 1904), p. xiii.

Part II Conclusion

Pritchett was correct in his assessment that Graham had been squeezed out of parliamentary politics. What separated him from a typical politician was not his class, his oratorical skill, his outspoken passion, or his unusual life experiences, but much more significantly, his political certainties. His views were predicated on his aesthetic and moral sense of value, resulting in an uncompromising semi-intellectual and semi-moralistic snobbery, inasmuch as he believed he possessed a clear and practical vision of the root causes of the society's ills and their cures, and anyone who did not concur was either bourgeois, corrupt, or a fool.

Graham would also be squeezed out of any significant role in the ILP due to his demeanour, and a rapid change in political fashion, whereby the patronage and legitimacy he had once offered were no longer seen as relevant, or, coming from a landowner, appropriate. Graham's hierarchy of needs was quite different from that of the party's new adherents, most of whom would no doubt have agreed with Brecht's famous line 'Grub first, then ethics',[1] which led to his disillusionment with the philosophical and moral basis of the new political entity. Getting working men into parliament had not been enough after all, and, notwithstanding the intellectual calibre of those elected, the nature of parliament itself was a barrier to change, defiling any member with pitch, whatever their party. As for the workers themselves, they did not embrace a noble, altruistic socialism, as he had hoped, but continued to vote for whomever they considered best served their interests.

Graham's subsequent criticism of what he saw as a lack of radical fervour from his erstwhile colleagues also blighted his reputation in the expanding Labour movement. At the other end of the social scale, he would remain toxic to the British establishment, and would receive no honours or patronage.[2] He was a political outsider, positioned between two armed camps and belonging to neither. Thus, he had an extraordinary ability to divide opinion, not along class lines, but between conservative and bourgeois elements in all classes, and those who admired his heroic qualities, whether they agreed with his political views or not. However, after forfeiting his seat, he lost much of his political influence, but he had served his purpose, for as Hardie wrote in another context, 'the work of the freelance is accomplished when the main body of the army comes up'.[3]

There were limits to Graham's egalitarianism; he was a champion of the people, not a man of the people, and believed that the division between employer and employee 'is only of a tailor's making',[4] while looking down on both. His elitism was not simply snobbery, as claimed by Glasier.[5] In 1909, in an interview with Robert Birkmyer, Graham said:

> Progress has always seemed to me to be misunderstood by most people. One cannot, of course, affect to despise the merely material progress, but too many seem to forget that material progress is a means and not an end . . . A soulless and material barbarian, although he is conveyed from London to Paris in a well-upholstered Pullman car, and can receive on the way the latest football and divorce news, still remains a barbarian. The progress that most interests me is *ethical*. Whilst being fully alive to the great advances made by applied science, I deplore that in ethics we seem to be absolutely stationary since the time of Plato.[6]

Harris wrote that Graham was on the side of the poor and the workers through his sense of justice and disdain for riches, but had 'an artist's contempt for their lack of vision, an adventurer's scorn for their muddy, slow blood'.[7] However, the contrast between his compassion and his moral stance was quite remarkable. Graham admired the heroic virtues he found in every class, perhaps again, drawn from his experiences abroad among people who led rough, dangerous, uncompromising, natural, 'harmonious' lives, unlike what he was now witnessing in the slums, sweatshops, and gentlemen's clubs at home. This may be termed 'heroic-élitism', where his admiration was reserved for the courageous individual, who was independent, self-sufficient, and self-realising. In 1929, a review of his *Thirty Tales & Sketches* in the *Saturday Review* succinctly summed this up:

> He is the aristocrat, the rebel, the man of heroic temper, suspicious of the morality of success, and the individualist's profound disbelief in the virtue of anything organized . . . an inverted, good-humoured Quixote who believes the armies he is charging are mere flocks of sheep.[8]

This fundamentalist world-view set Graham apart from, and in direct conflict with, most of humanity, and polarised opinion as to whether he was a hero or a dangerous eccentric. Compared to many of his near contemporaries, however, his disdain, particularly for the lower orders, was mild. In his book, *The Intellectuals and the Masses*,[9] John Carey presented illustrations of how a high proportion of Graham's contemporaries, including D. H. Lawrence, E. M. Forster, W. B. Yeats, G. B. Shaw, T. S. Eliot, Virginia Woolf, Thomas Hardy, and Ezra Pound, harboured a contempt for the common man that bordered on the genocidal.

Nonetheless, Graham's life was distinguished by an extraordinary resilience, and a catalogue of fortuitous events that led to unexpected consequences. After three years in the political wilderness, he was able to salvage another unpaid career in another solitary craft, that of a reborn social commentator, which flowered briefly during 1896 and 1897, where he attacked imperialism and the 'Kailyard' school of Scottish writers. Following this interlude, this study has asserted that in this new career, commentators have over-complicated his choice of literary medium, and not taken him at his word. Now constrained from writing polemic for a new and more conservative readership, which was his first instinct, and accepting that his imaginative storytelling talents were limited, Graham had little choice but to write factual or semi-factual memoirs, which were simply a development of his early foreign news reports. Moreover, while appearing to satisfy his readers' taste for exotic locations and adventure, he was obliged to frame his political pronouncements more subtly and obliquely, critiquing empire and so-called progress, and their deleterious effects on more traditional societies. Also, for someone who eschewed what he called 'invention', he was not only compelled to reach into his own experiences for inspiration, but to employ his emotionally reserved impressionistic skills to make his accounts more realistic. When he told Garnett that one of his pieces was 'an impression, nothing more . . . that is all I can do', he was being honest. Graham was not an Impressionist, he simply wrote impressions, which he usually wrapped around some central, often vague narrative or meditation. Garnett constantly encouraged him to extend himself by becoming more emotionally expressive, but Graham lacked either the confidence or the expressive apparatus to do so. Also, for the image he was creating for himself, of the distant aristocratic adventurer and committed radical, emotionally expressive writing would have been unmanly and inappropriate.

With some difficulty, he began to record his memories of Scotland, particularly his sometime home in Menteith, but these have also been interpreted incorrectly. Despite Graham's being quite explicit about his target in each, Walker failed to appreciate that his first three Scottish works were not 'bitter portrayals'. Each was a political diatribe, a protest against the popular sentimental representation of Scottish rural life, achieved by depicting a diverse and realistic Scotland, warts and all. Unlike Watts, Walker also failed to note that the remainder of his Scottish works, which had a much gentler and reflective quality, began immediately after his sad departure from his home, in which he recalled characters and scenes from an idealised past; they were documents of loss, and as such, motivationally and emotionally consistent with his sketches of change and loss in South America. Nostalgia, however, is mainly a luxury of the privileged, those who have the opportunity to enjoy things worth remembering, and have the time to reflect upon them.

Both Graham's South American and Scottish memories were of vanishing or vanished worlds, but when he came to describe them, the marked difference was that his foreign works were settings for some unfolding drama that he had witnessed. In his Scottish works there was no drama, the days of drama had gone, and he was obliged to rely only on descriptions of nature and local folklore, and portraits of diverse 'characters'. Harvie wrote that the reason realism had failed in Scottish writing of the period was that contemporary authors failed in probing individuality.[10] English novelists could span the classes, and were, more often than not, at home in the houses of the rich and eccentric, whereas Scottish writers and poets, up to this point, had focused on the lives (not necessarily the character) of lower-class country people, leaving a yawning gap in the Scottish literary canon. Graham's Scottish portraits, in contrast, did span the classes, particularly the eccentricities of the Scottish landed gentry, and the quirky and robust individuality of the lower orders. He is now mostly remembered for his adventurous life and his portrayal of exotic peoples and locations, but his irregular treasury of portraits, which documented the bygone characters and graces of the Forth Valley and southern Perthshire, seen through the eyes of someone who was half inside and half outside the rural community, were a unique contribution to Scotland's literary heritage. There is no evidence, however, that he wrote these as part of any particular cultural movement in Scotland; he simply reflected his continuing moral and political instincts, and he sits uncomfortably in MacDiarmid's Scottish Renaissance.

Latterly, Graham's impressionistic prose wandered into the realms of a mystic Celticism. The preoccupations of the Celtic Revivalists were, however, concerned with a hazy longing for an imaginary, other-worldly, fundamentally *unachievable* past, aimed at reinforcing or inventing a separate, mythical, and mystical cultural heritage. In contrast, Graham's works sought out landscapes where he perceived that the past still lingered,

particularly when climatic conditions wiped out the traces of man's presence, evoked the mystical ambience of Menteith, or rekindled his youthful
daydreams.[11] Watts described this as:

> His pervasive and almost narcissistic conservatism, for he is attempting per-
> sistently to conserve against time's corrosion of memory the experiences of
> his own past, the sights, smells, conversations and chance encounters.[12]

As for his growing attachment to Scottish nationalism, Graham had
long been disturbed by what he saw as Scotland's economic and cultural
subordination, which he believed home rule could remedy. Moreover,
the popular culture of his time simply projected a cosy complacency, and
was a standing insult in the face of glaring urban deprivation and squalor, and blatantly disregarded Scotland's diversity and ancient cultural
heritage, thereby stimulating a deeper patriotic anger. Graham's nationalism had now developed from the purely practical, a means by which
legislative anomalies could be addressed, to a more emotional patriotism,
an attempt to simultaneously return to, and proceed towards, an heroic
and harmonious existence, a means by which Scotland's distinctiveness
could be rescued from the erosion of progress and cultural absorption,
reclaimed, and developed.

Containing little action, his Scottish works were sometimes strained
and repetitious. Nevertheless, taken individually, they had a quiet, sad
beauty, and captured the atmosphere of a unique hybrid location, and of
a gentler, more harmonious, settled, hierarchical world. At this interme-
diate stage, Graham's socialism and nationalism can be linked directly to
his writing, and may simply have been a desire for respectful reciprocity
in both class and culture, in a more ordered and equitable society, which
he believed existed in former times among the peasantry, and even in
the paternalism between landlord and tenant. Ironically, after attempting to de-romanticise Scotland on departing Gartmore House, he began,
unconsciously, to re-romanticise it, but in a non-sentimental fashion, by
emphasising the unique character of the landscape, the culture, and the
diversity of his rural characters.

Graham, it seems, became increasingly stuck in his nostalgic, 'heroic'
past; his writings showed little or no sign of development, and it is
possible, also, that his political ideas increasingly began to reflect this.

Notes

1. 'Erst kommt das Fressen, dann kommt die Moral', from Brecht's *The Three-
   penny Opera*.
2. An obituary described Graham as 'a splendid firebrand', but his personality as 'radio-active' and 'not likely to meet with official recognition'. *The*

Observer, 22 March 1936, p. 28. Graham's name never appeared in *Who's Who*, which, we must assume, was his own choice.

3. Hardie, *Labour Leader*, 15 March 1893, p. 3.
4. Cunninghame Graham, 'Has the Liberal Party a Future?' p. 298.
5. Glasier described Graham as 'a species of inverted dilettantism'. Glasier, *James Keir Hardie*, p. 28.
6. Robert Birkmyre, 'An Appreciation of Cunninghame Graham', *The Idler*, February 1909, p. 480. My italics. Plato's *Republic* was the earliest and most influential discourse on ethics, justice, oligarchies, and the abuse of state power, and this statement suggests that it might have been another codifier of Graham's political philosophy, perhaps a fundamental one.
7. Frank Harris, *Contemporary Portraits*, p. 46.
8. 'Romance and Realism', *Saturday Review*, 2 November 1929, p. 515.
9. John Carey, *The Intellectuals and the Masses: Pride and Prejudice among the Literary Intelligentsia, 1880–1939* (London: Faber & Faber, 1992).
10. Harvie, *Scotland and Nationalism*, p. 99.
11. '[T]hat magic period, youth, when things impress themselves on the imagination more sharply than in after years.' Cunninghame Graham, *Thirteen Stories*, p. x.
12. Watts, *Joseph Conrad's Letters*, p. 30.

PART III

'THE FLESHLY TENEMENT', 1914–36

Part III Introduction

FOLLOWING THE SALE OF the *Saturday Review*, Frank Harris and Graham did not meet for almost fifteen years. When they did meet, in 1912, Harris noted that 'he [Graham] had altered indefinably . . . the fine colouring had faded, and the light of his eyes was dimmed. He had grown old, the spring of hope had left him.'[1] However, this was not borne out by his activities. The *Manchester Guardian* confirmed that he had lost none of his high profile, nor his enthusiasm for change:

> He is a well-known figure in the West End of London, not only in the clubs, but also in Trafalgar Square, where he has probably made more speeches than any other living man . . . and is always in the middle of any revolutionary movement. He does not favour the moderate groups of Socialists, but is generally to be found associated with the extremists.[2]

Graham had been politically active from the start of the new century, attacking imperialism, particularly international intrigues in Morocco, and he had lost none of his fire defending the unemployed, supporting socialist candidates, and attacking Labour. For example, he supported the 'Labour and Socialist' candidate, W. G. Leechman, at the Springburn by-election in Glasgow in 1912, but he accused Labour MPs of 'a lack of courageous action on behalf of those whose money sent them to the Commons'.[3]

The First World War would have the double effect of revitalising Graham by giving his life renewed purpose, and precipitating a major political watershed, wherein he became more cynical over the direction that socialism was taking, both nationally and internationally. This part of the study examines the possible causes of his cynicism, and his reactions. It also examines the roots of his surprising bellicosity over the war, wherein his previous anti-imperialism was silenced, and he developed a negative attitude towards political events in Ireland.

Moreover, as an unexpected outcome of his ill-conceived attempt to re-engage with post-war parliamentary politics, and despite his support for Britain's role in the recent conflict, he would find a new position as a political figurehead in a reborn Scottish national consciousness. This remains another landmark in Graham's current reputation in the world of Scottish politics, as one of the founders of modern Scottish nationalism, but an attempt is also made in the study to establish his true role and significance.

During this period, there would be a marked diminution in the frequency of Graham's writings, but the subject matter of nostalgic recollections of South America, and to a lesser extent, Scotland, remained unchanged. What did change was the vibrancy and tone, becoming even more reflective. We are now entering a phase where he became more politically detached and independent, and where Scotland would play an increasing part in his political, if not his literary life.

Notes

1. Harris, *Contemporary Portraits*, p. 55.
2. *Manchester Guardian*, 23 February 1914, p. 7.
3. *Glasgow Herald*, 27 September 1912, p. 8. Thomas Johnston was also on the platform.

14

Labour: Touched by Pitch

IN JANUARY 1914, SEVERAL newspapers announced Graham's selection as the 'socialist' candidate for the Rectorship of Glasgow University,[1] and the Marxist, John MacLean, was full of enthusiastic praise:

> We congratulate the students on their choice of the worthiest Scot to hold aloft the Red Flag of Socialism, knowing that thereby an increasing interest will be taken in our views and principles by students old and young through out the land; and we trust by November we can again congratulate them on electoral success, knowing that victory would bring a wealth of grist to the Socialist mill.[2]

At this time in Scotland, MacLean was the leading light of the loosely constituted British Socialist Party (BSP),[3] and at some point, Graham had joined the party. By 1916, the *Manchester Guardian*, described him as among the 'leading members' of the BSP.[4] This involvement was never mentioned by Graham, nor by his biographers, but it fits the now familiar pattern of inconvenient facts being omitted. Two days after the *Guardian* article, at their annual conference at Caxton Hall, Manchester, the BSP acrimoniously split between the pro and anti-war factions, and the party leader, Hyndman, led his 'Pro-Ally' group out, both sides vigorously singing 'The Red Flag' at each other.[5] For Graham, who previously had been anti-war, but who was one of those who had signed the BSP pro-war manifesto, this was his last direct involvement in purely socialist politics.

MacDiarmid would later write:

> The Labour and Socialist Movement in Scotland was unaccompanied by any counterpart of the slightest consequence in literature and the arts and failed even to yield any book that influenced the general development of British, let alone European Socialism'[6]

This was a typical overstatement. Hardie had published a well-argued and influential propagandist essay, *From Serfdom To Socialism*, in 1907,[7] and a year before that, in October 1906, a young pretender to the radical journalistic crown of Scotland emerged in the person of Thomas Johnston, who co-founded and edited the ILP newspaper, *Forward*,[8] with the stated intention 'to rouse Scotland, to stir the lethargic, to waken the dead'.[9] *Forward* was presented in an accessible and light-hearted style, and followed a left-wing, republican, pacifist, and home rule agenda. It mainly reported on disputes, with regular features on socialist doctrine, not dissimilar to the pieces that Graham had written twenty years earlier. It was surprising therefore, that Graham appears not to have directly contributed to it, apart from the very occasional letter, although it republished a few of his earlier political articles.[10] In the context of Scotland, this seems like a missed opportunity, but *Forward* was the house journal of the ILP in Scotland, and despite being admired by Johnston, Graham may have felt that his involvement was now inappropriate.

Johnston, thirty years Graham's junior, came from a relatively comfortable middle-class background, but could hardly have been more different from Graham in his demeanour. According to Emanuel 'Manny' Shinwell, Johnston was 'awkward and shy', and preferred writing to oratory,[11] but like Compton Mackenzie, he copied Graham's personal style. Galbraith wrote that 'Patrick Dollan[12] testified that next to R. B. Cunninghame Graham, he [Johnston] was the biggest swell in the [socialist] movement',[13] and despite Graham being a product of the very landowning class that Johnston attacked in his books, Johnston wrote of him:

> Those who have the personal friendship and acquaintance of the intrepid Socialist leader, have often hugged themselves as they visioned the occurrences that would of a surety arrive, were the Stuarts to return to the Scottish throne in the person of the man who wrote 'Success' and who went to gaol for the unemployed.[14]

Johnston had chaired a meeting in Glasgow in 1913, to which Graham had brought the Irish transport strike leader, Jim Larkin,[15] and he had campaigned for Graham during his aborted Glasgow University rectorship bid in 1914. However, post-war, their views would come into conflict.

In 1909, Johnston published his scurrilous but hugely influential *Our Scots Noble Families*,[16] written on the basis that '[a] democracy ignorant of the past is not qualified either to analyse the present or to shape the future'.[17] Although Johnston himself would later call it as 'historically one sided and unjust and quite unnecessarily wounding',[18] Robert Middlemass described it as 'the most caustic arraignment of the Scottish aristocracy ever committed to print',[19] and it apparently sold over 120,000 copies.[20] Johnston was no less passionate than Graham, but unlike the older man, he was politically focused, and attacked the institutions, particularly Scotland's aristocracy, whom he believed were little more than land-grabbers and robbers. This view had of course formed an integral part of Graham's early parliamentary campaigns, using the same language and critiques. For example, in his Introduction, Johnston took a similar 'Georgist' view to Graham that exclusivity in land was the basis of all Scotland's social ills, 'so long as half the race is compelled by dire necessity to kneel cap-in-hand before the Lord who "owns" the soil, so long will our rural populations be cast in an unmanly and spiritless mould',[21] echoing Graham's complaint that the peasantry had been robbed of their birthright and independence. This exclusivity, and the 'extortion' of rents, a grievous wrong, had not only driven the people from the land, it had shut them out from the beauties of nature, and herded them into smoky cities.[22] These criticisms had long since fallen away from Graham's campaigns, but Johnston went on to develop his ideas on land ownership in his celebrated book, *A History of the Working Classes in Scotland* (1920),[23] which was a 'first reader' for many socialists. In *Our Noble Families*, Johnston claimed that Scottish history had been 'inverted to fan their [the landowner's] conceits',[24] but in his new work, he set about correcting that inversion, and in the process, both books weaponised Scottish history. Although fundamentally socialist arguments, they provided valuable ammunition for both socialists and nationalists, by transforming the nation's history into a cavalcade of greed and oppression, easily transmitted from enthusiast to enthusiast, to be weaponised again and again, a propaganda success that Graham never came close to emulating.

Like Graham, Johnston was a man of action, but unlike Graham, when he became an MP, he worked within the political system, preferring persuasion to confrontation, and he eventually achieved high political office and great power. According to the historian Tom Devine, 'Johnston was a giant figure in Scottish politics and is revered to this day as the greatest Scottish Secretary of the [twentieth] century'.[25] Graham, by his very nature, attacked rather than compromised, and studiously avoided any executive or managerial involvements, ending up with no power, except the power to influence. These fundamental differences go a long way in highlighting his weakness not only as a serious politician, but also as a serious historian and writer. In his earlier, overtly polemical writings, Graham the dilettante displayed an imaginative whimsy, flitting from subject to subject, delivering short swipes at politicians and magnates. In contrast, Johnston's works, although showing no desire to present a balanced view of Scottish social history, involved a huge amount of laborious, detailed research and cogent argument that added up to a damning indictment of Scotland's ruling elites. As for Graham's 'historical' writings, which began in 1901 and at last began to display a storytelling ability, they lacked historical rigour.

On Sunday 2 August 1914, two days before Britain declared war on Germany, Graham, together with Hardie and other socialist leaders, addressed a tumultuous rally of an estimated twenty thousand people in Trafalgar Square. According to Hardie's biographer, William Stewart, Graham's speech:

> was said to have made the most profound impression, and to have been the best he had ever delivered, which was saying a great deal. 'Do not,' he implored, 'let us do this crime, or be parties to the misery of millions who have never done us harm.'[26]

Graham had long held an anti-war position,[27] and had described uniforms as 'a thing to be ashamed of',[28] but within two weeks of his Trafalgar Square speech, at the age of sixty-two, he volunteered for unpaid military service, and in November 1914, the *Glasgow Herald* reported that he had been given a commission by the War Office.[29] On 20 November, a letter from Graham appeared in the *Daily News & Leader* in which he said that Britain had been forced into war by Germany, and that 'we, perhaps by accident, have been forced into the right course, and that all smaller nationalities as Montenegro, Ireland, Poland, and the rest, would disappear on our defeat'.[30] Shortly afterwards, he departed for Montevideo where he spent six months buying horses for the war effort on behalf of the government.[31] Despite spending only a total of fifteen months overseas during the conflict, until the end of the war, newspaper reports of his activities at home were few.

Andrew Thorpe argued that the Labour party managed to retain cohesion and consistency throughout the conflict,[32] as, more recently, did Matthew Worley,[33] but not without many difficulties. Individual disputes continued within the socialist ranks, including for Graham. As an example of the animosity that now existed between erstwhile comrades over the war, in November of 1916, Glasier recorded in his diary that he had confronted Graham in the House of Commons lobby over his anti-German rhetoric. Graham had wished to be friendly, but Glasier snubbed him, and accused him of using William Morris's name to defame Germany:

> 'Was it fair, was it manly to do so in order to further influence the blind hatred of the British public against Germany?' I repeated the question again and again. He then confessed that 'perhaps he had made a mistake.' I then

spoke my mind to him about his wheel-around to 'patriotism', reminding him of his speech (when I supported him) at the Labour Conference upstairs on the very day that war was declared.[34] He shuffled, and just as it was getting rather warm . . . Graham said finally, 'But Glasier, we must not allow a thirty-year friendship to be broken by this stupid war' – or words to that effect. He is a poor creature.[35]

Three days after the Armistice, on 14 November 1918, Prime Minister Lloyd George called a general election. It was the first in eight years, and Graham was approached by the West Stirlingshire Liberal Association to stand as the 'Liberal Coalition' candidate, which, considering his previous record and experience with the party, is rather surprising – as was his acceptance. That said, the late war, which had been brought to a successful conclusion under the leadership of Lloyd George, had itself changed the political landscape, with the premier proclaiming that his task was to make Britain 'a fit country for heroes to live in'.[36] On 6 February 1918, for example, the Representation of the People Act was passed, enfranchising women over the age of thirty who met minimum property qualifications to vote for the first time. It no doubt appeared to many, including Graham, that the war would usher in a new dawn in which far-reaching reforms could take place, and he qualified his support for Lloyd George by saying that he would support him so long as he introduced progressive legislation.[37] By now, the Liberals would have been his only available political option. His friend and sometime publisher, James Leatham, explained, 'Graham, having no trade union connection or Labour Party backing, allowed himself once more to be nominated as a Liberal candidate for West Stirlingshire.'[38] However, he still retained kudos in the political arena. The *Stirling Observer* referred to him as 'an outstanding personality in the political world',[39] and as a local figure who had supported the late war, he obviously carried some weight in and around the garrison town of Stirling itself, where he drew large audiences.

At this election, Graham's stated aims were almost unchanged from his original parliamentary campaigns – the nationalisation of the mines, shipping, and eventually all the means of production, but he made no mention of the nationalisation of land, home rule for Ireland, nor the abolition of the House of Lords. He did, however, restate his support for women's suffrage, and 'he looked forward to the time when all sex disabilities would be removed, and women might aspire to the highest positions in the State'.[40] The *Stirling Observer* reported, at the beginning of his campaign at Bannockburn:

He in common with many other members of the community loyally supported the Premiership of Mr Asquith, and afterwards, that of Mr Lloyd

George, and it was his opinion to-day that it would be wise and well considered to entrust the Government which had been so successful in carrying the war to a victorious issue with the reconstruction and the dealing with the vast problems which would beset us in the immediate future. (*Applause.*)[41]

Obviously, he now saw himself taking part in the reshaping of this new post-war world.

Despite plaudits and assurances, it appears that the Liberal hierarchy had longer memories than those in Stirling, and Graham's position as the official candidate was unceremoniously usurped by the wartime 'Citizen's Coalition' with the imposition (or 'couponing') of a Coalition 'Unionist' candidate, Mr (later, Sir) Harry Hope, without the agreement of the two local party associations, which Graham quite rightly resented.[42] His other opponent, representing Labour, was his erstwhile supporter, thirty-seven-year-old Tom Johnston, and Leatham justifiably asked the question, 'Why did Graham stand as a Liberal against a good Labour man?'. Leatham's only explanation was that there was:

> a streak of wayward willfulness about him. By this time, Graham had no status within the Labour party, and had claimed that Liberalism was in no way a limiting factor, and had been Socialist or even Communist as the occasion seemed to demand.[43]

This was another informative affirmation of how Graham viewed political parties, but ignores the fact that the war had changed the political landscape. The ILP had made little electoral progress, Hutchison stating that 'Before 1914, the ILP never became a mass or even moderately popular party',[44] while the Liberals had seen a swing towards a more social agenda, and that 'Socialists on the eve of the war were left complaining that too many Scottish Liberal M.P.s were at least as far to the left as Labour, so that no breakthrough was achievable.'[45] Also, at a more immediate level, at an election meeting in Plean, Graham stated that despite Johnston standing on a platform that was almost identical to his own, he opposed him because he [Johnston] was a pacifist. (*Applause.*)[46] For his own part, Johnston seems not to have borne Graham any resentment, believing that the seat was unwinnable for him anyway.[47] In his memoirs, Johnston claimed that he never wanted to be an MP,[48] although he won the seat for Labour four years later (he retained it for only for two years).

Graham was received by large and enthusiastic audiences during his campaign,[49] but like his experiences in North-West Lanarkshire, although his policies appealed to rank-and-file Liberal members and the working classes, particularly the miners, the senior members of the association were less enthusiastic. This was no doubt because Graham still espoused controversial views, but more likely because he insisted on standing against the official Coalition candidate, with little chance of success, in the post-war euphoria. On 4 December, immediately after his nomination, Graham wrote to the Liberal Association withdrawing his candidacy because of the 'scant courtesy' extended to him.[50] This elicited a letter to the *Glasgow Herald* from the vice president of the local association stating that they had asked him to reconsider, as they believed that 'the Liberal prospects were never brighter in the constituency than under his candidacy'.[51] On the same page, the newspaper reported that Graham had changed his mind, and had withdrawn his withdrawal and would go to the poll. Meanwhile, the association claimed that it had been a 'misunderstanding'.[52] Despite his strident support for the war, in Lloyd George's 'Coupon Election' he came third, behind Johnston, both defeated by Hope.[53]

General Election Result, West Stirlingshire, *21 December 1918*

Harry Hope (Unionist)	6,893
Thomas Johnston (Labour)	3,809
R. B. Cunninghame Graham (Liberal)	2,582

Undoubtedly, Graham regretted standing, even before the election result was announced. Neil Munro recalled a letter from him, sent from Stirling on the eve of the poll, stating that he was sick of 'this infernal folly of elections'.[54]

Consequently, while he would periodically refer to himself as a socialist,[55] the general election of 1918 marked the end of Graham's personal parliamentary campaigns, and his engagement with socialism in general. There seems to have been two main reasons for this, one national, and the other international. Not only had the demeanour and attitudes of the country changed as a result of the war, so too had attitudes towards governmental bureaucracy. In June 1918, the Labour party adopted Sidney Webb's programme entitled *Labour and the New Social Order*, which committed the party to full employment, a comprehensive system of benefits, the nationalisation of land, the railways, electricity, and coal, and a wealth tax to pay for the war. This could be seen as the fruition of Graham's socialist dreams, but ironically, it was not. Thorpe wrote that Webb's programme was aimed at preserving the extended wartime state; that socialism could be 'an agent of national efficiency', offering 'bureaucratic top-down socialism', and the possibility of bringing about socialism by state action alone.[56] William Knox and Alan MacKinlay

wrote about the changes within the Labour party whereby the idealism that had inspired early adherents like Graham 'was to be dissipated
as electoral success and governmental responsibility shifted Labour to
a pragmatic political course, and to reliance on the bureaucrat and the
planner rather than the people'.[57] According to Knox and MacKinlay, in
later years, particularly during the Depression years of 1929 and 1932,
they believed that:

> Ethical socialism and a belief in working people's right to control their
> destiny gave way to belief in a strong, technocratic state . . . It was the task
> of the experts and technocrats to deliver the socialist commonwealth via
> planning, science, and technology.[58]

This was not Graham's idea of socialism. Despite his disillusionment
with working-class aspirations, he still believed that it should be a 'bottom-up' process whereby the workers and the poor themselves would
bring about their own enlightened emancipation, but what he felt he was
witnessing was bureaucratic diktat. MacDiarmid recalled an undated
speech in which Graham said that the Labour party was 'merely a third
party struggling for place, for office, and for the fruit of government,
all their high ideals lost, and all their aspirations locked away in some
dark corner of their souls'.[59] These sentiments would seem to confirm the
belief that fundamentally, the basis for his socialism was moral, and not
a little idealistic.

The late war fundamentally changed his attitude in another way.
Graham, who had been at the forefront of disputes and conflict only a
few years earlier, now, having witnessed the bloody results of 'bottom-up'
socialism in Russia, saw its influence threatening to spill over onto the
streets of Britain. There had been no comment from him on the Rent Strike
in Glasgow of 1915 (at which time he was back in Scotland), and there was
a marked silence during the General Strike in Glasgow in January 1919,
in which the 'Bolshevik' John MacLean was prominent, and the 'Bloody
Friday' riots in George Square. He may have regarded the Rent Strike as
justified, but at that time unpatriotic, and a distraction from the war in
France. As for the General Strike, there was undoubtedly a revolutionary
aspect to these agitations. In his 1918 election speeches he had expressed
strong antipathy to Bolshevism, and in that context, he expressed critical
views (it must be said, ironically) of the now imprisoned MacLean:

> [F]or whose cause he had no sympathy, nevertheless he thought he should be
> set at liberty. (*Applause.*) M'Lean [*sic*] he considered a harmless visionary,
> he believed a good citizen in private life, but with a super-abundant dose of
> vanity in his composition.[60]

In January 1918, MacLean had been appointed Bolshevik Representative in Scotland, and at the election meeting in Plean, a member of the audience asked if Graham would vote for recognition of Soviet Russia. Graham replied 'that the only recognition he would give the miserable blood-stained wretches, Lenin and Trotsky, would be at the end of a piece of hard rope on the gallows. (*Laughter and applause.*)'[61]

Notes

1. *Glasgow Herald*, 28 January 1914, p. 11. By September, Graham (whose great-grandfather, Robert, had been Rector from 1785 to 1787) had asked that his name be removed because of the war. *Glasgow Herald*, 16 September 1914, p. 9.
2. 'Gael' (John MacLean), 'Scottish Notes', *Justice*, 5 February 1914, p. 6.
3. The BSP was founded in 1911, and comprised members of the ailing SDF, and ILP dissidents, among others.
4. *Manchester Guardian*, 22 April 1916, p. 7.
5. Rosalind Hyndman, *The Last Years of H. M. Hyndman* (London: Richards, 1923), p. 120. She added, 'we began first'.
6. MacDiarmid, *Centenary Study*, p. 10.
7. Stewart described it as 'the most compact and vivid statement of the case for Socialism that has ever been written'. Stewart, *J. Keir Hardie*, p. 240. However, Benn conceded that 'Hardie as ideologue has never commanded respect from intellectuals'. Benn, *Keir Hardie*, p. 243.
8. The two major shareholders of Forward Printing & Publishing Company were Johnston and fellow socialist and ILP member, and later Scottish nationalist funder and propagandist, R. E. Muirhead, who would be Graham's support and encouragement in later years. George Bernard Shaw described *Forward* as 'the first newspaper worth a workman's tuppence'. Quoted by Douglas Young in Neil MacCormick, ed., *The Scottish Debate: Essays on Scottish Nationalism* (Oxford University Press, 1970), p. 11.
9. Thomas Johnston, 'Editorial', *Forward*, 13 October 1906, p. 4.
10. Graham's piece 'The Imperial Kailyard', which had first appeared in *Justice* in 1896, was reprinted in *Forward* on 31 August, 1907, p. 2, and his speech on women's suffrage in the St Andrew's Hall was also reported, *Forward*, 12 October, 1907, p. 6.
11. Quoted in Russell Galbraith, *No Quarter Given: A Biography of Tom Johnston* (Edinburgh: Mainstream Publishing, 1995), p. 8.
12. Patrick Dollan (1885–1963), socialist activist, later knighted. Lord Provost of Glasgow, 1938–41.
13. Quoted in Dollan's unpublished biography. Galbraith, *No Quarter Given*, p. 8.
14. Johnston, *Our Scots Noble Families* (Glasgow: Forward Publishing Company, 1909), p. 98.

15. *Glasgow Herald*, 11 December 1913, p. 10.
16. Johnston, *Our Scots Noble Families*. This book was compiled from articles that had previously been regular features in *Forward*.
17. Johnston, *Our Scots Noble Families*, p. xii.
18. Johnston, *Memories* (London: Collins, 1952), p. 35. Johnston halted publication when he joined Winston Churchill's Coalition cabinet in 1941 as Secretary of State for Scotland, and it was rumoured that he tried to buy copies back.
19. R. K. Middlemass, *The Clydesiders* (London: Hutchison, 1965), p. 47.
20. Johnston, *Memories*, p. 35.
21. Johnston, *Our Scots Noble Families*, p. ix. Johnston, however, repeatedly criticised George's economics from the pages of *Forward*, between 1907 and 1936.
22. Ibid., pp. ix–x.
23. Johnston, *A History of the Working Classes in Scotland* (Glasgow: Forward Publishing Company, 1920).
24. Ibid., p. viii.
25. T. M. Devine, *The Scottish Nation, 1700–2000* (London: Allen Lane, 1999), p. 521.
26. Stewart, *J. Keir Hardie*, p. 344. There was no record of this speech published in contemporary newspapers. However, in his biography of Graham, Tschiffely, presumably under Graham's direction, said the direct opposite of what Stewart claimed, stating: 'Instead of denouncing the war, as everybody expected he would, he said that England, the mother of freedom and the home of liberty, must throw her weight in the crises into the scale of humanity.' Tschiffely, *Don Roberto*. p. 360. This was another example of Graham adapting the past to suit how he wished to be remembered.
27. Graham had invited Joseph Conrad to a pacifist meeting in London in early 1899, but Conrad declined the invitation, with the words 'I am not a man of peace, nor a democrat'. Watts, *Joseph Conrad's Letters*, p. 116.
28. Cunninghame Graham, 'Futurism', p. 9.
29. *Glasgow Herald*, 4 November 1914, p. 6. Graham stated that he had been offered the grade of colonel, which he refused, 'thinking it ridiculous for a private citizen not a military man to hold such a title'. *Stirling Observer*, 2 December 1918, p. 3. Tschiffely wrote, however, that Graham had accepted the rank of colonel, but had refused to wear the uniform. Tschiffely, *Don Roberto*, p. 361.
30. *Daily News & Leader*, 20 November 1914, p. 4.
31. *Glasgow Herald*, 11 August 1917, p. 4. Graham returned to South America on 17 February 1917 to report to the British government on cattle resources, staying until 31 March, but he did not arrive back in Britain until the beginning of August. Only one report appeared in the newspapers that year, describing Graham's investigations in Columbia. *Glasgow Herald*, 11 August 1917, p. 4.
32. Andrew Thorpe, *A History of the British Labour Party* (London: Macmillan, 1997), p. 36.

33. Matthew Worley, *Labour Inside the Gate: A History of the British Labour Party Between the Wars* (London: I. B. Tauris, 2005), p. 31.
34. It was in fact held the day after, on 5 August 1914.
35. Laurence Thompson, *The Enthusiasts: A Biography of Bruce and Katharine Glasier* (London: Gollancz, 1971), p. 209.
36. Lloyd George, speech at Wolverhampton, 23 November 1918, reported in *The Times*, 25 November 1918, p. 13.
37. *Stirling Observer*, 2 December 1918, p. 2.
38. Leatham, *60 Years*, p. 159.
39. *Stirling Observer*, 23 November 1918, p. 4.
40. *Stirling Observer*, 26 November 1918, p. 5.
41. Ibid.
42. Ibid.
43. Leatham, *60 Years*, p. 160.
44. Hutchison, *Scottish Politics*, p. 22.
45. Ibid., p. 6.
46. *Stirling Observer*, 2 December 1918, p. 2. Johnston had repeatedly attacked the war through the pages of *Forward*.
47. Their combined vote would still not have beaten the 'coupon' candidate.
48. Johnston, *Memories*, pp. 46–7.
49. *Stirling Observer*, 26 November 1918, p. 5.
50. *Stirling Observer*, 7 December 1918, p. 5.
51. *Glasgow Herald*, 6 December 1918, p. 6.
52. Ibid.
53. Johnston believed that Hope won because he was even more bellicose over the war than Graham, and had a platform of hanging the Kaiser, and that the electorate believed that Graham 'would not pull the rope tight enough'. Johnston, *Memories*, pp. 46–7.
54. Munro, *The Brave Days*, p. 316.
55. *Glasgow Herald*, 30 October 1928, p. 9.
56. Thorpe, *History of the British Labour Party*, pp. 45–6.
57. W. W. Knox and A. MacKinlay, 'The Re-Making of Scottish Labour in the 1930s', *Twentieth Century British History* (Oxford University Press, 1995), p. 174.
58. Ibid., p. 181.
59. MacDiarmid, *Centenary Study*, p. 29. Graham repeated this sentiment at a speech on behalf of the National Party of Scotland in Kings Park, Stirling on 21 June 1930. *Scots Independent Supplement*, July 1930, p. 3.
60. *Stirling Observer*, 26 November 1918, p. 5. Graham's negative view of MacLean may also have been coloured by MacLean's pacifism. MacDiarmid doubted the two men ever met, stating, 'If they had met it is unlikely they would have got on together'. MacDiarmid *Centenary Study*, p. 9.
61. *Stirling Observer*, 2 December 1918, p. 2.

15

Empire and Colonialism: Volte-face

IN PARALLEL WITH HIS views expressed above, we now come to what his later biographers saw as Graham's volte-face over his attitudes to empire, with his enthusiastic support for what many saw as a capitalist war between the major European powers for imperial dominance. The consensus among historians was that the suddenness and unexpectedness of the war took many on the left by surprise, and created dilemmas both for political parties and individuals, including the consequential alliance with Czarist Russia.[1] Clayton, writing in 1926, believed:

> The actual declaration of war settled the matter as far as the majority was concerned. Hyndman and Cunninghame Graham . . . sought peace while it endured, but now that war had come, well, Socialists and Trade Unionists, like other people had got to see it through.[2]

Despite Graham's distaste for what he called 'oceans of false sentiment at home',[3] a later commentator, writing under the pseudonym 'Histronicus', wrote that Graham had been motivated by a sense of honour:

> Graham strongly opposed the government's attitude to war. In 1914, however, convinced that this was a war against tyranny, and because of his passionate love of liberty and keen sense of honour, he volunteered to go to South America on a horse-buying mission.[4]

In a similar fashion, Helen Smith wrote that Graham had 'protested vigorously against the prospect of conflict, but once it had commenced, he lent his support in the hope that the fighting would be brought to a swift conclusion.'[5] Moreover, his mother had apparently upset Garnett for 'as good as calling me [Garnett] pro-German',[6] which indicated strong prejudices within Graham's immediate family circle. Perhaps Hyndman summed up the position of many:

> As matters stand to-day, it is a choice of evils in all the affairs of life. When a man is called upon to act, he must put up the shutters on one side of

his intellect. The victory of Germany would be worse for civilization and humanity than success of the Allies.[7]

Graham's change of heart had been swift, and as early as 29 August 1914, his prejudices were expressed in a letter in the *Glasgow Herald* headed 'A Strange Patriot', in which he attacked a previous letter signed 'JFS' that supported Germany against the French. In this letter, he referred to the Germans as 'blood thirsty murderers of defenseless women, children, and non-combatants'.[8] His full support for the war was demonstrated in a letter to *The Nation* in August 1915, in which he attacked the press, particularly *The Times* and the *Daily Mail*, for their lack of support for the British war effort.[9] After the war, during his election campaign in 1918, Graham stated:

> He had with his own eyes seen evidence that placed the Boche outside humanity . . . These barbarous murderers must be made to pay to the uttermost farthing for all the misery and bloodshed they have brought upon the world . . . This was not a war of capitalists, it was the working men of Germany who sang the hymn of hate, tortured prisoners, and cheered on the Army so long as they were winning.[10]

Graham appears to have regarded the war, not as a capitalist war, like many of his erstwhile comrades, but as a people's war. One of only two sketches that referred to the war, 'Brought Forward' (1915),[11] set in the Parkhead Forge, was a lively dialogue between workmates who were concerned about the conflict, but the news of the death of one of their fellows at the Front resolved itself when one of the workers donned his jacket, and set off to seek personal, but noble, revenge.

Hardie, Ramsay MacDonald, and many within the ILP remained adamantly opposed to the conflict: in Stewart's words, 'What they were doing now was to clear themselves and their Party from responsibility for the crime, and, if possible, hold the Labour movement of this country true and faithful to the spirit and pledge of International Socialism'.[12] Nevertheless, by the end of August, the Labour Party had agreed an electoral truce, and it was soon supporting the war effort. Thorpe identified a 'patriotic surge, and most Labour leaders would not have been immune from it', but even the sceptics among them realised that 'Labour might cause itself great damage by going against the tide of patriotism sweeping the country.'[13] According to Clayton, most British socialists and trade unionists were as patriotic as the rest of the nation, and only a minority were pacifist.[14] This seeming paradox was addressed by G. K. Chesterton in an article in the *Illustrated London News* in 1915:

> It is the moderate Socialists who are Pacifists; the fighting Socialists are patriots. Mr. Ben Tillett who would have been regarded by Mr. Ramsay Macdonald as a

mere firebrand; but it is precisely because Mr. Tillet was ready to go on fighting Capitalism that he is ready to go on fighting Krupp. It is precisely because Mr. Macdonald was weak in his opposition to domestic tyrants, that he is weak in his opposition to foreign ones.[15]

Boiled down, Chesterton was proposing that it was not simply a matter of moral or political principle, but a matter of mental attitude towards oppression, from whichever direction it came. In addition, there was often a sentimental patriotism even among the most hardened anti-war socialists. Graham's erstwhile Labour colleague, Robert Smillie, wrote of his own conflicting feelings: 'In spite of all my misgivings, there was part of me that was so completely British that I could not help but hope that, whatever happened, we would be on the winning side.'[16] Claeys claimed that 'pro-imperial attitudes were much more wide-spread among social-ists than is usually assumed, to the degree that "socialist imperialism" may be described as a leading trend in the early twentieth century'.[17] This had obviously not previously applied to Graham, but at the outset of the conflict there may have been something else in his character that fed his prejudices and changed his mind: the *aesthetic* aspect to warfare. In his sketch 'Mudejar',[18] in which a soldier spared the destruction of an ancient tower, a literary critic wrote: 'For here he [Graham] admits that the soul of man expressed in art may be even more sacred than the body of man. The Germans who destroyed Rheims are worse sinners than the Germans who shot peasants.'[19] The past had created beauty as well as folly and ugliness, and this beauty was a precious link to that civilised past. To Graham, perhaps, anyone who had instigated its destruction, in what would be an ugly mechanistic struggle, was therefore a barbarian, outwith the bounds of common humanity. Added to this, was something that Mackenzie spoke of later, a fear that Graham no doubt shared:

We desired to delete [*sic*] Germany not because Germany was an Imperial rival, but because a prepotent Germany seemed to us a menace to what was left of individual freedom. To us the triumph of Germany meant the triumph of bureaucracy.[20]

This was the same bureaucracy that was creeping into the state socialism envisaged in Webb's programme.

After the war, Graham's anti-German position was in no way modi-fied. During his election campaign, he made several extremely bellicose remarks not only about Germans, but also about pacifists. At an election meeting in Banknock, when asked what he would do with conscientious objectors, he replied that he would release them, 'and give them each a petticoat at the national expense. (*Laughter.*)'[21] He amplified this at

Plean, when he told his audience that he would give 'the conchies' a pair of openwork silk stockings each.[22] At Cambuskenneth he added 'suspenders to the fit out'.[23] This intemperate and rather squalid language, if not simply an appeal to populism, seems unworthy of a man who had previously expressed contempt for the empire he now upheld, and who had opposed the conflict at the outset, but he obviously felt very strongly about the war and the moral position of those who opposed it, and it may indeed have been another motivation to stand for election.

Graham's political career was replete with passionate involvements and prejudices, and he alluded to a tendency towards extreme views and an all-or-nothing approach in his passions:

> [F]or all of my life I have called bread, bread, and wine, wine,[24] not caring for half measures, like your true Scot, of whom it has been said, 'If he believes in Christianity he has no doubts, and if he is a disbeliever he has none either.'[25]

A reviewer wrote in response, 'We fear that no half measures may be looked for from a Scot.'[26] This may have dictated Graham's attitude towards the war; having decided that Britain's role was just,[27] and that the Germans were pursuing an ugly, mechanistic aggression, Graham, who despite his militancy deprecated violence and brutality, threw himself wholly into supporting it. Also, his views on the significance of the British Empire's role in the conflict appear to have overridden his previous imperial scepticism. This was expressed at the launch of his electoral campaign in 1918, and the *Stirling Observer* reported these new sentiments:

> For four years they had been engaged in a war the influence of which had been felt all over the world, and the Empire had made an effort so colossal, so heroic, and so self-sacrificing that when the history of the war came to be written [,] all that Britain, all the Empire had done, would be a household word that the generation which came after them should enjoy that peace and those blessings for which this generation had suffered and endured and shed its blood.[28]

Here, it is necessary to draw a distinction between the instigators and exploiters of empire, particularly in the remoter and undeveloped areas of the world, whom Graham had railed against, and the products of empire, i.e. the sons and daughters of what Bell called 'the second settler empire'[29] in Canada and the Antipodes, who had come to the motherland's aid during the conflict, and whose actions and sacrifice far outweighed the negative aspects of localised imperial abuses.

Subsequent to his electoral defeat in 1918, Graham made no recorded statement on imperial matters. The war had ushered in many political changes, both nationally and internationally, and Worley highlighted a general mood in the country subsequent to the conflict: 'For some, the war had marked the end of the old order, paving the way for alternative political ideologies that would range from communism to socialism to fascism to syndicalism to overt nationalism.'[30] It would now be to nationalism, albeit with a socialist complexion, that Graham would increasingly turn.

Notes

1. Graham had protested the Czar's visit to Britain in 1909 owing to his imprisonment of Socialists and Liberals. Cunninghame Graham, letter to *Forward*, 1 May 1909, p. 2.
2. Clayton, *Rise & Decline of Socialism*, p. 166.
3. Cunninghame Graham, *Cartagena on the Banks of the Sinú* (London: Heinemann, 1920), p. xi.
4. *Methodist Times*, London, 1 July 1937, p. 7. The fact that he selected his beloved animals to be slaughtered in the conflict bears testament to his commitment.
5. Helen Smith, *The Uncommon Reader*, p. 246.
6. Ibid.
7. Rosalind Hyndman, *Last Years of H. M. Hyndman*, pp. 82–3.
8. Cunninghame Graham, letter to the *Glasgow Herald*, 29 August 1914, p. 3. Four days later, Graham had another letter published in the *Glasgow Herald*, calling the Germans 'Huns', and accusing them of being 'murderers of children, and violators of young girls'. 'Abuse of the White Flag', *Glasgow Herald*, 2 September 1914, p. 3.
9. Cunninghame Graham, letter to *The Nation*, 14 August 1915, p. 643.
10. *Stirling Observer*, 2 December 1918, p. 2.
11. Cunninghame Graham, 'Brought Forward', *English Review*, February 1915, pp. 285–89. Graham's second wartime sketch was 'Elysium', *The Nation*, 26 February 1916, pp. 759–60. Anthologised in *Brought Forward* (1916), pp. 60–5.
12. Stewart, *J. Keir Hardie*, p. 345.
13. Thorpe, *History of the British Labour Party*, p. 33.
14. Clayton, *Rise & Decline of Socialism*, p. 164.
15. G. K. Chesterton, 'Our Note Book', *Illustrated London News*, 3 July 1915, p. 3.
16. Torquil Cowan, ed., *Labour of Love: The Story of Robert Smillie* (Glasgow: Neil Wilson Publishing, 2011), p. 205.
17. Claeys, *Imperial Sceptics*, p. 8.
18. Cunninghame Graham, 'Mudejar', *English Review*, April 1915, pp. 45–9. Anthologised in *Brought Forward* (1916), pp. 120–9.
19. *The Observer*, 12 November 1916, p. 4.

20. Mackenzie, 'Safety Last'. Address delivered in the St Andrew's Hall, Glasgow, on 29 January 1932, on his installation as Rector of the University of Glasgow. Reprinted in *Scotland in Quest of Her Youth*, ed. by David Cleghorn Thomson (Edinburgh: Oliver & Boyd, 1932), p. 48.

21. *Stirling Observer*, 10 December 1918, p. 5. 'A young man stigmatised another as being a "conchie" or a skulker, and this led to blows between them. The police had to separate the combatants.' 'The candidate had nothing to do with it.'

22. Ibid.

23. Ibid.

24. An allusion carried forward into his essay on Wilfrid Scawen Blunt. 'Bread was bread, verily to him, and wine was wine; the two could never mix their essences and become the hotch-potch dear to politicians.' Cunninghame Graham, 'Wilfrid Scawen Blunt', *English Review*, December 1922, p. 488. Anthologised in *Redeemed* (1927), pp. 58–69.

25. Cunninghame Graham, 'Preface', *Brought Forward* (London: Duckworth, 1909), p. vii.

26. "'Adieu!' He Cried,'" *The Nation*, 21 October 1916, p. 108.

27. Alasdair MacIntyre defined a 'just' war as 'one in which the good to be achieved outweighs the evils involved in waging war and in which a clear distinction can be made between the combatants and non-combatants', which Graham would have agreed with. Alasdair MacIntyre, *After Virtue* (1981) (London: Bloomsbury Academic, 2011), p. 7.

28. *Stirling Observer*, 26 November 1918, p. 5.

29. Bell, *Reordering The World*, p. 266.

30. Worley, *Labour Inside the Gate*, p. 31.

16

Scotland: Awakening of a Nation

A T THE BEGINNING OF his 1918 election campaign, Graham made his first statement on Irish home rule for several years. He reminded his audience at the Town Hall in Bannockburn that he had stood on 'a thousand platforms' with Michael Davitt and Parnell, promoting Irish Home Rule, and he had been the only British MP to attend Parnell's funeral.[1] He also contended that it was wrong to suggest that Ireland had not done her duty in the recent conflict: 'There were nearly half a million gallant Irishmen from Ireland, the United States, and the colonial dominions who had fought and bled for the common cause'; the question of Ireland's status, which had been a disgrace to Britain for a hundred years should be settled quickly.[2] Again, in this immediate post-war period, all of his political statements were predicated on his support for the war and Britain's military might, which was a complete reversal of his previous position. Included in this was a threat to Sinn Fein, wherein they would be faced with that might if they threatened separation by force: 'they could not have separation without bloodshed'.[3] Like socialism's manifestation in the new Soviet Russia, events in Ireland had, in Mackenzie's words, prejudiced him against the Irish point of view.[4]

As we have seen, Graham had not always criticised the use of political violence as a means of gaining freedom from what he regarded as tyranny, but now the late war and its aftermath seem to have changed not only his views of empire, but his justification of British actions against Irish Republican Army attacks. On 21 November 1920, a team of undercover British intelligence agents, living and working in Dublin, were murdered by Irish republicans, acts that had quickly been followed by British reprisals. Graham sent a letter to R. E. Muirhead deprecating these events, as if linking the aspirations of the recently reformed SHRA with the methods of the IRA. Muirhead did not reply until a month later (blaming his company's stocktaking), assuring Graham that the SHRA also deprecated the killings on both sides, but reminding him of other acts of repression carried out by the British government in Ireland.[5] In previous times, Graham would have no doubt agreed, but in his reply, on 27 December, he stated that these reprisals had been nothing compared to the republican outrages, and defended British actions. In closing, an obviously angry Graham wrote that the SHRA should not 'fall into the mistake of meddling in the affairs of others'.[6]

Graham was now disturbed by assassination. In a letter of 27 November 1927, he wrote to the war correspondent, H. W. Nevinson, criticising Nevinson's praise for Graham and Conrad's old acquaintance, Sir Roger Casement[7] in his recent book, *Last Changes, Last Chances*: 'The shooting of men by batches revolted me. The exploits of the two bands of scoundrels, the Gunmen [the IRA] and the Black and Tans (*Arcades ambo*), filled me with disgust.'[8]

During his 1918 election campaign, Graham had continued to express the Scottish home rule sentiments that he had maintained throughout his political career, as reported in the *Stirling Observer*: 'Mr Graham as a strong Scottish Home Ruler specially resented all dictation from London.'[9] At Cambuskenneth, for example it was reported:

> [T]hat as a Scotsman he was in favour of Home Rule for Scotland, and the restoration of the Parliament in Edinburgh. He resented very much the influence of London as to who should be their candidates, and said that it might do well in England and Wales, but as regards Scotland he should say with all the force at his command, 'Hands off Scotland'![10]

This sentiment was repeated four days later at Lennoxtown, where he described London's interference in Scotland's electoral process (which included his own) as 'the mailed fist of political Prussianism'.[11]

With Graham's failure to win Stirlingshire West, he temporarily disappeared from the pages of national and local newspapers as a political activist for twenty months, except for periodic outbursts on animal cruelty, but reviews of his anthologies still appeared regularly. However, in what looks like yet another unintended outcome, his name began to reappear as an advocate for Scottish Home Rule, and we now move into what is considered a major part of his role in Scotland's political heritage.

On 3 August 1920, Graham wrote to Muirhead, declining an invitation to address a forthcoming rally,[12] but Muirhead persisted, and replied:

> During your campaign in Stirlingshire at the last election you delivered some very effective speeches in favour of Scottish Self-Government, I take it therefore that you are strongly convinced of the necessity of the establishing of a

Parliament in Scotland, that being the case I felt that if you could afford the time at you could be willing to do something to obtain Self-Government if for no other reason that it would enable you to feel more self-respect.[13]

This cleverly worded response contained the suggestion of a rebuke, and it seems to have been sufficient to convince Graham to change his mind, and to speak at the Wallace Day Commemoration at Elderslie, near Paisley, on 21 August. Many years later Muirhead wrote that Graham's change of mind had occurred in Glasgow 'as a result of some talks with him that he expressed his desire to join the Scottish Home Rule Association and he did so in August 1920'.[14] This initial correspondence established the pattern of address between the two men for the next fourteen years. Muirhead's letters were business-like, containing exchanges on the weather, news items, and latterly, the NPS's travails at elections, plus small blandishments, intended to encourage the now peripatetic Graham to speak at rallies.[15] Undoubtedly, Muirhead and the other SHRA members regarded Graham with some reverence, and saw him as a major asset as a crowd-puller, but the tone of their correspondence remained formal.

Leading up to the First World War, there had been a growing sense of reawakened Scottish national identity, manifesting itself, as stated previously, in an interest among certain individuals in Scotland's Celtic past. This was very slowly becoming politicised through various small and diverse groups, such as the Young Scots Society from 1900, *Comunn nan Albanach Lunnainn* (The Scots National League, London) from 1910, the rebirth of the SHRA in 1917, and Erskine of Marr's Scots National League from 1920.[16] Although, latterly, they would share speaking duties at NPS rallies, Graham may have avoided involvement with Erskine because of his avowed insistence on a religious element to his nationalism, which Graham, despite his sentimental interest in Catholicism in his youth, would have found anathema in the context of a projected new consensual movement. Graham's scepticism may also have been rooted in Erskine's attachment to what Finlay described as 'romantic notions of Celticism', which were eventually rejected by the Scots National League itself.[17] Finlay described the Scots National League as 'the most important of all the interwar nationalist groups'; it was established for the sole purpose of obtaining Scottish self-government, through the establishment of a new party that would run candidates at local and general elections, whereas the SHRA advocated autonomy within the existing structure of Britain, and cross-party cooperation.[18] These varying objectives would plague the nationalist movements for most of the 1920s, and also later, when the various groups amalgamated into the NPS and the SNP.

Again, a major motivating factor in this new nationalism was not simply economic but cultural, or perhaps the voices in what was seen as a new Scottish renaissance had the skills to express the various 'national' feelings more distinctly, and commentators found it easier to refer to these more recognisable adherents. In 1929, John Barbour launched an attack on this aspect of the nationalist case in the *Edinburgh Review*:

> A Scottish literary renaissance is in the air, fighting hard to break through the long mists of national self-denial. Scotland today swarms with minor poets – heralds, let us hope, of some new 'surpassing spirit.' Mr. Cunninghame Graham, Mr. C. M. Grieve [MacDiarmid], the Hon. Erskine of Marr – these are typical figures in the Scottish literary renaissance. Their chief weakness is their *impatient versatility* – best exemplified in the work of the ubiquitous Mr. Grieve.[19]

While it is problematic to place Graham among the leaders of any literary 'renaissance' (he had been writing similar material since at least 1900), he had certainly displayed an impatience throughout his political career. This general nationalist impatience, according to Barbour, stemmed from a shared belief that Scotland was in danger: 'All the tendencies reveal a nation slowly waking to the fear of being about to lose its soul, and striving to convince itself, with the aggressiveness of self-distrust, that it still has a personality of its own.'[20] Future Prime Minister Ramsay MacDonald put it thus:

> The Anglification of Scotland has been proceeding apace to the damage of its education system, its music, its literature, its genius, and the generation that is growing up under this influence is uprooted from its past, and, being deprived of the inspiration of its nationality, is also deprived of its communal sense.[21]

Graham's speech at Elderslie, on 21 August 1920, where he was described as 'the leading speaker',[22] was the first recorded speech on home rule for Scotland since he spoke in support of a Scottish Home Rule Bill in 1889. As in that speech (after the usual nationalist tropes about Bruce and Wallace,[23] and Graham's assertion that he was a direct descendant of Wallace's 'bosom friend' Sir John de Graham), he declared that he wished to see a Scottish Parliament that would make up for what he saw as a democratic deficit in the way that Scotland was governed. Moreover, in what was a departure from previous statements, he added, 'it could bring again the feeling of and sentiments of nationalism'.[24]

In 1923, Muirhead again asked Graham to speak at a 'Scotland's Day' rally on Glasgow Green, to be held on 25 August. Graham replied, accepting the invitation, but asking for a copy of the guest list, as he would not share a platform with anyone who had been pro-German during the war, or, if Irish, had murdered an unarmed man, Catholic or Protestant.[25]

As it transpired, due to an attack of rheumatism, Graham did not attend what turned out to be a large and well-attended historical pageant. The Labour MP James Maxton ably replaced him, certainly in terms of nationalistic fervour.[26] Maxton, who, like Graham, was charismatic, a firebrand speaker, and a natural rebel, acknowledged that 'hitherto there had been no real support for the demand for Scottish Home Rule', believing that the Scottish public representatives had passively accepted English domination. He himself had not been convinced of the need for a Scottish Parliament until he had been the member of an English one, but now he was absolutely persuaded of the necessity for a Scottish Parliament, 'absolutely free of the English people'. Finally, Maxton, who had been a conscientious objector, and who had been imprisoned for sedition in 1916, urged his audience 'to carry on the agitation for an independent parliament in Scotland, even though it meant a fight like that of Ireland,[27] a sentiment with which Graham would now have profoundly disagreed.[28]

During the early 1920s, Maxton and his Labour colleagues were the parliamentary standard bearers of Scottish home rule. With the Liberals in a steady national decline, and after the general election of 1923, it was believed that Ramsay MacDonald's minority government, with the tacit support of the Liberals, would enact the necessary legislation. Things reached a watershed when the Gorbals Labour MP, George 'Geordie' Buchanan, proposed a Government of Scotland Bill,[29] which received its second reading on 9 May 1924, seconded by Johnston.[30] It was talked out by the Tories, causing an uproar in the chamber, which led to the suspension of three Labour MPs, including Maxton and David Kirkwood. MacDonald's minority government was removed from office before any further legislation could be proposed. The SHRA, which was dominated by Labour members, was now at an impasse, and there were increasing calls for some new form of activity in order to circumvent the stranglehold of Labour's British interests.[31] Despite this, Muirhead was still writing to Graham in August of that year, expressing his optimism that the Labour government would enact a Home Rule Bill, and making no mention that the SHRA was deeply divided over its future. Simultaneously, Labour turned cool on the issue of Scottish home rule, and it was dropped from its manifesto.

Like Charles Waddie before him, Muirhead was the main promoter and funder of the SHRA. Hitherto it had been a loose confederation of cross-party enthusiasts, cultural organisations, affiliated socialist groups, and trade unionists, but it was now beginning to see a diminution in attendances at meetings and rallies. Muirhead still saw the need for action through parliament, if only, at this stage, to put more pressure on the other political parties, and this marks a significant milestone in the formation of a viable nationalist organisation. On 9 March 1926, Muirhead informed Graham that 'the question of the formation of a Scottish National Party is one which may be discussed at the Annual Meeting, having failed to reach a decision at the previous one'.[32] A Scottish National Convention was subsequently held, sponsored by the SHRA, in an attempt to bring the various parties together, and it drafted a further Home Rule Bill. This was proposed on 13 May 1927 by the Labour MP, the Reverend James Barr,[33] again seconded by Johnston, but again talked out.[34] It was at this juncture that we witness the beginnings of a major schism on the left of Scottish politics, one that continues to this day. It was not a matter of socialists versus home rulers – up to this point they were essentially the same people. It was a matter of priorities. One group believed that there was a strong prospect of extending socialist policies to the whole of Britain through the ballot box. The others, including Graham, whose experience had taught him otherwise, believed that this perception was flawed, and that socialism was only viable in an independent Scotland.[35] Thus, by default, it was the change of Labour Party policy that led to the creation of the NPS, and later the SNP, just as Liberal intransigence had inadvertently given birth to the SPLP, then the Labour party.

What was referred to as 'the inaugural meeting of the National Party of Scotland' was held on 24 March 1928, with the object of 'Self-Government for Scotland with independent national status within the British group of nations, together with the reconstruction of Scottish national life'. It also stipulated that it would not accept members of other parties, effectively excluding Labour loyalists like Maxton and Johnston.[36] A week later, on 2 April 1928, Muirhead again wrote to Graham, who had very recently returned from South America:

> Some of us have been working during the winter with the object of getting the Scottish National Movement focussed into one body. Last week a provisional Committee of Scottish nationalists was set up. A Constitution is being prepared and very soon I anticipate a Scottish National Party will take the field.

He added, that despite the Executive Committee being in favour of such a new body, the majority of SHRA members were not.[37] In addition, he shared some information that would prove extremely important to the final stage of Graham's political career:

> A particularly hopeful side of the movement which has developed during the last few months is the Glasgow University Scottish National Association. It is already some three hundred strong and is co-operating in the formation of a National Party . . . I understand that the Glasgow University Scottish

National Association have decided to approach you to invite you to stand as a Scottish National Candidate at the forthcoming Rectorial Election. I hope that you will be able to consider the proposal favourably.[38]

It is apparent that Muirhead was easing the way for the students, but also that much of the initiative was coming from the students themselves, led by twenty-three-year-old John MacCormick, another active member of the ILP. However, the choice of Graham as candidate for the Rectorship against the sitting Prime Minister, Stanley Baldwin, appears to have been arbitrary. After a refusal from J. M. Barrie, MacCormick recalled, 'It was then that the name of R. B. Cunninghame Graham came vaguely into my mind, but when I mentioned him to my student colleagues they all confessed that they knew nothing about him, and therefore, turned down my choice.'[39] This is at odds with a statement in the 1927 gossip column of the *Sunday Post* that 'There are few men nowadays so well known as Mr R. B. Cunninghame Graham',[40] that Graham had been a regular speaker at nationalist gatherings since 1920, and that his name had gone forward for Rectorship of Glasgow University in 1914.[41] Nevertheless, MacCormick persisted, took out Graham's anthology *Hope* from Glasgow's Mitchell Library, and became convinced that Graham should be their candidate:

> As I read I became fascinated both by the man and his writing. Here was really a great Scotsman and, although his name was unfamiliar to my own generation, I was sure we could soon remedy that. But what were his politics? I knew that in his young days he had been a Radical and had later taken part with Keir Hardie in the formation of the Labour Party. But, for many years, he had been missing from the political scene altogether and, seemed to have spent most of his time in South America.[42]

MacCormick convinced his fellow student nationalists that Graham was a good choice, and they approached him, and after meeting MacCormick's colleague James Valentine[43] in a Glasgow café, he agreed that he would stand. Valentine reported to his fellow students, 'we've got a candidate – and I think he's the greatest Scotsman alive!'[44]

MacDiarmid later wrote, 'At that time the Scottish Nationalist Movement was largely led by writers – Lewis Spence, Neil Gunn, Ruaraidh Erskine of Marr, William Gilles, Eric Linklater, and others, above all, a little later, Mackenzie.'[45] Compton Mackenzie would occupy an important position as a literary go-between, and on occasions stood in for Graham when Graham was in London, or increasingly on his foreign trips. On 10 May 1928, Mackenzie and Hugh MacDiarmid met for the first time at a conference organised by MacCormick to discuss the amalgamation of the various nationalist groups. The *Glasgow Herald* announced that following conversations between delegates of the Glasgow University Student Nationalist Association, the Scots National League, the Scottish National Movement, and the Scottish Home Rule Association, that the NPS had been formed.[46] It was expressly stipulated that the Party would contest parliamentary and local government elections, and would not lend its support to candidates other than those put forward under its auspices.[47] The report then went on to detail the new constitution and rules, particularly the aim of its promoters to obtain such powers of self-government as would ensure Scotland independent national status within the British group of nations. It also stipulated that elected members would not take positions in any Westminster government; that Scotland would withdraw from Westminster after gaining a majority of parliamentary seats, and again, that prominence would be given to the reconstruction of Scottish national life. Among those who had already joined the party were:

> Mr R. B. Cunninghame Graham, Mr Compton Mackenzie, the Hon. R. Erskine of Marr, Mr Lewis Spence, Mr William Gilles, Mr R. E. Muirhead, the Rev. Walter Murray, Mr C. M. Grieve [MacDiarmid], amongst other prominent nationalists.[48]

The day after the 10 May conference, after the withdrawal of G. K. Chesterton and Hilaire Belloc, Mackenzie addressed the Students Union at Glasgow University and informed them that Graham was intending to stand at the rectorial election. Mackenzie recalled the background and the event in his autobiography:

> At this date a law student at the University, J. B. MacCormick, had parted company with the Labour Party and founded the Glasgow University Nationalist Association with the intention of putting up R. B. Cunninghame Graham as their candidate in the Rectorial election next October. This remarkable young man, seconded by James Valentine, another remarkable young man, had been able to convince various seniors like Lewis Spence and R. [E.] Muirhead that if the National movement was to make real headway it was vital to amalgamate the various Home Rule associations already in existence into what should be called the National Party of Scotland. A conference was held in Glasgow at the beginning of May at which this amalgamation became an accomplished fact. I was appointed a member of the Council, and John MacCormick asked me to make the announcement of Cunninghame Graham's candidature for the Rectorship in the Glasgow University Union.[49]

On 16 May, Muirhead wrote to Graham in London: 'The Glasgow University students were very highly pleased with the Compton Mackenzie meeting last week at which your name was put forward as Scottish

Nationalist candidate for Lord Rectorship.'[50] Muirhead obviously saw that part of his role was to placate and encourage Graham, if this sometimes meant not being entirely forthright and honest, for the *Glasgow Herald* reported that the students had given Mackenzie, initially at least, a rough reception.[51] Later, Graham wrote to Muirhead, 'I feel my chance for the university is not good for Baldwin is heavy metal.'[52]

MacCormick later claimed that he and his colleagues ran 'the greatest Rectorial campaign ever known in Glasgow University', adding, '[W]e coolly commandeered the platform of all our opponents and ultimately by various devices took over their social functions as well.'[53] On the day of the poll, 27 October 1928, the NPS held a demonstration in the Usher Hall, Edinburgh, and Graham was the principal speaker. Afterwards, Mackenzie accompanied Graham to the Caledonian Hotel to await the result, which arrived by telegram; 'only sixty-six votes behind Baldwin', he [Graham] murmured, 'well, in the circumstances I think that is as good as a victory, better indeed because I shall escape the boredom of having to prepare and deliver a Rectorial Address.'[54]

University of Glasgow Rectorial Election Results, *27 October 1928*

Stanley Baldwin (Conservative)	1,044
R. B. Cunninghame Graham (Scottish Nationalist)	978
Sir Herbert Samuel (Liberal)	396
Rosslyn Mitchell (Labour)	66

Despite Graham coming second, *The Observer* commented:

> Glasgow University Rectorial Election took place yesterday and resulted in the return of Mr. Baldwin . . . The result was considered a triumph for Scottish Nationalists. The voting of the men students showed a clear majority for Mr. Cunninghame Graham, but the women's vote turned the scale in favour of the Premier.[55]

In January 1929, the *Contemporary Review* recalled the result: 'The country was astounded, and even the Press was unprepared.'[56]

MacCormick believed that Graham had the majority of the male vote 'across four "nations," but that the women's vote from the "flappers" had gone to Baldwin because he had given them the franchise earlier that year'.[57] From Graham's account, Tschiffely confirmed this, stating:

> After the election, several delegations consisting of young ladies, called at 'Ardoch' House to explain that although they would normally have voted for Don Roberto, they felt it was their duty to elect the Prime Minister who had supported and put through women's suffrage.

Tschiffely, however, added a note: 'As we have seen, Don Roberto was one of the first supporters of women's suffrage, before Mr. Baldwin came on the political scene. Obviously the students didn't realise this.'[58]

Directly after his defeat, there occurred the most significant unexpected outcome in Graham's later life, for his near-success had stimulated great enthusiasm among the Home Rule supporters, and a public meeting was arranged at St Andrew's Hall two days later. The *Glasgow Herald* reported that it attracted almost three thousand Glasgow citizens, presided over by the Duke of Montrose, and Graham was the principal speaker. The audience had been very enthusiastic, and 'any pithy claim for Scottish self-government aroused great applause'.[59] Graham's speech repeated his previous practical preoccupations that Scotland was poorly governed, and that unemployment and housing were worse than in England. He also focused on identity politics, and included statements such as 'There has been a tendency in Scotland for us to become pale copies of our Southern brethren. That is a tendency that I have always deplored.' He asserted that he was still a socialist, but believed that a Scottish Parliament would provide a better theatre in which socialists could 'ventilate their grievances and with a better chance of being heard', however, he believed that Scottish politics had become too tame, and that 'the Predominant Partner has always looked upon Scotland as a Cinderella not worthy of consideration'.[60]

The Scotsman, typically, dismissed the new party: 'Mr Cunninghame Graham's position in the Glasgow Rectorial election has no political significance whatever.' It saw no need for Home Rule, and turned the tables on the nationalists, inverting their claims:

> Are we Scotsmen not able to hold our own in union with England? Is the union with England sapping our independence, robbing us of our national heritage in language and literature, making us poor, mean spirited creatures, without a home or country of our own?[61]

Obviously, a number of people *did* believe that Scotland had been, and was, the inferior partner, and that national life *was* endangered, but they were still few. MacCormick's autobiography was a catalogue of high ideals and hopes, amateurish political organisation, and lost deposits, as the party failed to make any electoral headway.[62] However, at the beginning at least, the main protagonists of the new party seemed in no way abashed. *The Scotsman* reported that Graham, fresh from his near-victory, would be one of the NPS candidates in Paisley at the general election. It also reported that Graham had written in the Glasgow University Magazine that he had 'advocated the restoration of the ancient Scottish

Parliament for forty years', adding, 'rather than face another forty years of my speaking, the youth of Scotland has risen up in self-defence, and insisted in taking the words out of my mouth.'[63] Graham did not stand at Paisley; he had already written to Muirhead in July of 1928 stating that:

> I cannot see my way to allow my name to be put forward as a parliamentary candidate. I am too much occupied in literary work to think of politics and the last thing in the world I should like is to see myself elected. Believe me I can do far better work outside direct politics. To go forward as a candidate would be I feel sure to forfeit any little influence I may have. Moreover the dunghill of active politics is a young man's game. It is a dunghill I know for I have been on (or in) the hill.[64]

This statement is another confirmation of Graham's belief that he was now above, or rather beyond, party politics. Nonetheless, his near-success had re-inspired him, and he was active in promoting NPS candidates, including in January 1929 on behalf of Lewis Spence[65] at a by-election campaign in North Midlothian.[66] During April 1929 a nationwide recruitment campaign was launched, in which he spoke between foreign travels, and several new branches were founded.[67]

Graham would be a regular speaker at the NPS's annual 'Scotland's Day' rallies at Kings Park in Stirling, and at Elderslie, but by 1932 it was obvious that his views on independence had hardened, when at Elderslie he declared that he would repeal the Union, and then make a solemn declaration of Scottish sovereignty, followed by a treaty between Scotland and England. In his brave new world, Scotland would have its own military forces, its own coinage, postage stamps, and power to send ambassadors overseas. It would also have the power to institute its own fiscal system. He also asserted that the king was King of Scotland, and should be crowned in Edinburgh.[68]

In 1928, Graham had been elected President of the NPS, and a member of the Executive of the National Council,[69] but it was clear from the minutes that despite initial enthusiasm after its foundation, and its high aspirations, the new party was suffering from disputes between the various groups that had come together to form it.[70] Even by the mid-1950s, nationalist propagandist, Oliver Brown, would say of them, '[T]he nationalist movement is all individuals and fragments, a collection of oddities and hopefuls with a bewildering history of schism.'[71] There were frequent resignations and continual financial crises, and by August 1932, the party was running on an overdraft of £50.[72] It was also clear, that like his previous political involvements, Graham took very little interest in day-to-day matters. There is no mention of him attending any National Executive meeting until 18 April 1931,[73] and not again until 29

September 1932, when he chaired an Extraordinary Executive Meeting to discuss unemployment, but left half way through.[74] There is also no record of him attending an executive meeting subsequently, and in a letter, written in November 1932, he wrote, 'I am just off to the Holy Land, for the Renfrewshire election.'[75] However, Graham was not alone in his impatience with discussions on internal policy and the squabbles that beset the new party. As early as 28 December 1928, Mackenzie wrote to MacDiarmid, 'The last Council meeting nearly sent me off my head.'[76] It is not clear whether this was the result of factionalism, or the tedium of committee work, but it indicated that the 'men of letters' within the party, which included Graham, were a different breed from the committee men who were attempting to hold it together, and Graham's actual contribution to its survival was small, apart from his by now traditional role of a figurehead.[77]

The party's financial tribulations continued, and in July 1933, a letter was sent to all the branches requesting a donation of £5, the outcome of which would determine 'the stand or fall of the party'.[78] In May of that year there was a request for 'an interview' from the right-of-centre Scottish Party, led by the Duke of Montrose, which MacCormick had been delegated to arrange,[79] and over the next months, discussions were held in an attempt to resolve policy differences.[80] Matters were resolved by the end of 1933, and Muirhead wrote to Graham on 23 December stating that 'yesterday a joint committee met and agreed to amalgamate the NPS and Scotland's Party. They agreed to call it The Scottish National Party',[81] and a joint conference was proposed for 7 April 1934.[82] At this conference, Graham was apparently involved in unrecorded discussions on unification, and these were successful. Montrose was elected President, and Graham, Honorary President.[83] MacCormick recalled Graham's participation:

> I well remember the final meeting of the joint negotiating committee when we gathered to celebrate the success of our endeavours. Cunninghame Graham, who had throughout encouraged us in the policies which we had followed, entertained us all to dinner at the Central Hotel.[84]

This impression of consensus runs contrary to Mackenzie's statement in his obituary of Graham in 1936. Mackenzie wrote that Graham had regretted the amalgamation, but thought it his duty to avoid the appearance of disruption within the nationalist ranks, 'and out of regard for him I abstained from denouncing what I held to be disastrous policy of reconciliation; an opinion which has been strengthened by events of the last two years'.[85] Mackenzie did not explain why Graham opposed it, but it was undoubtedly because he felt uncomfortable that the NPS, whose main promoters had formerly been members of the ILP, should merge with a right-of-centre party, thus losing its distinctly socialist identity. Nevertheless, although Graham stopped speaking at rallies after 1932, his general enthusiasm for the independence cause did not diminish, and three exuberantly patriotic feature articles appeared in the *Scots Independent*,[86] one of which expressed a sentiment that would have been unthinkable before the war:

> [T]he enemies of Scottish nationalism are not the English, for they were ever a great and generous folk, quick to respond when justice calls. Our real enemies are amongst us, born without imagination.[87]

After the formation of the SNP, Graham volunteered to help at the general election of 1935,[88] and as Honorary President, he had sent a message of encouragement to the Bannockburn Day Celebration, stating that he believed that the party was moving towards victory.[89] However, electorally, the SNP fared no better than the NPS, Finlay describing its performance as 'a dismal failure'.[90]

Notes

1. *Stirling Observer*, 26 November 1918, p. 5.
2. Ibid.
3. Ibid.
4. Compton Mackenzie, 'R. B. Cunninghame Graham Scottish Nationalist', *Outlook & The Modern Scot*, May 1936, p. 21.
5. R. E. Muirhead, letter to Cunninghame Graham, 23 December 1920. Muirhead Papers.
6. Cunninghame Graham, letter to R. E. Muirhead, 27 December 1920.
7. Sir Roger Casement was executed for treason in 1916 in Pentonville Prison (where Graham had been incarcerated) for attempting to enlist German support for an Irish uprising during the First World War. Casement greatly admired Graham's South American sketches. *Manchester Guardian*, 18 July 1912, p. 5.
8. Graham continued: 'His father was deputy grand master of the Orange Lodges of Armagh. Sir Roger was a bitter, black Ulster Protestant, who, when Conrad and I knew him first, had no words but of contempt for Irish Catholics.' Cunninghame Graham, letter to H. W. Nevinson, dated 27–8 November 1927. Quoted in Tschiffely, *Don Roberto*, pp. 391–3. Since this letter appeared in Tschiffely's biography, it appears that Graham, a Scottish nationalist, wished to clarify his stance regarding such actions.
9. *Stirling Observer*, 26 November 1918, p. 3.
10. Ibid., 2 December 1918, p. 3.
11. Ibid., 30 November 1918, p. 5.

12. Muirhead, letter to Cunninghame Graham, 5 August 1920. Muirhead Papers.
13. Muirhead, letter to Cunninghame Graham, 5 August, 1920.
14. Muirhead, 'Foreword' to MacDiarmid's *Centenary Study*, p. 5.
15. Graham spent three months abroad every winter, three months at his Scottish home at Ardoch, and the remainder of his time in London's Belgravia. Tschiffely, *Don Roberto*, p. 390.
16. Finlay, *Independent and Free*, p. 29.
17. Ibid., p. 50.
18. Ibid., p. 2.
19. John Barbour, 'Scotland – The New Dominion', *Edinburgh Review*, April 1929, pp. 325–6. Original italics.
20. Ibid.
21. J. Ramsay MacDonald, *Socialism: Critical and Constructive* (London, Cassell, 1921), p. 249. In 1888, MacDonald had established the London General Committee of the Scottish Home Rule Association, and had been its Secretary. Austen Morgan, *J. Ramsay MacDonald* (Manchester City Art Gallery, 1987), p. 17. Rothenstein wrote that MacDonald considered Graham 'a great man, a delightful fellow and a gallant gentleman'. Rothenstein, *Since Fifty: Recollections* (London: Faber & Faber, 1939), p. 270. However, the novelist Arnold Bennett recorded that Graham told him that fellow socialists referred to MacDonald as 'MacChadband' (*Bleak House*), because he preached so much, and Graham regarded him as 'a Judas'. Arnold Bennett, *The Journals* (London: Penguin, 1954), p. 480. Graham vehemently denied this, as reported in the *Glasgow Herald*, 16 May 1933, p. 10.
22. *Glasgow Herald*, 30 August 1920, p. 9.
23. 'Wallace made Scotland, he is Scotland; he is the symbol of all that is best and purest and truest and most heroic in our national life. So long as grass grows green, or water runs, or whilst the mist curls through the corries of the hills, the name of Wallace will live.'
24. *Glasgow Herald*, 30 August 1920, p. 9.
25. Cunninghame Graham, letter to R. E. Muirhead, 7 July 1923. Muirhead Papers.
26. Maxton had been a member of the re-formed SHRA since its foundation. Muirhead, letter to Cunninghame Graham, 17 June 1925. Muirhead Papers.
27. 'Scotland's Day: A Glasgow Pageant', *Glasgow Herald*, 27 August 1923, p. 12.
28. It is possible that Graham had demurred from speaking when he found that Maxton was on the speaker's list, due to Maxton's pacifism. Johnston, like Maxton, had joined the second SHRA at its formation.
29. Government of Scotland Bill, Hansard, 9 May 1924, Vol. 173, cc 789–874.
30. At this time, Johnston was the MP for Stirling and Clackmannan West, but he would lose the seat five months later.

31. Finlay, *Independent and Free*, p. 16.
32. Muirhead, letter to Cunninghame Graham, 9 March 1926. Muirhead Papers.
33. Reverend James Barr (1862–1949), MP for Motherwell (1924–31), and Coatbridge (1935–45).
34. PP. Government of Scotland Bill, Hansard, 13 May 1927, Vol. 206, cc 865–7. Barr at this time was president of the SHRA.
35. Fundamental to this stance was the belief that independence would also lead to Scotland's cultural salvation and regeneration.
36. Minutes of National Party of Scotland Inaugural Meeting. 24 March 1928. James Halliday Papers, NLS. Acc.13417/1.
37. Presumably, those SHRA members whose allegiance remained with the Labour Party.
38. Muirhead, letter to Cunninghame Graham, 2 April 1928. Muirhead Papers.
39. MacCormick, *The Flag in the Wind*, pp. 26–7. MacDiarmid concurred, and was dismayed: 'When I addressed the students supporting Cunninghame Graham's candidature for Lord rectorship of Glasgow University . . . and found that they knew nothing or next to nothing of his writings.' MacDiarmid, *Centenary Study*, p. 19. Also MacDiarmid, 'The Significance of Cunninghame Graham', in his *Selected Essays*, p. 122.
40. *Sunday Post*, 13 November 1925, p. 15.
41. Extraordinarily, Malcolm Petrie wrote that at this time, MacCormick was 'apparently unaware of the Scottish Home Rule Association'. Malcolm Petrie, 'John MacCormick', *Scottish National Party Leaders* (2016), p. 48.
42. MacCormick, *The Flag in the Wind*, p. 27.
43. Dr James Valentine (1906–2007). Later, he became a noted clinical psychiatrist.
44. MacCormick, *The Flag in the Wind*, p. 28.
45. MacDiarmid, *Centenary Study*, p. 10. Mackenzie was obviously a great admirer of Graham, and like Graham he was born in England, with wide international interests. He claimed that he had first met Graham in May 1903, at a garden party in Worcester College, Oxford, but they did not meet again until the formation of the National Party in 1928. Mackenzie, 'Don Roberto', p. 868. Mackenzie was also known for his charm, his distinctive dress-sense, his pointed beard, and his barely legible handwriting. Andro Linklater wrote of him in words that by now have a familiar resonance: 'In the end it is clear that his true genius was theatrical, but that instead of confining his talents to the stage he created around him a stage on which he could represent himself . . . In the Quixotic, extravagant performance of his own life he achieved his real masterpiece.' Andro Linklater, *Compton Mackenzie: A Life* (London: Chatto & Windus, 1987), p. 324.
46. It was not officially inaugurated until 23 June at a rally in King's Park, Stirling, presided over by Graham. *Glasgow Herald*, 25 June 1928, p. 14.

47. *Glasgow Herald*, 14 May 1928, p. 9.

48. Ibid.

49. Compton Mackenzie, *My Life and Times*, Octave Six, 1923–30 (London: Chatto & Windus, 1967), pp. 132–3. MacCormick made no mention of Mackenzie taking this initial role, stating instead: 'When we came to announce our candidate's name at an open meeting at the Union (the tradition being that it should be held secret until then) we could find no sponsoring speaker from outside and I, therefore, undertook the task myself.' John MacCormick, *The Flag in the Wind*, p. 28. This was incorrect, as reported in the *Glasgow Herald* next day. *Glasgow* Herald, 11 May 1928, p. 11. Mackenzie was however mentioned by MacCormick as attending a later meeting in the Union in support of Graham. MacCormick, *The Flag in the Wind*, p. 31.

50. R. E. Muirhead, letter to Cunninghame Graham, 16 May 1928. Muirhead Papers.

51. *Glasgow Herald*, 15 May 1928, p. 9.

52. Cunninghame Graham, letter to R. E. Muirhead, 22 July 1928. Muirhead Papers.

53. MacCormick, *The Flag in the Wind*, pp. 28–9. Pitched battles raged among the students, which included the throwing of an estimated twenty thousand eggs, as well as soot, flour bombs, and fireworks. *Manchester Guardian*, 27 October 1928, p. 13.

54. Mackenzie, 'Don Roberto', p. 869.

55. *The Observer*, 28 October 1928, p. 15.

56. 'Scottish Nationalism', *Contemporary Review*, January 1929, p. 208.

57. MacCormick, *The Flag in the Wind*, p. 30.

58. Tschiffely, *Don Roberto*, p. 395. *The Scotsman* stated that of the male vote, Graham beat Baldwin by 712 to 501. *Scotsman*, 23 March 1936, p. 10. Graham made a miscalculation when he again stood for the Lord Rectorship of Glasgow University, as recalled by Mackenzie: 'I was rather distressed to learn in 1934 that he had allowed himself to be nominated as the Nationalist candidate for the rectorship for the second time, because he was in his eighty-third year, and there was a long tradition that a Rectorial candidate never succeeded at the second time of standing. To my grief he was beaten.' Mackenzie, 'Don Roberto', p. 869. This was disingenuous. In his 1936 obituary of Graham, Mackenzie claimed that he had persuaded the 'most unwilling' Graham to stand. Mackenzie, 'Cunninghame Graham Scottish Nationalist', p. 22.

59. 'Scots Nation: The New Party in Glasgow', *Glasgow Herald*, 30 October 1928, p. 9.

60. Ibid.

61. *Scotsman*, 31 October 1928, p. 10.

62. Finlay, 'Pressure Group or Political Party? The Nationalist Impact on Scottish Politics, 1928–1945', *Twentieth Century British History*, Vol. 3, No. 3, 1993, p. 275.

63. *Scotsman*, 22 November 1928, p. 14.

64. Cunninghame Graham, letter to R. E. Muirhead, 22 July 1928. Muirhead Papers.

65. Lewis Spence (1874–1955). Journalist and folklorist. Founder of The Scottish National Movement.

66. *Scotsman*, 12 January 1929, p. 12. Spence had been the first NPS parliamentary candidate. Graham wrote to Muirhead from Tenerife, regretting Spence's poor result at the polls. Cunninghame Graham, letter to R. E. Muirhead, 8 February 1929. Muirhead Papers.

67. *Scotsman*, 13 April 1929, p. 11.

68. *Glasgow Herald*, 22 August 1932, p. 7.

69. Muirhead, letter to Cunninghame Graham, 18 April 1928. Muirhead Papers.

70. Finlay stated that this was due to the lack of consensus over 'the kind of relationship a self-governing Scotland would have with the British Empire and Commonwealth, and hence with the rest of the United Kingdom', with each side 'struggling to establish their own particular version of home rule as the accepted orthodoxy'. Richard J. Finlay, 'For or Against? Scottish Nationalists and the British Empire, 1919–39', *Scottish Historical Review*, Vol. LXXI, Nos 1/2, 1992, pp. 184–5.

71. Oliver Brown, *The Observer*, 2 August 1954.

72. Minutes of the National Executive of the National Party of Scotland, 4 August 1932. Halliday Papers.

73. Ibid., 18 September 1931.

74. Ibid., 29 September 1932.

75. Graham, Letter to Richard Curle, 21 November 1932. Herbert Faulkner West Collection, Dartmouth College.

76. Compton Mackenzie Papers, EUL, MS 2954.8: Mackenzie, letter, 28 December 1928. In 1932, Mackenzie again wrote to MacDiarmid suggesting that he attend the NPS conference, 'even if you have to go out of it immediately afterwards, possibly in my company'. Ibid., Mackenzie, letter, 10 October 1928. At this time, MacDiarmid worked for Mackenzie in London, as editor of Mackenzie's radio review magazine, *Vox*, and later they were both involved in setting up the secret nationalist organisation, Clann Alba.

77. Much later, MacDiarmid wrote about how he saw the relationship: 'Cunninghame Graham and Mackenzie in council with the officials and branch delegates of the Scottish Nationalist Party were like a pair of golden eagles, with their wings clipped, in a crowded poultry run, full of poultry far gone with the "gapes".' MacDiarmid, *Selected Essays*, pp. 127–8. On 19 May 1933, MacCormick wrote to MacDiarmid, explaining that the NPS had no room for extremists, and Alan Bold wrote that 'Party policy was to present a moderate front to the Scottish people by getting rid of men like MacDiarmid'. Alan Bold, *MacDiarmid* (London: Paladin, 1990), pp. 331–2.

78. Minutes of the National Executive of the National Party of Scotland, 13 July 1933. James Halliday Papers.
79. Ibid., 11 May 1933. James Halliday Papers.
80. Graham was invited to chair such a meeting, but did not attend. Ibid., 17 August 1933.
81. Muirhead, letter to Cunninghame Graham, 23 December 1933. Muirhead Papers.
82. Halliday Papers, 1 February 1934.
83. This was undoubtedly a gesture by the executive of the NPS to cement Scotland's Party into the new alliance. However, in May 1935, the Duke announced opposition to SNP policy, and his renewed allegiance to the Liberals. Letter to *Glasgow Herald*, 4 May 1935, p. 6.
84. MacCormick, *The Flag in the Wind*, p. 86.
85. Mackenzie, 'Cunninghame Graham Scottish Nationalist', p. 21.
86. 'Scotland's Day: The New Covenant', *Scots Independent*, July 1930 (Supplement), p. 1; 'McSneeshin', *Scots Independent*, January 1931, p. 1 (see Appendix IX); and 'The Awakening of a Nation', *Scots Independent*, October 1932, p. 184.
87. 'McSneeshin', *Scots Independent*, January 1931, p. 1.
88. Cunninghame Graham, letter to R. E. Muirhead, 26 October 1935. Muirhead Papers.
89. Leaflet, Muirhead Papers.
90. Finlay, 'Pressure Group or Political Party?' p. 275.

17

Continuing Literary Works: Things Unalike

IN 1914, SIXTEEN OF Graham's Scottish works, mostly portraits, were collected in his *Scottish Stories*[1] some of which had been included in previous anthologies (which perhaps explains why the book was hardly reviewed). *The Academy* briefly reviewed it thus:

> This is a mature work of a master of words, a brilliant achievement in literature, taking the word in its highest sense . . . Not only is the spirit of the work good, but the form is also exquisite; the world will be richer for such a little volume as this, though the work is too fine and delicate to attain to popularity.[2]

This latter point may be true, but it may also be true that very few people, even in Scotland, had experienced or understood the specific, unique, and deeply historical ambience and moods of the district about which Graham wrote. Also, their impact was lost because they were so separated and distanced in his anthologies. Earlier that year, another reviewer expressed his surprise that someone who held such zealous opinions, could preserve such impartiality in his literary works, concluding, 'The truth is, Mr. Cunninghame Graham on the platform is an impatient idealist; Mr. Cunninghame Graham in the study, is to a great extent, a patient realist.'[3]

It was not until Graham's next anthology, *Brought Forward* (1916), which contained sketches originally published in 1914 and 1915, that we can begin to see the effect of recent events and a more melancholy strain, a critic commenting that the war 'has cast a gloom upon this last volume'.[4] The theme of death was illustrated in a sketch entitled 'Fidelity',[5] which concerned a dying bird and its mate's devotion, which may have reflected on the death of Gabrielle in 1906. As he put it, in another sketch in this anthology, 'When a man's lost his wife it leaves him, somehow, as if he were like a 'orse hitched on one side of the wagon-pole, a-pullin' by hisself'.[6] Perhaps of even more relevance was the tale in which an idealistic lay preacher addressed a small and diminishing audience:

'Love suffereth all things, endureth all things, createth all things.' He paused, and looked round, saw that he was alone . . . The speaker sighed, and wiped the perspiration from his forehead with a soiled handkerchief. Then, picking up his hat and his umbrella, a far off look came into his blue eyes as he walked homewards almost jauntily, conscious that the inner fire had got the better of the fleshly tenement, and that his work was done.[7]

It is difficult not to draw parallels between the subject of this piece and Graham's own political situation, where he was still motivated to speak out, but the world was no longer willing to listen in the current political climate of war fever; nor, at this period, did he have any serious political attachments or influence.

Graham had announced in the preface to *Brought Forward* that this was to be his last book: 'Tis meet and fitting to let free the horse or pen before death overtakes you, or before the gentle public turns its thumbs down and yells, "Away with him".'[8] A reviewer for *The Observer* included another sentence: 'So I shall write no more of these short stories, tales, sketches, or what you like to call them, for I perceive that in the writing of them I have written my life's story, and it can never be recalled.'[9] This sentence did not appear in the original 1916 edition or the 1917 reprint, but it may have appeared in a review copy, which might indicate that Graham considered it too final to be included in the published version. In 1927 he wrote, 'Thinking upon a vow I registered eleven years ago (Postume, Postume!)[10] not to write any more short stories',[11] confirming that this was indeed his original intention. Graham concluded his preface with the word *Vale* ('Farewell'), but he was still physically active, and it is not clear why he decided to stop at this point.

In the few reviews of *Brought Forward*, each critic regretted Graham's decision to lay down his pen. Amy Wellington, for example, wrote in 1918 about the intended conclusion of Graham's literary career:

With the North-East Wind [his sketch of Hardie's funeral] seems to close the book of Cunninghame Graham's own long and chivalrous fight for the despised and rejected of this earth; just as, a little later, he attaches his formal farewell as a writer to the preface of his final volume, *Brought Forward*. Both artist and fighter have grown a little cynical and very weary.[12]

It was by no means his last book, but his articles for journals greatly reduced between 1916 and 1925, apart from his obituaries of the Colombian writer and campaigner Santiago Pérez Triana,[13] the traveller

Wilfrid Scawen Blunt,[14] Conrad,[15] and a piece on the forgotten grave of the Ogallala Sioux, Long Wolf.[16] No new anthology of his works, appeared until 1927, although eight individual history books were published during the period, mostly on South American subjects,[17] and Graham's political beliefs remained clear in all of them. As early as 1904, a critic had written about Graham's history *Hernando De Soto*: 'A careful reading . . . shows that it is not modern life or modern men that against which the author shoots his shafts of wit so much as against the modern man's cant about all our superior motives, actions, and ideals.'[18] In 1921, another critic wrote, 'Mr. Cunninghame Graham is fonder than ever of annotating his narrative with satirical jibes at modern European civilization, but he writes so well that his pungent digressions season the dish.'[19] Graham's political and moral preoccupations continued in his writings, but his political activities slowed considerably, apart from annual addresses at nationalist gatherings and his letters to the press on animal welfare. References to him in newspapers reduced to a trickle.

The year 1925 saw Graham's re-engagement with the *Saturday Review*, with five pieces, rising to six the following year, then a final piece in 1931. His first ambient Scottish sketch for twelve years was 'Inch Cailleach',[20] a return to his previous preoccupations, where the spirits of the past rose up from beneath the earth, and within the mist was another world composed of mist, a world of the past, of ancient earls and warriors, that could, when conditions were right, reimpose itself on the present. This theme continued in his next and final Scottish sketch (and second last for the *Saturday Review*), 'Euphrasia', which was a short, sentimental meditation on a war grave on Skye.[21]

The reason for this slowing in Graham's productivity may simply be attributable to his age, which was undoubtedly a factor, but there was, perhaps, a less conspicuous cause. His early polemical essays were no longer appropriate to his statesmanlike literary persona, his memories may have become exhausted, or perhaps too insubstantial or fleeting to be turned into sketches, and his life story had in fact been written. There was, perhaps, simply no more material to draw upon, and even his Scottish sketches no longer drew on portraiture, but increasingly only on the evocation of mystical landscapes, and were now becoming tired and repetitive.

Another more 'factual' literary outlet was his contributions to the works of others. Between 1897 and his death in 1936, Graham had written almost fifty prefaces and forewords, which, when the subject of the book engaged him, were opinion pieces. These were mostly to books on travel, but in the Scottish context, four pieces stand out. The first, written in 1902, was an Introduction to John Morrison Davidson's book *Scotland for the Scots: Scotland Revisited*.[22] Though it dealt mostly with Graham's bizarre encounter with a fellow Scot in Argentina (which gave him another opportunity to display his knowledge of Scots dialect), the last three paragraphs were taken up with Davidson's Scottish nationalism. This introduction was an early manifestation of Graham's growing national sentiment: that the Scotland that they both wished to see was not a Scotland of the Enlightenment, but a 'return to a more national spirit and a revival of the ancient Scottish Type which ruled the roost before the Ten per Centlings rose, making poor Scotland stink before the world with their base peddling ways'. (For full text, see Appendix VI.)

The next short foreword was to a book entitled *Inchmahome and the Lake of Menteith* (1931), by John A. Stewart, which was unremarkable, except, again, for overt nationalist sentiments, with a reference to the signatories of the 'Ragman's Roll' by which the nobility and gentry of Scotland had given their allegiance to King Edward I of England.[23] Graham described them as 'false loons, no true Scots but henchmen of the Southron enemy',[24] and declared that the island of Inchmahome, 'in which so many of our ancestors – their life's crusade achieved – await our coming'.[25]

Graham's foreword to Thomas Dick Lauder's *The Wolf of Badenoch* (sixth edition) was also brief, but contained similar overtly nationalist sentiments:

> For a century Scotsmen have been content to remain pale copies of our 'ancient enemy' from beyond the Tweed. Some denigrate sons of Scotia, even today, attribute the economic progress of Scotland to the Act of Union and forget their own share in the job. A new generation of race-conscious Scotsmen is arising, and to it the republication of a Scottish novel will be a boon.[26]

This theme of 'race consciousness' would be repeated two years later in Graham's overtly nationalist article 'The Awakening of a Nation', where, describing the things that others would describe as peculiarly Scottish, he regarded them as being 'as admirable in themselves as flies in amber, [and] ... a poor substitute, for me, at least, for race consciousness'.[27] Similar hard-line sentiments had been expressed four years earlier at a public meeting in Edinburgh, where Graham said, 'There had been too little bitterness in Scottish politics. It wanted more bitterness to draw the people together.'[28]

The most relevant piece, in his later years, and in the context of this study, was Graham's 1933 Introduction to Robert Kirk's *The Secret Commonwealth* (c. 1691).[29] Graham, of course, was following in the footsteps of Andrew Lang's extensive Introduction to his own 1893 edition, though he was no scholar like Lang.[30] That said, he was admirably suited to the task, being at one time very local to the setting ('a descendant of men long domiciled within sight of the Fairy Hill'), infused since childhood with the legends ('though an infrequent worshiper of any kind of Gods'), and, as we have seen, in later years, interested in fairy lore. It also appears that Graham, like Lang, had 'stood sponsor' for this edition, like Walter Scott, who had sponsored its original publication in 1815.[31]

The great enigma surrounding Kirk was that, as a Christian clergyman, he had produced a reasoned argument for the existence of another world, a magical world that mirrored our own, which was not dissimilar to Graham's own mist-shrouded imaginings of another Scotland, a parallel world easily accessed by those who wished, or who had the ability, to imagine it. Gregory Smith believed that this was a distinctive quality of Scottish writing, 'this strange combination of things unalike, of things seen in the everyday world and things which, like the elf-queen herself neither earth nor heaven will claim'.[32] Graham wrote that he had sponsored the book because it was 'a style of literature that long has disappeared, and had "a curiosa felicitas" [a felicity of expression] that shows the writer to have been a man of parts and a believer "quia impossibilis" in all he writes about'.[33] However, Kirk's descriptions had little of the ethereal childlike feyness and late Victorian wistfulness. They had a primitive reality, very much part of the history of Graham's own locality, that appealed to the same desire to evoke the past, and perhaps even a rebellion against conformity and the bourgeois norm.

Robert Crawford wrote that the early growth of Scottish nationalism, was 'closely enmeshed with artistic production';[34] the new movement included many writers, and the growth of national sentiment was to find a cultural expression as much as a political one. The early roots of this literary reawakening were complex, but the Scottish author and editor, George Blake, put it simply:

A 'consciousness of Scottishness' came to us after the War. We began to see – or believed we saw – that the Scottish spirit had been misrepresented in literature by kailyard pawkiness on the one hand, and whaup-and-leather romance on the other.[35]

According to Blake, something was stirring, but the use of the word 'Renaissance' was to him (writing in 1932) premature, and led to the assumption 'that the actual products of the movement were numerous and substantial, whereas they were, and are, not'.[36] In contrast, Crawford described the National Renaissance, orchestrated by MacDiarmid, as 'erupting', 'making Scotland rather than London the focus of Scottish writers' activities'.[37] MacDiarmid wrote that he had first met Graham in the early 1920s. It was from this meeting that he decided 'to make the Scottish Cause, cultural and political, my life-work dates from that moment',[38] and he had 'lamented Graham's long absences from Scotland',[39] writing in 1926:

> He began well: but for those of us who are connected with either the Scottish Nationalists or the Socialist movements he has become like a curious and unseizable dream by which we are tantalizingly haunted but which we can by no means effectively recall.[40]

These were highly significant statements, and reflected on the unquantifiable impact that Graham had on at least two generations, who themselves would go on to inspire others.

The sources of MacDiarmid's attraction to Graham were obvious: Graham's radicalism, his elitism, his polemics, his anti-bourgeois sentiments, his socialism,[41] his internationalism, and his nationalism.[42] It might also be added that MacDiarmid was drawn to aristocrats; he proudly proclaimed the help and kindness offered to him by the Duke of Hamilton and his brother the Earl of Selkirk,[43] and praised the 3rd Marquess of Bute (1847–1900) for being 'notably nationalist'.[44] Bold described MacDiarmid's character in terms that could equally be applied to Graham: 'His problem was not duality, but plurality. When his intellectual elitism clashed with his socialism he felt that the only sure synthesis was his own personality.'[45] In other words, like Graham, he had turned himself into an original. Above all, it was perhaps the 'zig-zag of contradictions',[46] the contrary nature of Graham's character, that MacDiarmid found so interesting – here, at last, was a man in whom extremes met. This 'Caledonian antisyzygy' was the bedrock of a book that greatly influenced MacDiarmid (Gregory Smith's *Scottish Literature*, 1919),[47] but perhaps MacDiarmid found, in Graham's writings, the strange combination of things unalike that Smith identified as defining the uniqueness of Scottish literature.

MacDiarmid used his book *Contemporary Studies* as a platform to attack almost every aspect of Scottish life, literature, and attitudes. Neil Munro was dismissed as a poor writer, at best 'a respectable craftsman',[48] while Stevenson was virtually ignored. Socialists and nationalists like Graham and William Power were, however, widely praised, but Graham's neglected position was used by MacDiarmid as an example of what he considered fundamentally wrong with Scottish life and letters. He described Graham as a man of 'exceptional brilliance',[49] but despite this plaudit, he also described him as 'the only Scotsman of his generation to win to the second rank of as an imaginative artist – the second rank, be it remarked, in the British, not in the European or World, scale',[50] but who 'calculated to open the windows of most of his countrymen's minds for the first time and let in the pure air'.[51] MacDiarmid believed, moreover, that Graham was the subject of bias: 'The Anglo-Scottish press were dead against him, as were the stuffy yes-men of the status quo of the university authorities. He was never given his due in Scotland.'[52] MacDiarmid was trying to co-opt Graham into his otherwise rather threadbare Scottish renaissance, even though Graham had been writing on the same subject matter, and in the same way, for the previous thirty years.

Notes

1. Cunninghame Graham, *Scottish Stories* (London: Duckworth, 1914).
2. *The Academy*, 20 June 1914, p. 795.
3. *The Nation*, 24 January 1914, p. 718.
4. *English Review*, 'Essays and General Literature', November 1916, p. 476.
5. Cunninghame Graham, 'Fidelity', *The Nation*, 27 November 1915, pp. 323–4. Anthologised in *Brought Forward* (1916), pp. 30–9.
6. Cunninghame Graham 'In A Backwater', *English Review*, October 1914, p. 280. Anthologised in *Brought Forward*, pp. 97–105.
7. Cunninghame Graham 'A Minor Prophet', *English Review*, July 1915, p. 401. Anthologised in *Brought Forward*, pp. 130–45.
8. Cunninghame Graham, *Brought Forward*, pp. x–xi.
9. *The Observer*, 24 September 1916, p. 4.
10. From Horace's ode, *Eheu Fugaces*: 'Alas . . . the years glide swiftly by, nor will righteousness give pause to wrinkles, to advancing age, or Death invincible.'
11. Cunninghame Graham, Preface to *Redeemed* (London: Heinemann, 1927), p. 12.
12. Wellington, 'Artist-Fighter', p. 158.
13. In *Hispania: Politica, Comercio, Literatura, Artes y Ciencias*, London, 27 June 1916, pp. 1617–19. Triana had founded this publication.
14. Cunninghame Graham, 'Wilfrid Scawen Blunt', pp. 486–92.
15. Cunninghame Graham, 'Inveni Portum', *Saturday Review*, 16 August 1924, pp. 162–3. Anthologised in *Redeemed* (1927), pp. 161–71.
16. A member of 'Buffalo Bill's Wild West'. Cunninghame Graham, 'Long Wolf', *Scribner's Magazine* (New York), June 1921, pp. 651–4. Anthologised in *Redeemed* (1927), pp. 70–81. Almost a hundred years after Long Wolf's death, Graham's article was read by Elizabeth Knight of Worcestershire, who rediscovered his grave in London. In 1997, after a lengthy campaign, his remains were reinterred near the site of the Wounded Knee massacre.
17. The major exception was his biography of his great-great grandfather, Robert Graham of Gartmore. Cunninghame Graham, *Doughty Deeds*.
18. *The Speaker*, 23 January 1904, p. 412.
19. 'Cartagena and the Banks of the Sinu', *The Spectator*, 1 January 1921, p. 25.

20. Cunninghame Graham, 'Inch Cailleach', *Saturday Review*, 5 September 1925, pp. 253–4. Anthologised in *Redeemed* (1927), pp. 103–9.
21. Cunninghame Graham, 'Euphrasia', *Saturday Review*, 25 September 1926, p. 331. Anthologised in *Redeemed* (1927), pp. 172–6.
22. Cunninghame Graham, 'Introduction' to John Morrison Davidson's *Scotland for the Scots: Scotland Revisited* (see *passim*). Davidson (1843–1916), a left-wing Scottish patriot, barrister, journalist, and campaigner, was a regular contributor to Tom Johnston's *Forward*. Davidson claimed that he had established that Graham, as a direct descendent of King Robert II, was *de jure* monarch of the United Kingdom. *Edinburgh Evening News*, 18 September 1895, p. 3. The English author, Ford Maddox Ford, recalled the following incident: 'Once, driving with Mr. Graham from Roslyn Castle to Edinburgh I heard a politically minded lady say to him: "You ought, Mr. Graham, to be the first president of a British Republic." "I ought madam, if I had my rights," he answered sardonically, "to be the king of this country. And what a three weeks that would be!"'
Ford Maddox Ford, *Return to Yesterday* (1931) (Manchester: Carcanet, 1999), p. 38.
23. Perhaps also a swipe at a declaration signed in 1932 by members of Scotland's nobility and business leaders, opposing Scottish home rule.
24. Cunninghame Graham, 'Foreword' to John A. Stewart's *Inchmahome and the Lake of Menteith* (printed privately, 1933), p. 9.
25. Ibid., p. 10.
26. Cunninghame Graham, 'Foreword' to Thomas Dick Lauder's *The Wolf of Badenoch* (Stirling: Eneas Mackay, 1930), p. 7.
27. Cunninghame Graham, 'The Awakening of a Nation', *Scots Independent*, October 1932, p. 184.
28. *Glasgow Herald*, 29 October 1928, p.8. This article was adjacent to a report of a speech by Sir William Noble, who expressed fears about the rise of Irish immigration into Scotland and his belief that Scottish culture was being swamped.
29. Cunninghame Graham, 'Introduction' to Robert Kirk's *Secret Commonwealth* (Stirling: Eneas Mackay, 1933), pp. 11–18.
30. Graham described Lang as being 'steeped to the lips in all the lore of fairydom, of elves, of doublegangers [sic], peghts, brownies, banshees, and the second sight'. Ibid., p. 11.
31. Scott had described the locale and traditions in *Rob Roy* (1817), and the beliefs and misfortunes of Kirk[e] in his *Letters on Demonology and Witchcraft* (1830). Doon Hill is still a place of pilgrimage and oblation for those fascinated by fairy lore.
32. Gregory Smith, *Scottish Literature*, p. 35.
33. Graham, 'Introduction' to *Secret Commonwealth*, p. 12. This phrase may have been Graham borrowing an early Christian doctrine of faith, *Certum est quia impossibile est*, inferring that something is certain because it is

impossible. This also reflected Kirk's concerns over Sadduceeism; i.e. if one did not accept the existence of the supernatural, it was a step closer to denying the existence of God. My thanks to Professor Richard J. Finlay for this insight.

34. Robert Crawford, *Devolving English Literature* (Oxford: The Clarendon Press, 1992), p. 569.

35. George Blake in *Scotland in Quest of Her Youth* (Edinburgh: Oliver & Boyd, 1932), p. 158.

36. Ibid., p. 159.

37. Crawford, *Devolving English Literature*, p. 544.

38. MacDiarmid, *Centenary Study*, p. 9.

39. Bold, *MacDiarmid*, p. 267.

40. Grieve, *Contemporary Scottish Studies*, p. 54.

41. Grieve (MacDiarmid) had been an active member of the ILP in South Wales, where he had sought out Keir Hardie in 1911.

42. Bold recorded that MacDiarmid was fond of saying that 'to be international, one had to have a nation to be "inter" about'. Alan Bold, 'Introduction' to MacDiarmid's *Aesthetics in Scotland* (Edinburgh: Mainstream Publishing, 1984), p. 14.

43. Hugh MacDiarmid, *The Company I've Kept* (London: Hutchison, 1966), p. 256.

44. *Western Mail*, 7 March 1927, p. 3. John Crichton-Stuart, 3rd Marquess of Bute, architectural patron and philanthropist, was reputedly the richest man in Europe. He built Cardiff Castle, the fantastical Mount Stuart, and endowed Bute Hall at the University of Glasgow.

45. Bold, *MacDiarmid*, p. 77.

46. Gregory Smith, *Scottish Literature*, p. 4.

47. Grieve, *Contemporary Scottish Studies*, p. 19.

48. Ibid., p. 49.

49. MacDiarmid, *The Company I've Kept*, p. 75.

50. Grieve, *Contemporary Scottish Studies*, p. 51.

51. Ibid., p. 56.

52. MacDiarmid, *Selected Essays*, p. 122.

18

Obituaries and Appreciations: An Immortal Type

GRAHAM, WHO SUFFERED FROM bronchitis, caught a chill, most likely from standing knee-deep in a cold Argentinian stream, and died of pneumonia in Buenos Aires on 20 March 1936, at the age of eighty-three. Such was his celebrity, on his death, and for several months after, there were over two hundred reports, obituaries, and tributes in newspapers and periodicals, both at home and overseas, including twenty in *The Scotsman*, eighteen in the *Glasgow Herald*, ten in *The Observer*, and six in *The Times*.[1] Any such assessments of Graham's legacy, however, must be seen in the context of his long life, during which time not only his own views but also political fashions and social mores changed, but also the inherently eulogistic nature of the newspaper obituary. The *Glasgow Herald* reported:

> He was a political freelance . . . He was not made of the docile stuff essential in the good party politician . . . the party managers were not loth to be rid of so disturbing an element . . . at this period he was regarded merely an eccentric figure in public life, a political farceur. Later, all sections came to recognise as a man of splendid personality and brilliant talents. He was an idealist who chased his ideals in a specious world of his own. The constitution of this country and the temperament of its people afford no scope for giving realisation to the views he so strenuously preached.[2]

The Scotsman opined that Graham could not be said to have achieved what the world counts as success, but he was:

> Unique in an age which cannot boast too many outstanding men. His far sighted views made him appear to have been born a century before his time; but, on the other hand, there was a certain touch of the crusader about him – the word seems most appropriate – which made one feel whilst listening to him that he was born three centuries too late.

The obituarist believed, further, that his distinctive style marked him out as one of the foremost present-day exponents of the art of essay writing.[3]

The Times described Graham as 'the most picturesque Scot of his time . . . In him Spain and Scotland met.' He was 'a cowboy-dandy', but he was neither an essayist nor an historian'.[4] The *Manchester Guardian* obituarist believed that he was better understood in the last years of his life, 'since our more stirring century began, than before'. In keeping with the change in political fashion, it added that in the previous century he was regarded as something of a 'freak' or 'phenomenon', but that it also found it difficult to describe him as a success.[5] Most acerbically, Malcolm Muggeridge wrote that Graham was one of those humanitarians to whom adventure seemed the greatest good. Like Don Quixote he needed a crusade, hence his adherence to the socialism of William Morris. He hated the unheroic, abstract, calculating world of the capitalists against which he set an 'heroic world, full of richness and colour, with proud values', but since men were not as heroic as he would like to think, he had to 'content himself with dreams, and self-dramatisation and heroic episodes'.[6]

The *Buenos Aires Herald* reported the day after his death that 'Graham could claim to be the greatest stylist in the English language during the last half century'.[7] A month after his death, his friend Fernando Pozzo wrote, 'Graham was perhaps the Englishman [*sic*] imbued with the spirit of the Argentine plains, which helped him to realise his youthful dreams.'[8] The Argentinian cultural magazine *Nostoros* published several articles about him, one commentator believing that:

> Graham knew and loved the Argentine pampa. His work, which reveals a nostalgia for types and customs now dead, is, above all, descriptive and pictorial. On his final visit he no longer found the visions of his youth.[9]

The most comprehensive, informed, and reflective commentaries, however, appeared in three consecutive articles in May 1936 in the short-lived *Outlook & The Modern Scot*, by Henry Nevinson,[10] Compton Mackenzie, and George Scott Moncrieff. Nevinson believed that Graham was

> a 'throw-back' – to the age of romance and unselfish devotion. Bonnie Prince Charlie in his best years of his youth may have looked like that, and have exerted the same kind of personal attraction upon all who came under his charm.[11]

Graham's personality, he believed was finer and more influential than his writings, 'but all his writings strike the same high note of genuine sympathy with the depressed and those who have never enjoyed the opportunity for the fullest life of which their nature was capable'.[12] (For full text, see APPENDIX X.) Mackenzie approached Graham's life from a political angle, and no doubt reflecting his own current disillusionment with the SNP, wrote that his death might prove a mortal blow to Scottish nationalism, and that nationalists must recognise that Graham was one of the few leaders of the movement able and willing to confront the full implications of the political and economic freedom at which he aimed. He added that it was tragic that Graham was already so old when the NPS was formed with such hopes,[13] and that the current SNP 'possessed neither the spiritual, nor moral, intellectual, nor the political force it possessed eight years earlier'.[14]

Moncrieff's article was a rebuttal of Muggeridge's critique, and he believed that any study of Graham's writing 'is less a study of his literary style than of the bone and the philosophy of his work'. Critics might find fault with his grammatical lapses, but to Graham 'the substance of the work was of so much greater importance than the manner of its presentation', and his work 'is worthy of the consideration when modern works so much of which are "scrimpet and vapid"'. Finally, Moncrieff attempted to sum up the intrinsic meaning in his writings:

> It is a philosophy that takes the utmost pleasure obtainable from the many-coloured shadows of life, yet is perpetually aware of, at once humbled by, and exalted by, the underlying substance of a conscious or unconscious immortality: one that can find consummation in failure.[15]

Edward Garnett, the man who probably knew Graham and his works best, wrote an appreciation in the *London Mercury* that, although, eulogistic, had some valid insights. Garnett believed that his main traits were his 'trenchant philosophy and his pulverising contempt for worldly humbug', his interest in practical matters, his sense of human drama,[16] his keen eye for character (although he had no power to create it), and his challenge to Victorian shibboleths of the white man's burden. Garnett also discussed his lack of popularity as a writer, which Graham was aware of; none of his books 'sold', as publishers put it, and only one reached a second edition. His works, according to Garnett, were 'devoid of "moral uplift" and sentimental camouflage', and lacked a sentimental appeal to women, all of which Garnett considered fatal in the ordinary reader's eyes.[17]

Notes

1. 'Mr Cunninghame Graham: A Scottish Hidalgo', *The Times*, 23 March 1936, p. 18.
2. *Glasgow Herald*, 21 March 1936, p. 11.

 3. *Scotsman*, 23 March 1936, p. 10.
 4. *Times*, 23 March 1936, p. 18.
 5. *Manchester Guardian*, 21 March 1936, p. 19.
 6. Muggeridge, 'Cunninghame Graham', pp. 440–1.
 7. *Buenos Aires Herald*, 21 March 1936, p. 4.
 8. Fernando Pozzo, *La Literatura Argentina*, No. 88, April 1936, p. 79.
 9. Carlos Ibarguren, 'Un Gran Espiritu' (A Great Spirit), *Nosotros*, April 1936, p. 26.
10. Henry Woodd Nevinson (1856–1941), English war correspondent, campaigning journalist, socialist, and suffragist.
11. Henry Nevinson, 'A Rebel Aristocrat', *Outlook & The Modern Scot*, May 1936, p. 18.
12. Ibid., p. 20.
13. Ibid., p. 21.
14. Ibid., p. 22.
15. Moncrieff, 'Cunninghame Graham and a Contemporary Critic', pp. 25–8.
16. Garnett introduced his own drama by telling his readers that Tschiffely had told him of Graham's presentiment that he did not expect to return alive from Argentina. Garnett himself was to die only eight months after this article was published.
17. Garnett, 'R. B. Cunninghame Graham: Man and Writer', pp. 125–9.

Part III Conclusion

GRAHAM HAD STOPPED WRITING overtly propagandist material because it would have compromised his position as an elder statesman, while the younger man, Johnston, suffered from no such inhibitions until he too gained visibility and influence. The fundamental difference between Graham and Johnston was that Johnston was an optimist who believed that 'there was very little wrong with Scotland that her sons and daughters might not speedily put right',[1] while Graham became increasingly mired in pessimism, since the old, brave, romantic world that he had cherished was increasingly eroded.

His volte-face over the war and the empire was, like his other crusades, based on a moral revulsion, for which, with some justification, he blamed Germany, but also, having been obliged to choose sides as a man for whom 'bread was bread, and wine was wine', as usual he took an uncompromising stance, giving him another cause for which to strive. Nevertheless, it was undoubtedly also a major watershed in his political views, to which his silence over post-war strikes and civil unrest at home stands testament. Also, despite his occasional attraction to, and encouragement of, direct and even violent action, when Graham witnessed events in Ireland during and after the war, Mackenzie wrote that he became 'naturally prejudiced against the Irish point of view'.[2]

Graham increasingly looked like an isolated figure, a non-party man, at a time when 'party men' would predominate. He had distanced himself further from the Labour party by standing against Johnston on basically the same political platform. Now, and for decades to come, many of the left's intelligentsia, of which, at one time, Graham had stood on the periphery, would look towards Soviet Russia for their inspiration, but he hated what he saw as Soviet barbarity.

His decision to stand as a Liberal in 1918 is perplexing, and his political allegiances appear promiscuous, but the Liberals now embraced many of the policies that he had campaigned for, and perhaps he saw an opportunity to advance these even further, and, as previously stated, he was less interested in party labels than political action. But why stand at all, having already been 'defiled by the pitch of politics' and protested so vigorously against the House of Commons? It looks like an odd decision, but the fact remains that between 1885 and 1918, Graham had put himself forward for election to parliament five times, being successful only once. It is more likely that his motivation to stand was (as usual) entirely personal, for a man who was passionate for the moment, and since the sale of Gartmore House, his debts had gone and he was in funds.[3] But it seems that, even before his defeat, he regretted standing. Moreover, his bellicose statements during the 1918 general election campaign are difficult to explain, and appear to be completely at odds with his life and philosophy hitherto, leading Neal Ascherson to speculate:

> The old boy seemed to be going potty. But it was just a bad patch. In his commitment to Scottish Nationalism, which followed, Graham returned to his normal acid sanity and talked again like a practical socialist.[4]

In 1916, Graham had prematurely announced his retirement from writing. He may have felt disappointed by his lack of commercial success, or that his literary contributions would now be outdated by the cultural and political changes that the war would bring, or simply that the sources of his inspiration – his recollections – had dried up. Apart from a brief re-engagement with the *Saturday Review*,[5] his literary output greatly reduced, and his focus moved away from his memories to more factual and historical material. Only occasionally did he reminisce in his inconclusive sketch style, but these pieces lacked the political impetus of his previous works. His letters to the press also declined in number, and he rarely reacted to outside agency, as he had so strongly in the past. It appears that despite maintaining a socialist conscience, the socialism now being demonstrated in world affairs no longer appealed. Consequently, Graham's political activities became increasingly focused on the smaller and more comprehendible canvas of Scotland.

In a now familiar generational cycle, between conflicts, an interest in, and enthusiasm for, Scottish home rule had again blossomed in various forms, led by articulate and committed individuals, whose followers, however, comprised a loose collection of eccentrics and dreamers. It was a populist fad that gained renewed momentum only after Labour dropped its long-held home rule policy, precipitating a schism in the

Labour-dominated SHRA, and the subsequent call to amalgamate the factional nationalist interests. The central figures in this amalgamation were Muirhead and MacCormick, who had the vision and the ability to compromise that helped consolidate the groups into the NPS, while Graham's re-engagement with nationalist politics was initially tentative. From correspondence, it appears that he was at first goaded, then constantly encouraged by Muirhead into becoming more active, but age and temperament would keep him distant from the day-to-day business and machinations of its other adherents. Muirhead saw that part of his function was to keep Graham engaged by informing him of the latest developments. However, contrasting the correspondence between them with the reports on the internal difficulties faced by the SHRA and the NPS, and the sometimes rancorous negotiations between the nationalist groups, it is clear that Muirhead mostly kept him in the dark as to the challenges.

Graham's enthusiasm had been rekindled by his near success at the Rectorial Election, and perhaps the feeling that he was again politically relevant, but his role has been overstated. Among the students he was unknown; it was MacCormick who engineered his nomination, and MacCormick and Mackenzie who managed his campaign, with Graham, as was customary, making no appearance.[6] Nonetheless, it was this establishment upset that led directly to the consolidation and growth of the NPS, which itself can be regarded as a significant achievement – for the students, particularly MacCormick. However, translating this success from the Gothic cloisters on Gilmorehill to the pitheads, factory gates, and kail-yards of the rest of Scotland would prove considerably more problematic, as the initial excitement of the possible, was, as is common, overwhelmed by the practical mundanities of the actual.

As in the early years of the SPLP, Graham, a man who was already well known to the older generation, was given the role of an inspirational figurehead in the NPS, where, apart from MacDiarmid and Mackenzie, the other nationalist functionaries were entirely unknown.[7] MacDiarmid, however, took his normal, jaundiced view, believing that Graham's talents were misused:

> The trouble was not that he was unpractical in this sense, not that he failed to do the donkey-work – but that donkey-work was almost all that circumstances allowed him to do, and that he was never enabled to serve the movement effectively on his own best plane. It was all right for most of the others, but he and Mackenzie were used by the Nationalist Party, so far as suspicion and jealousy and sheer incomprehension permitted the Nationalist Party to avail themselves of their services at all.[8]

In contrast, Taylor, in concluding her biography, saw him latterly as a sad figure in the nationalist ranks:

> His political career begun so early and with such passionate effect upon the hearts and minds of the industrial workers of the West of Scotland ended at the summer outings of the National Party of Scotland where, a painfully thin but still upright and dapper figure, microphone in hand he bid for the attention of the picknickers around him.[9]

Both MacDiarmid's and Taylor's assessments were overstated. MacDiarmid, who had been expelled from the NPS in 1933 for his Communist sympathies and anti-English extremism, did not understand Graham's relationship with the nationalists as it manifested itself through the only substantive sources, his correspondence with Muirhead, and the records of the NPS, which showed that he was a very infrequent participant. Graham, who was spending more time abroad, or in London, was temperamentally unsuited to the donkey-work of party affairs – ironically like MacDiarmid himself, who regarded the NPS organisation as 'hopelessly inadequate'.[10] MacCormick more accurately wrote of Graham:

> [He] was in politics (and in the best sense of the word) an adventurer who took keen delight in crossing swords with party Goliaths and who gave little thought to any practical considerations with might weigh with other men.[11]

It also appears, from Mackenzie's cryptic statement, that Graham was unhappy with the amalgamation of the NPS with Scotland's Party, and, had he lived longer, he might have displayed the same disenchantment toward the SNP as he had done with the Liberals and the Labour Party. It is thus difficult to understand why Graham was given a chapter in Mitchell and Hassan's 2016 book *Scottish National Party Leaders*, while Muirhead, the tireless campaigner, part-funder, SNP President (1936–50), and organiser of the modern nationalist movement who campaigned into his nineties, was not.[12]

Taylor also failed to understand Graham's position in this new party: he was making his contribution in the only way he was now capable of, as a respected ageing icon, and like his idealistic preacher, addressing no one, conscious that the inner fire had got the better of the fleshly tenement, and that his work was done.

Notes

1. Quoted in Galbraith, *No Quarter Given*, p. 7.
2. Mackenzie, 'Cunninghame Graham Scottish Nationalist', pp. 21–4.
3. On his death, Graham's personal estate was valued at £100,426. *Scotsman*, 20 July 1936, p. 13.

4. Neal Ascherson, 'Cunninghame Graham: A Critical Biography', *Spectator Review*, 14 July 1979, p. 19.
5. Ten pieces published over a period of one year, in very short bursts, indicating, perhaps, Graham's increasing absence from British shores.
6. A more realistic outcome can be witnessed four years later, when, without the enthusiastic support of MacCormick and the students, Graham was badly beaten.
7. These two men presented their political enemies with an opportunity to accuse the NPS of being composed entirely of Communists and Roman Catholics. Following the decision of a branch in Glasgow to sever its connection with the NPS following a speech by Mackenzie, Muirhead, for the sake of unity, wrote to Graham asking him to use his influence to dissuade Mackenzie from discussing his Catholicism at public meetings. R. E. Muirhead, letter to Cunninghame Graham, 12 December 1928. Muirhead Papers.
8. MacDiarmid, *Selected Essays*, p. 127.
9. Taylor, *The People's Laird*, p. 334.
10. MacDiarmid, *Selected Essays*, p. 123.
11. John MacCormick, *The Flag in the Wind*, p. 34–5.
12. James Mitchell and Gerry Hassan, eds, *Scottish National Party Leaders* (London: Biteback Publishing, 2016), pp. 4–5. Grieve (MacDiarmid) described Muirhead as 'the mainspring' of the nationalist movement, Grieve, *Contemporary Scottish Studies*, p. 262, and a man of 'extraordinary tenacity', p. 265.

Conclusion

ANY ATTEMPT TO ANALYSE Graham is fraught with difficulties, even his close associates found him hard to fathom.[1] His early publisher and long-time acquaintance, Frank Harris, said of him, '[H]ow little I knew Graham; how reticent he was or proud with that curious secretive pride which is so Scotch and so Spanish.'[2] MacDiarmid described him as an enigma,[3] and the critic Frederick Watson considered him 'a very elusive personality'.[4] Exasperated by his contradictions, Watts described him as 'a plethora of paradoxes'.[5] The waters were muddied further by half-truths and myths, some of which Graham helped elaborate into the legend of the hybrid Spanish *hidalgo* and adventurous Scottish laird, but there has been no shortage of willing accomplices. Perhaps it was, as the ever-tactful Maitland suggested, that 'life has been turned into art thereby representing real life more vividly'.[6] In other words, the truth was embellished to make it truer. This closely resembles what Terry Eagleton described as 'Truth, the cognitive, becomes that which satisfies the mind . . . Morality is converted to a matter of style, pleasure and intuition. How should one live one's life properly? By turning oneself into an artefact',[7] which, to resolve his paradoxes and contradictions, is exactly what Graham succeeded in becoming. But there was also a strong streak of cultured perversity in his character that Professor John Mackenzie wisely recognised. Quoting from Disraeli's novel *Sybil*, Mackenzie wrote of Graham's attraction to life's absurdities, 'I rather like bad wine, one gets so bored with good wine'.[8] More importantly, perhaps, he had a patrician's scorn for mere wealth, and understood that any form of success was ultimately distorting, corrosive, and disappointing.

Describing Graham as a socialist also remains problematic. At the beginning of his political career he was an inspired late Victorian rebel, and like Hyndman and Champion, two other widely travelled political itinerants, he was a 'Tory socialist',[9] more than satisfying Walter Bage-hot's studied judgement that 'the essence of Toryism is enjoyment'.[10] Instinctively anti-authoritarian, confident, and self-willed, he sought out and co-opted idealistic socialistic doctrines to advance what was a naively optimistic but deeply reactionary conservatism, opposing over-whelming tides of economic, technological, scientific, and social change. Graham stood against the modern world wherein the rise of industrialism and capitalism during the nineteenth century had brought with it huge social disparity and dislocation, the triumph of the commercial classes, the enlargement of an impoverished and often destitute urban proletar-iat, and the near-destruction of traditional rural life. He was perhaps a socialist in the abstract, MacDiarmid maintaining that his socialism was not based on an adequate theory of social causation: 'He was "one of these damned *aristos* who had embraced the cause of the people" – and as a consequence fell between two stools.'[11]

Graham was no intellectual: his inspiration came from generalists and amateurs like Owen, George, and Morris, not political economists and social theorists like Malthus, Mill, Hobson, or Marx.[12] He had com-bined Owen's heroic ruralism, retrospective social ideals, and bonds of community, with Ruskin and Morris's industrial romanticism, in which an enlightened proletariat would willingly work towards the common weal. His socialism was akin to the idealism of his friends Wilde[13] and Kropotkin,[14] men from privileged backgrounds who envisaged societ-ies based on mutual aid, voluntary cooperation, self-sufficiency, and individualism, sometimes called 'primitive communism', similar to the less developed societies that Graham so admired and cherished.[15] These were extremely unrealistic aims in the dynamic and expansive late Victorian world, and despite his denials, they smacked of utopianism. His uniqueness found strong parallels in Buchan's precise analysis of their compatriot, Sir Walter Scott:

> He had mingled ultimately with every class and condition of men; he had enough education to broaden his outlook but not enough to dim it; he was familiar alike with city and moorland, with the sown and the desert, and he escaped the pedantry of both the class-room and the drawing-room; above all he had the good fortune to stand at the meeting-place of two worlds.[16]

Graham never gained a reputation as a serious political thinker – a vic-tim of the very attributes that made him such a unique personality – his restless whimsicality, and his sardonic and anarchic wit. He produced no cohesive political manifesto, his quixotic political perceptions being con-fined to the platform, and scattered across the pages of little-read socialist

journals. Excited and motivated by ideas, not by theories or administration, as a consolation prize, this political dilettante was obliged to
accept honorary positions in every organisation with which he became
involved, with veneration and influence, but with little executive power.
This extended to his significance within the Scottish national movement,
which has been overstated. By this time in his life, he was spending more
time abroad and in London, and had little interest in political involvement other than as a figurehead, an occasional speaker, and an ambassa-
dor for independence. However, his participation, no matter how distant,
would have been inspirational to many, particularly the young. Equally,
to the more conservative elements, opponents of home rule, and those
with long memories, he would have been the recognisable face of a lunatic
fringe whose stated aim was to dismember the British state with potentially disastrous consequences for the monarchy, the political establishment, the landowning elites, and the empire – the same institutions that
he had so fervently attacked throughout his political career.

Graham's politics transcended conventional economic and social
models; the source of his discontent, the source of his contradictions,
and the primary and universal driving force behind all of his political and
literary activities, notwithstanding his personal vanity, was overwhelm-
ingly *moral*. This was not the common morality of the times, which he
considered false, hypocritical, bourgeois, and an impediment to the reordering of society. Neither was it religious; it was what the Greek philosophers had called *arete* or 'virtue',[17] sometimes described as moral
excellence, with its emphasis on 'ethics', a word that Graham frequently
used to describe his own underlying philosophy. Most significantly, for
Graham, it was derived not only from his conscience, and his sense of
duty, but also from his sense of honour, and the joy of personal fulfilment. The most important virtue to the ancient Greeks was justice, and
the absence of justice, whether to the poor, women, ethnic groups, or
animals, was the target of Graham's altruistic moral rage and impulsive,
occasionally manic behaviour. As he was unable or unwilling to bridle
these instincts, in 1916, a critic remarked that despite Graham's airy
panache, at the first sign of abuse and arrogance, 'his air of disengage-
ment and supercilious dash vanishes, and, sword out, he leaps before the
victim, fixing an implacable gimlet eye on the offender'.[18]

His ethical and moral pursuits not only defined his political campaigns,
they also pervaded his literary works. All his descriptions of native societies, his obituaries, and his Scottish portraits, described those whom he
considered possessed virtue, and his social critiques of home, hubris, and
decadence, and his descriptions of imperial and colonial abuses, were of

those whom he considered did not. Thus, this study has asserted that his writings were, like the basis of his politics, intrinsically moral, and just as fundamentally conflicted in their irreconcilable desire for change and for historical continuity. With many others, this also defined his Scottish nationalism.

From the outset of his political career, Graham's energies were directed towards attacking the institutions that he believed propagated and maintained injustice, including parliament and the political, landed, and industrial establishments. Inspired by Morris, as a first step towards his insubstantial ideals, it was his overarching and overreaching ambition to empower the working class politically; and it appears, albeit from scant recorded evidence, that he was the catalyst and prime mover in the foundation of the first party of labour, which has not previously been verified. Although small, and itself inconsequential, it was the seed of a mass working-class movement that would fundamentally change the direction of British politics and eventually succeed in implementing many of his political aspirations some time after his death. In an age of deference, Graham, as a 'toff' and a Member of Parliament, was in a strong and unique position to give vent to progressive opinions, and he became an inspirational rallying point for many who shared his extreme minority views, which have now become mainstream.

It was his elitism that finally terminated Graham's parliamentary career. His uncompromising stance made it impossible for him to cooperate within the broad church of Liberalism, or in the highly competitive but negotiable world of the House of Commons, and he became an incongruous and isolated figure. He had taken on the plutocrats and the wire-pullers, and had been out-manoeuvred, and with the loss of his seat went much of his public prestige and kudos. It was also his elitism that inevitably led to the fracturing of his ties to his Labour colleagues. This was not simply because of his demeanour and his paradoxical social position, but because it prevented him from providing leadership, which he would have considered vulgar, until suddenly that kind of philanthropic patronage was no longer valued. For someone who had no respect for working-class attitudes and aspirations, and no patience with those who pursued only their own narrow sectional interests, he was overtaken by the more focused efforts and the personal ambitions of others. When the party he had envisaged, and was instrumental in creating, moved away from him, he found himself criticising its lack of idealism and radical fervour from the sidelines and was exiled to the margins of Labour history. Thus, the great irony of his political life was that having dedicated much of it to empowering the masses, when at last they began to seize the day and wield that power through industrial action, combined with post-war statism and the growth of mass culture, he found it abhorrent, and not at all what he had envisaged. On 11 December 1919, in a letter to the dramatist, Henry Arthur Jones, Graham wrote that he had hoped that socialism would have produced the demise of selfishness and a better feeling between men, adding, rather forlornly:

> You will admit, I think, that my ambition was not a low ambition. That I was deceived, and that all the golden dreams of Morris have vanished in nine bestial and inarticulate years . . . has not been my fault.[19]

Consequently, subsequent to the First World War, he made no statements on workers' rights or on mass unemployment and the strikes and hunger marches of the 1920s and 1930s.

Another irony was that despite criticising city life, particularly the poverty, wealth, power, and corruption that he witnessed in London, it was that city that rescued him from the political and cultural wilderness, and where he continued to spend a large part of his time until his death.[20] It was in London that this extraordinary wild-man-tamed was most admired and celebrated, and through his many contacts in the political and literary elites, it was there that his early political journalism found a home. It would be there also that his new-found literary career would be established, and irony of ironies, in publications read by the very people whom he most deprecated and criticised.

Although he contributed to other journals, the *Saturday Review* became the mainstay of Graham's literary career, but they were strange bedfellows, and it was his celebrity as much as his literary talents that initiated and sustained the relationship. Once he had brought them under control, however, these talents were considerable. He possessed an extraordinary facility for recollection, and a felicity of expression that could conjure convincing, often startling exotic settings and incidents.[21] However, such works, even in anthology, were never going to achieve wide popularity, and they are too protracted and periphrastic for modern literary tastes. As Andrew Long put it, perhaps unfairly, 'he wrote in a verbose and turgid style that appealed to a specific readership – that is, to an educated middle-class register'.[22]

Self-indulgently, Graham wrote as he remembered, but through the prism of partiality. He was a *raconteur* in the original sense of the word, a recounter of events that had stirred his imagination, events through which he could perceive, or attach, a deeper moral meaning, or at least make his readers reflect. But when his memories became exhausted, so did their spontaneity. Paradoxically, despite his passionate attachments, because either his social position and public persona put reins on his expressiveness, or he was afraid to confront his deeper emotions, his works failed to touch the hearts and pockets of the general reading public. Graham had been entirely honest when he told Leslie Chaundy that he wrote largely for his own amusement, but his own amusement included too many unnecessary digressions. As John Galsworthy noted, with reference to Graham, the short story form required:

> an almost superhuman repression of the writer's self . . . Very much of an artist, he is yet too much of a personality ever to be quite the pure artist; the individuality of the man will thrust its spear-head through the stuff of his creations.[23]

Graham's writings were too distinctive and personal, selected and skewed, to express and satisfy his nostalgic impulses, his passionate moral drives, and his need to sermonise about high and low human instincts. Also, the tame and domestic beauties of Dorset and Lincolnshire had more commercial appeal than the mysteries and characters of Menteith. It was, perhaps, as Jeffrey Meyers observed, that he spread his talents too thinly and achieved little of enduring importance.[24] If he had pandered to popular tastes and attained a wider popularity as a writer in his lifetime, his name and reputation would have survived longer. Or, if he had focused his talents on a smaller canvas, for instance, on his portraits of Menteith, then he might have established himself more firmly in the public imagination, albeit, perhaps, at a local level. But for this campaigning memoirist, with such a broad range of adventurous experiences to draw upon, that would never have been a serious option. Thus, ironically, although displaying a strong underlying unity of sentiment and purpose, the international, cross-cultural and diverse subject matter that distinguished Graham from other Scottish writers were the very qualities that diluted and eventually dissipated his literary standing in the eyes of both reader and critic. In addition, like his position in the world of politics, although he was difficult to ignore, it was in the interest of very few within the literary establishment to champion his works, and it was left to personal acquaintances and political fellow-travellers to extol his literary virtues. Although a highly gifted writer, it was also his untrammelled productivity, his lack of editorial discipline, and his emotional reticence, that prevented him from attaining greatness, and his position in the pantheon of Scottish literary artists remains inconclusive.

Graham undoubtedly led an extraordinary and meaningful life. It was not simply diverse and adventurous, it inspired many others, including subsequently brighter stars in the Scottish firmament, such as Hardie, Johnston, MacDiarmid, Mackenzie, and MacCormick, who were the childless Graham's spiritual and political heirs. As Nevinson observed, 'His personality was finer and more influential than his writings',[25] and personality cannot be discounted. By lending his personality, he advanced the causes of the Labour party and the NPS, and as he himself wrote, with typical self-regard:

> There is a personality about some men, which even if they never get a chance to excel, still makes them in themselves superior to their fellows. Sometimes a man who neither writes, nor speaks, nor has excelled in his profession, yet in himself excels.[26]

But *post mortem*, such personalities are devilishly difficult to conjure, and their lasting impact is impossible to quantify. Thus, the continuing imponderable is to what extent Graham's personality and his life story have now, like then, dominated opinion and eclipsed any tangible or lasting achievements, preventing us from seeing a little further into the dark. With such scant and diffuse evidence, his achievements remain for the most part nebulous, and thus the very existence of such a man has inevitably become the focus. This, perhaps alone, has periodically kept his name alive, while others have been sucked back into the shadows.

Graham's most significant and lasting legacy was not his prescient radicalism nor his large literary canon. In Scotland, it was his hybrid, pragmatic, cosmopolitan localism, which, albeit sporadically, distracted the nation from its sentimental, cultural, and political navel gazing, and directed that gaze towards a broader horizon, with an ambition for Scotland, mankind, and the natural world that was prophetic, relevant, and inspirational.[27] On that broader horizon, his was a much-needed voice of opposition to conformity and complacency: an heroic voice of courage and independence, which, in its time, excelled all others. Frank Harris most eloquently described what he saw as Graham's noble and heroic qualities:

> He was born to wealth and place, dowered with perfect health and great personal charm; tempted as only such a man is, he might have been forgiven if he had chosen the primrose way and lazied through life relishing all the flowers and tasting all the sweets. Instead of that, he left his caste and spoke and wrote and worked for the poor and the outcast and the dispossessed. He braved the scorn and hatred of men when he might easily have enjoyed their applause and honour. He faced blows and indignities and imprisonment when he could have reckoned on welcome as a distinguished guest in Courts and Throne-rooms; by choice he took the martyr's way and gave the best of his life to the meanest of his fellows.[28]

To his eager champions, Graham was, and remains, a hero, and for the rest of us, as Carlyle reminds us: 'Great Men are profitable company. We cannot look, however imperfectly, upon a great man, without gaining something by him.'[29] Yet the title of hero applied to Graham is not without its appeal. Heroes act alone, without endorsement, guided by a moral compass to pursue a single-minded vision, and are discouraged by neither defeat, vilification, nor shame. Careless of approval, the admiration of their peers, the hope of reward, the promise of retroactive affection, or some other emotional compensation, such individuals prize only their sense of honour and fulfilment. There is no doubt that Graham met many of these criteria, and at a time of precious few heroes, despite his flaws, paradoxes, and downright contradictions, he set the standard for integrity and personal courage. Certainly, Shaw would have included him in the following passage:

> The free-thinking English gentlemen-republicans of the last half of the nineteenth century ... great globe-trotters, writers, *frondeurs*, brilliant and accomplished cosmopolitans so far as their various abilities permitted, all more interested in the world than in themselves, and in themselves than in official decorations; consequently unpurchasable, their price being too high for any modern commercial Government to pay.[30]

Graham has indeed become an artefact, a mirror that continues to sparkle in a cynical and humdrum age, one in which his admirers can bask in the reflected glories of an imagined heroic past, or project their dreams of future utopias.

*If to ride and dream and plan and speak and act
like a gentleman, a patriot and a scholar is to be a
Don Quixote, then let him be called Don Quixote.
Yet for a visionary who looked so fearlessly into
the cold eyes of truth I should prefer the epithet
less suggestive of an outlived chivalry. If in Scottish
history he be doomed to remain just another of
our picturesque failures, the blame and shame will
rest upon Scotland which allows some thousands
of Scots bleating round London in comic tam-
o'-shanters that a Hottentot would spurn, to be
accepted as a more representative expression
of the nation's life and the nation's pride than
Cunninghame Graham.*

R.I.P.

Compton Mackenzie

Notes

1. In an obituary, Pritchett wrote: 'When men become legends, as Cunninghame Graham did, this private character becomes elusive.' Pritchett, 'New Literature', p. 339.
2. Frank Harris, *Contemporary Portraits*, p. 57.
3. MacDiarmid, *Cunninghame Graham: A Centenary Study*, p. 23.
4. Frederick Watson, 'R. B. Cunninghame Graham', p. 174.
5. Watts, 'Janiform Genius', p. 2.
6. Maitland, *Robert and Gabriela Cunninghame Graham*, p. 15.
7. Terry Eagleton, *The Ideology of the Aesthetic* (Oxford: Basil Blackwell, 1990), p. 368.
8. John M. Mackenzie, 'The Local and the Global: The Multiple Contexts of Cunninghame Graham', in *Empires and Revolutions: Cunninghame Graham & His Contemporaries*, pp. 18–19.
9. Engels described Hyndman as 'an arch-Conservative'. Bottogelli, *Friedrich Engels: Correspondence*, p. 389. However, Pelling wrote that Champion's 'Tory Socialism', represented 'an intelligible point of view'. Pelling, *Origins of the Labour Party*, p. 150.
10. *The Works & Life of Walter Bagehot*, Vol. II (London: Longman's, 1915), p. 100.
11. MacDiarmid, *Centenary Study*, p. 9.
12. Cunninghame Graham described Mill and Malthus as 'writers of the dismal science [Carlyle], now dead and damned for dullness'. 'The Bloody City', *People's Press*, 16 August 1890, p. 9.
13. As expressed in Wilde's essay *The Soul of Man Under Socialism* (1891), which David Goodway believed was 'unquestionably an anarchist text'. David Goodway, *Anarchist Seeds Beneath the Snow* (Liverpool University Press, 2006), p. 73. Graham also shared Wilde's distaste for charity, 'which debases those who give as well as those who receive it'. Cunninghame Graham, 'Aspects of the Social Question', *English Review*, December 1908, p. 166.
14. Principally described in Kropotkin's books, *The Conquest of Bread* (1892) and *Mutual Aid* (1902).
15. Described in Engels's book: *The Origin of the Family, Private Property and the State* (1884).
16. Buchan, *Sir Walter Scott* (London: Cassell, 1932), p. 43.
17. 'I believe in virtue, magnanimity, righteousness.' Cunninghame Graham, 'The Imperial Kailyard', p. 3.
18. *New Statesman*, 11 November 1916, p. 134.
19. Doris Arthur Jones, ed., *Taking the Curtain Call*, p. 304.
20. After the sale of Gartmore House, Graham rented various apartments in London's fashionable Mayfair and Belgravia.
21. An unnamed reviewer in the *Saturday Review* wrote of his talents: 'Mr. Cunninghame Graham is not altogether a good story-teller: indeed,

he is not exactly a story-teller at all. He has a remarkable power of calling up an atmosphere, as if by a kind of careless enchantment . . . a narrative full of gesture, interrupting itself.' 'The Unlucky Number', *The Saturday Review*, 29 September 1900, p. 400.

22. Long, 'A Refusal and Traversal, p. 390.

23. John Galsworthy, 'Notes on R. B. Cunninghame Graham', *Forsytes, Pendyces and Others* (London: Heinemann, 1935), pp. 273–4. (For full text, see APPENDIX VIII.)

24. Meyers, *Fever at the Core*, p. 39.

25. Nevinson, 'A Rebel Aristocrat', p. 20.

26. Cunninghame Graham, 'The Admiral', *Saturday Review*, 3 November 1900, pp. 546–8. Anthologised in *Hope* (1910), pp. 216–30.

27. Graham was the embodiment of the words 'Think global, act local', attributed to his compatriot, Patrick Geddes.

28. Frank Harris, *Contemporary Portraits*, pp. 59–60.

29. Carlyle, *On Heroes, Hero-Worship and the Heroic in History* (1841) (University of Nebraska Press, 1996), p. 1.

30. George Bernard Shaw, *Pen Portraits and Reviews* (London: Constable, 1932), p. 129.

The Literature

SHORT BIOGRAPHIES

THERE WAS A LARGE catalogue of short biographies of, and references to, Graham published in his lifetime, most of which were eulogies. Those of interest include Robert Birkmyre's 'An Appreciation of Cunninghame Graham' (1908), which was based on an interview with his subject, and which described Graham as 'a protean personality capable of the most chameleon-like variations'.[1] Amy Wellington's more incisive 'An Artist-Fighter in English Prose' (1918) described Graham as 'the boldest, most original and unpopular of living British writers',[2] and Robert Lynd's *Old and New Masters* (1919), described him as a grandee of contemporary literature and of revolutionary politics.[3] Bernard Muddiman's *Men of the Nineties* (1920),[4] lavished praise on Graham's evocations of exotic lands, and C. Lewis Hind's *More Authors and I* (1922) described 'this grandee of the mob' as someone who wrote of things seen on the byways of life, 'which he finds more vitalising than the high-roads'.[5]

Similar praise continued after his death. A typical example, entitled 'Don Roberto', was published by the author and playwright Samuel Levy Bensusan, and described Graham as essentially democratic, a friend of all classes, a linguist, a fine storyteller, and a master of style equal to Anatole France. All his work was an expression of his fundamental sympathy for the underdog and contempt for material commercialism.[6] A trickle of articles continued through the 1940s, including in a book entitled *Twentieth Century Authors*, in which Graham was described as:

> One of the great British 'aberrants', along with Doughty, Burton and Trelawney. Although his Spanish blood made him look like a Velazquez portrait, the Celt in him produced the adventurer and the eccentric. Though he has been neglected by 'right-minded' men, few writers less deserve neglect.[7]

The centenary of Graham's birth in 1952 briefly generated renewed interest, and perhaps a more questioning approach to how he had previously been depicted. Hamish Henderson's article, referenced in the Introduction, critiqued Paul Bloomfield's anthology of Graham's sketches,[8] and criticised Graham's early biographers, declaring that Graham, like Robert Burns, was honoured for wrong or at least irrelevant reasons. Henderson insisted that it was not for being a legendary figure that Graham should be remembered, but rather fancifully, that he emerged from the recognisable Scottish traditions of 'the soldier of fortune and the wandering scholar . . . the penniless clansman who regarded himself as the equal of any king'.[9]

Much later, the prolific American biographer, Jeffrey Meyers, dedicated a chapter to Graham in his book on political rebels, *Fever At the Core: Six Studies of Idealists in Politics* (1976),[10] which focused on the adventurous aspects of Graham's life, particularly his charging of police lines in Trafalgar Square.

Biographical details also appeared in the biographies of Graham's friends and contemporaries, particularly of Joseph Conrad, Keir Hardie, W. H. Hudson, and Edward Garnett.

PERSONAL MEMOIRS

There were many personal recollections of Graham in articles and autobiographies. Of note was the novelist George Moore's *Conversations in Ebury Street*,[11] which discussed his extensive literary knowledge. In his book *Men and Memories*, Graham's artist friend, Sir William (Will) Rothenstein, described Graham as 'the most picturesque and picaresque figures of the day, and extremely entertaining. He had a witty and caustic tongue, and told the best Scotch stories I have ever heard.'[12] Another distinguished painter, who rendered Graham in oils, was the Irish artist John Lavery, who described his friendship with Graham in his autobiography, *The Life of a Painter* (1940), adding the revealing comment, 'I think that I did something to help Graham in the creation of his own masterpiece – himself.'[13]

George Bernard Shaw described him as an 'incredible personage'.[14] Galsworthy regarded Graham's literary talents as 'peculiar and unique', but felt he had too much of a personality to be a true artist,[15] nevertheless, he believed that Graham was a 'gallant foe of oppression, of cruelty, of smugness, and fatty degeneration; a real tonic salt to the life of an age that needs it'.[16] (For full text, see Appendix VIII.) Much later, Frank Harris wrote that Graham's physical advantages and wealth prevented him from being a great writer, and referred to him as 'an amateur of genius'.[17]

Among those Scots who knew him, Neil Munro, in his memoir *The Brave Days* (1931), dwelt on Graham's personality rather than his writing skills, describing him as 'noble, gallant; always distinguished; sometimes a little daft'.[18] Munro also wrote that there were 'more inconsistencies to the chapter in Mr. Cunninghame Graham than in any writer I know'.[19] In Richard Curle's *Caravansary and Conversation* (1937), Graham was described as 'one the most remarkable men of his period . . . more often painted than any other contemporary figure'.[20] A socialist fellow-traveller was the author and publisher James Leatham, who recalled in *The Gateway* Graham and Keir Hardie's early campaigns, describing Graham as 'a writer in a perfectly unique vein and style'.[21] Another anecdotal eulogy was included as a chapter in the autobiography of Graham's friend, the noted electrical and mining engineer, Sam Mavor (1940).[22]

A friend of both, and sharing Graham and MacDiarmid's political views, Compton Mackenzie recorded his memories of Graham in his autobiography, *My Life and Times* (1967).[23] This was another useful first-hand account of Graham's early involvement with Scottish nationalism, particularly his candidature for the Rectorship of Glasgow University in 1928. Mackenzie also wrote an appreciation of Graham on his death,[24] which gave an insight into his own, and Graham's attitude to the SNP.

Graham's remarkable maiden speech in parliament received plaudits from political diarists, but the first commentary on his parliamentary performances was written by an anonymous Irish MP in the popular journal *United Ireland*, which described him as one of the most remarkable men in the new parliament.[25] (For edited text, see Appendix IV.) Graham's name also appeared in memoirs of his early socialist colleagues. The most valuable was by the journalist David Lowe in his *Souvenirs of Scottish Labour* (1919),[26] and Lowe's newspaper articles of the 1930s.[27] Two other rare and valuable eyewitness accounts of those early days discussed in this study appeared in the autobiographies of the trade unionists Robert Smillie[28] and his colleague, Alexander 'Sandy' Haddow.[29]

EAGER CHAMPIONS

Graham's earliest and most consistent champion, the man who got his works anthologised, was the hugely influential publisher's reader and editor Edward Garnett,[30] who also wrote an insightful obituary.[31] Later, William Power, mentioned above, would praise Graham in newspaper reviews, and in three books.[32]

Thirty years after Graham's death, the foremost of his champions was another Scot, Professor John Walker, who described Graham as 'a Scots literary giant', and optimistically predicted the revival of his name and reputation.[33] Between 1966 and 1986, Walker published nine articles on Graham, and three anthologies of his sketches, including *The Scottish Sketches of Cunninghame Graham* (1982),[34] which has been critiqued in this study. Walker's anthologies were accompanied by percipient commentaries on the works, and he did much to keep Graham's name alive during that otherwise fallow period.

CONTEMPORARY LITERARY CRITICISM

In 1916, the critic Frederick Watson wrote that Graham had a genius 'for the phrase that bites into the mind and haunts the memory'. His travel sketches glowed with 'powerful impressive metaphor', but there was nothing superficial, dazzling, or exaggerated about his art. However, success had eluded him because people hate being instructed.[35] In 1918, Harold Williams complimented Graham for being endowed with gifts of style and language, and observational skills, which shrank from nothing.[36] In 1925, the poet and critic Arthur Symons recalled that Joseph Conrad had once said to him, 'Could you conceive for a moment that I could go on existing if Cunninghame Graham were to die?'[37] Symons himself was more caustic, describing Graham as 'a wanderer with so many purposes as to be without a purpose. Don Quixote with something of the humorous soul of Sancho Panza.'[38]

Hugh MacDiarmid, writing under his given name, C. M. Grieve, gave the first comprehensive appreciation of Graham and his writings in his *Contemporary Scottish Studies* (1926).[39] MacDiarmid regarded him highly; however, this acerbic work was MacDiarmid's first attempt to use Graham as an example of how the Scottish establishment had rejected its best talents, stating that Scottish culture was beset by mediocrities, whilst the few with real talent, such as Graham, 'who was *potentially* the greatest Scotsman of his generation',[40] were driven out. Nevertheless, he classed Graham as belonging to the second rank of imaginative artists, but one who was virtually unknown in Scotland due to Scotland's debasement as a cultural nation.[41]

In 1929, Edwin Clark wrote that Graham was sadly neglected, and despite being admired in certain quarters, 'he has failed to excite popular interest';[42] but in 1932, the writer and critic V. S. Pritchett wrote that Graham was 'one of the very best writers in the English language'.[43] Another globe-trotting Scot, the journalist and travel-writer Stephen Graham, wrote a chapter on his namesake, entitled 'Laird and Caballero' in his memoir, *The Death of Yesterday* (1930). In this he maintained that Graham's 'ever-persisting wit and humour tell of the myriad-fold complex currents of the mind of the Anglo-Saxon and the Scot', and that his books were an attempt to 'strip before the public eye', and 'to equalise himself even with the lowest of the low'.[44]

Graham's name also occasionally appeared in contemporary literary companions, meriting a chapter in W. M. Parker's florid and romantic *Modern Scottish Writers* (1917), where Parker confidently predicted that 'his fame is assured'.[45]

LATER LITERARY CRITICISM

On the centenary, MacDiarmid wrote the most spirited defences of Graham, both as a politician and as a writer, in two studies. In the first, 'The Significance of Cunninghame Graham',[46] MacDiarmid again used Graham as a means by which he could attack the Scottish literary and political establishments, including the SNP, and offered a splendidly biased first-hand account of Graham's role within that organisation. The second, *Cunninghame Graham: A Centenary Study*, was more celebratory, but he could not resist further jibes. Tellingly, for someone who knew and admired him, MacDiarmid admitted that Graham had left 'the enigma of his personality unsolved'.[47]

In 1953, Mark Longaker's *Contemporary English Literature* compared Graham's works to those of Galsworthy as 'sometimes approaching the short story, sometimes the essay'.[48] Moreover, Longaker believed that Graham was:

> A Spanish hidalgo of the fifteenth century strayed into the twentieth century. He saw the world through the eyes of a free man who carries his honor through a world open to his fortune. The degradation of the individual in the regimented societies dominated by money provoked his scorn, in such a world success is vulgar, only defeat is honorable . . . his prevailing tone when writing of the modern world is one of fierce aristocratic contempt. These qualities have won the appreciation of the few he esteemed but have denied him a wider popularity.[49]

In the same year, Maurice Lindsay complimented Graham's stylishness,[50] and in his *History of Scottish Literature* (1977), he described Graham as one 'who wrote of Scotland from the outside, looking in', and his prose works as vivid, full of sharp insights and strong narrative threads, but his characterisations were broad and colourful rather than psychologically subtle. He also believed that Graham's sketch-tale 'Beattock for Moffat' deserved a place in most anthologies of Scottish short stories.[51]

In the various academic companions to English and Scottish literature, with a few exceptions, Graham's name is notable by its absence. In *The Concise Cambridge History of English Literature* (1970), George Sampson stated, 'Unfortunately, he [Graham] lavished much of his literary skill on South American adventurers and dictators who have little appeal to English readers',[52] and in *British Commonwealth Literature* (1971), edited by David Daiches, Graham's sketches were described as 'good reflective *rapportage*, rather than original creation'.[53] Daiches subsequently described Graham as 'one of the puzzles of Scottish literary history'.[54] Roderick Watson included Graham's name in his *Literature of Scotland* (1984) and described him as 'some unlikely collision between Oscar Wilde, John Buchan and Hugh MacDiarmid', and wrote of his prose: 'hovering somewhere between sketch, free reminiscence and fiction, it is usually controlled by his own alert and astringent sense of irony – a style admired by many of his more famous writer friends.'[55] Graham was never afraid to put his spurs to sacred cows, and with MacDiarmid, he 'shared his delight in slashing artistic mediocrity and bourgeois values whenever possible'.[56]

A rare modern academic assessment of Graham the politician and writer, was published by Professor Chris GoGwilt in 'Broadcasting News from Nowhere: R. B. Cunninghame Graham and the Geography of Politics in the 1890s' (1996).[57] In this, GoGwilt declared that Graham was situated 'at the key turning points in the histories of early modernism and democratic socialism',[58] and that his written works were 'a mixture of the "low" literary form of his early political journalism and the "high" art form perfected in collaboration with Garnett and Conrad'.[59]

THE LABOUR PARTY

Graham's influence on Keir Hardie was acknowledged in William Stewart's official biography of Hardie, but there is no mention of any pivotal role in the founding of the SPLP.[60] In 1926, however, Joseph Clayton, a journalist and ILP organiser, described Graham as 'a leading spirit' of the SPLP, along with Hardie and Dr Gavin Clark.[61] In George Cole's *British Working Class Politics, 1832–1914* (1941), Graham was referred to several times, but only as an associate of Hardie, who was 'the principal organiser'.[62] In Francis William's history of the Labour Party, *Fifty Year March* (1949), Graham was mentioned three times: as 'a Scottish laird and Radical MP, a wild, quixotic and fantastically distinguished figure',[63] while Hardie again took centre stage.

In his biography of Hardie, Emrys Hughes described the close relationship between the two men,[64] but in 1975, Iain MacLean, another biographer of Hardie, wrote, 'After being badly defeated in 1892 General Election he [Graham] disappeared from British domestic politics, to reappear in the late 1920s as a Scottish Nationalist.'[65] This was demonstrably incorrect, but the misconception was repeated in T. C. Smout's *A Century of the Scottish People* (1987).[66] A more comprehensive reading can be found in Henry Pelling's *Origins of the Labour Party, 1880–1900* (1965), wherein Graham's role in the development of the first party of labour in Britain was acknowledged, meriting a dozen references, but he was not part of a central narrative, flitting in as an extraordinary, exposed, and ultimately doomed political figure.[67]

Modern texts have either omitted Graham, or used his name to enliven biographies and histories. One exception was A. J. Davies's *To Build A New Jerusalem* (1996), where he was described as 'an extraordinary character', but his involvement in early Labour politics was credited as 'demonstrating that any new venture would not be exclusively a proletarian grouping'.[68] Of the later Hardie biographers, Caroline Benn was the only writer who gave Graham a significant role in early Labour history.[69]

SCOTTISH HOME RULE

Apart from contemporary newspaper reports and brief references in early biographies, very little has been written about Graham's participation in the early Scottish home rule movement of the late nineteenth century. It was not until 1955 that John MacCormick's book *The Flag In the Wind* described Graham's very significant candidature in the rectorial election at the University of Glasgow as a Scottish nationalist.[70] Much of this was collaborated in Compton Mackenzie's autobiography.[71]

H. J. Hanham's *Scottish Nationalism* (1969),[72] and Keith Webb's *Growth of Nationalism in Scotland* (1977),[73] which were key texts during the nationalist resurgence, made only the briefest mention of Graham, and notwithstanding his high offices in the early and later nationalist movements, he was treated as a marginal figure. Surprisingly, there was no reference to Graham's involvement with the nationalist cause in Douglas Young's contribution to *The Scottish Debate: Essays on Scottish Nationalism* (1970),[74] or in Christopher Harvie's *Scotland and Nationalism* (1977), only his membership of the SPLP,[75] which was repeated in Iain Hutchison influential book, *A Political History of Scotland* (1986). Graham received several brief mentions in Michael Keating and David Bleiman's volume *Labour and Scottish Nationalism* (1979), but only as a 'nationalist enthusiast' who 'had been prominent in the Labour Party in Keir Hardie's day'.[76] However, Richard J. Finlay briefly mentioned him as lending credibility to the NPS's image in his *Independent and Free: Scottish Politics and the Origins of the Scottish National Party, 1918–45* (1994), but he did not believe that Graham played a significant role in the party's formation, that accolade going to MacCormick.[77]

Notes

1. Birkmyre, 'An Appreciation of Cunninghame Graham', pp. 476–82.
2. Wellington, 'Artist-Fighter', p. 155.
3. Robert Lynd, 'Mr. Cunninghame Graham', *Old and New Masters* (London: Unwin, 1919), pp. 184–7.
4. Bernard Muddiman, *Men of the Nineties* (London: Henry Danielson, 1920), pp. 65–7.
5. Hind, 'R. B. Cunninghame Graham', pp. 72–3.
6. Samuel Levy Bensusan, 'Don Roberto', *Quarterly Review*, Vol. CCLXX, April 1938, pp. 292–306.
7. *Twentieth Century Authors* ed. by Stanley J. Kunitz and Howard Haycraft (New York: H. W. Wilson, 1942), pp. 340–1.
8. Bloomfield, *The Essential Cunninghame Graham*.
9. Philip Henderson, *Letters of William Morris*, p. 319.
10. Meyers, *Fever at the Core*, pp. 39–58.
11. George Moore, *Conversations in Ebury Street* (London: Heinemann, 1936), pp. 157–66.
12. Rothenstein, *Men and Memories*, p. 180.
13. Lavery, *Life of a Painter*, p. 92. Lavery's celebrated full-length portrait of Graham hangs in the Kelvingrove Art Gallery and Museum in Glasgow.
14. George Bernard Shaw, 'Notes to *Captain Brassbound's Conversion*'.
15. Galsworthy, 'Notes on R. B. Cunninghame Graham', p. 274.
16. Ibid., p. 276.
17. Frank Harris, *Frank Harris: His Life And Adventures* (London: The Richards Press, 1947), p. 476.
18. Munro, *The Brave Days*, p. 317.
19. Neil Munro, 'A Group of Writing Men', *The On-Looker* (Edinburgh: Porpoise Press, 1933), pp. 301–2.
20. Richard Curle, *Caravansary and Conversation: Memories of Places and Persons* (New York: Frederick A. Stokes, 1937), p. 31. Richard Henry Parnell Curle (1883–1968). World traveller and author, assistant, and literary executor to Graham's friend Joseph Conrad, whom he met through Edward Garnett. He was part of Garnett's literary circle.
21. Leatham, *60 Years*, p. 153.
22. Sam Mavor, 'Robert Bontine Cunninghame Graham', in *Memories of People and Places* (London: William Hodge, 1940), pp. 69–82.
23. Compton Mackenzie, *My Life and Times*, Octaves Four and Six (London: Chatto & Windus, 1965 and 1967).

24. Mackenzie, 'Cunninghame Graham Scottish Nationalist', p. 21.

25. 'Portraits in the House', by 'A Young Parliamentary Hand'. *United Ireland*, 3 March 1888, p. 6.

26. Lowe, *Souvenirs of Scottish Labour*.

27. In 1937, Lowe published a series of articles for the *Glasgow Evening Times* on Graham and his relationship with Hardie, and accounts of the early SPLP.

28. Smillie, *My Life For Labour*.

29. 'Sandy' Haddow, 'Reminiscences', p. 6.

30. Edward Garnett (1886–1937). English literary editor for T. Fisher Unwin, Duckworths, and Jonathan Cape. He advanced the careers of many famous writers, including Conrad, D. H. Lawrence, and Galsworthy, who described Garnett as a man who 'has done more for English fiction than any living critic'. Galsworthy, 'Notes on R. B. Cunninghame Graham', p. 262.

31. Edward Garnett, 'R. B. Cunninghame Graham: Man and Writer', *London Mercury*, Vol. XXXIV, June 1936, pp. 125–9.

32. William Power, *My Scotland* (Glasgow: Porpoise Press, 1934), pp. 196–7, p. 300; *Literature and Oatmeal*, pp. 168–9; and *Should Auld Acquaintance* (London: Harrap, 1937), pp. 44–5, p. 54, p. 128, p. 140, pp. 166–8, p. 177, p. 187, p. 201.

33. John Walker, 'The Revival of a Scots Literary Giant', *Scotsman Magazine*, June 1981, p. 8.

34. Walker, *Scottish Sketches*.

35. Frederick Watson, 'R. B. Cunninghame Graham', p. 176.

36. Harold Williams, *Modern English Writers* (London: Sidgwick & Jackson, 1918), p. 328.

37. Symons, *Notes on Joseph Conrad*, p. 31.

38. Ibid., pp. 32–3.

39. C. M. Grieve, *Contemporary Scottish Studies*, First Series (London: Leonard Parsons, 1926). In this work, MacDiarmid compared Graham's presence in the House of Commons to 'a blood-mare among donkeys, or an eagle in a hen-house', p. 51.

40. Ibid., p. 49. My italics. There were also passing references to Graham in MacDiarmid's autobiography, *Lucky Poet*, and *The Company I've Kept*.

41. Ibid., p. 51.

42. Edwin Clark, *New York Times Book Review*, 6 October 1929, p. 2.

43. V. S. Pritchett, 'A Reviver of Chivalry in English Prose', *Current Literature*, Vol. LIII, October 1932, pp. 470.

44. Stephen Graham, *Death of Yesterday*, p. 47 and p. 52.

45. W. H. Parker, *Modern Scottish Writers* (1917) (Books for Libraries Press, 1968), p. 210.

46. MacDiarmid, 'The Significance of Cunninghame Graham' (1952) in *Selected Essays*.

47. MacDiarmid, *Cunninghame Graham: A Centenary Study* (Glasgow: Caledonian Press, 1952), p. 23.

48. Mark Longaker, *Contemporary English Literature* (New York: Appleton-Century Crofts, 1953), p. 458.
49. Ibid., p. 459.
50. Maurice Lindsay, *The Lowlands of Scotland: Glasgow and the North* (London: Robert Hale, 1953), p. 113.
51. Maurice Lindsay, *A History of Scottish Literature* (London: Robert Hale, 1977), pp. 433–4. Lindsay repeated his praises in David Daiches's *A Companion to Scottish Culture* (1981), where he described Graham as 'a passionate champion of the underdog, a man of flamboyant style and a rapier wit', p. 89.
52. George Sampson, *The Concise Cambridge History of English Literature*, 3rd edition (Cambridge University Press, 1970), p. 689.
53. *British Commonwealth Literature*, ed. by David Daiches (London: Penguin, 1971), pp. 220–1.
54. David Daiches, 'Don Roberto', *London Review of Books*, Vol. 5, No. 3, 1983, p. 17.
55. Roderick Watson, *The Literature of Scotland* (Basingstoke: Macmillan, 1984), pp. 342–3.
56. Ibid., pp. 343–4.
57. GoGwilt, 'Broadcasting News from Nowhere', pp. 235–52.
58. Ibid., pp. 237–8.
59. Ibid., p. 241.
60. Stewart, *J. Keir Hardie*. Stewart had been selected to write the biography by Hardie's Memorial Committee, after the death in 1920 of their first choice, Bruce Glasier. Stewart, *J. Keir Hardie*, p. vii.
61. Joseph Clayton, *The Rise & Decline of Socialism in Great Britain, 1884–1924* (London: Faber & Gwyer, 1926), p. 66.
62. Cole, *British Working Class Politics*, p. 129.
63. Francis Williams, *Fifty Years' March: The Rise of the Labour Party* (London: Odham's Press, 1946), p. 61.
64. Hughes, *Keir Hardie*, pp. 33–4.
65. Iain MacLean, *Keir Hardie* (London: Allen Lane, 1975), pp. 33–4.
66. T. C. Smout, *A Century of the Scottish People* (London: Fontana, 1987), pp. 254–5.
67. Pelling, *Origins of the Labour Party*, p. 105.
68. A. J. Davies, *To Build A New Jerusalem* (London: Abacus, 1996), p. 27.
69. It might be noted, that Benn's husband, Tony Benn, who was from an aristocratic background, also dedicated himself to working-class and labour politics against his own best interests.
70. John MacCormick, *The Flag in the Wind: The Story of the National Movement in Scotland* (London: Victor Gollancz, 1955), pp. 26–30.
71. Mackenzie, *My Life and Times*, Octave Six.
72. Hanham, *Scottish Nationalism*, p. 40.
73. Keith Webb, *The Growth of Nationalism in Scotland* (Abingdon: Taylor & Francis, 1977), p. 89.

74. Neil MacCormick, *The Scottish Debate*.
75. Christopher Harvie, *Scotland and Nationalism* (London: Routledge, 2004), p. 22.
76. Michael Keating and David Bleiman, *Labour and Scottish Nationalism* (London: Macmillan, 1979), p. 104.
77. Richard J. Finlay, *Independent and Free: Scottish Politics and the Origins of the Scottish National Party, 1918–45* (Edinburgh: John Donald, 1994), p. 80.

APPENDICES

Appendix I

THE *STAR* ON CUNNINGHAME GRAHAM'S 'COPY', *PEOPLE'S PRESS*, 3 SEPTEMBER 1890

Mr. Cunninghame Graham, says our contemporary the *Star*, has unwittingly gone within an ace of bringing about a strike and causing a revolution in his office. He sent us a letter the other day from Liverpool. That letter was 24 pages long, and was headed 'Dancing and Barricades.' It has made everyone dance who touched it, and still remains an insurmountable barricade. It cannot be read. Mr. Graham's handwriting is sometimes crotchety, but this specimen of his calligraphy was about as legible as Egyptian hieroglyphics. The letter has been touring about the office for several days – from the editor to the printer, from the printer to the reader, from the reader to the sub-editor, and back to the printer again in a cycle – a cycle which threatened to end in revolution. Everyone has wrestled with it, but no one has been able to dig a continuous story out of it. The head printer put on his glasses and tore his hair over it, until he now wears an aged look and a wig. And expert comp was called in, but the only evidence he gave was that in Clowes' office[1] the men refused to set Mr. Graham's copy. A strike was ordered at once unless the copy was withdrawn. It was withdrawn and handed to the reader, who found his occupation gone, and gave notice. The sub-editor has had a tussle with it, took it home to sleep over, but has not slept or worked since. The application of a microscope only diminished the legibility, and a magnifying glass only increased our difficulties. The copy remained undecipherable.

(We tearfully sympathise with the men of the *Star*. Two of our own most valued men, after a prolonged struggle with one of Graham's articles, retired to the peaceful seclusion of a padded room at Colney Hatch.[2] Ed. *The People's Press*.)

Graham attributed his disability to an accident with a horse. In a letter to Henry Arthur Jones in 1919, he wrote:

> I gained this infamous handwriting, owing to a twist with a lazo, which was not improved by another I received three years ago in the Argentine Republic, saddling a horse for one of our troopers to ride subsequently at the Front.[3]

Notes

1. William Clowes, Ltd. A British printing company founded in London in 1803. It grew to be one of the world's largest printing houses by the mid-nineteenth century.
2. Colney Hatch Lunatic Asylum (later, Friern Hospital) in North London.
3. Doris Arthur Jones, ed., *Taking the Curtain Call*, p. 304.

Appendix II

MAIDEN SPEECH, 1 FEBRUARY 1887, R. B. CUNNINGHAME GRAHAM (NORTH-WEST LANARKSHIRE)[1]

A debate on the Queen's Speech forms the best occasion for a new Member to lose his political virginity (*Laughter.*), and, therefore, I cast myself at once on the forbearance and the generosity of the House.

On glancing over the Queen's Speech, I am struck with the evident desire which prevailed in it to do nothing at all. There was a similarity in its paragraphs to the laissez-faire school of political economy. Not one word was said in the Speech about lightening the taxation under which Her Majesty's lieges at present suffered; not one word to make that taxation more bearable; not one word to bridge over the awful chasm existing between the poor and the rich; not one word of kindly sympathy for the sufferers from the present commercial and agricultural depression (*Hear, hear!*) – nothing but platitudes, nothing but views of society through a little bit of pink glass. To read Her Majesty's Speech, one would think that at this present moment this happy country was passing through one of the most pronounced periods of commercial activity and prosperity it has ever known. One would think that wheat was selling at 50 shillings a-quarter, and that the price of bread had not gone up. One would think that poverty, drunkenness, prostitution, and wretchedness were in a fair way to be utterly extirpated; and one would think further that Great Britain had made the first important step towards that millennium when the Irish landlord would cease from troubling, and when the landlords and tenants would lie down in amity, and finally be at rest. (*Laughter.*)

Of course, it is matter for congratulation that this country was not suddenly called upon to enter upon a Quixotic crusade to place Prince Alexander of Battenberg[2] upon the Throne of Bulgaria.

We are thankful for small mercies, and I supposed we must be content. If this unlucky nation had to forego the pleasure of paying for the vagaries of Prince Alexander, it had still a pretty large group of needy Royalties who were placed on the Civil List of this country. (*Laughter and Radical cheers.*)

It is not to be expected that Her Majesty's Government would vouchsafe to the House any idea of when the British troops might be withdrawn from Egypt. That is expecting far too much. But, surely, it would be wise to let the House know when it was intended to withdraw those troops from their inactivity in that pestilential region, and from playing the ungrateful role of oppressors of an already down-trodden nationality. (*Radical cheers.*) But no. The bondholders must have their pound of flesh. We must also protect the so-called high road to India by the Suez Canal, in order that the very last straw might be laid on the unfortunate fellaheen,[3] and that British money and British treasure might be poured out like water. I had forgotten the 'cent per cent.' (*A Laugh.*) I had forgotten by whose advice we were in Egypt – that it was by the advice of that illustrious statesman and economist who has raised the art of carpet-bagging from its primitive rudeness into a political science, (*Laughter.*) and who so well illustrated the Scriptural injunction, 'When they persecute you in one city, flee to another.'[4] (*Great Laughter.*)

With reference to our latest filibustering exploit in Burmah, it was a matter of great congratulation – it was something on which a Christian might truly plume himself, to hear that Her Majesty's Government were in process of rapidly suppressing brigandage, which had grown up in the country, and in putting down bands of marauders. 'Marauders,' like 'mobled Queen,'[5] was 'good,' very good, when applied to poor, unfortunate, misguided people, who, in their pig-headed way, were endeavouring to defend their own country. Does the House recognise how a band of marauders was put down? I do; I have seen it done often. Surely, it can be no great matter of self-congratulation for Britons with arms of precision to shoot down naked savages. It can be no feather in a soldier's cap to suppress these unfortunate wretches with all the resources of civilisation at his command. When the telegrams came from Burmah we slapped our hands on our chests, quite regardless of damage to our shirts, (*Applause.*) and talked of British gallantry; and so we laughed like parrots at a bagpiper, when we looked at the sketches in the illustrated papers depicting Natives running away from our troops. A native wounded to death, I take it, and tormented by mosquitoes in the jungle, felt his misery as acutely as the best be-broadclothed gentleman among us, even though he should happen to be a chairman of a School Board;

but what is all that to the Government? The Government, like an American hog, must root or die.

The question is, how did this Government come in? That is the humour of it. They came in by the help of the pseudo-Liberals – the crutch-and-toothpick Gentlemen (*Laughter.*) – through the assistance of that feeble Union ladder which, having been used and abused, was now about to be cast aside and been kicked into the dunghill. I was delighted to see how the noble Lord [Lord Randolph Churchill][6] last night treated his Unionist allies – to observe that, having betrayed their master, like Judas Iscariot, there was but one resource left for them, and that was to go out and hang themselves (*Great Laughter.*) – and to see how these superior persons fell out and bespattered one another, and I thought to myself, 'How these mugwumps[7] love one another.' This Government reminds me of Pope's flies in amber:- 'Things in themselves though neither rich nor rare, One wonders how the devil they got there.'[8]

The noble Lord [Churchill], with that retiring modesty which was his great characteristic, left the government to seek obscurity or popularity as the case may be. His alleged pretext was economy. Well, it was easy to wish for economy, but to follow it was quite a different affair. What was the use of his preaching economy in the face of an ever-increasing army? (*Radical cheers.*) The army was the first branch of expenditure where economy might be practiced. What should a small democratic State like this want with an army? Its only use could be to wring another million or two out of stout patient ass, the British Public. (*Great Laughter.*)

I do not wish to be understood to say a word against the navy, or any money that ought to be spent upon it. (*Cheers.*) I do not impugn the skill of our military officers, or the gallantry, prudence, and daring of our brave troops, but they should not be allowed to exercise their gallantry, bravery, and daring at the public expense. (*Laughter.*) I deprecate still more the spending of any public money to find places for the younger sons of our plutocrats and autocrats. (*Hear, hear.*) I deprecate spending the money of this country to forward the ambition of soldiers and diplomats who made the name of Britain execrated in the four corners of the globe. (*Irish cheers.*)

Personally, I regret the resignation of the noble Lord the Member for South Paddington. He was a type in times of dull uniformity, and from the depth of his obscurity I admire the noble Lord's parabolic course. (*Laughter.*) The noble Lord's resignation has saddened me as children are saddened when they see a rocket spout up, and were all unaware that it would fall down a stick (*Laughter.*) – as was well said by Ben Jonson: 'He was a child that so did thrive in grace and feature, (*Laughter.*) As Heaven and nature seemed to strive which owned the creature.'[9] Where is the noble Lord now? Yesterday he was, to-day he was not – gone like the froth on licensed victualler's beer, or the foam on petroleum champagne, leaving Her Majesty's Government, alone and unaided, to wrestle with the difficulties of the situation, and to give 'their careful consideration to all the matters' pertaining to their functions. (*Laughter.*)

With respect to Ireland, I have eminent qualifications for dealing with that subject, for many reasons. First of all, I have never been there (*Laughter.*); secondly, sitting next to Nationalist Members, I have gained, of late, something of National colour; and I had once known an Irish commercial traveller, who imparted to me various facts quite unattainable by the general public. I have also gained much information from the hon. Member for Camborne (Mr. Conybeare), who has recently been staying with the nobility and gentry of that country. From these sources, I have conceived a warm respect and regard for that much-abused and downtrodden class – the Irish landlords, who are held in the deepest affection by their tenants. As to the Glenbeigh evictions, the landlords have been held up to most unjust obloquy, as they have ever been most kind to their tenants, whom, in fact, they have kept in cotton wool. It is the pride and the privilege of the Irish landlord to look after the interests, creature as well as spiritual, of his tenants; and, such is the relation of class to class that, so far from turning them out on a bleak, cold winter's night, the landlord has provided his dependents with a fire to warm their hands; only, through a pardonable inadvertence, it was their houses that had furnished the blaze.

The Government has lighted a light that will serve to light the Liberals on their path. The homes destroyed in Glenbeigh were, no doubt, as dear to the poor peasant (*Irish cheers.*) in his lonely village on the stony mountain side in the far west, as is the shoddy mansion in South Kensington to the capitalist, as is Haddon Hall to its owner, or as is Buckingham Palace to the absentee owner of that dreadful building. (*Cheers and great laughter.*) Who can say that the affairs of this handful of obscure tenants in a wind-swept and rain-bedewed, stony corner of Ireland, might not prove to have given the first blow to that society in which one man worked and another enjoyed the fruit – that society in which capital and luxury makes a Heaven for 30,000, and a Hell for 30,000,000 – that society whose crowning achievement is this dreary waste of mud and stucco – with its misery, its want and destitution, its degradation, its prostitution, and its glaring social inequalities – the society which we call London – that society which, by a refinement of irony, has placed the mainspring of human action, almost the power of life and death, and the absolute power to pay labour and to reward honour, behind the grey tweed veil which enshrouded the greasy pocket-book of the capitalist. (*Laughter.*)

Notes

1. Transposed into the first person from Hansard and the *Airdrie Advertiser* (5 February 1887).
2. A nephew by marriage to Tsar Alexander II of Russia, and uncle to Earl Mountbatten of Burma. He was elected Prince of Bulgaria in 1879, but forced to abdicate in 1886.
3. Arabic = An agricultural labourer.
4. Matthew 10:23.
5. Hamlet, Act II, Scene ii: 'O, who had seen the mobled [swaddled] queen –'.
6. Father of future prime minister, Winston Spencer Churchill.
7. Usually, a person who stands aloof from sordid party politics, but in this case, it refers to certain US Republicans, who, in 1884, voted against their own presidential nominee.
8. Alexander Pope, 'An Epistle to Arbuthnot' (1734). John Arbuthnot (1667–1735), a celebrated Scottish physician, satirist and polymath.
9. Ben Jonson, 'An Epitaph on S.P.' (1616).

Appendix III

BLOODY SUNDAY

At around 4pm on Sunday, 13 November 1887, several marches converged on Trafalgar Square in support of the unemployed, and the imprisoned Irish nationalist and editor of *United Ireland*, William O'Brien MP. Public meetings in the square had been banned, and it was ringed by policemen, supported by the Life Guards, displaying fixed bayonets. Graham had been scheduled to speak at the rally, but finding his way barred, in a reckless, but certainly premeditated act,[1] he charged the police cordon arm in arm with fellow socialist, John Burns, followed by between seventy and a hundred others, and was severely beaten.[2] Sir Edward Reed MP wrote the following account in the *Pall Mall Gazette*:

> After Mr. Graham's arrest was complete, one policeman after another, two certainly . . . stepped up from behind and struck him in the head . . . with a violence and brutality which was shocking to behold. Even after this, and when some five or six other police were dragging him into the Square, another from behind seized him most needlessly by the hair . . . and dragged his head back, and in that condition he was forced forward many yards.[3]

Graham, Burns,[4] and Hyndman were taken to Bow Street Magistrate's Court and charged with 'Unlawful assembly, assault of the police, along with other evil-disposed persons, thereby endangering public peace.' Their trial, which began on 16 January 1888, lasted three days, during which several witnesses testified that hitherto the rally had been orderly, and that Graham, who was defended in court by the future Prime Minister, Herbert Asquith, had not assaulted the police. Immediately prior to sentencing, Graham was reported to have 'divided his attention between bowing to his friends in the body of the Court, arranging his luxuriant locks, and admiring the brilliant bouquet which he displayed in his button-hole'.[5] Graham and Burns were found guilty of unlawful assembly, and were sentenced to six weeks in prison, without hard labour,[6] while Hyndman was acquitted on all charges. (At this time, Graham still held the office of Justice of the Peace in three counties, and was Deputy-Lieutenant of Dunbartonshire.[7]) William Morris wrote of the event: 'His conduct will long be remembered, one would hope, by lovers of freedom; but he must expect for some time to come to be a pariah among M.P.s. To do him justice he is not likely to care much about that.' Shaw wrote much later:

> The battle of Trafalgar Square, in which he [Graham] personally and bodily assailed civilization as represented by concentrated military and constabular forces of the capital of the world, can scarcely be forgotten by the more discreet spectators, of whom I was one. On that occasion, civilization, qualitatively his inferior, was quantitatively so huge in excess of him that it put him in prison, but had not sense enough to keep him there. Yet getting out of prison was nothing compared to his getting into the House of Commons.[8]

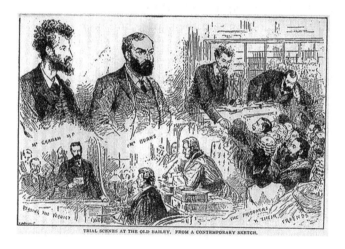

TRIAL SCENES AT THE OLD BAILEY, FROM A CONTEMPORARY SKETCH.

Of all the events in his extraordinary life, it was his actions in Trafalgar Square that created the greatest sensation. A 'London Correspondent' to the *Coatbridge Express* wrote: 'One of the most popular men in London at present is Mr Cunninghame Graham',[9] and on his release from prison, he was given a hero's reception. However, although he enjoyed adulation amongst the rank and file, many senior Liberals were not amused:

> Sir, I must express my indignation at the second resolution which was proposed at the conference on Tuesday, viz – 'That this Council of the Scottish Liberal Association protests against the imprisonment of Mr. R. B. Cunninghame Graham, M.P., for his attempt to vindicate the right of public

meeting in Trafalgar Square, London.' The above individual is not a political martyr, he has been imprisoned like any disorderly person, and like many sound Liberals, I regret his locks have not been cut, as it might help to cool his ardour. The recognition of such a person will do a great deal of harm to the Liberal party, and the Council had surely very little to talk about when they had such a miserable second resolution to propose. It would have been quite in order, if the following words had been added: 'That the Council also protests against the imprisonment of drunks and disorderlies connected with the Liberal party.'

I am, &c, A Chairman of a Liberal Association.[10]

Oscar Wilde, along with Morris, had rushed to Bow Street to support Graham after the riot, and Wilde's wife, Constance, was in attendance throughout his trial: 'Oscar, busy in Tite Street making plans for *The Woman's World* did not attend. His own date with the Bow Street dock was yet to come.'[11] Constance and Graham remained friends, and Graham's close companion in Morocco, Walter Harris, was godfather to the Wildes' first child, Cyril. Tschiffely recorded Graham's tragic encounter with Wilde in Hyde Park soon after Wilde had been charged with gross indecency,[12] and four years after Wilde's death, Graham wrote a personal and moving appreciation of Wilde's masterwork, *De Profundis* for the *Saturday Review*.[13]

Notes

1. It appears to have been a deliberate and foolhardy act of provocation, for, two days prior to the riot, at a meeting in Broxburn, Graham said that he intended to 'test' the authorities in Trafalgar Square. *Airdrie Advertiser*, 12 November 1887, p. 4. It might be considered that if he had not been so enthusiastic about confrontation, the rally might have passed off more peacefully, and the many injuries and imprisonments would have been avoided.
2. It had been a blow to the head, while on military service in Ireland, that had confined Graham's father to an institution under restraint until his premature death, and family and friends feared that history might repeat itself.
3. *Pall Mall Gazette*, 14 October 1887, p. 8.
4. John Burns (1858–1943). Son of a Scottish railwayman, he was an independent radical who became MP for Battersea in 1892. In 1914 he was briefly President of the Board of Trade.
5. 'Cunninghame Graham Trial', *Glasgow Herald*, 19 January 1888, p. 4. Graham was reported to have paid his other defence counsel, Sir Charles Russell, over £1,000 in fees. *Glasgow Herald*, 23 September 1891, p. 7.
6. They were released after a month, on 18 February 1888. Graham's prison experiences were recalled in his essay 'Sursum Corda', published in the

Saturday Review, 19 June 1897, pp. 681–3, and anthologised in *Success* (1902), pp. 86–99.

7. 'Mr. Graham's Arrest', *The Times*, 15 November 1887, p. 5. Despite his imprisonment, Graham seems to have retained these offices until his death. Hugh MacDiarmid was also a JP.

8. George Bernard Shaw, 'Notes to *Captain Brassbound's Conversion*', p. 287.

9. *Coatbridge Express*, 7 December 1887, p. 1.

10. *Coatbridge Express*, 22 February 1888, p. 1.

11. Fanny Moyle, *Constance: The Tragic and Scandalous Life of Mrs. Oscar Wilde* (London: John Murray, 2011), p. 149.

12. Tschiffely, *Don Roberto*, p. 349. Wilde had broken down in tears when Graham had jokingly suggested that he might consider suicide as a solution to his situation. Wilde had replied, 'I know, it's the only way out, but I haven't the courage.' Apparently, Graham deeply regretted his 'gaffe' until his dying day.

13. 'Vox Clamantis', *Saturday Review*, 4 March 1905, p. 266–7.

Appendix IV

'PORTRAITS IN THE HOUSE', BY 'A YOUNG PARLIAMENTARY HAND' (ABRIDGED), *UNITED IRELAND*, 3 MARCH 1888, P. 6

From the beginning Cunninghame Graham was regarded as one of the most remarkable men in the new Parliament. His appearance alone was eminently calculated to single him out from the ordinary run and ruck of new members who huddled (timidly) together in the lobbies of Westminster after a general election. Some of those who first stared in amazement at the stranger – slight, slim, aquiline, eager, with keen bright eyes, a head of curling hair, and a pointed beard of the kind the Valois loved.

If Mr. Cunninghame Graham only carried himself a little less erectly, if his closely-knit frame had been a little less sinewy, and his movements less limber, he might very well have passed muster as the representative of a certain school of art.[1] But anyone who carried investigation beyond the cursory glance soon noticed muscularity in the body which never came from wielding a paint-brush, a tan upon the firm flesh which never was due to the cool light and shade of stuccoed studios. In fact, the critical observer noted something about Cunninghame Graham that was of a soldierly smack, but not quite soldierly either. That the man was a mighty rider was obvious to the experienced eye in a little, but his movements were not that of a cavalryman: they were freer, less stiff, simpler.

London, more eager than Athens of old for something new, was pleased, at the time, to take a great deal of interest in and manifest a vast amount of enthusiasm for that curious production of American frontier life, the Cow-boy. Buffalo Bill and his merry men were the heroes of the hour, and in certain circles, while the craze lasted, little was talked or thought but the Cow-boy . . . The Cow-boy fever ran its course and died away as all such frenzies do in a great capital where people hunger and thirst after any new excitement.

If Cunninghame Graham had been content to call himself 'Mexican Jack' and to sport a sombrero, he would have obtained what the French call a *succès fou*,[2] but he was a man with a mission, and languid London does not love men with missions. He was a Radical in the true sense of the term – a Radical with that touch of Quixotism without which few reforms would ever come to anything. He saw that there was work to be done, and he set himself to do it with the same fiery energy and indomitable determination which he had shown during his former travels in wild lands. He entered Parliament not to play the part of the silent member, but to plead vehemently for all the causes dearest to his heart.

It is needless to say that he made himself at once amazingly unpopular with all the 'classes', with advocates of things as they are, and that if there was one individual whom the average Tory hated almost as much as any Irish member, it was the impetuous, red-haired Cunninghame Graham.

Notes

1. The Aesthetic Movement.
2. French = An extraordinary success.

Appendix V

MOTIONS: HOME RULE FOR SCOTLAND, 9 APRIL 1889, R. B. CUNNINGHAME GRAHAM (NORTH-WEST LANARKSHIRE)

I wish in a very few words to support the Motion of the hon. Member for Caithness [Dr. Gavin Clark], but I wish to do it on vastly different grounds and reasons from any of those which have been urged by hon. Members who have spoken to-night. I do not wish to support this proposal especially on national grounds. I thoroughly agree with an observation that fell from the hon. Member for Caithness when he said that though there was a great and growing feeling in favour of Home Rule in Scotland it runs on other lines than those of the Radical programme. I believe, Sir, that there is a great and growing demand for Home Rule in Scotland, but it comes, in my opinion, from no sentimental grounds whatever, but from the extreme misery of a certain section of the Scottish population, and they wish to have their own Members under their own hands, in order to extort legislation from them suitable to relieve their misery. That may seem an extreme proposition to state in this House. Hon. Members from Scotland are often fond of representing Scotland as a sort of Arcadia, but I think that, in face of the misery existing in the Highlands and Islands, that we have women in Aberdeen today toiling for 6s. or 7s. a week; that we have 30,000 people in Glasgow who herd together in one room; and in face of the fact that we have a Socialistic agitation on foot in the East and West of Scotland, I must say I do not think the condition of the poor in that country is one very much to be envied. I think it will be found that the same reasons which impel a certain section of the Scottish people to be dissatisfied with the legislation served out to them from this Parliament are not the reasons which have been alleged by other hon. Members. On many public questions public opinion is far riper for legislation than in this country. Not one member who has spoken[,] although it must be patent to all hon. Members[,] has referred to the rising opinion in favour of land legislation in Scotland. I should like to ask the hon. Member for Roxburghshire [Mr. Arthur Elliot] whether he could go down to his constituency and speak to the free and independent electors there, and say much against the theories of Henry George, for example? And I would like, furthermore, to point out to the house that on the question of labour legislation in Scotland we are much further advanced as a country than in England, especially on the eight hours' question. In the matter of free education and many other questions, the people of Scotland are greatly in advance of those of England, and it is for these reasons, and not for sentimental or national ones, that I think this House will soon be called on to face the demand for a Legislature for Scotland. We have an absolute detestation in Scotland of all propositions dealing with the solution of the land question by means of emigration. It would not, I fancy, tend to enhance the popularity of any hon. Member in Scotland to go down to his constituency and propose to emigrate the crofters *en masse*. He would soon be met by the suggestion that some of the landlords and capitalists of the country could be emigrated with much greater benefit to the country. It has been said that in the event of the institution of a Scottish Legislature we should be represented by the merchants of the country. To that statement I say, God forbid! I believe I speak the feelings of a large section of the Scottish people when I emphatically state that, were such a Legislature ever created, we should find the working classes much more represented than is the case here. Thus, I think that, taking into account the large expression of opinion that has undoubtedly been given to-day by the Scottish Members, and taking into consideration the great pressure that will soon be brought to bear from social causes upon this House from the electorate of Scotland, we have not come here with an absolutely futile or fatuous proposition when we have, for the first time, endeavoured to press the cause of Scottish Home Rule upon the House of Commons.

Appendix VI

CUNNINGHAME GRAHAM, 'INTRODUCTION' TO *SCOTLAND FOR THE SCOTS: SCOTLAND REVISITED*, BY MORRISON DAVIDSON (1902)

Scottissimus Scotorum – Surely to no one more than to the author of 'Scotland Revisited' does the above phrase apply. A Scot of Scots! although he apparently imagines that he has recently revisited Caledonia, I cannot think that he really left it for an hour.

Born in Buchan, perhaps to refute the saw,[1] 'there's rowth o' a' thing in Buchan haud awa' freet'[2] – he carries Buchan with him everywhere he goes.

What is it that makes your true Scot, him I mean of the *perfervidum ingenium*,[3] so intensely national? It is, I think, because of those very qualities, the decay of which the Author bewails in his present book.

I remember once, in South America, having gone out to look for some strayed horses, and not having found them, that I ascended a little hill and sat me down to smoke. Below me rolled the Pampean ocean of brown grass: grass, grass, and still more grass: grass which the breeze from the south-west had set in motion in long waves: grass which, where rivers in the middle distance crossed it, was cut by strips of 'Argentina,' looking like silver bands: Grass in which deer and ostriches passed happy lives, so happy that the Gauchos knew the former as the 'desert mirth': Brown waves of grass in which roamed cattle and sheep innumerable, and over which the Tero-Teros flew uttering their haunting cry.

And as I sat and smoked –

Upon a thin old chestnut horse, with a torn English saddle, over which a sheepskin had been laid, a man of about fifty years of age appeared. Dressed in a suit of Scottish homespun, such as our farmers wore, but twenty years ago, before the looms of Bradford and of Leeds had clothed them all in shoddy, with a grey flannel shirt without a collar, and the whole man surmounted by a battered, flat straw-hat, which might have made an indifferent strawberry pottle[4] I at once descried a brother Scot. Dismounting and hobbling his horse, he drew a short clay pipe out of his pocket, capped with a tin cover that workmen in the North used to affect, in the pre-briar-root days, and greeting me in a strange Doric[5] Spanish, he sat down to smoke.

Some time he talked, till in compassion I said, 'Friend, you appear to make but middling weather of it in the Spanish tongue.' No sign he gave of the least astonishment, but between two draws, as he rammed the 'dottle'[6] hard into his pipe, he said, 'I see ye speak the English pretty well.' I, though at the time, just at the age, when a man speaks, rides and shoots better than any other man in all the world, suppressed a smile, and said, 'Yes; how do you like the view?'

'A bonny view, sir, aye, ou aye; I'd no say onything against the view: but man, maybe ye ken a hill – they ca' it the Dumyet[7] – just abune Brig o' Allan?' I did so, having climbed it as a boy, and watched the Forth wind out, a silver ribbon towards Aberfoyle.[8]

'Weel, weel, if ye ken it, ye'll ken there's a far brawer view frae the Dumyet than frae the wee boranty[9] that we're sittin' on the noo.'

When he had got upon his horse and schauchled[10] down the hill, I fancied that I could smell the heather and sweet gale, hear the whawps[11] calling on the moor, and in the towns see drucken folk a-stotterin'[12] from the public house.

Something of this compound essence of the North our Author has. Something of the pre-bawbean[13] times, something of those old shirt-less Scottish scholars who, in the Middle-Ages, over-ran Europe, 'gaun aboot bodies'[14] with a tattered Homer in their hand, Andrew Ferrara[15] on their hip and with a plenteous lack of pelf in the lean deer-skin pouch they carried at their side. So, naturally enough, the Scotland of to-day seems to him wersh,[16] the national character becoming moulded after the Southern form; the whisky no sae nippy in the mooth, religion turned but a dreich[17] Erastian affair, and even hell-fire merely a wee bit spunky in the lum.[18]

But he has put his finger on the blot, and pointed out (his bagpipe certainly gives no uncertain sound) our national vice of snobbism. Pity to see a Scot 'attempt the English' and essay in havering[19] tones to clip the Doric, and, worst of all, to see our country clean despoiled of brains, and all her sons run off to London, for the gatherin' o' the gear. The Highlands too delivered over to the Yank, and the whole land become a cross between a rich man's playground and a sweater's hell he marks with disapproval, and looks back to Fletcher, him of Saltoun,[20] who believed in the divine right of princes to be hanged.

He mourns our Scottish Parliament, that 'lang auld sang' which Southern wiles and gold brought to an end, leaving the House disconsolate, and a mere stamping ground for Advocates, who, like the devil, walk to and fro seeking for those they may devour.[21]

Therefore he advocates Home Rule.

Not a return to those blithe days when in Auld Reekie[22] folks cried 'Gardey-Loo,'[23] and on the causeway sword-and-buckler men fought for the 'croon,' whilst Highland chairmen carrying old gentlemen to routs,[24] paused not an instant though the bottom of the chair fell out, causing their fares desperately to run, and to exclaim on landing 'that but for the honour o' the thing they had as lieve hae[25] walked.'

But to return to a more national spirit and a revival of the ancient Scottish Type which ruled the roost before the Ten per Centlings[26] rose, making poor Scotland stink before the world with their base peddling ways.

Notes

1. A saying.
2. Obscure. Perhaps, 'There's an abundance of everything in Buchan, don't be concerned'.
3. Latin: *Perfervidum ingenium Scotorum* = The intensely earnest character of the Scots.
4. Scots = A conical punnet for fruit.
5. A distinctive dialect spoken in the north east of Scotland.
6. A plug of unburnt tobacco.
7. Dumyat ('Hillfort of the Maeatae tribe'). A hill to the north-east of Stirling, commanding the River Forth.
8. A small town adjacent to Graham's old estate at Gartmore.
9. Scots = A mound or tumulus. The diminutive of 'burian'.
10. Scots = Shambled.
11. Scots = Curlews.
12. Scots = Staggering.
13. Pre-materialistic.
14. Scots = Wanderers, travellers.
15. More correctly, 'Andrea Ferrara', the generic name for a basket-hilted broadsword.
16. Scots = Flavourless.
17. Scots = Dismal.
18. Scots = A small spark in the chimney. Spunkie = Will o' the Wisp.
19. Scots = Babbling, talking nonsense.

20. Andrew Fletcher of Saltoun (1655–1716). Scottish writer, politician, and opponent of the 1707 Act of Union between Scotland and England.
21. 1 Peter 5:8.
22. Scots = Old smoky = Edinburgh.
23. French/Scots = 'Beware of the water'. A common cry from an upper storey, before a chamber pot was emptied onto the street below.
24. Street gatherings.
25. Scots = Might as well have.
26. Capitalists.

Appendix VII

EXTRACT FROM 'R. B. CUNNINGHAME GRAHAM: JANIFORM GENIUS', BY PROFESSOR CEDRIC WATTS, ASLS CONFERENCE, STIRLING, 4 JULY 2015

R. B. Cunninghame Graham was amply a plethora of paradoxes. A romantic and a cynic; an idealist and a sceptic; a Don Quixote and a Hamlet; a nationalist and an internationalist; a socialist and a conservative; a revolutionary and a gradualist; a nobleman and a cowboy; a South American cattle-rancher and horse-trader who was also 'the uncrowned King of Scotland'; a dandy and a convict; a Justice of the Peace who headed a riot; an anti-racist and an anti-Semite; an atheist and a defender of Jesuits. He opposed the Great War but then worked for the War Office; he opposed cruelty to animals but selected horses to suffer and die in battlefields; he was a Scottish landowning aristocrat who advocated the nationalisation of the land; an anarchist who was proud of his descent from King Robert II; a Marxist (according to Engels), yet he hoped to see Lenin hanged. He was a striving radical who declared the futility of such striving: 'It results in nothing at the end,' he said.

Appendix VIII

'NOTES ON R. B. CUNNINGHAME GRAHAM', BY JOHN GALSWORTHY[1]

In these very few words I speak of Cunninghame Graham rather as a writer, than as man. His peculiar and quite unique talent has been given so far as I know entirely to short stories, and in one book of travels. I confine myself to his short stories, the more absorbing topic of a fellow-writer.

The short story is a form of fiction in which but few English have excelled, and none have reached the super-eminence of de Maupassant or of Anton Tchekov. It is a form in which, for perfection, an almost superhuman repression of the writer's self must go hand in hand with something that one can only describe as essence of writer – a something unmistakable but impalpable, and not to be laid a finger on. In the perfect short story one is unconscious of anything but a fragrant trifle, so focused and painted before our minds, that it is as actual and yet as rounded, as deep in colour, as fine in texture as a flower, and which withal disengages a perfume from – who knows where, and makes a carnation not a rose, a Maupassant, not a Tchekov.

Now Cunninghame Graham sometimes – as in *Hegira*, *A Hatchment*, and other stories – approaches this perfection. I am not sure if he ever quite reaches it, for a reason that, curiously, is his real strength as a writer. Very much of an artist, he is yet too much of a personality ever to be quite the pure artist; the individuality of the man will thrust its spear-head through the stuff of his creations. I may be wrong, but I cannot honestly recall any story of his in which his knight errant philosophy does not here and there lift its head out of the fabric of his dreams, if not directly, then through implicit contrast, or in choice of subject. One can readily understand the queer potency which this particular quality gives to his tales, in an age and country very much surrendered to money and materialism. It is not that he is a romantic; on the contrary he is a realist with a steel-keen eye, and a power of colouring an exact picture hardly excelled. It is his clear, poignant realism that makes his philosophy ring out so convinced and convincing, and gives it the power to rip the gilding off the shoddy and snobbishness of our civilisation.

The bent of his soul, and the travels of his body have inclined him to those parts of the earth – the pampas, Morocco, Spain, Scotland – where there are still gleams at all events of a life more primitive, more æsthetically attractive, and probably saner than our own: and when, as in *Un Monsieur* and such studies as *Appreciation*, he pitches on a purely 'civilised' setting, he rides home, indeed.

It is a rather strange thing, and a great tribute to his personality, that throughout what is really a sustained attack on certain habits of existence, and the bloated house they have succeeded in building for themselves, he never once gives the feeling of attacking for the sake of attacking. The assault is delivered, as it were, not by his reason and mind, but by his spirit and his nerves. As if, while he wrote, the music of our high civilisation would keep intruding its blusterous, rich, and flabby harmonies on his strange ears, so that he must leap from his chair, and, sitting down again, die, or insert in his screed the word 'accursed.'

And the real beauty of him is that the things of which he writes that word, directly or by implication, in a hundred tales, are really mean and sordid in that true sense of the word which has not, as so many journalists appear to imagine, any connection with absence of income, or presence of human nature in the back streets.

With his style I personally have sometimes a fault or two to find, but I recognise in it to the full those qualities of colour, vibration, and sense of the right word that alone keep life beating in a tale. Without high power of expression philosophy is of little use to the artist, weighting his pockets till he is sitting in the road instead of riding along it with his head up, as this writer always does. He has a manner, and a way with him, valuable at a time when certain leading writers have little or none at all. And he has a passion for the thing seen, that brings into his work the constant flash of revelation. He makes us see what he sees, and what he sees is not merely the surface.

Withal he is a gallant foe of oppression, of cruelty, of smugness, and fatty degeneration; a real tonic salt to the life of an age that needs it.

Note

1. Galsworthy, 'Notes on R. B. Cunninghame Graham', pp. 273–6.

Appendix IX

CUNNINGHAME GRAHAM, 'McSNEESHIN', *SCOTS INDEPENDENT*, JANUARY 1931

From the beginning the McSneeshin clan have been the greatest enemy Scotland has known. The Spanish saying runs, 'There is no worse thief than the thief in your own house' (*no hay peor ladron, que el de casa*). Scotland has suffered bitterly, if not from thieves, at least by traitors in her house. They, one and all, disguise it as they may, were but mere pensioners of England, taking her money quite contentedly, so that, as Murray, Morton, and many other Scottish noblemen, they were allowed to browse upon the spoils of the monasteries, and to preserve their power and their position of pre-eminence inviolate. All were McSneeshins to a man, and anti-patriots, content to do the bidding of a foreign potentate, as long as a full mess of beef and beer supplied the absence of the soul that they had bartered for it.

John Balliol McSneeshin

Balliol[1] was a good douce[2] noble. No doubt a gentleman, but not a 'parfait knight.' As a Norman noble, holding estates on both sides of the Tweed, and also in both Aquitaine and Normandy, he was more to be excused than were the above referred to English pensioners. Brought up in courts and probably speaking Norman French as his mother tongue, no doubt he looked upon the Scots as mere barbarians. He saw that England was more advanced in arts and chivalry than Scotland. He probably admired sincerely the stern warrior Edward, perhaps the ablest king who ever sat on England's throne. He saw the English knights were sheltered in Milan steel and rode destriers[3] from Naples and from Spain, whilst those from Scotland had to be content with Galloways, or at the best with heavy flat-footed animals from Flanders. What he did not see was that the wildest Johnstone, Jardine or Turnbull, upon his little hackney, 'that was never putte to hard meete', as Froissart[4] tells us, but who remained a Scot at heart, was, as far as Scotland was concerned, a prince compared to the McSneeshin chivalry.

Balliol bowed the knee, no doubt, in the first place for the crown, but perhaps as much because he saw something superior to the Scot in 'Goddes owne Englishman.' So he came beneath the spell, as so many of his spiritual descendants of today. Wealth, power, refinement, luxury, the gorgeous tournament, the cultured Court, the well armed knights, the ladies in bower, whose beauty was enhanced by all that wealth can bring (the Scottish lady had but her fresh complexion and her snood,[5] except in rarest cases), all was designed to catch McSneeshin's eye.

He then, as now, had his excuse, that it was well to keep in with your neighbours, that we could use their wealth and better opportunities to our own ends. No doubt they said, just as they say today, a Scot, put him in far Cathay, remains a Scot at heart. No doubt the Scots of those days had their equivalent of 'A Nicht wi' Burns,' when round the festive bowl they trolled their ditties of some popular poet of the time. Without a shadow of a doubt they ate their haggis when it could be procured in exile, and over their French doublets or Italian silks they tied a tartan scarf. Just as they do to-day they thought that nationalism was a thing to put on once or twice a year. Meanwhile, the Saxon smiled beefily, and winked the other eye.[6]

The Modern McSneeshins

These were the members of the historic clan in former days. To-day their position, though in the main the same, that is spread-eagled (or perhaps better, frog-marched) to the south, they take a different attitude. We are the men, they tell us. We rule the British Empire. See how McWharble is Under-Secretary for Useless Affairs, McDoodle (of the Doodles of that ilk) the High Commissioner for Tristan d'Acunha [*sic*], and my Lord Moneypenny bears a pewter rod about the court! We are all proud of being Scots, they say, and prove it in the tongue of Grub Street, 'up to the hilt,' by wearing kilts at public banquets, and bellowing maudlin ditties about Alloway Kirk, and Bonnie Lassies O'. Thus having publicly professed their patriotism, and their descent from Wallace apostolically, they still continue to praise the Lord and cheat when the church bell chaps out, or competition renders it expedient.

The McSneeshin Delusions

The pity of it is, the McSneeshin up-to-date is in the main an honest fellow, blinded by what he reads in newspapers, and never having peered beneath the surface of the society in which he moves. He takes for granted that such national prosperity as we enjoyed before the War, for he dimly perceives that all is not right in the state of Scotland to-day, came from the Union (bless the word!) with England. He thinks, apparently, that it has always been the keen desire of English legislators to forward Scotland's interests. Blinded to economic facts, he still believes that it is possible to build up once more our old prosperity on the old lines, not seeing that the whole conception of law, of order, commerce, and international relations has entirely changed, whilst he has been enjoying his after-dinner nap. Of course the typical McSneeshin of these days is a good Liberal, a member of that fast decaying race of pterodactyls that is being ground into extinction between the upper and the nether millstones of Toryism and Socialism.

Still, in the grinding he protests, just as the wheat emits a sound of gentle wailing during its attrition in an old-fashioned hand mill in Morocco or Spain. That kind of McSneeshin always wants to get back to Liberal principles, such as he remembered them in the halcyon days, when the pound sterling had hardly fallen to the level of the old Scots pound.

The McSneeshin Consolations

What has been, clearly was ordained by Heaven, and one of Heaven's first laws was to hold fast to the union with the greater partner, brought about as we know by the venality of the Scottish aristocracy.

Our consolation is that somewhere in the selvage of the Union Jack a microscopic cross of St. Andrew still exists, but unobtrusively, 'only a little,' as the Frenchman said when asked if he was wed. Still it is there, and our good friend McSneeshin, when he sees it, rubs his belly like an old-time Gold Coast negro used to do before his fetish. Then looking upwards to his emasculated flag he thanks his Maker that his election is a dead sure thing, as after all he rules the British Empire, although the other fellow holds the whip.

The Honest Scot

I have typified the honest, pig-headed Scot of these days under the name that I have chosen as a title to these lines. He is far from being a conscious traitor to his country, as were the anti-patriots of old. Our present representative of the type does not take bribes from English statesmen, nor would he take them, even if they came his way. His fault is lack of imagination, a fault that has made many more angels fall into the pit than did ambition.

Our fellow-countryman, who does not see that only he who wears the shoe can feel the pinch, is to be commiserated. Although he holds an antique creed, for him Triton will never wind his wreathed horn, or if he sounds it, it will fall upon deaf ears.

This little allegory, dip into history, or reflection on the present time, or what you will, I commend to all those Scotsmen who having eyes to see, see not, and having ears to hear, hear nothing.

L'Envoi

Yes, fellow-Scots, the enemies of Scottish nationalism are not the English, for they were ever a great and generous folk, quick to respond when justice calls. Our real enemies are amongst us, born without imagination, bound in the fetters of their own conceit, impervious to progress, and who fail to see that what was right and just last year, to-day may have become through altering conditions, rank injustice.

Notes

1. John Balliol (1249–1314). King of Scots from 1292 to 1296. Sometimes referred to as 'toom tabard': Scots = empty jacket. His father founded Balliol College, Oxford.
2. Scots = Sober.
3. War-horses.
4. Jean Froissart (c.1337–c.1405). Flemish medieval author and poet.
5. A hairband originally worn by Scottish women as a symbol of virginity.
6. Lied.

Appendix X

OBITUARY: 'A REBEL ARISTOCRAT', BY HENRY W. NEVINSON (ABRIDGED), *OUTLOOK & THE MODERN SCOT*, **MAY 1936**

The sudden news in the middle of March that Cunninghame Graham had died startled me. Ever since I came to know him fifty years ago he had always seemed to me an immortal type rather than an actual man subject to change and death like the rest of us. In the Trafalgar Square Riots of 1887, there he was, with John Burns, Hyndman and William Morris protesting against the violent suppression of a great meeting called on behalf of persecuted Ireland. Tall, very slim, with sharply pointed beard and masses of brown hair, speaking with restrained gestures in a fearlessly penetrating voice, dressed quietly, but to perfection, he stood conspicuous among all the crowds, the very model of a fine and knightly figure. He seemed a return – a 'throw-back' – to the age of romance and unselfish devotion. Bonnie Prince Charlie in the best years of his youth may have looked like that, and have exerted the same kind of personal attraction upon all who came under his charm.

Except for whitening his hair and deepening the wrinkles on his thin and active face, age did not change his appearance much, and never changed his spirit at all. In the preface to *Captain Brassbound*, Bernard Shaw thus described him in 1901:

> Everything that has ever happened to him seems to have happened in Paraguay or Texas instead of in Spain or Scotland. He is, I regret to add, an impenitent and unashamed dandy: such boots, such a hat, would have dazzled D'Orsay himself. With that hat he once saluted me in Regent Street, when I was walking with my mother. Her interest was instantly kindled, and the following conversation ensued: 'Who was that?' 'Cunninghame Graham.' 'Nonsense! Cunninghame Graham is one of your Socialists; that man is a gentleman.'

Mrs. Shaw was quite right. Cunninghame Graham, though a Socialist, always remained a gentleman. Our history has supplied us with many of those aristocrat and wealthy people – Byron, Shelley, William Morris – who were always on the side of the common people, and Cunninghame Graham was another conspicuous example. His personality was finer and more influential than his writings, but all his writings strike the same high note of genuine sympathy with the depressed and those who have never enjoyed the opportunity for the fullest life of which their nature was capable.

The sufferings of all animals, especially of horses, are, as he wrote in his last book, 'infinitely sad to anyone cursed with imagination, the gift that makes life sometimes unbearable.' When mounted, he became part of the horse in mind as in movement. His natural and spiritual home was on horseback, galloping over the wide plains of South America or the deserts of Morocco. Epstein's bust of him is fine, but the best portrait is the sketch of him as a Gaucho, the frontispiece in *The Ipané*. He is riding a largish horse, seated upright, with a large hat and Spanish cloak and heavy silver spurs – a knightly figure, careless of opinion as of the common world in which success is counted on very different terms from his own. If you want to know fellow-feeling with horses, read 'Calvary,' the life of a common hansom [cab] horse, in *Thirteen Stories*, or read 'Inmarcesible' in his latest book *Mirages*, telling of the massacre of 400,000 untrained horses in the Boer War, where I myself saw thousands simply die from exhaustion and want of care. If you want to realise how true a Socialist this born aristocrat was at heart, read his collection called *Success*, on which he pours scorn on all the standards of upper-class existence. And again, if a Scot can endure to read the finest satire upon his own race ever written by a true Scotsman, let him read the chapter called 'Salvagia,' also in *The Ipané*.

But I must now again say farewell to this noble and most attractive figure, with whom for so many years, with but one unhappy break,[1] I have remained on the most friendly and admiring terms.

Note

1. This presumably referred to Graham's angry letter to Nevinson, criticising Nevinson's praise of Roger Casement.

Bibliography

CUNNINGHAME GRAHAM'S POLITICAL AND LITERARY ARTICLES (QUOTED)

'A Plea for the Chainmakers', in *The Nail and Chainmakers*, Labour Platform Series, No. 2, 1888.

'Has the Liberal Party a Future?' *Contemporary Review*, February 1888.

'The People's Parliament', *Labour Elector*, 13 July 1889.

'Lisbon Revisited', *Labour Elector*, 21 December 1889.

'Foreign Notes', *Labour Elector*, 25 January 1890.

'An Open Letter to Prince Kropotkin', *Labour Elector*, 8 February 1890.

'Parable of the Paitans', *Knights of Labor*, 13 March 1890.

'Horses of the Pampas', *Time* (London), 1 April 1890

If Cock Robin is Dead – Who Will Kill King Capital?' *People's Press*, 5 July 1890.

'Notions', *People's Press*, 15 November 1890.

'Joined to Their Idols', *People's Press*, 22 November 1890.

'Home Rule', *People's Press*, 20 December 1890.

'The American Indians: Ghost Dancing', *Daily Graphic*, 29 November 1890.

'Ca' Canny', *People's Press*, 29 November 1890.

'The Scotch Strike', *People's Press*, 17 January 1891.

'Evolution of a Village', *The Albemarle*, June 1892.

'China Dogs', *Labour Prophet*, May 1892.

'A Jesuit', *Saturday Review*, 3 August 1885.

'Fraudesia Magna', *Saturday Review*, Part I, 21 March 1896; Part II, 4 April 1896.

'A Survival', *Saturday Review*, 3 May 1896.

'The Imperial Kailyard' *Justice*, 5 September 1896.

'Salvagia', *Saturday Review*, 12 September 1896.

'Heather Jock', *Saturday Review*, 30 January 1897.

'Bloody Niggers', *Social Democrat*, April 1897.

'Expansion of Empire', *Sunday Chronicle* 13 June 1897.

'Snaekoll's Saga', *Saturday Review*, 18 December 1897.

'Bristol Fashion', *Saturday Review*, 5 February 1898.
'The Voyage of the Tourmaline I', *Saturday Review*, 4 June 1898.
'The Voyage of the Tourmaline II', *Saturday Review*, 18 June 1898.
'Higginson's Dream', *Saturday Review*, 1 October 1898.
'Un Angelito', *Ipane* (London: T. Fisher Unwin, 1899).
'A Veteran', *Saturday Review*, 14 April 1900.
'The Pyramid', *Justice*, 1 May 1900.
'The Admiral', *Saturday Review*, 3 November 1900.
'The Failure of Success', *Saturday Review*, 17 May 1902.
'Polybaglan', *The Speaker*, 28 November 1903.
'*An Tighearna*: A Memory of Parnell', *Dana* (Dublin), November 1904.
'The Grey Kirk', *Guth na Bliadhna*, February 1906.
'Ha Til Mi Tualiadh', *The Speaker*, 17 February 1906.
'An Idealist', *Saturday Review*, 25 August 1906.
'Lochan Falloch', *Saturday Review*, 4 January 1908.
'The Real Equality of the Sexes', *New Age*, 11 July 1908.
'At the Ward Toll', *Saturday Review*, 7 November 1908.
'Aspects of the Social Question', *English Review*, December 1908.
'At Dalmary', *Saturday Review*, 4 December 1909.
'A Retainer', *English Review*, July 1910.
'Caisteal-Na-Sithan', *Saturday Review*, 15 April 1911.
'San Andrés', *English Review*, July 1911.
'A Braw Day', *English Review*, November 1911.
'Mists in Menteith', *Saturday Review*, 5 April 1913.
'The Beggar Earl', *English Review*, July 1913.
'Futurism', *Justice: Organ of Social Democracy*, 30 April 1914.
'Brought Forward', *English Review*, February 1915.
'A Minor Prophet', *English Review*, July 1915.
'With the North-East Wind', *The Nation*, 23 October 1915.
'Fidelity', *The Nation*, 27 November 1915.
'Wilfrid Scawen Blunt', *English Review*, December 1922.
'Inch Cailleach', *Saturday Review*, 5 September 1925.
'Euphrasia', *Saturday Review*, 25 September 1926.

CUNNINGHAME GRAHAM'S BOOKS (QUOTED)

Notes on the District of Menteith (Edinburgh: Adam & Charles Black, 1895).
Father Archangel of Scotland (London: Adam & Charles Black, 1896).
Aurora La Cujini: A Realistic Sketch in Seville (London: Leonard Smithers, 1898).
Mogreb-El-Acksa (1898) (London: Century, 1988).
The Ipané (London: T. Fisher Unwin, 1899).
Thirteen Stories (London: Heinmann, 1900).
Success (London: Duckworth, 1902).

Progress and Other Sketches (London: Duckworth, 1905).
His People (London: Duckworth, 1906).
Faith (London: Duckworth, 1909).
Hope (London: Duckworth, 1910).
Charity (London: Duckworth, 1912).
A Hatchment (London: Duckworth, 1913).
Scottish Stories (London: Duckworth, 1914).
Brought Forward (London: Duckworth, 1916).
A Brazilian Mystic (New York: Dodd, Mead, 1920).
Cartagena on the Banks of the Sinú (London: Heinemann, 1920)
Doughty Deeds (London: Heinemann, 1925).
Redeemed (London: Heinemann, 1927).
Thirty Tales & Sketches (London: Duckworth, 1929).
Writ In Sand (London: Heinemann, 1932).
Mirages (London: Heinemann, 1936).
Rodeo (London: Heinemann, 1936).

CUNNINGHAME GRAHAM'S INTRODUCTIONS AND FOREWORDS (QUOTED)

J. L. Mahon, *A Labour Programme*, Labour Platform Series, No. 1, 1888.
John Morrison Davidson, *Scotland for the Scots: Scotland Revisited* (Edinburgh: F. R. Henderson, 1902).
Ida Taylor, *Revolutionary Types* (London: Duckworth, 1904).
Charles Ruddy, *Companions in the Sierra* (London: John Lane, 1907).
Thomas Dick Lauder, *The Wolf of Badenoch* (Stirling: Eneas Mackay, 1930).
Robert Kirk, *The Secret Commonwealth of Elves, Fauns and Fairies* (New York: Dover Books, 2008)
John A. Stewart, *Inchmahome and the Lake of Menteith* (Printed Privately, 1933).

MANUSCRIPT MATERIALS

John Burns Collection, Senate House Library, University of London.
John Burns Library, University of Warwick.
Cunninghame Graham Papers, NLS.
Collection of Admiral Sir Angus Cunninghame Graham, Manuscript Collection, NLS.
Faulkner West Collection, Rauner Library, Dartmouth College, NH.
Haldane of Cloan Papers, NLS.
James Halliday Papers, NLS.
Compton Mackenzie Papers, EUL.
R. E. Muirhead Papers, NLS.
Rosebery Papers, NLS.

NEWSPAPERS AND PERIODICALS

The Academy, 1898–1914.
Airdrie Advertiser, 1885–90.
The Albemarle, June 1892.
American Journal of Economics and Sociology, 1987.
The Athenaeum, 15 November 1902.
Blackwood's Edinburgh Magazine, August 1889.
Buenos Aires Herald, 21 March 1936.
Caledonian Mercury, 5 February 1855.
Chiswick Gazette, 15 September 1906.
Coatbridge Express, 1885–91.
The Commonweal, 1885–90.
Contemporary Review, 1888, 1929.
Daily Graphic, 1890–1.
Daily News & Leader, 20 November 1914.
Daily Worker, November 1952.
Edinburgh Evening News, 1885–7, 1902.
Edinburgh Review, April 1929.
English Review, 1908–22.
Freeman's Journal, 19 September 1888.
Fortnightly Review, May 1936.
Forward, 1906–10.
Gateway, 1912, 1916, 1936.
Glasgow Evening News, 25 June 1892.
Glasgow Evening Times, 1937–8.
The Glasgow Herald, 1886–1936.
Guth na Bliadhna, February 1906.
Hispania: Politica, Comercio, Literatura, Artes y Ciencias, 1916.
Journal of the Knights of Labour, 13 March 1890.
Justice: The Organ of Social Democracy, 1896–1914.
Labour Leader, 1889–93.
Labour Elector, 1888–93.
The Labour Prophet: The Organ of the Labour Church, 1892.
Labour Tribune, 12 May 1888.
Library Review, Winter 1932.
London Mercury, 1936, 1938.
London Review of Books, 1983.
Manchester Guardian, 1888–1936.
Methodist Times, 1 July 1937.
The Miner, August 1888.
The Nation, 1907–16.
New Age, July 1908.
Nineteenth Century, 1893–94, 1999.
The Observer, 1910–36.

Outlook, 1899, 1900.
Outlook & The Modern Scot, May 1936.
Pall Mall Gazette, 14 October 1887.
People's Press, 1890–1.
Quarterly Review, April 1938.
Saturday Review, 1895–1936.
Scots Independent, 1930–2
The Scotsman, 1887–1936.
Scribner's Magazine, June 1921.
Social Democrat, 1897.
South London Chronicle, 9 June 1888.
The Speaker, 1903–4, 1921.
Spectator, 1888–1891.
The Star, 25 August 1890.
Stirling Observer, 28 August 1884, November–December 1918.
Sunday Chronicle, 13 June 1897.
Time (London), 1 April 1890.
Time and Tide, 28 March 1936.
Times (London), 1879–1936.
Vanity Fair (London), 25 August 1888.
Western Mail, 7 March 1927.
Westminster Gazette, 1899.

PARLIAMENTARY PAPERS

Hansard, 1887–9.

PUBLISHED SOURCES

Abse, Joan, *John Ruskin: The Passionate Moralist* (London: Quartet Books, 1980).
Ascherson, Neal, 'Cunninghame Graham: A Critical Biography', *Spectator Review*, 14 July 1979.
Bagehot, Walter, *The Works & Life of Walter Bagehot*, Vol. II (London: Longman's, 1915).
Baines, Jocelyn, *Joseph Conrad: A Critical Biography* (London: Weidenfeld & Nicolson, 1960).
Barbour, John, 'Scotland: The New Dominion', *Edinburgh Review*, April 1929.
Barker, Ernest, *Political Thought in England From Herbert Spencer the Present Day* (London: Williams & Norgate, 1915).
Bax, Ernest Belfort, *The Religion of Socialism* (1886) (New York: Books for Libraries Press, 1972).
Bell, Duncan, *Reordering the World: Essays on Liberalism and Empire* (Princeton University Press, 2016).
Benn, Caroline, *Keir Hardie* (London: Hutchinson, 1992).

Bennett, Arnold, *The Journals* (London: Penguin, 1954).

Bensusan, Samuel Levy, 'Don Roberto', *Quarterly Review*, Vol. CCLXX, April 1938.

Birkmyre, Robert, 'An Appreciation of Cunninghame Graham', *The Idler*, February 1909.

Blackie, John Stuart, *The Scottish Highlanders and the Land Laws* (London: Chapman & Hall, 1885).

Blake, George, in *Scotland in Quest of Her Youth* (Edinburgh: Oliver & Boyd, 1932).

Blake, George, *Barrie and the Kailyard School* (London: Arthur Barker, 1951).

Bloomfield, Paul, *The Essential Cunninghame Graham* (London: Jonathan Cape, 1952).

Blunt, Wilfred Scawen, *My Diaries*, Vol. II (New York: Alfred A Knopf, 1921).

Boardman, Philip, *The Worlds of Patrick Geddes* (London: Routledge & Kegan Paul, 1978).

Boehmer, Elleke, *Colonial and Postcolonial Literature: Migrant Metaphors* (Oxford University Press, 1995).

Bogdanor, Vernon, *Devolution in the United Kingdom* (Oxford University Press, 1999).

Bold, Alan, *MacDiarmid* (London: Paladin, 1990).

Bold, Alan, 'Introduction' to MacDiarmid's *Aesthetics In Scotland* (Edinburgh: Mainstream Publishing, 1984).

Boos, Florence, ed., 'William Morris's Socialist Diary', *History Workshop Journal*, Issue 13, Spring 1982.

Bottogelli, Émile, ed., *Friedrich Engels: Correspondence*, Vol. II (London: Lawrence & Wishart, 1959).

Buchan, John, *The Thirty-Nine Steps* (1915) (Ware: Wordsworth Classics, 1994).

Buchan, John, *Sir Walter Scott* (London: Cassell, 1932).

Campbell, Ian, *Kailyard: A New Assessment* (Edinburgh: Ramsay Head Press, 1981).

Carey, John, *The Intellectuals and the Masses: Pride and Prejudice among the Literary Intelligentsia, 1880–1939* (London: Faber & Faber, 1992).

Carlyle, Thomas, *On Heroes, Hero-Worship and the Heroic in History* (1841) (University of Nebraska Press, 1996).

Chamberlain, Joseph, 'True Conception of Empire' (1897) in *Mr Chamberlain's Speeches*, ed. by C. W. Boyd (London: Constable, 1914).

Chaundy, Leslie, *A Bibliography of the First Editions of the Works of R. B. Cunninghame Graham* (London: Dulan, 1924).

Chesterton, G. K., 'Our Note Book', *Illustrated London News*, 3 July 1915.

Chesterton, G. K., *Robert Louis Stevenson* (London: Hodder & Stoughton, 1927).

Claeys, Gregory, *Imperial Sceptics: British Critics of Empire, 1850–1920* (Cambridge University Press, 2010).

Clark, Edwin, *The New York Times Book Review*, 6 October 1929.

Clarke, P. F., *Lancashire and the New Liberalism* (Cambridge University Press, 1971).

Clayton, Joseph, *The Rise & Decline of Socialism in Great Britain, 1884–1924* (London: Faber & Gwyer, 1926).

Cole, G. D. H., *British Working Class Politics, 1832–1914* (London: Routledge, 1941).

Cook, Richard, 'The Home-Ly Nation: Nineteenth Century Narratives of the Highland Myth of Merrie Old Scotland', *Nineteenth Century*, Winter 1999.

Cornford, J. P., 'The Parliamentary Foundations of the Hotel Cecil', in *Ideas and Institutions of Victorian Britain*, ed. by Robert Robson (London: G. Bell, 1967).

Coupland, Reginald, *Welsh & Scottish Nationalism* (London: Collins, 1954).

Cowan, Torquil, ed., *Labour of Love: The Story of Robert Smillie* (Glasgow: Neil Wilson Publishing, 2011).

Crane, Walter, *An Artist's Reminiscences* (London: Macmillan, 1907).

Crawford, Robert, *Devolving English Literature* (Oxford: The Clarendon Press, 1992).

Crewe, Robert, *Life of Rosebery*, Vol. 1 (Edinburgh: John Donald, 1931).

Cunninghame Graham, Jean, *Gaucho Laird: The Life of R. B. 'Don Roberto' Cunninghame Graham* (Long Riders' Guild Press, 2004).

Curle, Richard, *Caravansary and Conversation: Memories of Places and Persons* (New York: Frederick A. Stokes, 1937).

Curle, Richard, ed., *W. H. Hudson's Letters to R. B. Cunninghame Graham* (London: Golden Cockerel Press, 1941).

Daiches, David, ed., *British Commonwealth Literature* (London: Penguin, 1971).

Daiches, David, ed., *A Companion to Scottish Culture* (London: Edward Arnold, 1981).

Daiches, David, 'Don Roberto', *London Review of Books*, Vol. 5, No. 3, 1983.

Davies, A. J., *To Build A New Jerusalem* (1992) (London: Abacus, 1996).

Davies, Laurence, 'R. B. Cunninghame Graham: The Kailyard and After', *Studies in Scottish Literature*, Vol. 11, No. 3, 1974.

Devine, T. M., *The Scottish Nation, 1700–2000* (London: Allen Lane, 1999).

Dryden, Linda, 'Literary Affinities and the Postcolonial in Robert Louis Stevenson and Joseph Conrad', in *Scottish Literature and Postcolonial Literature: Comparative Texts and Critical Perspectives*, ed. by Michael Gardiner and Graeme Macdonald (Edinburgh: Napier University, 2012).

Eagleton, Terry, *The Ideology of the Aesthetic* (Oxford: Basil Blackwell, 1990).

Engels, Friedrich, *The Condition of the Working-Class in England* 1845) (Oxford University Press, 1993).

Engels, Friedrich, *The Origin of the Family, Private Property and the State* (1884) (London: Penguin, 1985).

Erickson, Sandra S. Fernandes and Glenn W. Erickson, 'Cunninghame Graham's Plagiarism of da Cunha's *Os Sertões*, and its Role in Vargas Llosa's *La Guerra del Fin del Mundo*', *Luso-Brazilian Review*, Vol. 29, No. 2, 1992.

Faulkner West, Herbert, *Cunninghame Graham: His Life and Works* (London: Cranley & Day, 1932).

Finlay, Richard J., 'For or Against? Scottish Nationalists and the British Empire, 1919–39', *Scottish Historical Review*, Vol. LXXI, Nos 1/2, 1992.

Finlay, Richard J., 'Pressure Group or Political Party? The Nationalist Impact on Scottish Politics, 1928–1945', *Twentieth Century British History*, Vol. 3, No. 3, 1993.

Finlay, Richard J., *Independent and Free: Scottish Politics and the Origins of the Scottish National Party, 1918–45* (Edinburgh: John Donald, 1994).

Fraser, Ian M., *R. B. Cunninghame Graham, Fighter for Justice: An Appreciation of his Social and Religious Outlook* (self-published, 2002).

Fraser, W. Hamish, 'Trades Councils in the Labour Movement in Nineteenth-Century Scotland', in *Essays in Scottish Labour History*, ed. by Ian MacDougall (Edinburgh: John Donald, 1978).

Fraser, W. Hamish, *Scottish Popular Politics: From Radicalism to Labour* (Edinburgh: Palgrave, 2000).

Friedl, Augustine, 'Lagging Emulation in Post-Peasant Society', *American Anthropologist*, June 1965.

Galbraith, Russell, *No Quarter Given: A Biography of Tom Johnston* (Edinburgh: Mainstream Publishing, 1995).

Galsworthy, John, 'Notes on R. B. Cunninghame Graham', in *Forsytes, Pendyces and Others* (London: Heinemann, 1935).

Garnett, David, ed., *The Selected Letters of T. E. Lawrence* (London: World Books, 1941).

Garnett, David, *The Golden Echo* (London: Chatto, 1953).

Garnett, Edward, 'The Prospectus for the Overseas Library', reprinted in John Gaggin, *Among the Man-Eaters*, Vol. 8 (London: Unwin, 1900).

Garnett, Edward, 'R. B. Cunninghame Graham: Man and Writer', *London Mercury*, Vol. XXXIV, June 1936.

Gatrell, V. A. C., 'Introduction' to Robert Owen's *A New View of Society: Report to the County of Lanark* (London: Penguin, 1969).

Geikie, Archibald, *Scottish Reminiscences* (Glasgow: James MacLehose, 1904).

George, Henry, *Progress and Poverty* (1879) (New York: Doubleday & Page, 1879. Reprinted in London: The Henry George Foundation of Great Britain, 1931).

George, Henry, *Social Problems* (London: Kegan Paul, 1884).

George, Henry, *Protection and Free Trade* (London: Kegan Paul, 1886).

Gilmour, Robin, 'Regional and Provincial in Victorian Literature', in *The Literature of Region and Nation*, ed. by Ronald P. Draper (London: Macmillan, 1989).

Glasier, James Bruce, *James Keir Hardie: A Memorial* (Manchester: The National Labour Press, 1919).

Glasier, James Bruce, *William Morris and the Early Socialist Movement* (London: Longman's, 1921).

GoGwilt, Christopher, 'Broadcasting News from Nowhere: Utopian Narrative and the Sketch Artistry of R. B. Cunninghame Graham', in *High and*

Low: Moderns Literature and Culture 1889–1939, ed. by Maria DiBattista and Lucy McDiarmid (Oxford University Press, 1996). Reprinted as 'Broadcasting News from Nowhere: Utopian Narrative and the Sketch Artistry of R. B. Cunninghame Graham', in GoGwilt, *The Fiction of Geopolitics: Afterimages from Wilkie Collins to Alfred Hitchcock* (Stanford University Press, 2000).

Goodway, David, *Anarchist Seeds Beneath the Snow* (Liverpool University Press, 2006).

Graham, Stephen, *The Death of Yesterday* (London: Ernest Benn, 1930).

Gregory Smith, G., *Scottish Literature* (London: Macmillan, 1919).

Grieve, C. M. (Hugh MacDiarmid), *Contemporary Scottish Studies*, First Series (London: Leonard Parsons, 1926).

Haddow, Alexander 'Sandy', 'Reminiscences of the Early Socialist Movement in Scotland', *Forward*, 8 May 1909.

Haddow, William Martin, *My Seventy Years* (Glasgow: Robert Gibson, 1943).

Haldane, R. B., 'The Liberal Party and its Prospects', *Contemporary Review*, January 1888.

Hanham, H. J., 'Mid-Century Scottish Nationalism: Romantic and Radical', in *Ideas and Institutions of Victorian Britain*, ed. by Robert Robson (London: G. Bell, 1967).

Hanham, H. J., *Scottish Nationalism* (London: Faber & Faber, 1969).

Hardie, James Keir, in *Review of Reviews*, June 1906.

Hardie, James Keir, *From Serfdom to Socialism* (London: G. Allen, 1907).

Harris, Frank, *Contemporary Portraits*. Third Series (privately printed, 1920).

Harris, Frank, *My Life and Loves*, Vol. II (privately printed, 1925).

Harris, Frank, *Frank Harris: His Life And Adventures* (London: The Richards Press, 1947).

Harris, Wendell V., 'R. B. Cunninghame Graham', *English Literature in Transition, 1880–1920*, Vol. 30, 1987.

Harvie, Christopher, *Scotland and Nationalism* (London: Routledge, 2004).

Haymaker, Richard E., *Prince-Errant Errant and Evocator of Horizons: A Reading of R. B. Cunninghame Graham* (Printed Privately, 1967).

Hayward, Jennifer, 'R. B. Cunninghame Graham and the Argentinian Angelito', in *Empires and Revolutions: Cunninghame Graham and His Contemporaries* ed. by Carla Sassi and Silke Stroh (Scottish Literature International, 2017).

Healy, Philip, 'Introduction' to Graham's *Mogreb-El-Acksa* (London: Century, 1988).

Hechter, Michael, *Internal Colonisation: The Celtic Fringe in British National Development, 1536–1966* (London: Routledge & Kegan Paul, 1975).

Henderson, Hamish, 'Who Remembers Cunninghame Graham?' *Daily Worker*, November 1952. Reprinted in *Alias, MacAlias: Writing on Songs, Folk and Literature* (London: Polygon 1992).

Henderson, Philip, ed., *The Letters of William Morris to His Family and Friends* (London: Longman's, 1950).

Herzfeld, Michael, *Cultural Intimacy: Social Poetics and the Real Life of States, Societies, and Institutions* (London, Routledge, 2016).

Hewison, Robert, *Ruskin and His Contemporaries* (London: Pallas Athene, 2018).

Heyck, T. W. and William Klecka, 'British Radical M.P.s, 1874–1895: New Evidence From Discriminant Analysis', *Journal of Interdisciplinary History*, Vol. 4, No.2, 1973.

Hind, C. Lewis, 'R. B. Cunninghame Graham', in *More Authors and I* (London: John Lane, The Bodley Head, 1922).

Hughes, Emrys, *Keir Hardie* (London: George Allen & Unwin, 1956).

Hulme, T. E., 'Romanticism and Classicism', in *The Collected Writings of T. E. Hulme*, ed. by Karen Csengeri (Oxford: Clarendon Press, 1994).

Hunter, James, *The Last of the Free* (Edinburgh: Mainstream Publishing, 1999).

Hutchison, I. G. C., *A Political History of Scotland, 1832–1924* (Edinburgh: John Donald, 1986).

Hutchison, I. G. C., in *The Working Class in Glasgow, 1750–1914*, ed. by R. A. Cage (London: Croom Helm, 1987).

Hutchison, I. G. C., *Scottish Politics in the Twentieth Century* (Basingstoke: Palgrave, 2001).

Hyndman, H. M., 'Introduction' to William Morris's *How I Became A Socialist* (London: Twentieth Century Press, 1896).

Hyndman, H. M., *The Record of An Adventurous Life* (London: Macmillan, 1911).

Hyndman, Rosalind, *The Last Years of H. M. Hyndman* (London: G. Richards, 1923).

Ibarguren, Carlos, 'Un Gran Espiritu', *Nosotros*, April 1936.

Jackson, Holbrook, 'R. B. Cunninghame Graham: The Man and His Work', *To-day*, Vol. VII, March 1920.

James, William, *The Principles of Psychology II* (1890) (New York: Dover Books, 1950).

Johnston, Thomas, *Our Scots Noble Families* (Glasgow: The Forward Publishing Company, 1909).

Johnston, Thomas, *A History of the Working Classes in Scotland* (Glasgow: Forward Publishing Company, 1920).

Johnston, Thomas, *Memories* (London: Collins, 1952).

Jones, Doris Arthur, ed., *Taking the Curtain Call: The Life and Letters of Henry Arthur Jones* (London: Victor Gollancz, 1930).

Jones, Peter d'A., 'Henry George and British Labor Politics', *American Journal of Economics and Sociology*, Vol. 46, No. 2, 1987.

Jurado, Alicia, *El Escocés Errante: R. B. Cunninghame Graham* (Buenos Aires: Emecé Editores, 1978).

Keating, Michael and David Bleiman, *Labour and Scottish Nationalism* (London: Macmillan, 1979).

Kellas, James, 'The Mid Lanark Election and The Scottish Labour Party (1888–1894)', *Parliamentary Affairs*, No. 18, 1964.

Kellas, James, 'The Liberal Party in Scotland 1876–1895', *Scottish Historical Review*, Vol. XLIV, No. 37, 1965.

Kelvin, Norman, ed., *The Collected Letters of William Morris*, Vol. II (Princeton University Press, 1987).

Kiberd, Declan, *Inventing Ireland: The Literature of a Modern Nation* (London: Jonathan Cape, 1995).

Kidd, Colin, 'Sentiment, Race and Revival: Scottish Identity in the Aftermath of the Enlightenment', in *A Union of Multiple Identities: The British Isles, c. 1750–1850* ed. by Lawrence Brockliss and David Eastwood (Manchester University Press, 1997).

Knowles, Thomas, *Ideology, Art & Commerce: Aspects of Literary Sociology in the Late Victorian Scottish Kailyard* (Gothenburg: Acta Universitatis Gothoburgensis, 1983).

Knox, W. W. and A. MacKinlay, 'The Re-Making of Scottish Labour in the 1930s', *Twentieth Century British History* (Oxford University Press, 1995).

Koestler, Arthur, *The Act of Creation* (London: Hutchinson, 1969).

Lascano Tegui, Vizconde de, 'Don Cunninghame Graham', *Nosotros*, 1 May 1936.

Lavery, John, *The Life of a Painter* (London: Cassell, 1940).

Lawrence, Elwood P., *Henry George in the British Isles* (Michigan State University Press, 1957).

Laybourn, Keith, *The Rise of Labour* (Polytechnic of Huddersfield, 1990).

Leatham, James, 'Barren Labourism', *The Gateway*, July 1912.

Leatham, James, 'The Passing of "Don Roberto"', *The Gateway*, March 1936.

Leatham, James, *60 Years of World Mending* (1940) (Turriff: Deveron Press, 2016).

Liebknecht, Wilhelm, *Briefwechsel mit Karl Marx und Friedrich Engels*, ed. by George Eckert (The Hague: Mouton, 1963).

Lindsay, Maurice, *The Lowlands of Scotland: Glasgow and the North* (London: Robert Hale, 1953).

Lindsay, Maurice, *A History of Scottish Literature* (London: Robert Hale, 1977).

Lindsay, Maurice, 'Cunninghame Graham', in *A Companion to Scottish Culture*, ed. by David Daiches (London: Edward Arnold, 1981).

Linklater, Andro, *Compton Mackenzie: A Life* (London: Chatto & Windus, 1987).

Lloyd Jones, Naomi, 'Liberalism, Scottish Nationalism and the Home Rule Crisis, c.1886–93', *English Historical Review*, Vol. 129, No. 539, 1 August 2014.

Long, Andrew C., 'A Refusal and Traversal: Robert Cunninghame Graham's Engagement with Orientalism in *Mogreb-El-Acksa*', *Nineteenth-Century Literature*, Vol. 63, No. 3, 2008.

Longaker, Mark, *Contemporary English Literature* (New York: Appleton-Century Crofts, 1953).

Lowe, David, *Souvenirs of Scottish Labour* (Glasgow: W. R. Holmes, 1919).

Lowe, David, 'The First Time It Has Been Told: Why Cunninghame Graham Left the Labour Party', *Glasgow Evening Times*, 11 February 1938.

Lowe, David, 'The Old Scottish Labour Party', *Glasgow Evening Times*, 18 February 1938.

Lyall, Scott, ed., 'Hugh MacDiarmid's Impossible Community', in *Community in Modern Scottish Literature* (Amsterdam: Rodop, 2016).

Lynd, Robert, 'Mr. Cunninghame Graham', *Old and New Masters* (London: Unwin, 1919).

MacCormick, John, *The Flag in the Wind* (London: Victor Gollancz, 1955).

MacCormick, Neil, ed., *The Scottish Debate: Essays on Scottish Nationalism* (Oxford University Press, 1970).

MacDiarmid, Hugh, 'The Caledonian Antisyzygy', in *Scottish Eccentrics* (London: Routledge, 1936).

MacDiarmid, Hugh, *Lucky Poet: A Self Study* (London: Methuen, 1943).

MacDiarmid, Hugh, *Cunninghame Graham: A Centenary Study* (Glasgow: Caledonian Press, 1952).

MacDiarmid, Hugh, *The Company I've Kept* (London: Hutchison, 1966).

MacDiarmid, Hugh, *The Selected Essays of High MacDiarmid*, ed. by Duncan Glen (London: Jonathan Cape, 1969).

MacDonald, J. Ramsay, *Socialism: Critical and Constructive* (London, Cassell, 1921).

MacIntyre, Alasdair, *After Virtue* (1981) (London: Bloomsbury Academic, 2011).

Mackail, J. W., *The Life of William Morris*, Vol. II (1899) (New York: Dover Books, 1995).

Mackenzie, Compton, 'Safety Last', in *Scotland In Quest of Her Youth*, ed. by David Cleghorn Thomson (Edinburgh: Oliver & Boyd, 1932).

Mackenzie, Compton, 'R. B. Cunningham Graham Scottish Nationalist', *Outlook & The Modern Scot*, May 1936.

Mackenzie, Compton, 'Don Roberto: On the Centenary', *The Listener*, 29 May 1952.

Mackenzie, Compton, *My Life and Times*, Octave Four (London: Chatto & Windus, 1965).

Mackenzie, Compton, *My Life and Times*, Octave Six (London: Chatto & Windus, 1967).

MacKenzie, John M., 'The Local and the Global: The Multiple Contexts of Cunninghame Graham', in *Empires and Revolutions: Cunninghame Graham & His Contemporaries*, ed. by Carla Sassi and Silke Stroh (Glasgow: Scottish Literature International, 2017).

Mackenzie, Norman, ed., *The Letters of Sidney and Beatrice Webb* (Cambridge University Press, 1978).

MacLean, Iain, *Keir Hardie* (London: Allen Lane, 1975).

Maddox Ford, Ford, *Return to Yesterday* (London: Victor Gollancz, 1931).

Maitland, Alexander, *Robert and Gabriela Cunninghame Graham* (Edinburgh: William Blackwood, 1983).

Mann, Tom, *Tom Mann's Memoirs* (London: The Labour Publishing Company, 1923).

Mavor, Sam, *M&C Apprentices' Magazine*, Vol. XX, Summer, 1936.

Mavor, 'Robert Bontine Cunninghame Graham', in *Memories of People and Places* (London: William Hodge, 1940).

Melville, Herman, *Typee* (1846) (Ware: Wordsworth Classics, 1994).

Menikoff, Barry, *Robert Louis Stevenson and The Beach of Falesá* (Edinburgh University Press, 1984).

Meyers, Jeffrey, *Fever At the Core: Six Studies of Idealists in Politics* (London Magazine Editions, 1976).

Middlemass, R. K., *The Clydesiders* (London: Hutchison, 1965).

Mill, John Stuart, *Principles of Political Economy*, Preface to 3rd edition (London: John W. Parker, 1852).

Mill, John Stuart, *On Liberty* (1859) (Cambridge University Press, 2004).

Mill, John Stuart, *Dissertations and Discussions: Political, Philosophical, and Historical*, Vol. 3 (New York: 1874).

Millar, J. H., 'The Literature of the Kailyard', *New Review*, April, 1895.

Millar, J. H., *A Literary History of Scotland* (London: T. Fisher Unwin, 1903).

Mitchell, James and Gerry Hassan, eds, *Scottish National Party Leaders* (London: Biteback Publishing, 2016).

Mitchell, W., *Is Scotland to Be Sold Again?* (Edinburgh: Scottish Home Rule Association, 1892).

Moncrieff, George Scott, 'Cunninghame Graham and a Contemporary Critic', *Outlook & The Modern Scot*, May 1936.

Moore, George, *Conversations In Ebury Street* (London: Heinemann, 1936).

Morgan, Austen, *J. Ramsay MacDonald* (Manchester City Art Gallery, 1987).

Morgan, Kenneth O., *Keir Hardie: Radical and Socialist* (London: Phoenix, 1988).

Morris, May, ed., *The Collected Works of William Morris*, Vol. II (London: Longman's, 1910).

Morris, William, *How I Became a Socialist* (London: Twentieth Century Press, 1896).

Morton, Graham, 'The First Home Rule Movement in Scotland, 1886–1918', in *The Challenge to Westminster*, ed. by H. T. Dickinson and Michael Lynch (East Linton: Tuckwell Press, 2000).

Moyle, Fanny, *Constance: The Tragic and Scandalous Life of Mrs. Oscar Wilde* (London: John Murray, 2011).

Muddiman, Bernard, *Men of the Nineties* (London: Henry Danielson, 1920).

Muggeridge, Malcolm, 'Cunninghame Graham', *Time and Tide*, Vol. XVII, 28 March 1936.

Muir, Edwin, *Scottish Journey* (1935) (London: Flamingo, 1985).

Muir, Edwin, *Scott and Scotland: The Predicament of the Scottish Writer* (New York: Speller, 1938).

Munro, Neil, *The Brave Days: A Chronicle of the North* (Edinburgh: Porpoise Press, 1931).

Munro, Neil, 'A Group of Writing Men', *The On-Looker* (Edinburgh: The Porpoise Press, 1933).

Nash, Andrew, *Kailyard and Scottish Literature* (Amsterdam: Rodopi, 2007).

Nevin, Donal, ed., *Between Comrades, James Connolly, Letters and Correspondence, 1889–1916* (Dublin: Gill & Macmillan, 2007).

Nevinson, Henry W., 'A Rebel Aristocrat', *Outlook & The Modern Scot*, May 1936.

Oliphant, Margaret, 'The Window in Thrums', *Blackwood's Edinburgh Magazine*, August 1889.

Owen, Robert, *A New View of Society: Report to the County of Lanark* (1821) (London: Penguin, 1969).

Parker, W. H., *Modern Scottish Writers* (1917) (New York: Books for Libraries Press, 1968).

Paulin, Tom, 'Cunninghame Graham: A Critical Biography', *New Statesman*, 24 August 1979.

Pelling, Henry, *Origins of the Labour Party, 1880–1900* (Oxford University Press, 1965).

Porter, Bernard, *Critics of Empire: British Radicals and the Imperial Challenge* (London: I. B. Tauris, 2008).

Power, William, *My Scotland* (Glasgow: Porpoise Press, 1934).

Power, William, *Literature and Oatmeal* (London: George Routledge, 1935).

Power, William, *Should Auld Acquaintance* (London: Harrap, 1937).

Pozzo, Fernando, *La Literatura Argentina*, No. 88, April 1936.

Pritchett, V. S., 'A Reviver of Chivalry in English Prose', *Current Literature*, Vol. LIII, October 1932.

Pritchett, V. S., 'New Literature', *London Mercury*, Vol. XXXVII, January 1938.

Redmond, James, 'Introduction' to Morris's *The News from Nowhere* (London: Routledge & Kegan Paul, 1977).

Regan, Stephen, 'Introduction: The Return of the Aesthetic', in *The Politics of Pleasure* (Open University Press, 1992).

Renan, Ernest, *Poetry of the Celtic Races* (London: Walter Scott Publishing, 1896).

Renwick, W. L., 'Introduction' to *W. E. Aytoun: Stories and Verse* (Edinburgh University Press, 1964).

Rickett, A. C., *William Morris* (London: Herbert Jenkins, 1913).

Roosevelt, Theodore, *Ranch Life and The Hunting Trail* (1888) (New York: Century, 1911).

Rothenstein, William, *Men and Memories 1900–22* (London: Faber & Faber, 1931).

Rothenstein, William, *Since Fifty: Recollections* (London: Faber & Faber, 1939).

Ruskin, John, *Modern Painters*, Vol. II (1846) (London: George Allen, 1906).

Ruskin, John, 'On the Nature of the Gothic', in *The Stones of Venice* (1853) (New York: National Library Association, 2009).

Ruskin, John, *Unto This Last and Other Writings* (1860) (London: Penguin, 1997).

Sampson, George, *The Concise Cambridge History of English Literature* (Cambridge University Press, 1970).

Scott, Walter, *The Minstrelsy of the Scottish Border* (1802–3) (Edinburgh: Adam & Charles Black, 1873).

Seeley, John Robert, *The Expansion of England* (1883) (Cambridge University Press, 2010).

Shaw, George Bernard, 'Notes to *Captain Brassbound's Conversion*: Sources of the Play', in *Three Plays For Puritans* (1901) (London: Penguin, 2000).

Shaw, George Bernard, *Pen Portraits and Reviews* (London: Constable, 1932).

Shaw, George Bernard, *Morris As I Knew Him* (New York: Dodd & Mead, 1936).

Shepherd, Gillian, 'The Kailyard', in *The History of Scottish Literature*, Vol. 3, ed. by Douglas Gifford (Aberdeen University Press, 1988).

Slater, Joseph, ed., *The Correspondence of Emerson and Carlyle* (Columbia University Press, 1964).

Smillie, Robert, *My Life For Labour* (London: Mills & Boon, 1924).

Smith, Helen, *The Uncommon Reader: A Life of Edward Garnett* (New York: Farrar, Straus and Giroux, 2017).

Smith, James Steel, 'R. B. Cunninghame Graham as a Writer of Short Fiction', *English Literature in Transition*, Vol. XII, No. 2, 1969.

Smout, T. C., *A Century of the Scottish People* (London: Fontana Press, 1987).

Snowden, Philip, *An Autobiography* (London: Ivor, Nicholson & Watson, 1934).

Stansky, Peter, *Ambitions and Strategies: The Struggle For the Leadership of the Liberal Party in the 1890s* (Oxford: Clarendon Press, 1964).

Stansky, Peter, *William Morris* (Oxford University Press, 1987).

Stewart, William, *J. Keir Hardie* (London: Cassell, 1921).

Symons, Arthur, *Notes on Joseph Conrad and Some Unpublished Letters* (London: Myers, 1925).

Taylor, Anne, *The People's Laird* (Edinburgh: Tobias Press, 2005).

Thomas, Edward, ed., *A Selection of Letters to Edward Garnett* (Edinburgh: Tragara Press, 1981).

Thompson, E. P., *William Morris: Romantic and Revolutionary* (London: Pantheon Books, 1976).

Thompson, Laurence, *The Enthusiasts: A Biography of Bruce and Katharine Glasier* (London: Gollancz, 1971).

Thorpe, Andrew, *A History of the British Labour Party* (London: Macmillan, 1997).

Tillett, Ben, *Is the Parliamentary Labour Party a Failure?* (London: Twentieth Century Press, 1908).

Tindall, George and David Shi, *America: A Narrative History* (New York: W. W. Norton, 1999).

Tinker, Edward Larocque, 'New Editions, First and Otherwise', *New York Times Book Review*, 29 November 1936.

Tschiffely, Aimé Félix, 'Reminiscences: Letters Destroyed', *The Scotsman*, 19 October 1936.

Tschiffely, Aimé Félix, *Don Roberto: Being the Account of the Life and Works of R. B. Cunninghame Graham, 1852–1936* (London: Heinemann, 1937).

Veitch, James, *George Douglas Brown* (London: H. Jenkins, 1952).

Wade, Allan, ed., *The Letters of W. B. Yeats* (London: Hart-Davis, 1954).

Walker, John, 'The Revival of a Scots Literary Giant', *The Scotsman Magazine*, June 1981.

Walker, John, ed., *The Scottish Sketches of R. B. Cunninghame Graham* (Edinburgh: Scottish Academic Press, 1982).

Walker, John, 'Cunninghame Graham and the Critics', *Studies in Scottish Literature*, Vol. 19, 1984.

Walker, John, ed., *The North American Sketches of R. B. Cunninghame Graham* (Edinburgh: Scottish Academic Press, 1986).

Watson, Frederick, 'R. B. Cunninghame Graham', *The Bookman*, March 1916.

Watson, Roderick, *The Literature of Scotland* (Basingstoke: Macmillan, 1984).

Watts, Cedric, 'A Letter from W. B. Yeats to R. B. Cunninghame Graham', *Review of English Studies*, Vol. XVIII, 1967.

Watts, Cedric, ed., *Joseph Conrad's Letters to R. B. Cunninghame Graham* (Cambridge University Press, 1969).

Watts, Cedric, *R. B. Cunninghame Graham* (Boston: Twaynes English Authors, 1983).

Watts, Cedric, 'R. B. Cunninghame Graham: Janiform Genius', in *Empires and Revolutions: Cunninghame Graham & His Contemporaries*, ed. by Carla Sassi and Silke Stroh (Glasgow: Scottish Literature International, 2017).

Watts, Cedric and Laurence Davies, *Cunninghame Graham: A Critical Biography* (Cambridge University Press, 1979).

Webb, Keith, *The Growth of Nationalism in Scotland* (Abingdon: Taylor & Francis, 1977).

Webb, Sidney and Harold Cox, *The Eight Hours Day* (London: W. Scott, 1891).

Weller, Peter, *The New Liberalism: Liberal Social Theory in Great Britain, 1889–1914* (1982) (London: Routledge, 2016).

Wellington, Amy, 'An Artist-Fighter in English Prose: Cunninghame Graham', *The Bookman* (New York), April 1918.

Westcott, B. F. 'The Empire', in *Lessons From Work* (New York: Macmillan, 1901).

Williams, Francis, *Fifty Years' March: The Rise of the Labour Party* (London: Odham's Press, 1946).

Williams, Harold, *Modern English Writers* (London: Sidgwick & Jackson, 1919).

Williams, Raymond, *Culture and Society, 1780–1950* (London: Chatto & Windus, 1967).

Williamson, Edwin, 'Argentina: The Long Decline', in *The Penguin History of Latin America* (London: Penguin, 2009).

Wilmer, Clive, ed., 'Introduction' to John Ruskin's *Unto This Last* (London: Penguin, 1997).

Wittig, Kurt, *Scottish Tradition in Literature* (Edinburgh: Oliver & Boyd, 1958).

Worley, Matthew, *Labour Inside the Gate: A History of the British Labour Party Between the Wars* (London: I. B. Tauris, 2005).

Yeats, W. B., 'A Visionary', in *The Celtic Twilight: Faerie and Folklore* (1893) (London: Prism Press, 1990).

THESES

Davies, Laurence, 'R. B. Cunninghame Graham and the Concept of Impressionism', DPhil, University of Sussex, 1972.

Reid, Fred, 'The Early Life and Political Development of James Keir Hardie, 1856–92', DPhil, University of Oxford, 1969.

Summers, David F. 'The Labour Church and Allied Movements of the Late 19th and Early 20th Centuries', DPhil, University of Glasgow, 1958.

Index